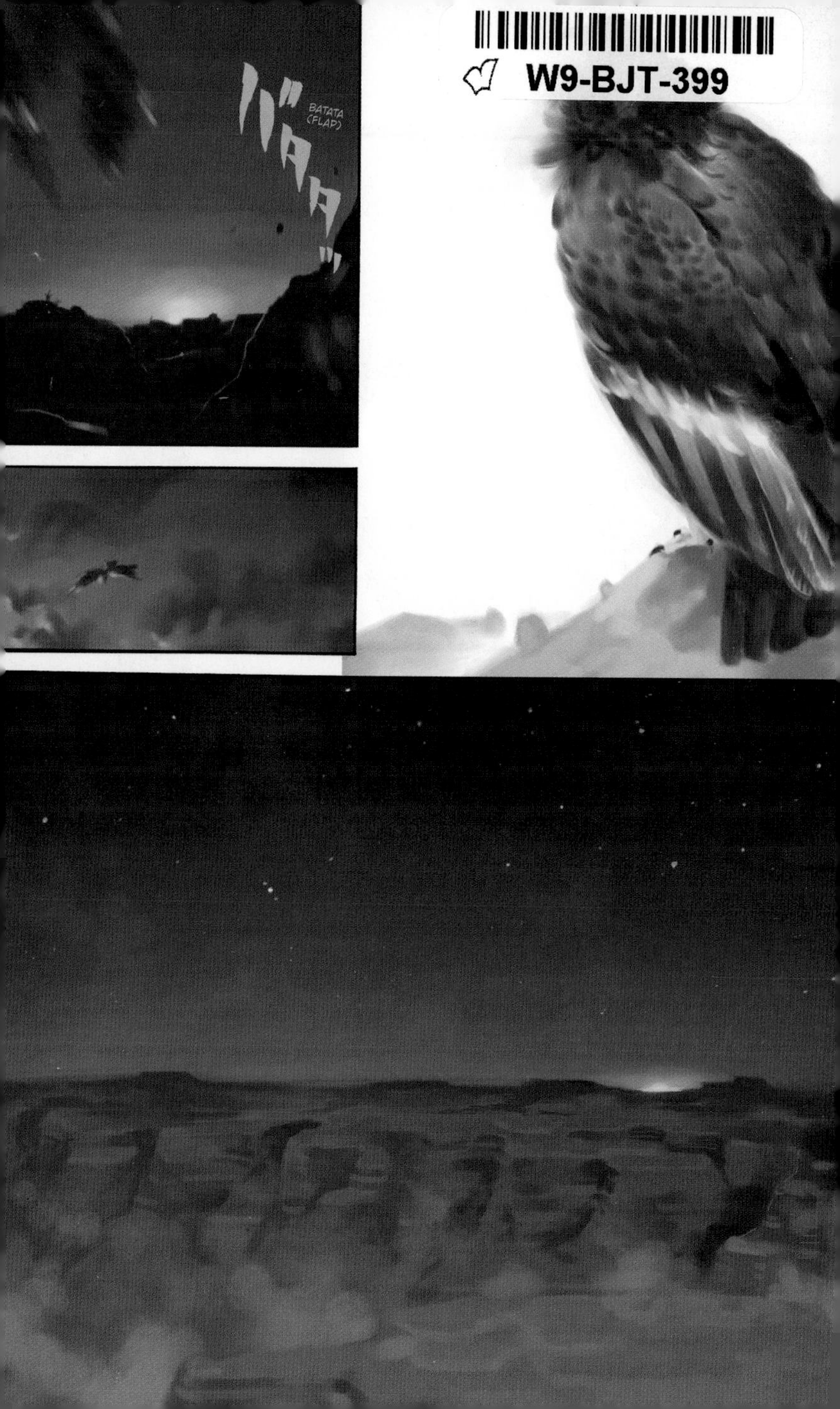
バタタッ
BATATA (FLAP)

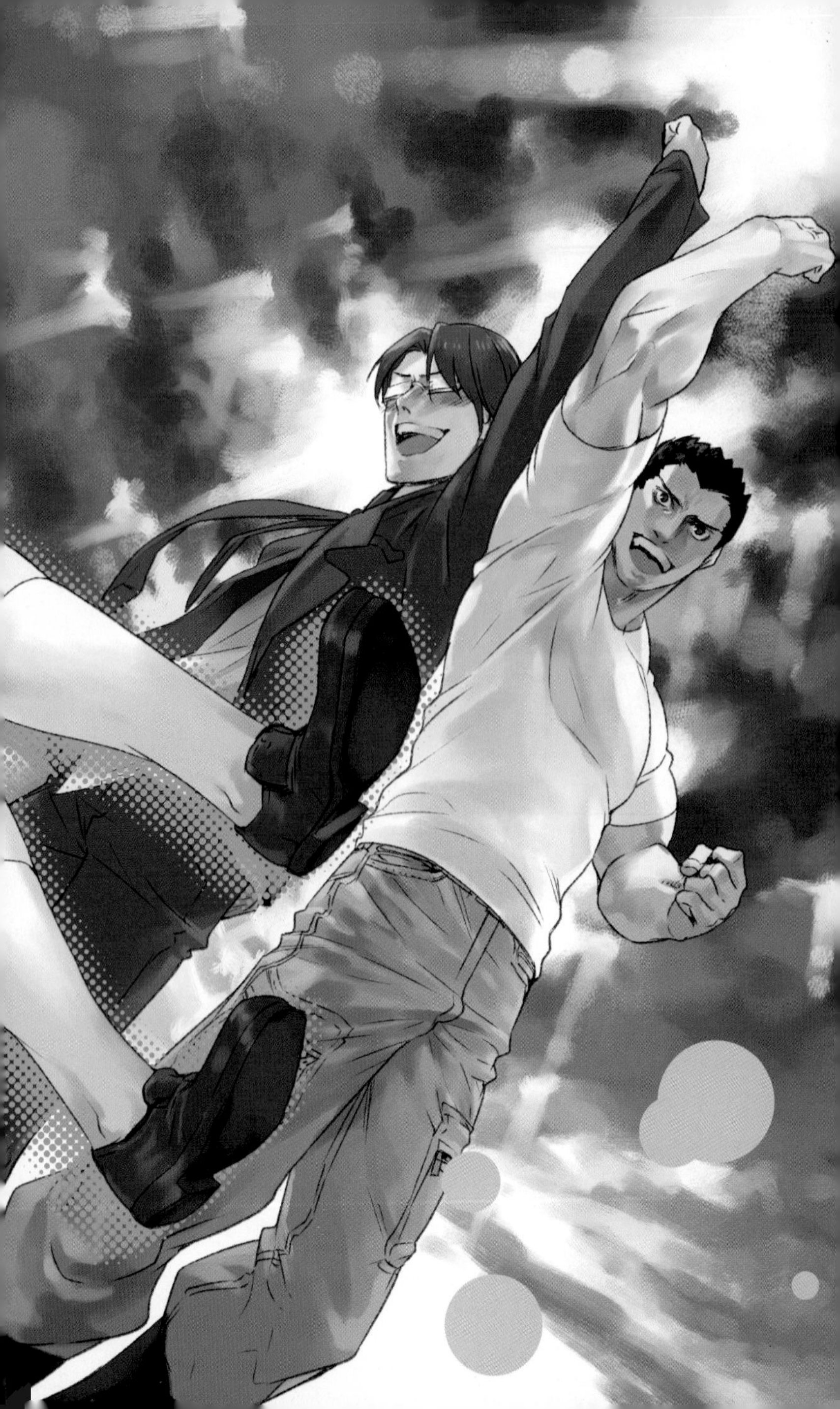

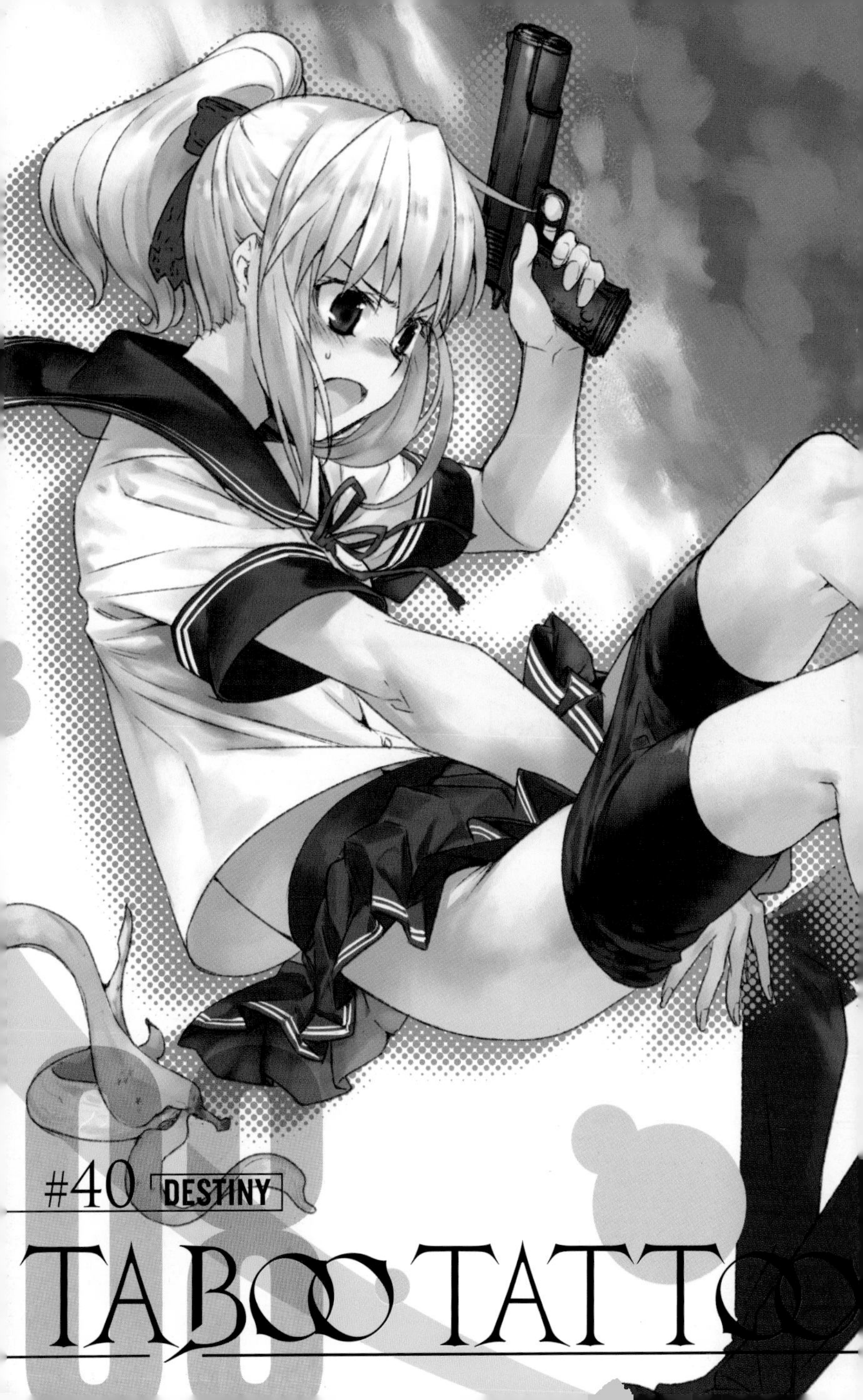

#40 DESTINY

TABOO TATTOO

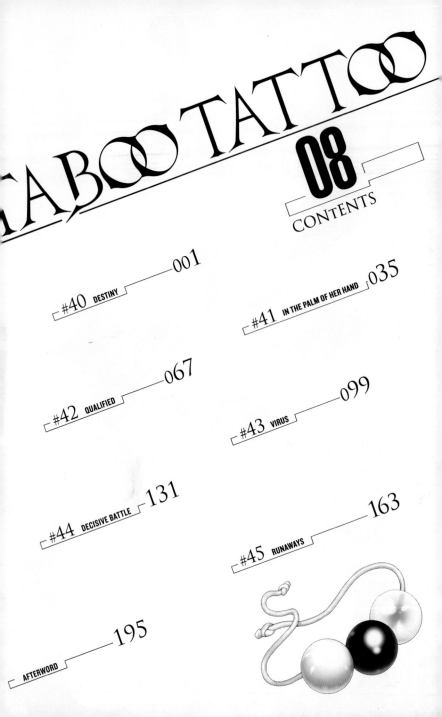

TABOO TATTOO

08

CONTENTS

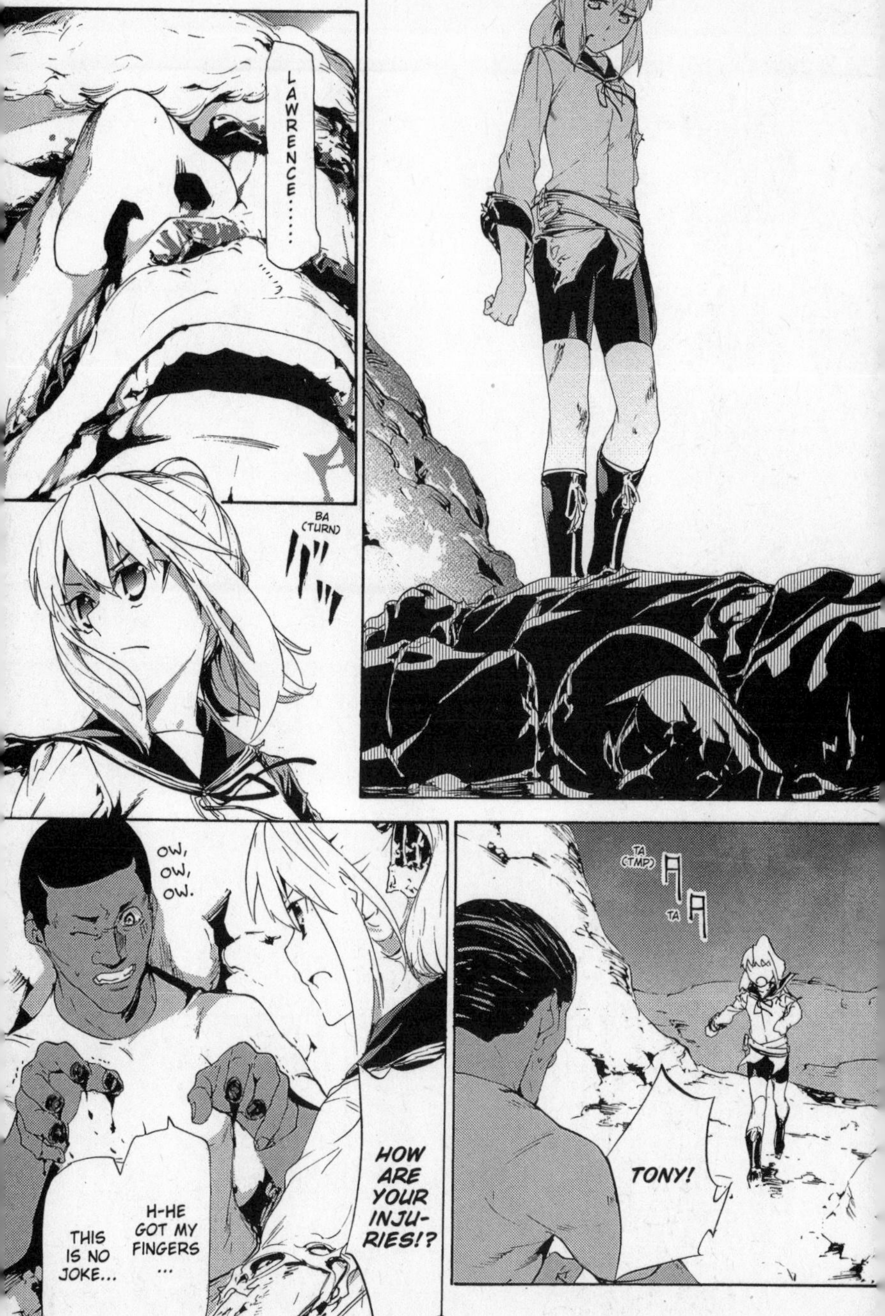
LAWRENCE......
BA (TURN)
TA (TMP) TA
TONY!
OW, OW, OW.
HOW ARE YOUR INJURIES!?
H-HE GOT MY FINGERS ...
THIS IS NO JOKE...

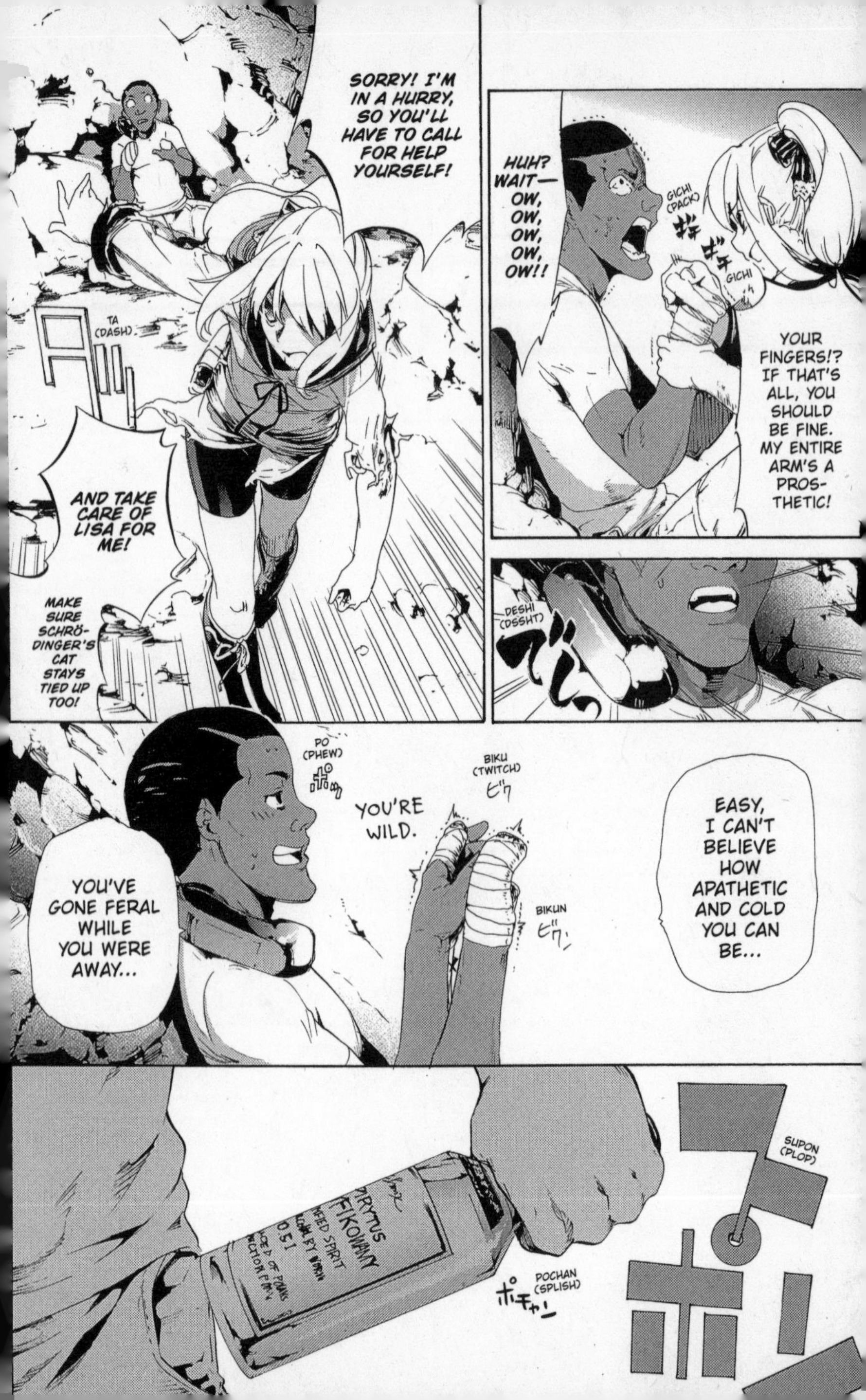
GICHI (PACK)
HUH? WAIT— OW, OW, OW, OW, OW!!
GICHI
YOUR FINGERS!? IF THAT'S ALL, YOU SHOULD BE FINE. MY ENTIRE ARM'S A PROS-THETIC!
DESHI (DSSHT)
SORRY! I'M IN A HURRY, SO YOU'LL HAVE TO CALL FOR HELP YOURSELF!
TA (DASH)
AND TAKE CARE OF LISA FOR ME!
MAKE SURE SCHRÖ-DINGER'S CAT STAYS TIED UP TOO!
EASY, I CAN'T BELIEVE HOW APATHETIC AND COLD YOU CAN BE...
BIKU (TWITCH)
YOU'RE WILD.
PO (PHEW)
BIKUN
YOU'VE GONE FERAL WHILE YOU WERE AWAY...
SUPON (PLOP)
POCHAN (SPLISH)

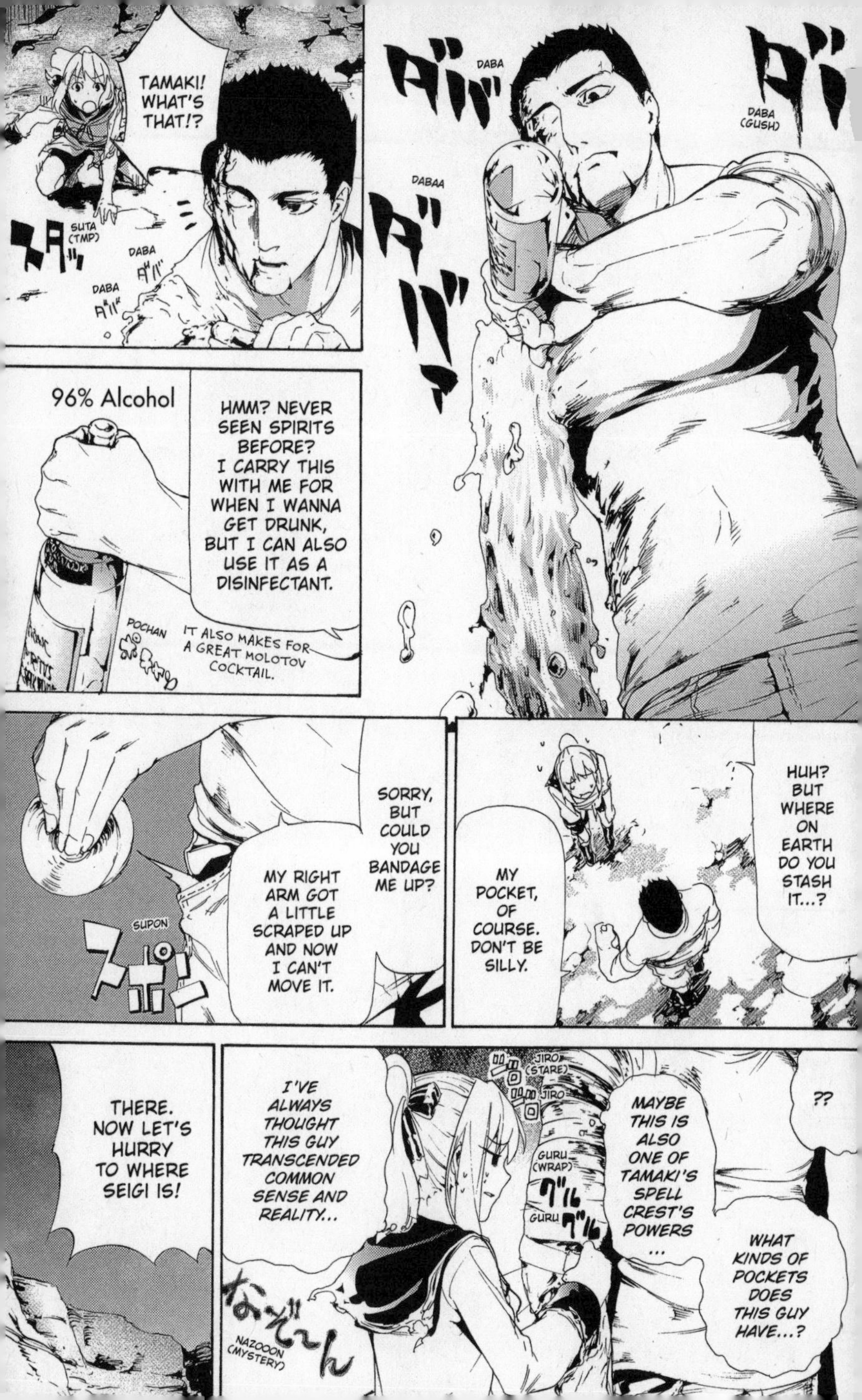
DABA (GUSH)
DABA
DABAA
TAMAKI! WHAT'S THAT!?
SUTA (TMP)
DABA
DABA
HMM? NEVER SEEN SPIRITS BEFORE? I CARRY THIS WITH ME FOR WHEN I WANNA GET DRUNK, BUT I CAN ALSO USE IT AS A DISINFECTANT.
96% Alcohol
IT ALSO MAKES FOR A GREAT MOLOTOV COCKTAIL.
POCHAN
HUH? BUT WHERE ON EARTH DO YOU STASH IT...?
MY POCKET, OF COURSE. DON'T BE SILLY.
SORRY, BUT COULD YOU BANDAGE ME UP?
MY RIGHT ARM GOT A LITTLE SCRAPED UP AND NOW I CAN'T MOVE IT.
SUPON
??
WHAT KINDS OF POCKETS DOES THIS GUY HAVE...?
MAYBE THIS IS ALSO ONE OF TAMAKI'S SPELL CREST'S POWERS...
JIRO (STARE)
JIRO
GURU (WRAP)
GURU
I'VE ALWAYS THOUGHT THIS GUY TRANSCENDED COMMON SENSE AND REALITY...
NAZOOON (MYSTERY)
THERE. NOW LET'S HURRY TO WHERE SEIGI IS!

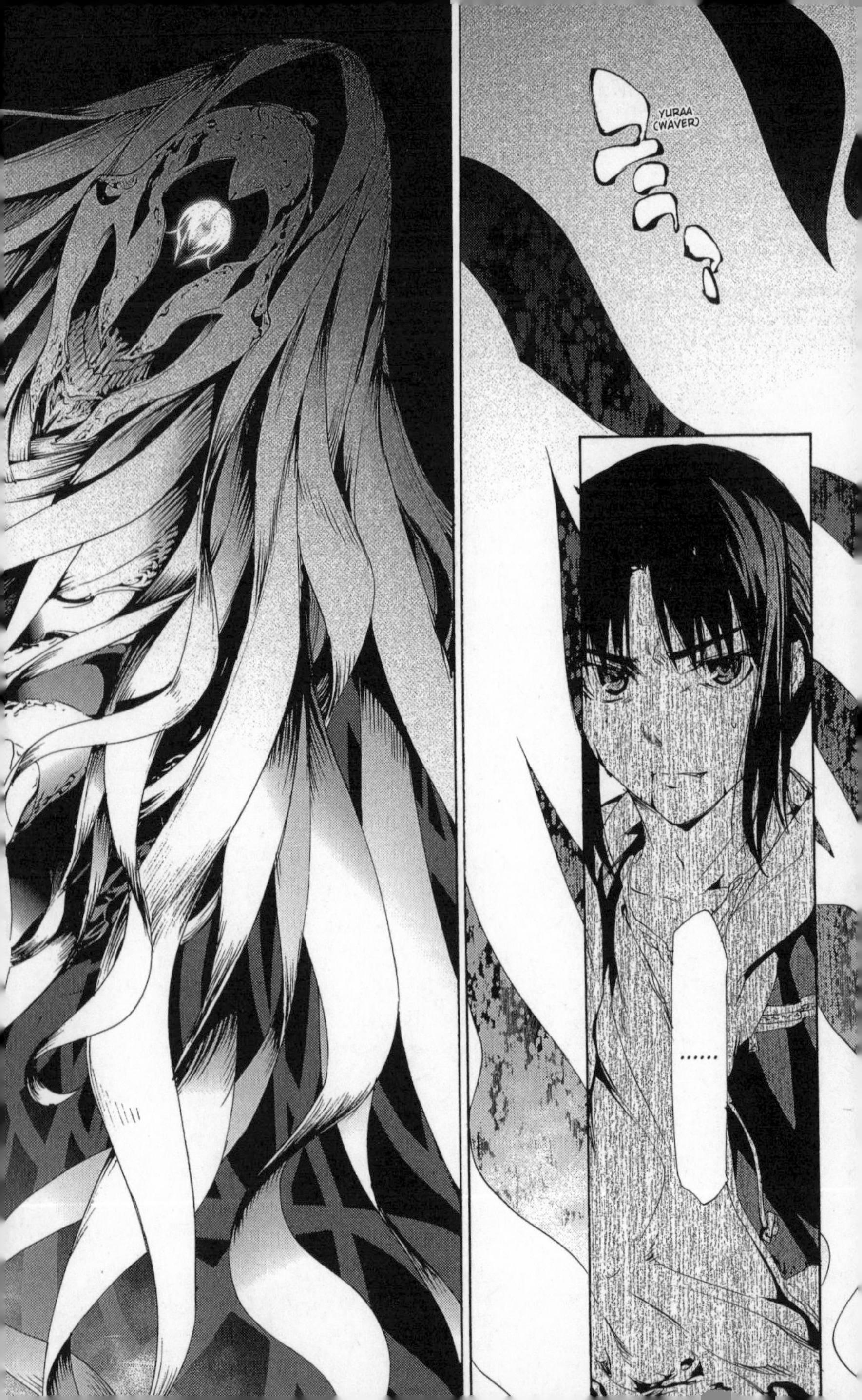
YURAA (WAVER)
……

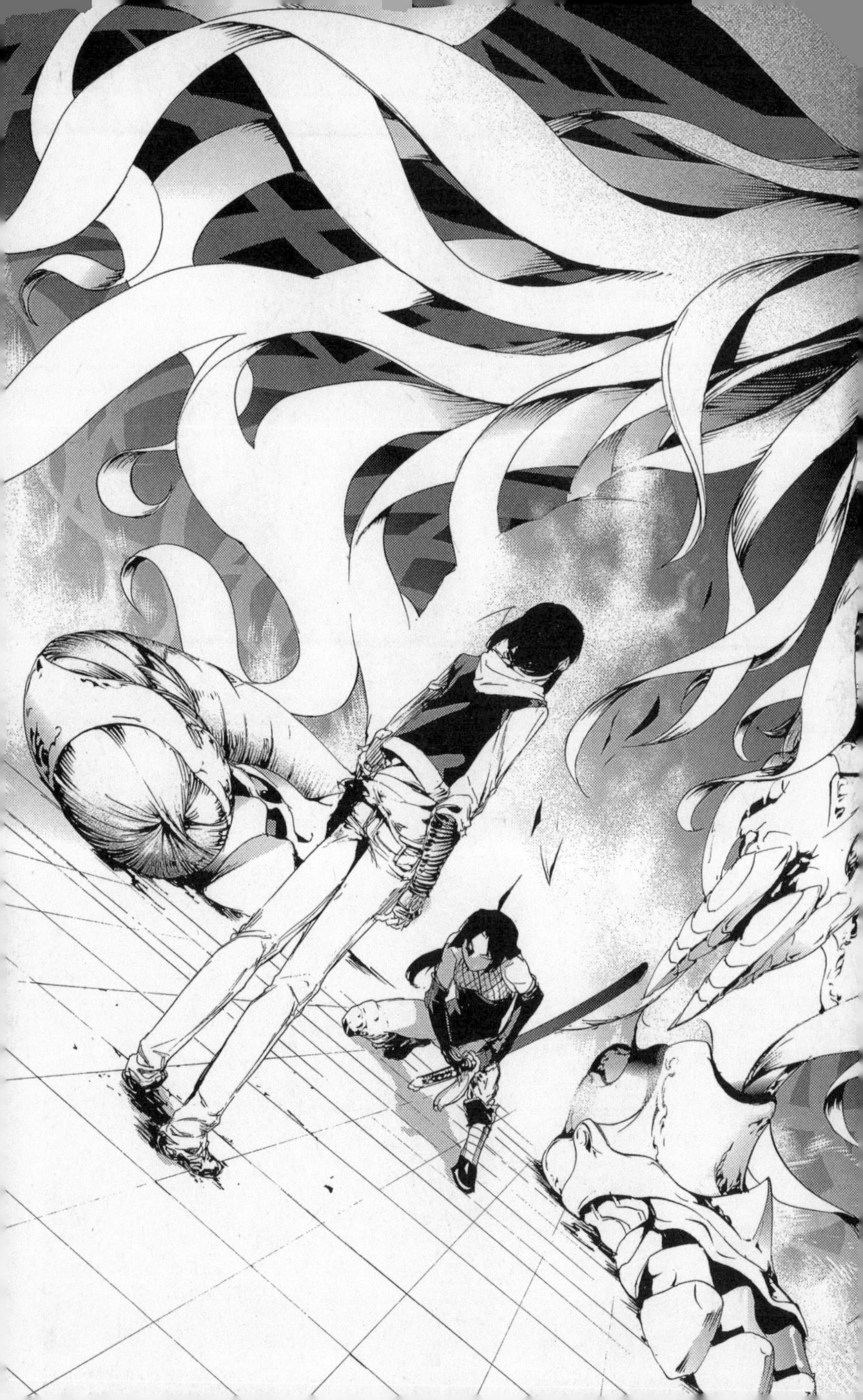

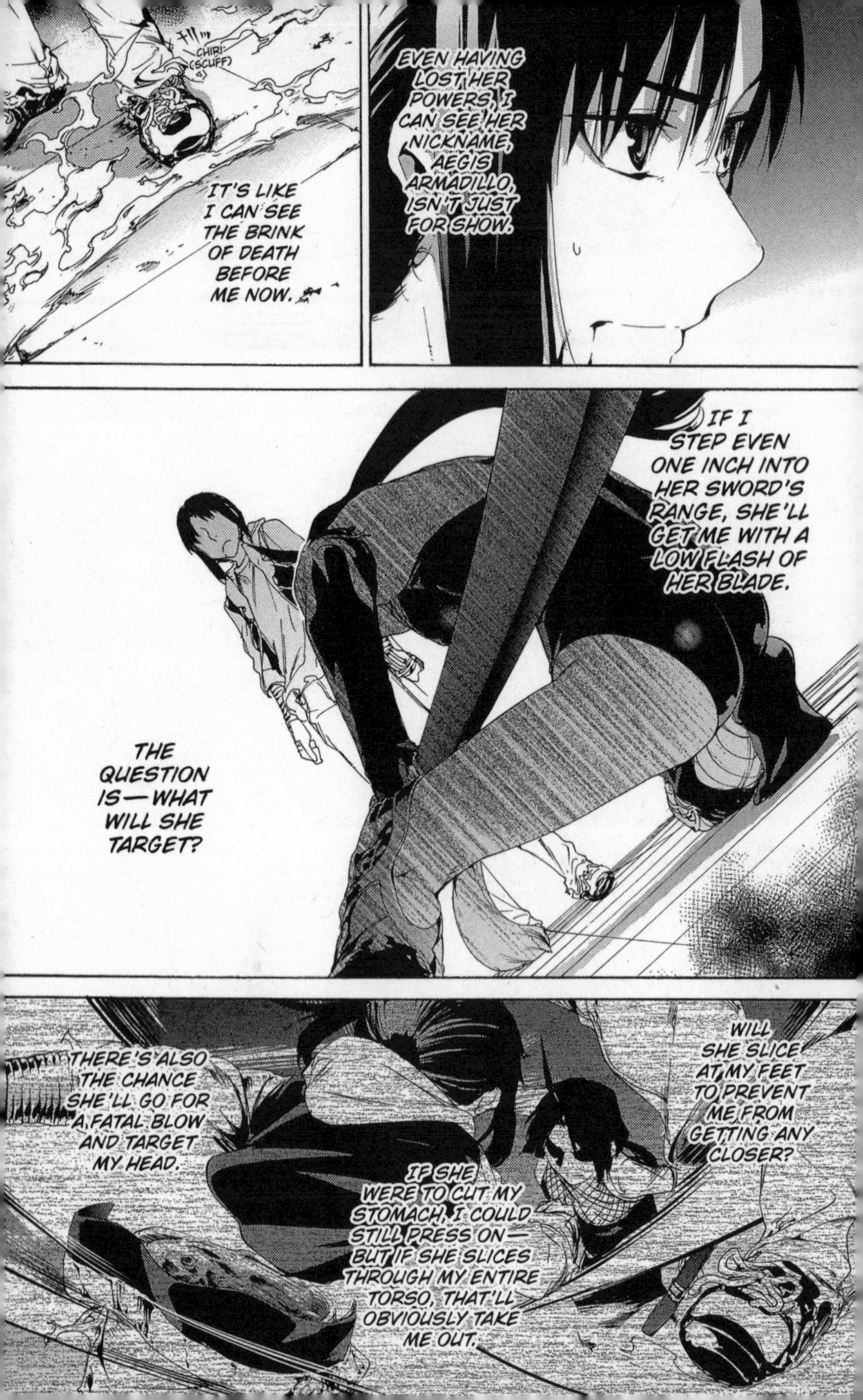
EVEN HAVING LOST HER POWERS, I CAN SEE HER NICKNAME, AEGIS ARMADILLO, ISN'T JUST FOR SHOW.
CHIRI (SCUFF)
IT'S LIKE I CAN SEE THE BRINK OF DEATH BEFORE ME NOW.
IF I STEP EVEN ONE INCH INTO HER SWORD'S RANGE, SHE'LL GET ME WITH A LOW FLASH OF HER BLADE.
THE QUESTION IS—WHAT WILL SHE TARGET?
WILL SHE SLICE AT MY FEET TO PREVENT ME FROM GETTING ANY CLOSER?
IF SHE WERE TO CUT MY STOMACH, I COULD STILL PRESS ON—BUT IF SHE SLICES THROUGH MY ENTIRE TORSO, THAT'LL OBVIOUSLY TAKE ME OUT.
THERE'S ALSO THE CHANCE SHE'LL GO FOR A FATAL BLOW AND TARGET MY HEAD.

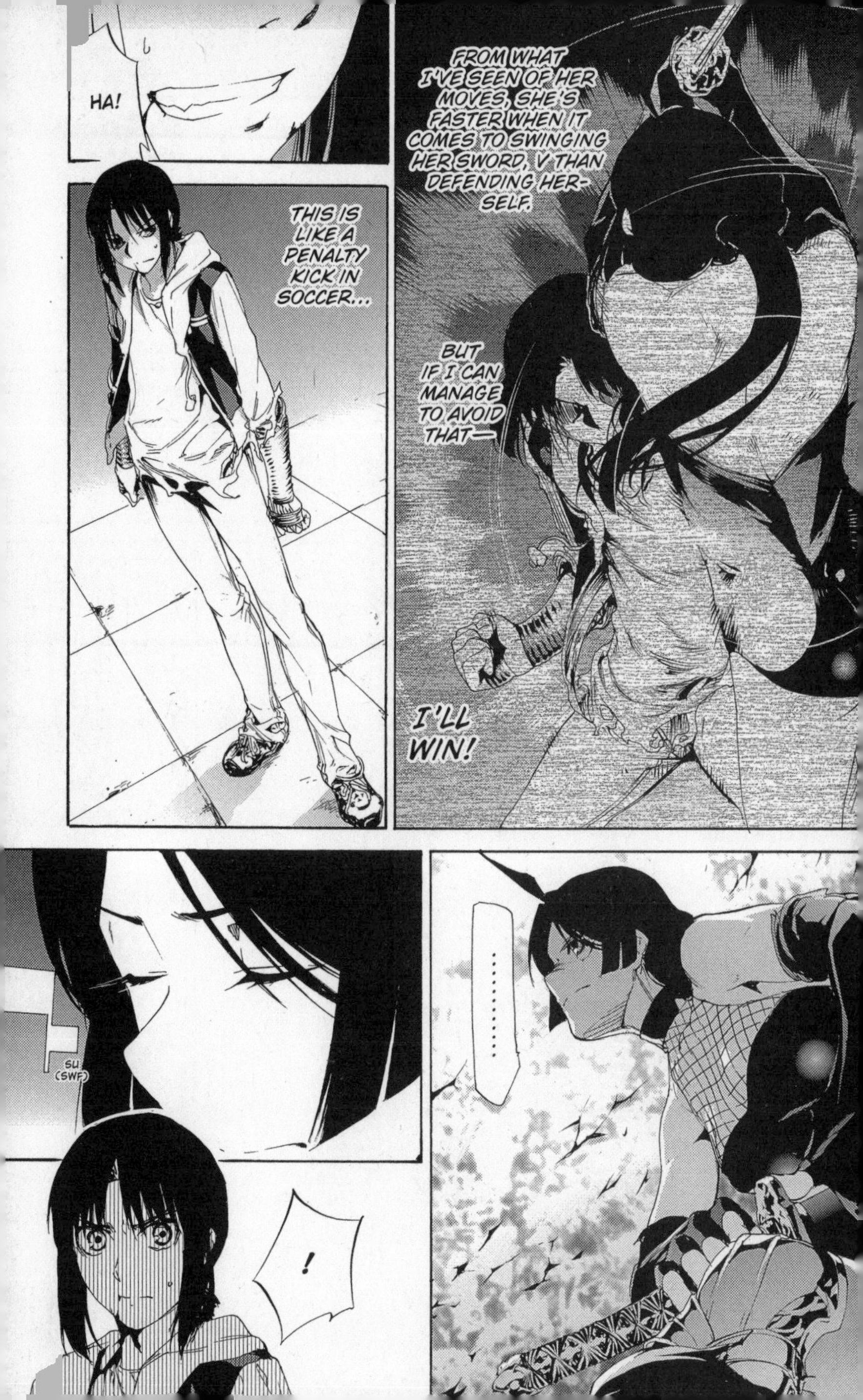
FROM WHAT I'VE SEEN OF HER MOVES, SHE'S FASTER WHEN IT COMES TO SWINGING HER SWORD, V THAN DEFENDING HER-SELF.
BUT IF I CAN MANAGE TO AVOID THAT—
I'LL WIN!
HA!
THIS IS LIKE A PENALTY KICK IN SOCCER...
......
SU (SWF)
!

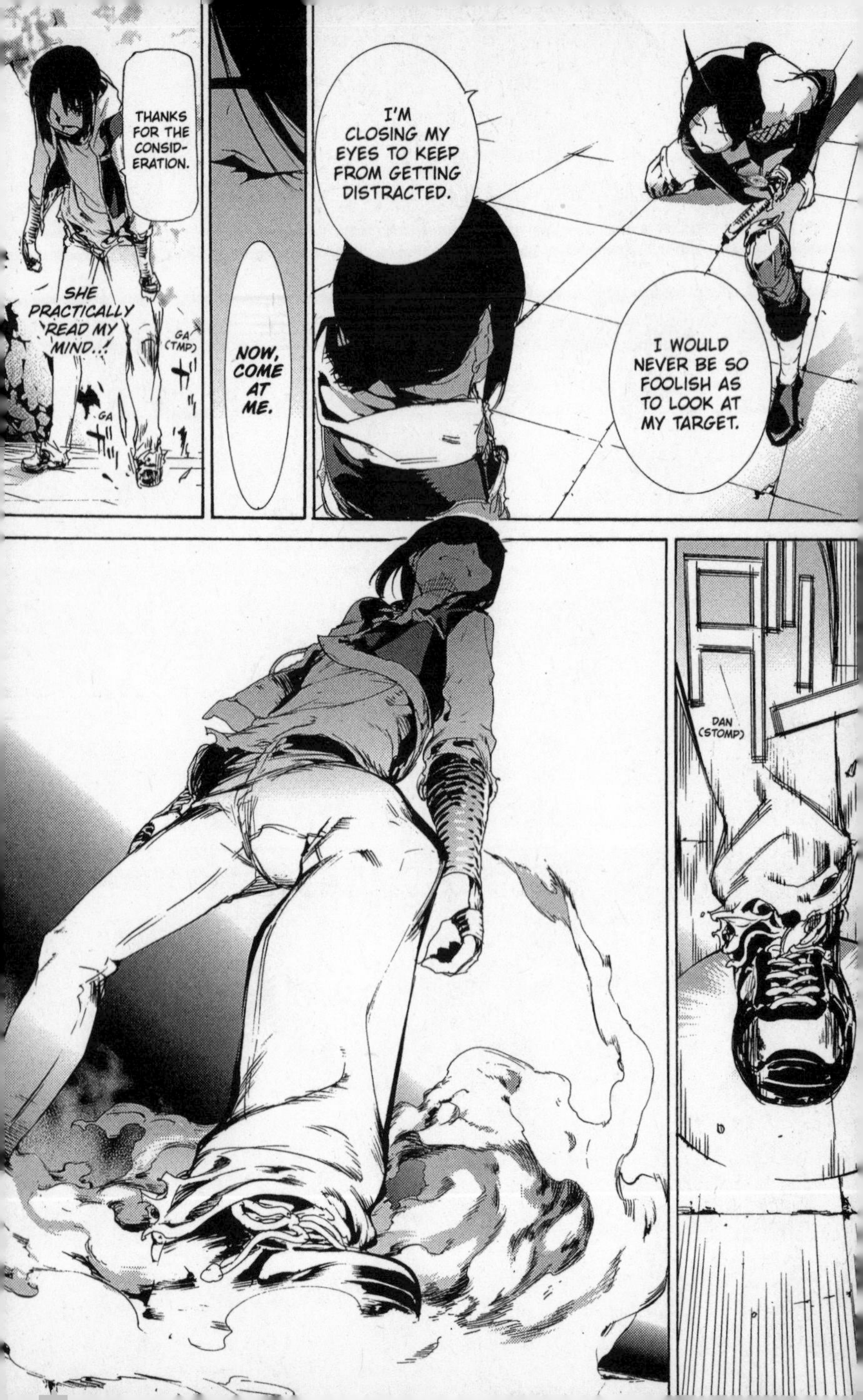
I'M CLOSING MY EYES TO KEEP FROM GETTING DISTRACTED.
I WOULD NEVER BE SO FOOLISH AS TO LOOK AT MY TARGET.
NOW, COME AT ME.
THANKS FOR THE CONSID-ERATION.
SHE PRACTICALLY READ MY MIND...
GA (TMP)
GA
DAN (STOMP)

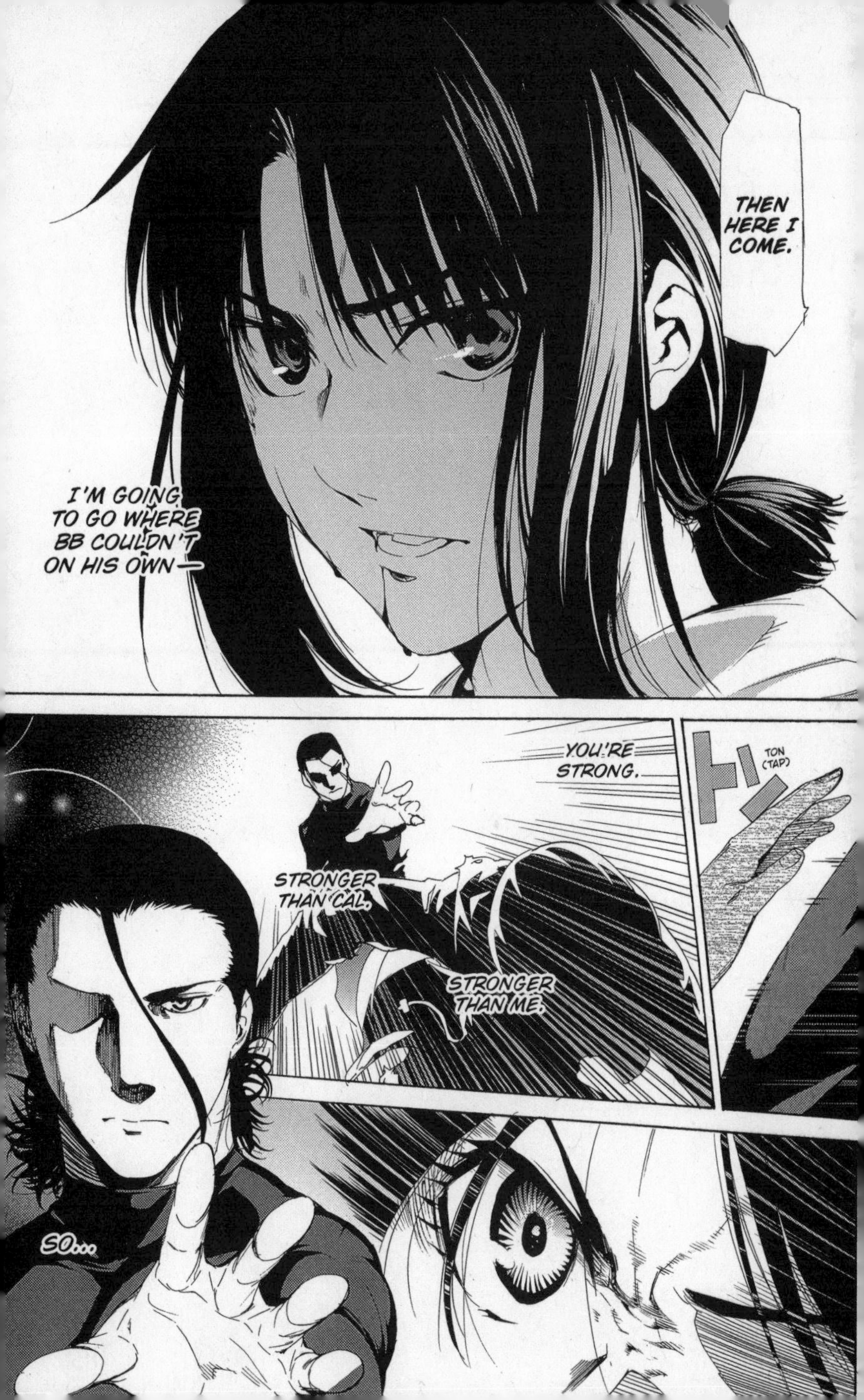
THEN HERE I COME.
I'M GOING TO GO WHERE BB COULDN'T ON HIS OWN—
TON (TAP)
YOU'RE STRONG.
STRONGER THAN CAL.
STRONGER THAN ME.
SO...

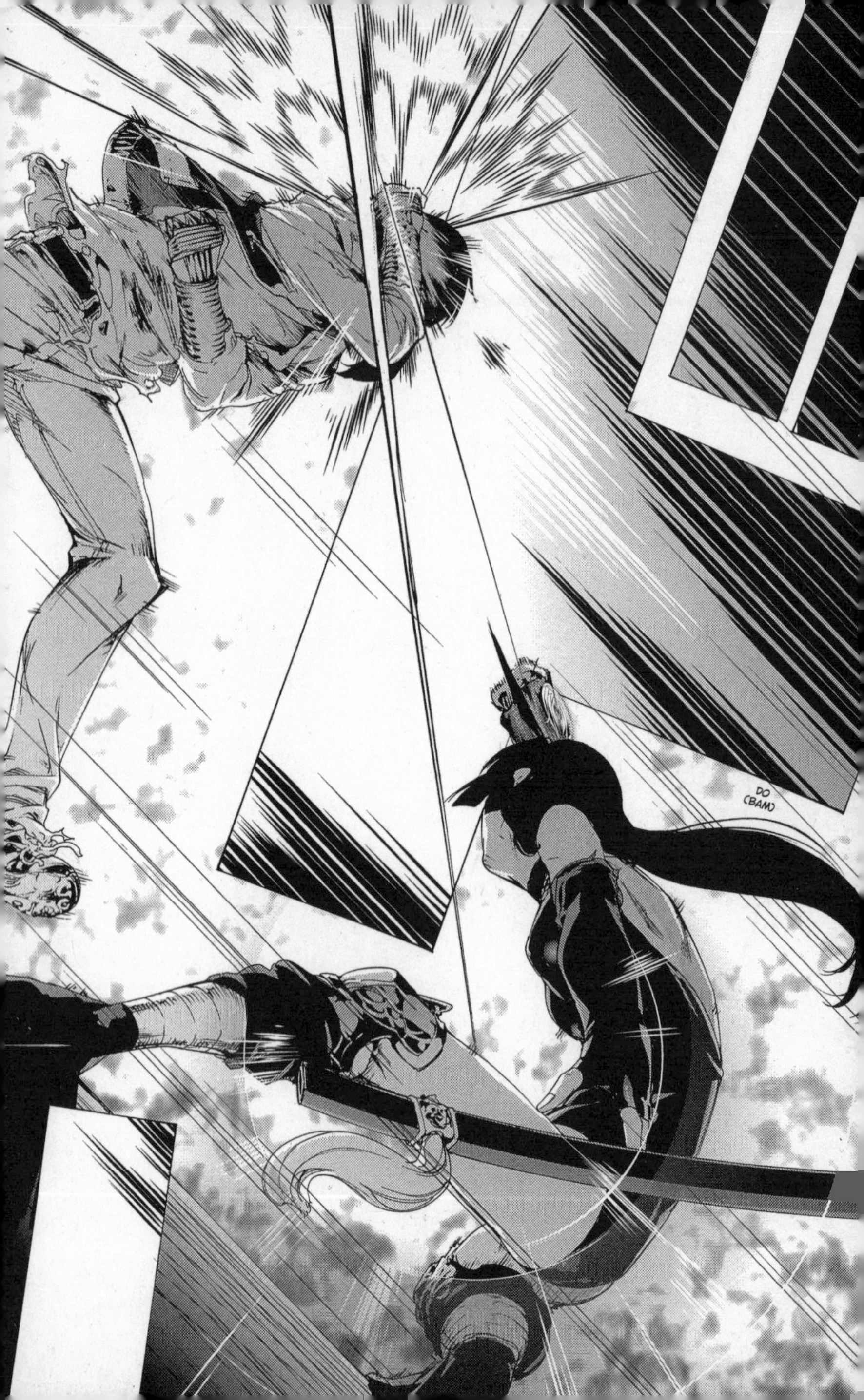
DO
(BAM)

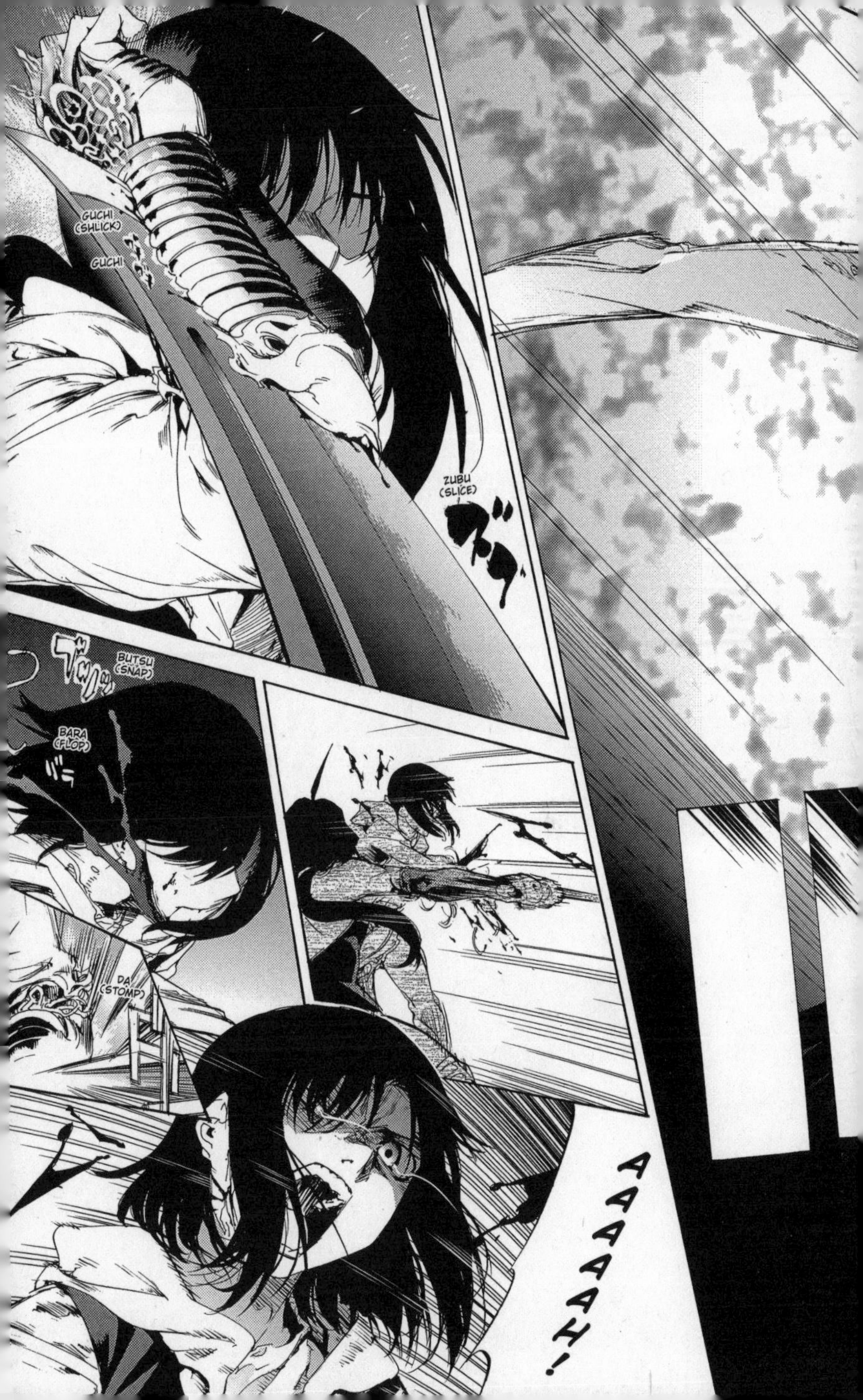
ZUBU (SLICE)
GUCHI (SHLICK)
GUCHI
BUTSU (SNAP)
BARA (FLOP)
DA (STOMP)
AAAAAAH!

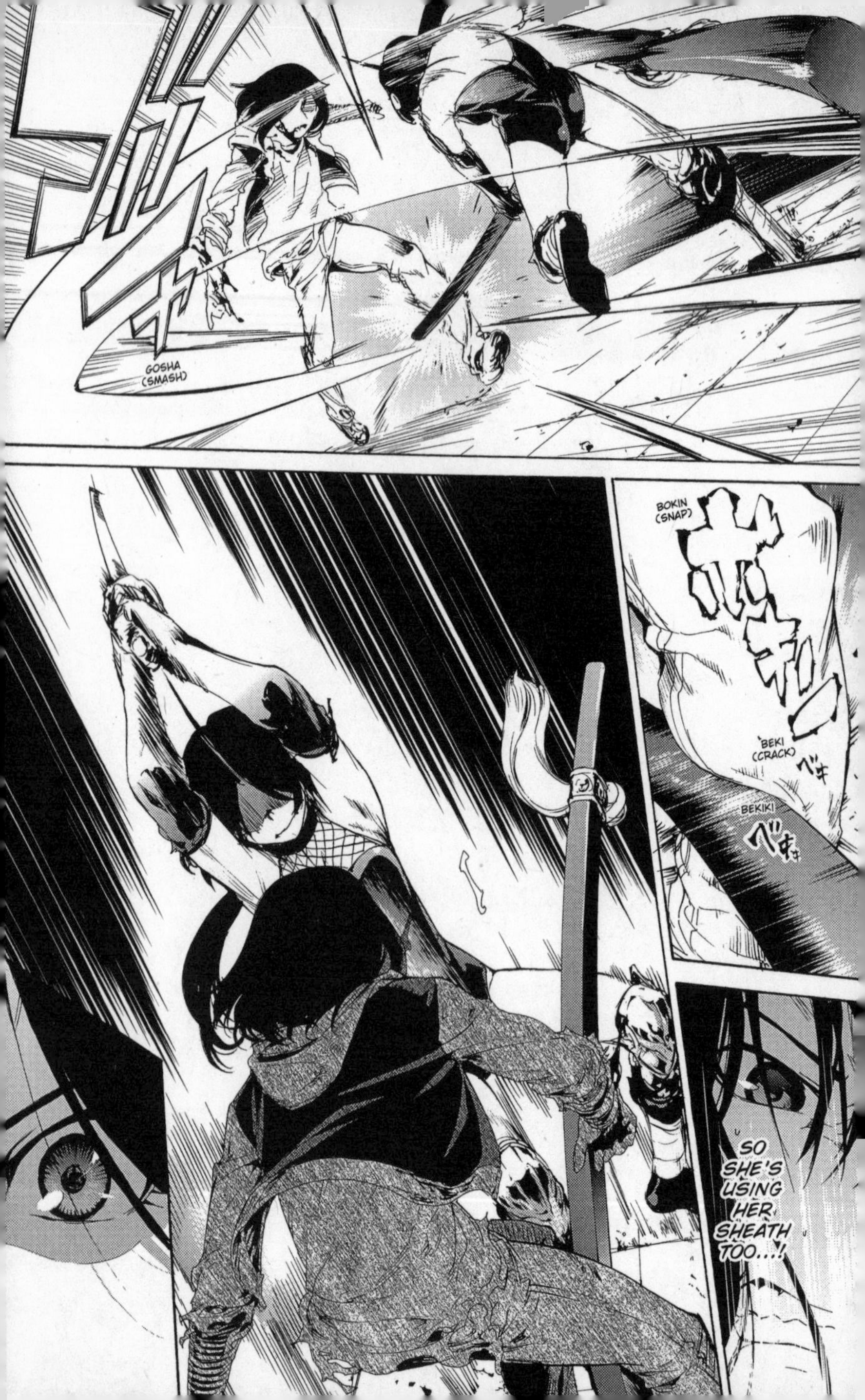
GOSHA (SMASH)
BOKIN (SNAP)
BEKI (CRACK)
BEKIKI
SO SHE'S USING HER SHEATH TOO...!

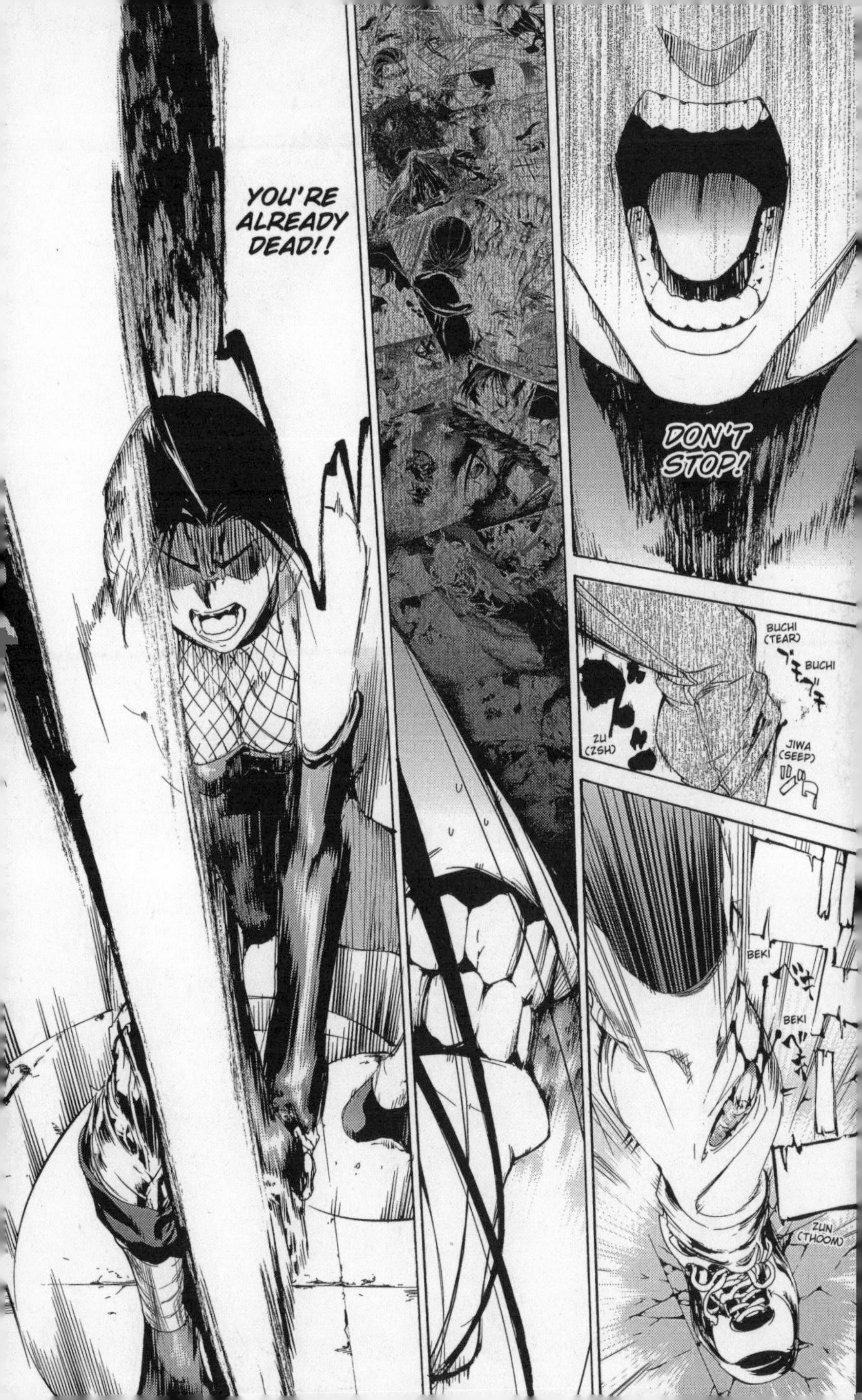
DON'T STOP!
BUCHI (TEAR)
BUCHI
JIWA (SEEP)
ZU (ZSH)
BEKI
BEKI
ZUN (THOOM)
YOU'RE ALREADY DEAD!!

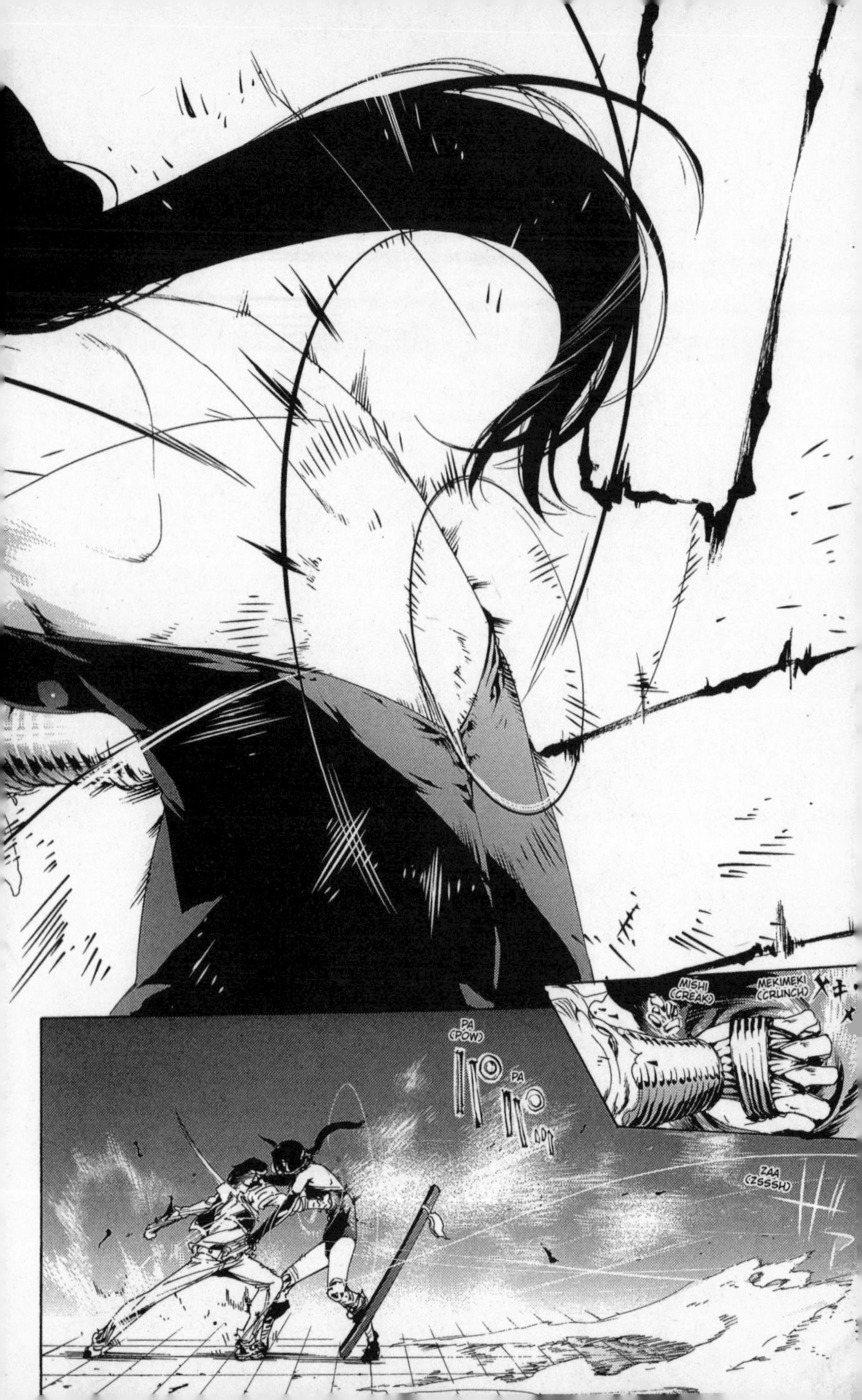
MEKIMEKI (CRUNCH)
MISHI (CREAK)
PA (POW)
PA
ZAA (ZSSSH)

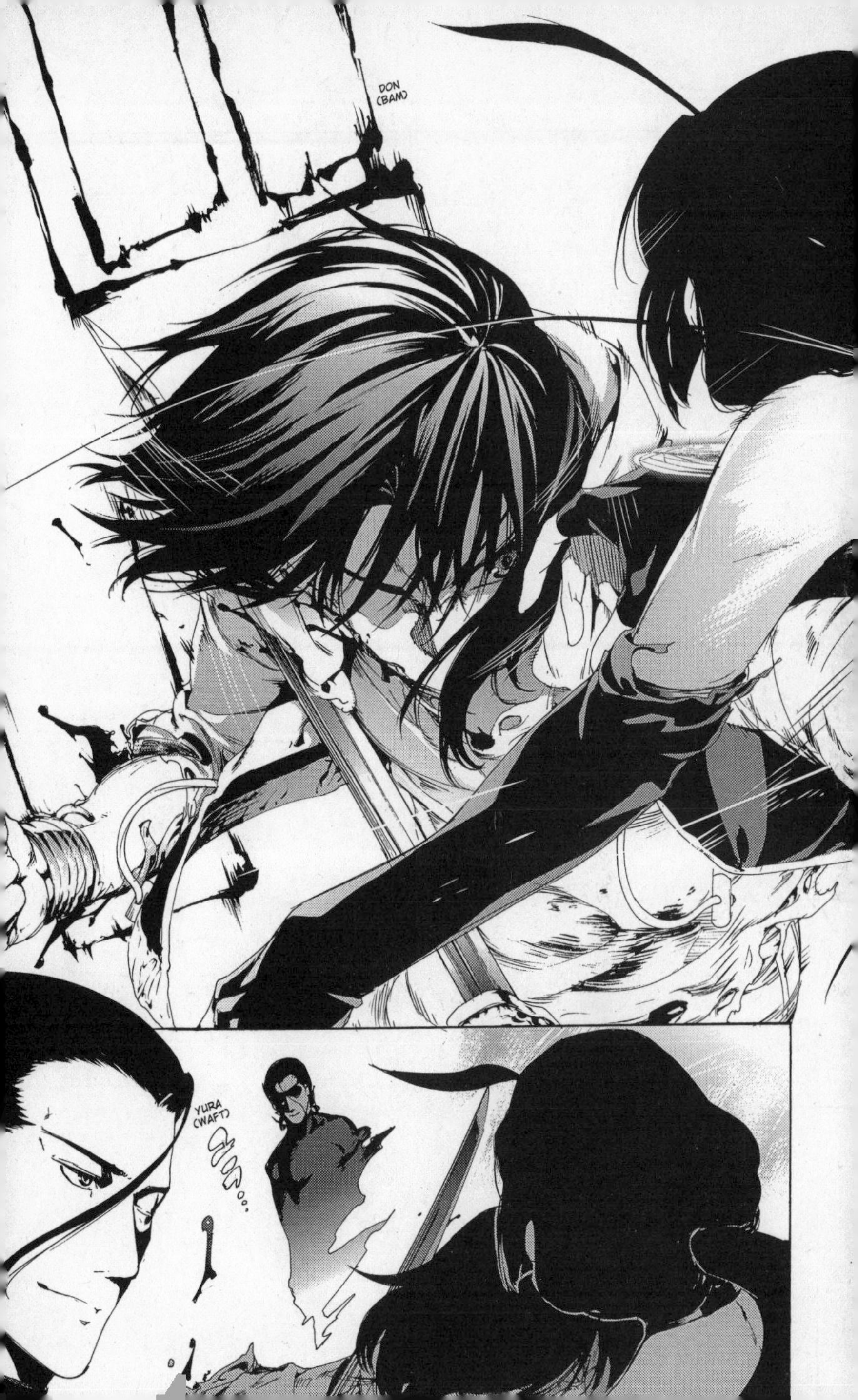
DON (BAM)
YURA (WAFT)

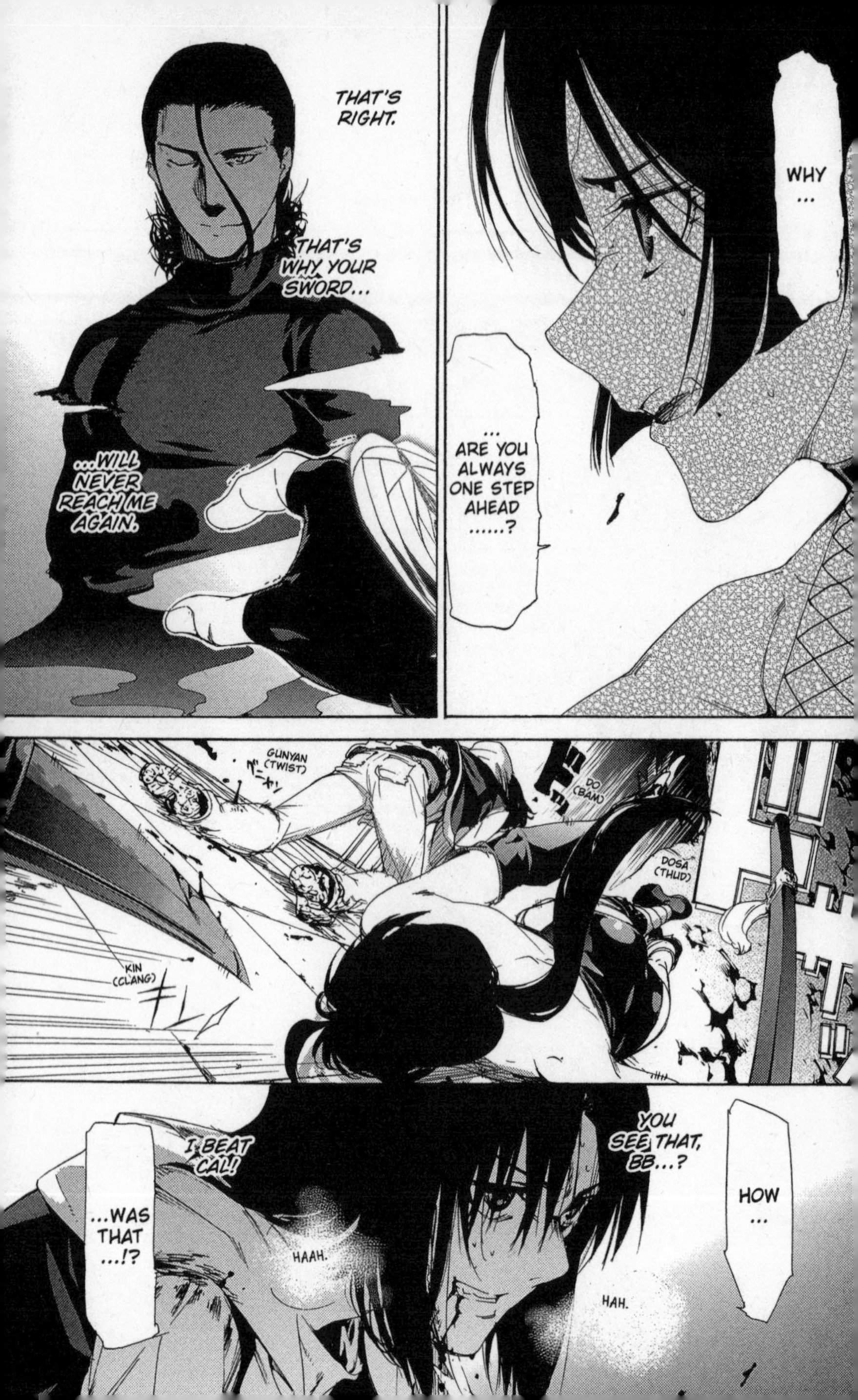
WHY...
...ARE YOU ALWAYS ONE STEP AHEAD......?
THAT'S RIGHT.
THAT'S WHY YOUR SWORD...
...WILL NEVER REACH ME AGAIN.
DO (BAM)
GUNYAN (TWIST)
DOSA (THUD)
KIN (CLANG)
YOU SEE THAT, BB...?
HOW...
I BEAT CAL!
HAH.
...WAS THAT...!?
HAAH.

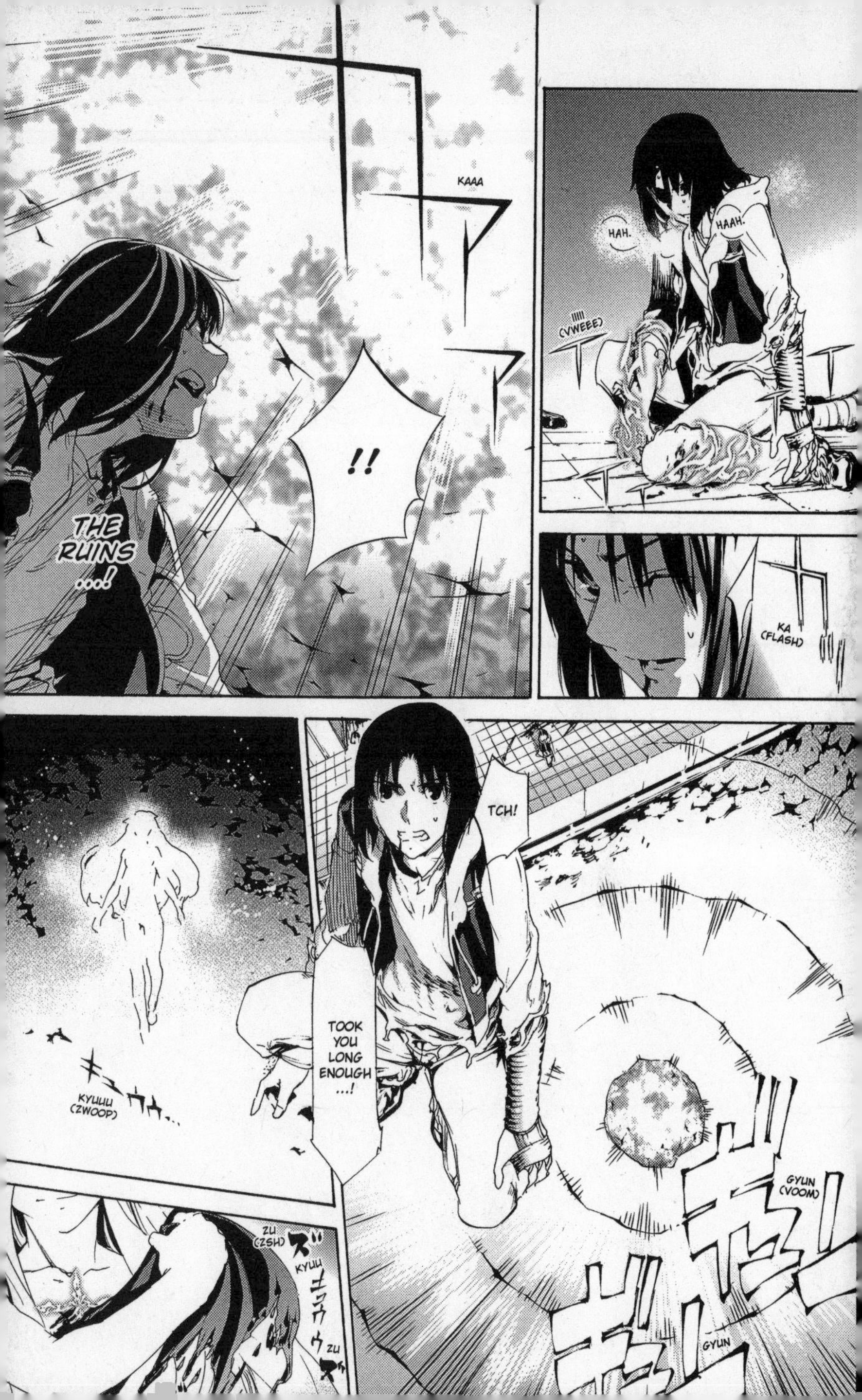
HAH.
HAAH.
IIIII (VWEEE)
KA (FLASH)
KAAA
!!
THE RUINS ...!
TCH!
TOOK YOU LONG ENOUGH ...!
GYUN (VOOM)
GYUN
KYUUU (ZWOOP)
ZU (ZSH)
KYUU
ZU

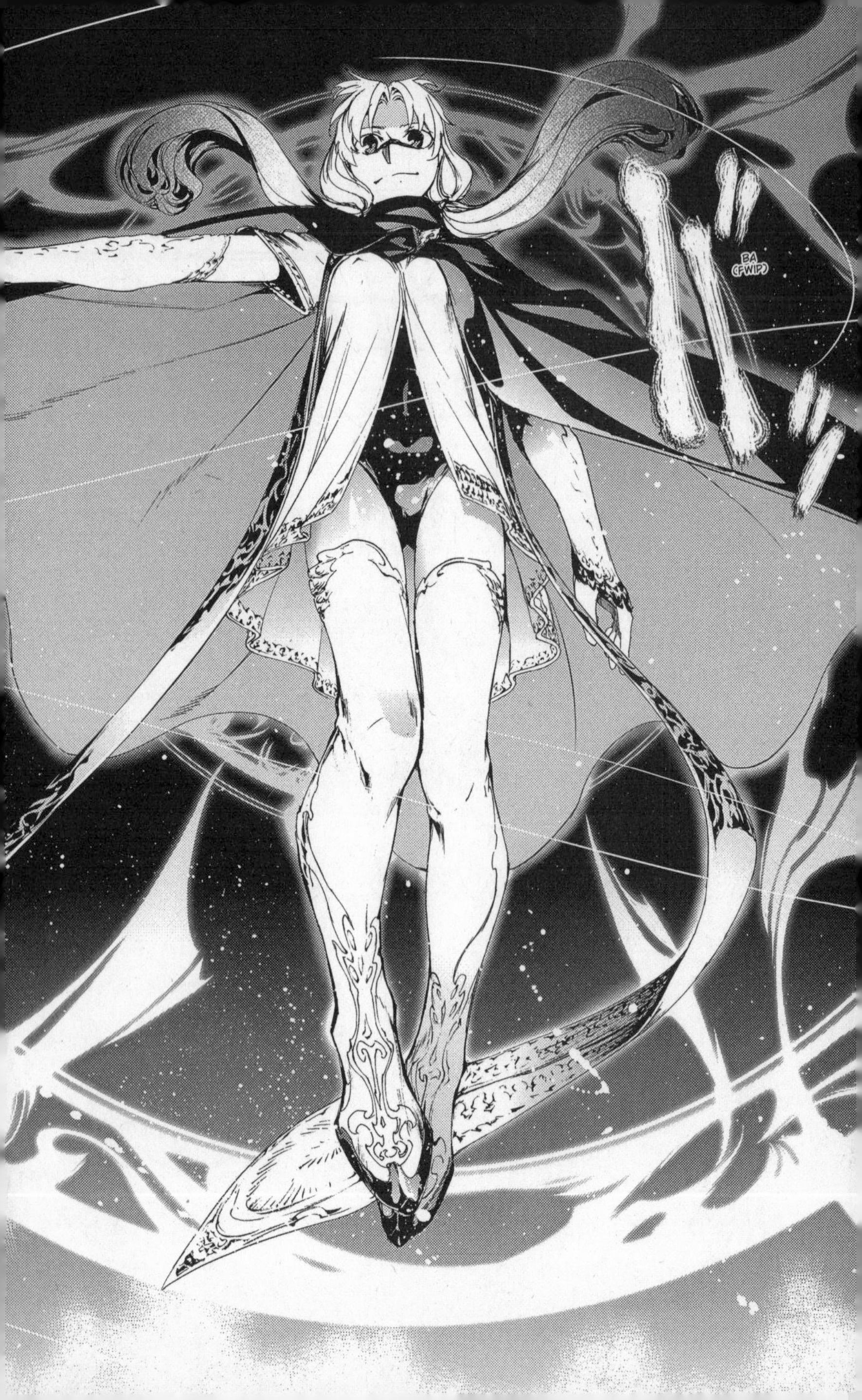
BA
(FWIP)

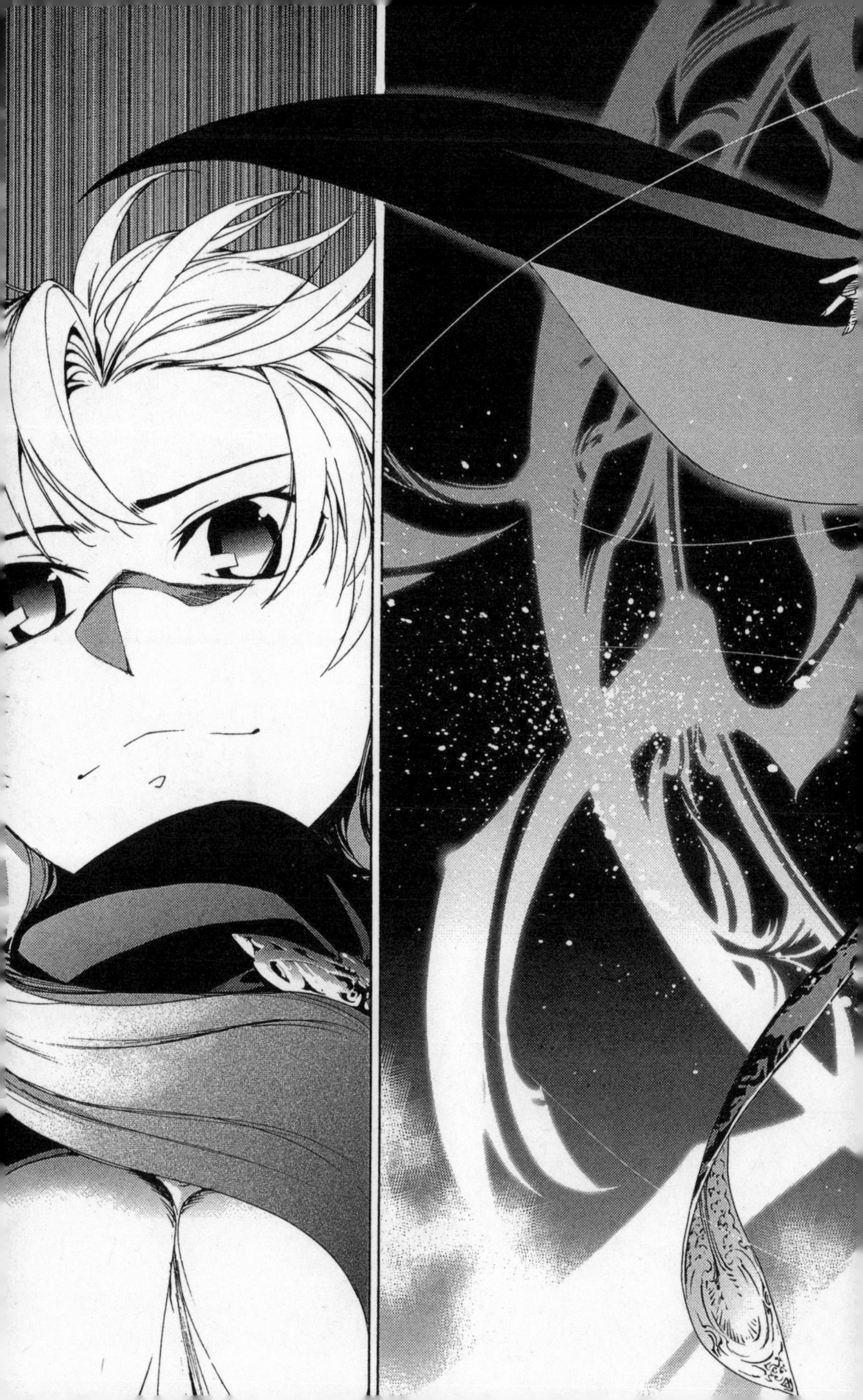

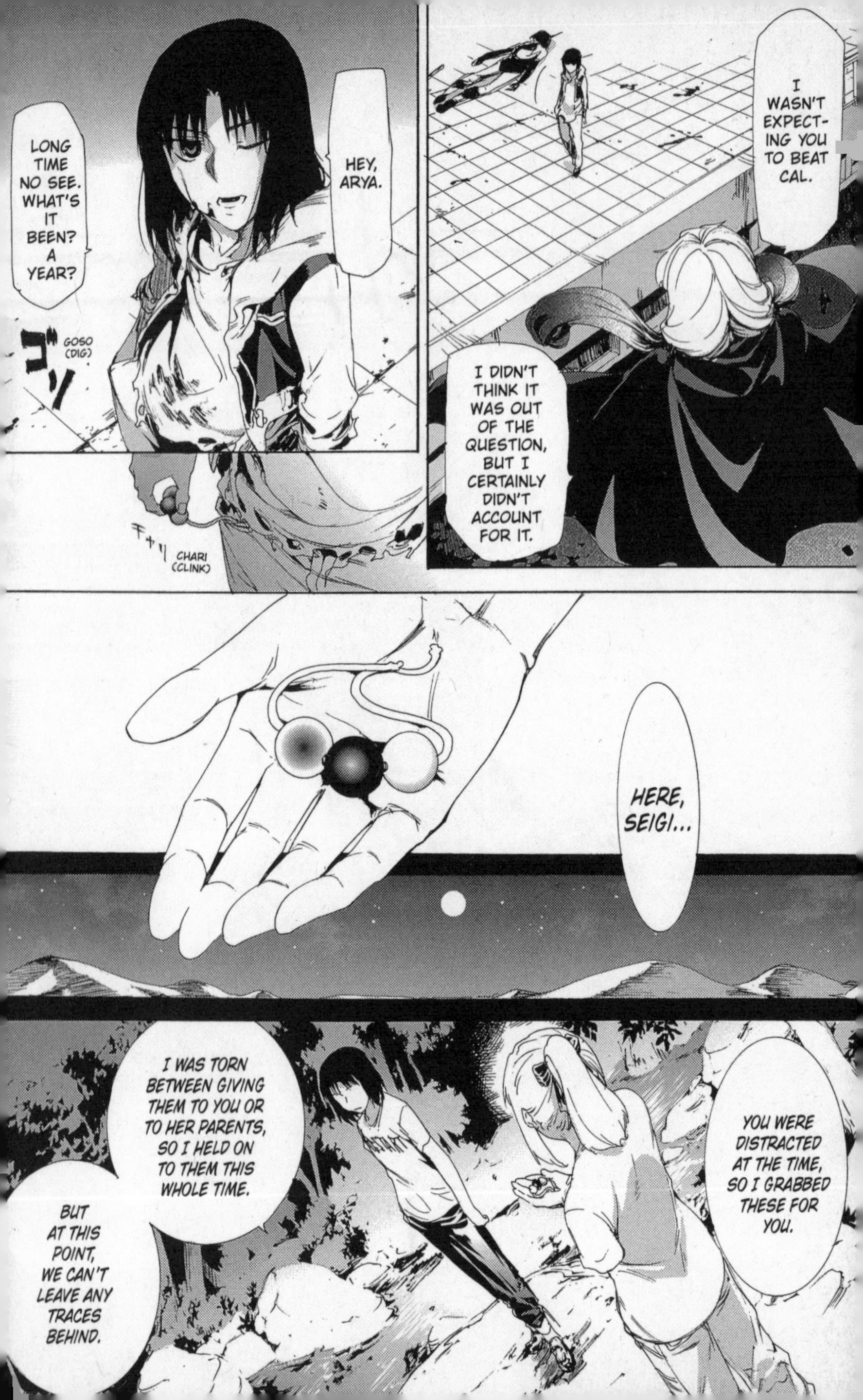

I WASN'T EXPECTING YOU TO BEAT CAL.
I DIDN'T THINK IT WAS OUT OF THE QUESTION, BUT I CERTAINLY DIDN'T ACCOUNT FOR IT.
HEY, ARYA.
LONG TIME NO SEE. WHAT'S IT BEEN? A YEAR?
ゴソ GOSO (DIG)
チャリ CHARI (CLINK)
HERE, SEIGI...
YOU WERE DISTRACTED AT THE TIME, SO I GRABBED THESE FOR YOU.
I WAS TORN BETWEEN GIVING THEM TO YOU OR TO HER PARENTS, SO I HELD ON TO THEM THIS WHOLE TIME.
BUT AT THIS POINT, WE CAN'T LEAVE ANY TRACES BEHIND.

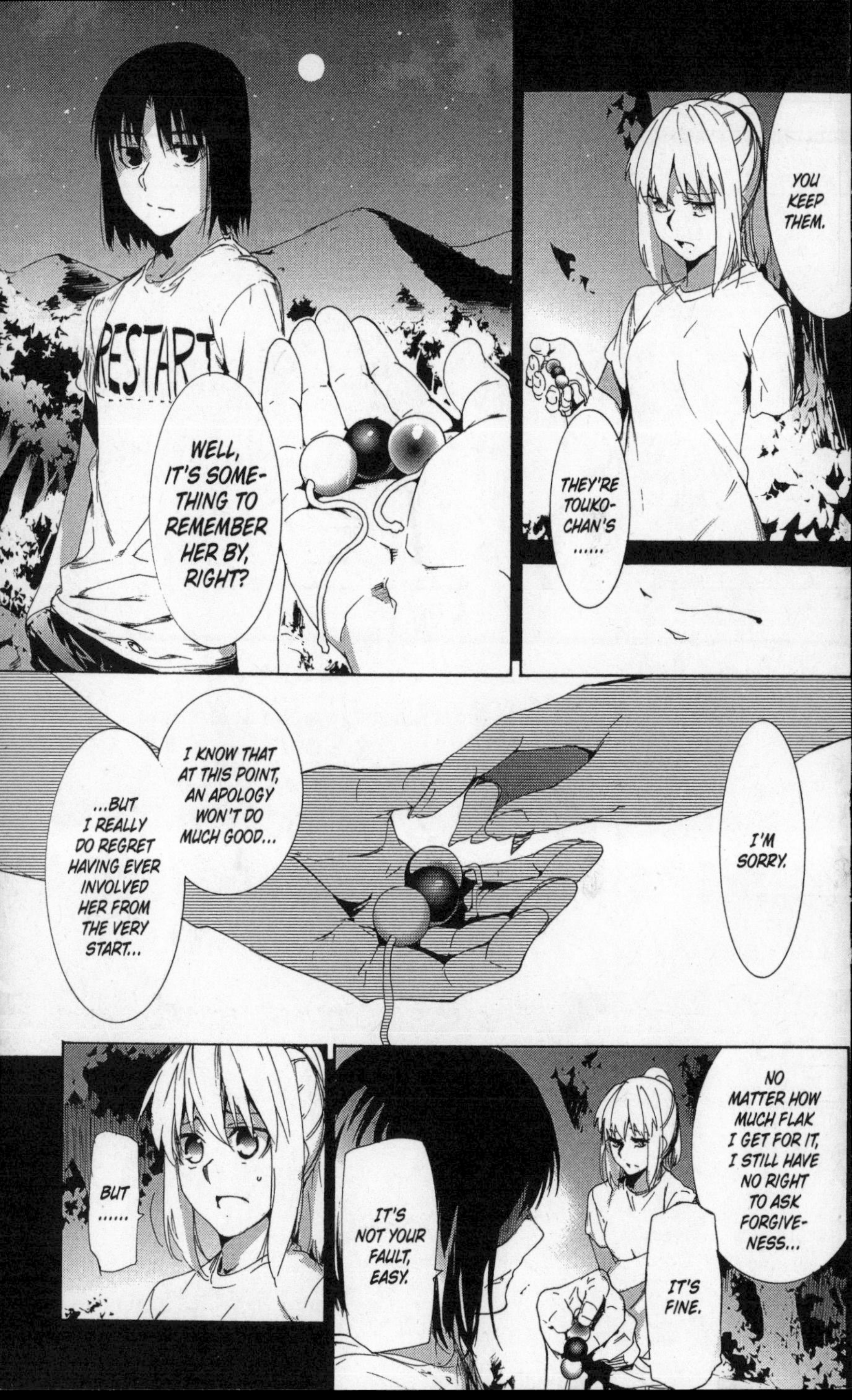

YOU KEEP THEM.
THEY'RE TOUKO-CHAN'S ......
WELL, IT'S SOMETHING TO REMEMBER HER BY, RIGHT?
I'M SORRY.
I KNOW THAT AT THIS POINT, AN APOLOGY WON'T DO MUCH GOOD...
...BUT I REALLY DO REGRET HAVING EVER INVOLVED HER FROM THE VERY START...
NO MATTER HOW MUCH FLAK I GET FOR IT, I STILL HAVE NO RIGHT TO ASK FORGIVENESS...
IT'S FINE.
IT'S NOT YOUR FAULT, EASY.
BUT ......

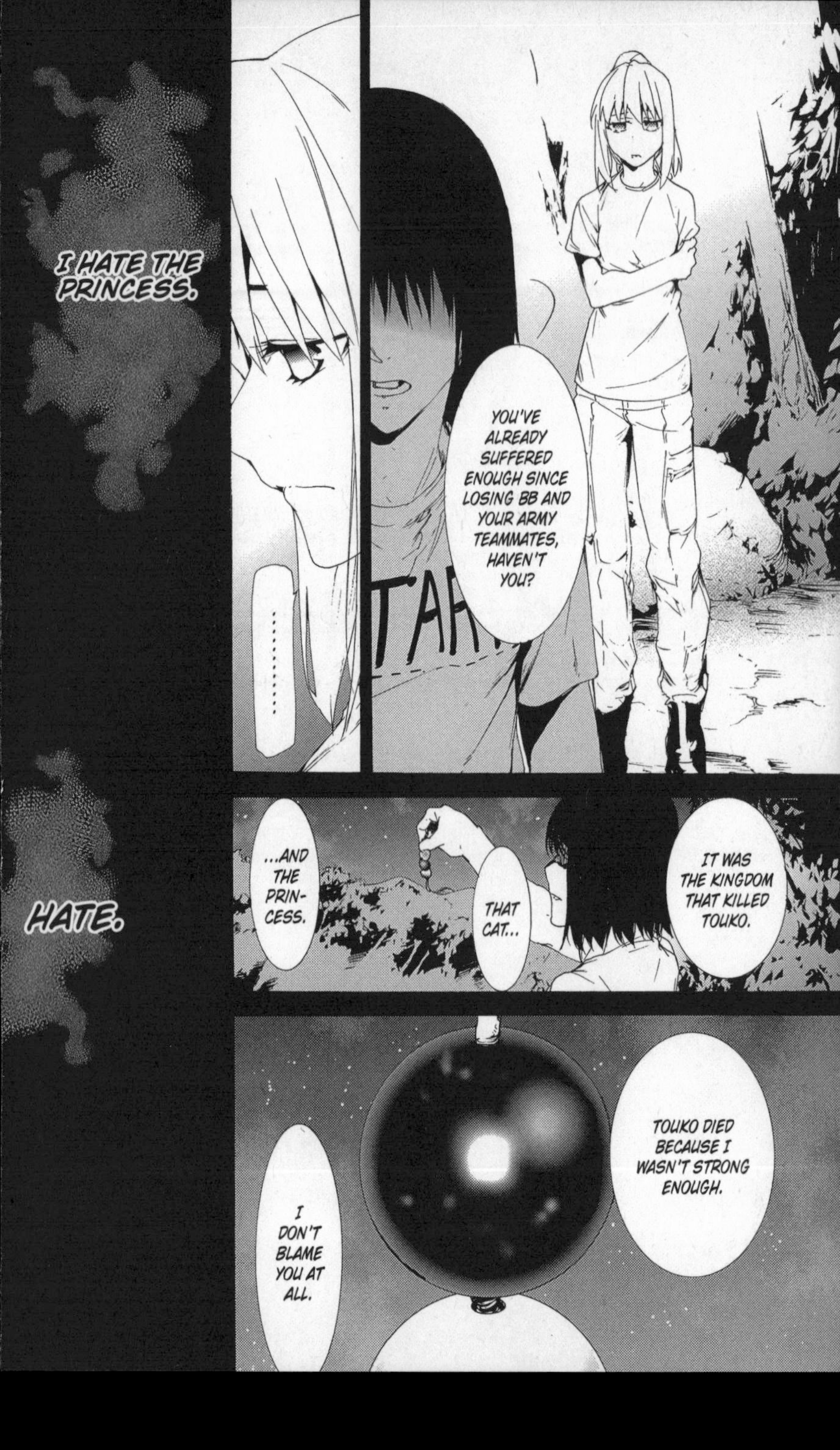
YOU'VE ALREADY SUFFERED ENOUGH SINCE LOSING BB AND YOUR ARMY TEAMMATES, HAVEN'T YOU?
......
IT WAS THE KINGDOM THAT KILLED TOUKO.
THAT CAT...
...AND THE PRIN-CESS.
TOUKO DIED BECAUSE I WASN'T STRONG ENOUGH.
I DON'T BLAME YOU AT ALL.
I HATE THE PRINCESS.
HATE.

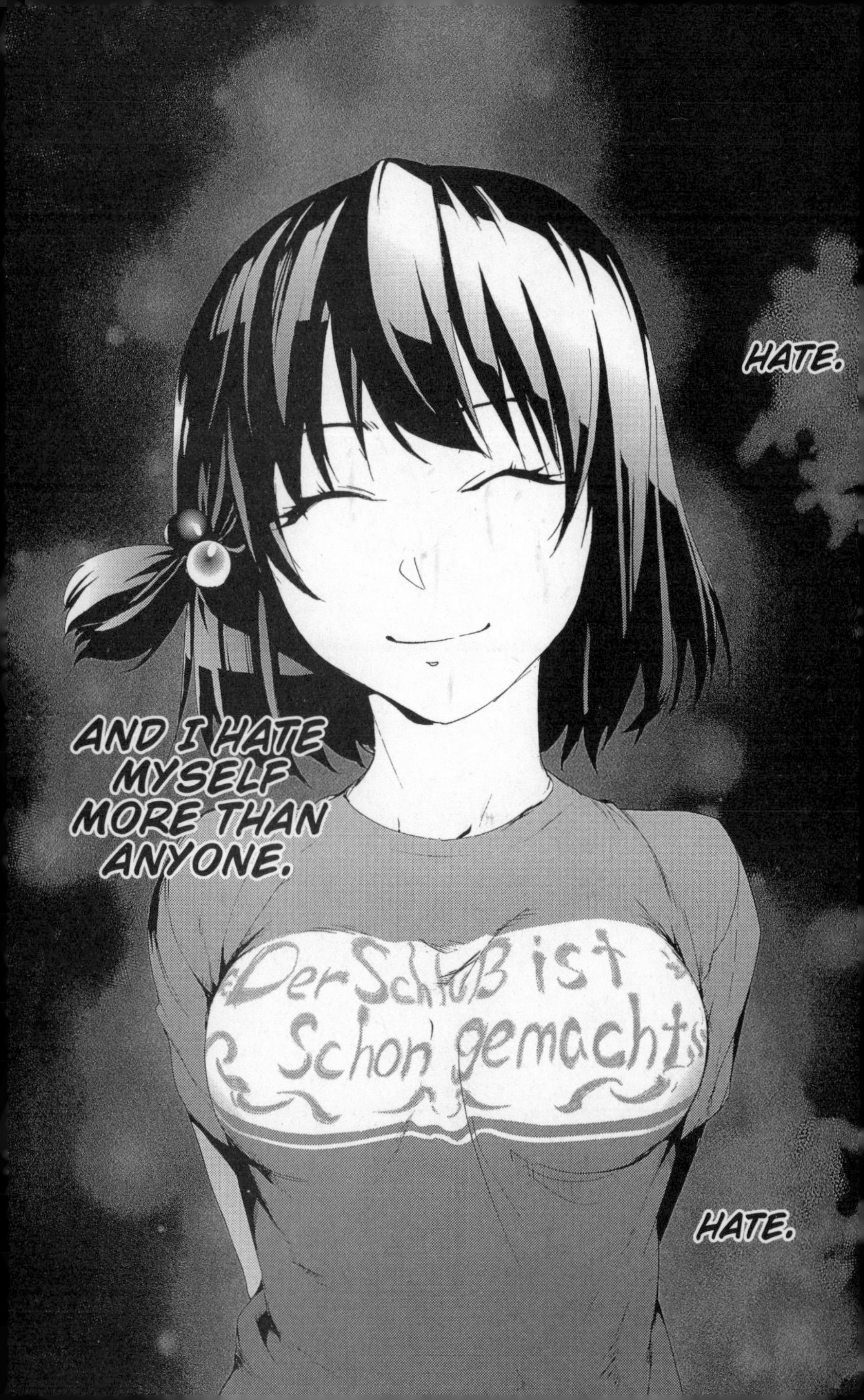
HATE.
AND I HATE MYSELF MORE THAN ANYONE.
Der Schluß ist Schon gemacht
HATE.

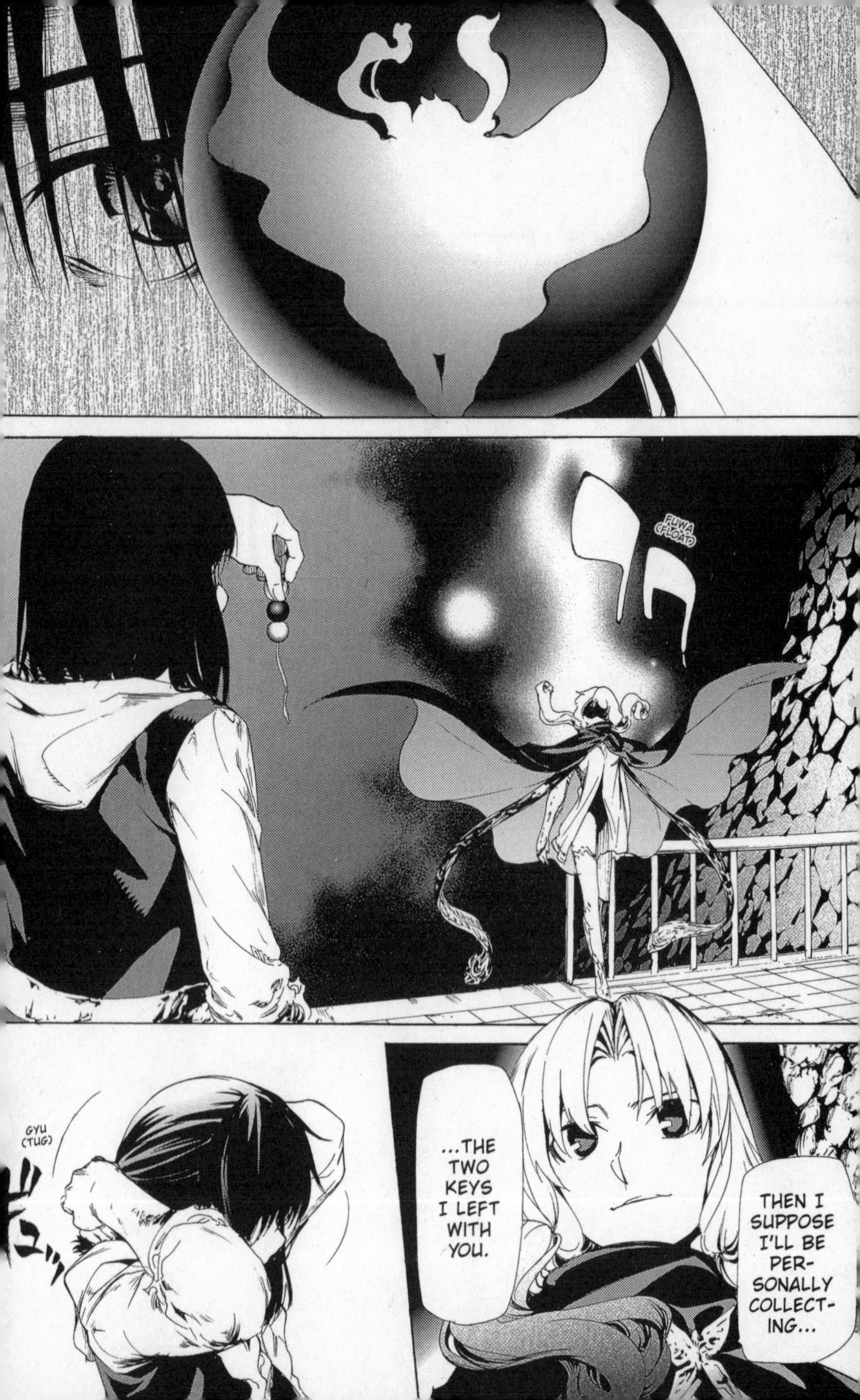
FUWA (FLOAT)
THEN I SUPPOSE I'LL BE PER-SONALLY COLLECT-ING...
...THE TWO KEYS I LEFT WITH YOU.
GYU (TUG)
ギュッ

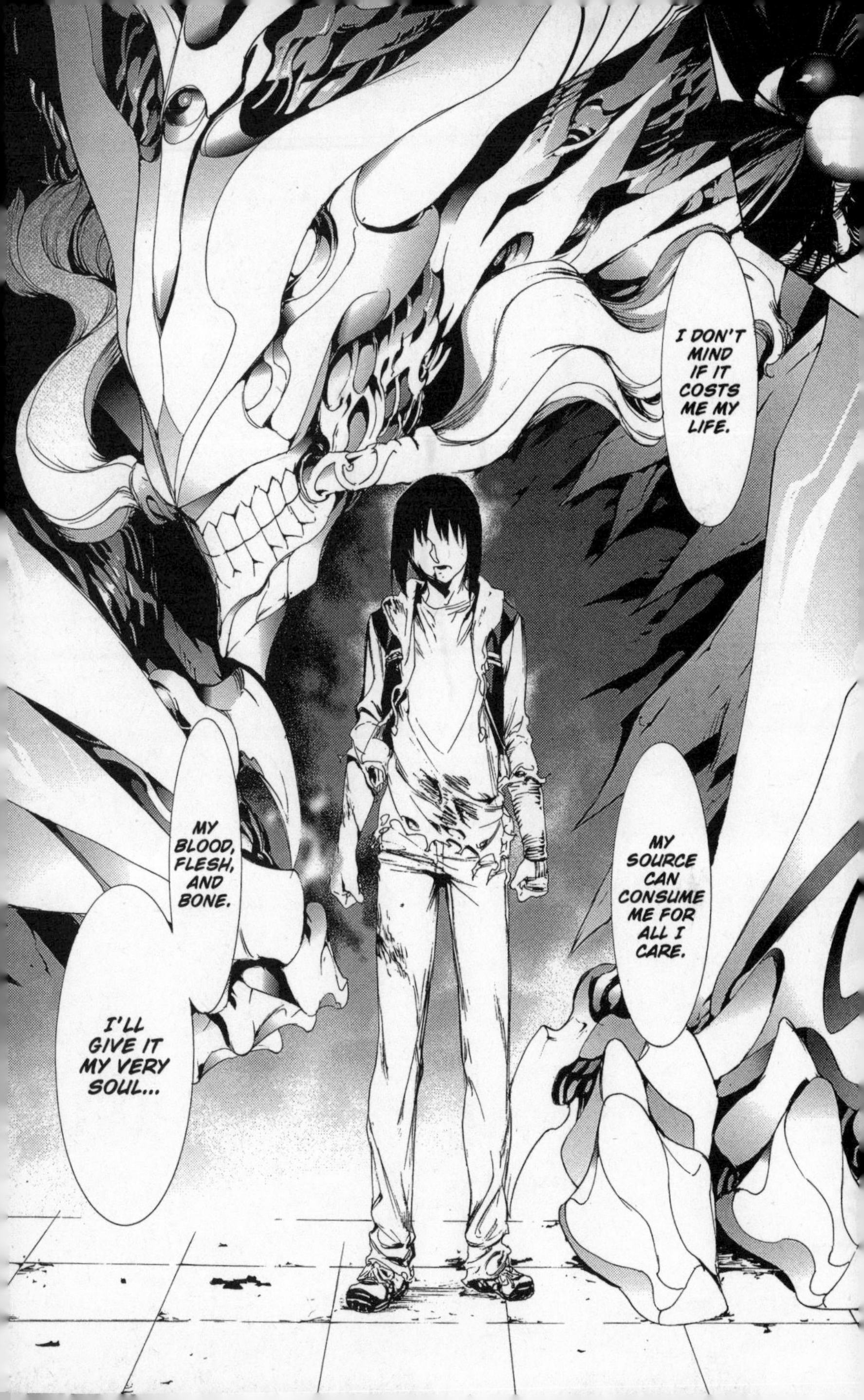
I DON'T MIND IF IT COSTS ME MY LIFE.
MY SOURCE CAN CONSUME ME FOR ALL I CARE.
MY BLOOD, FLESH, AND BONE.
I'LL GIVE IT MY VERY SOUL...

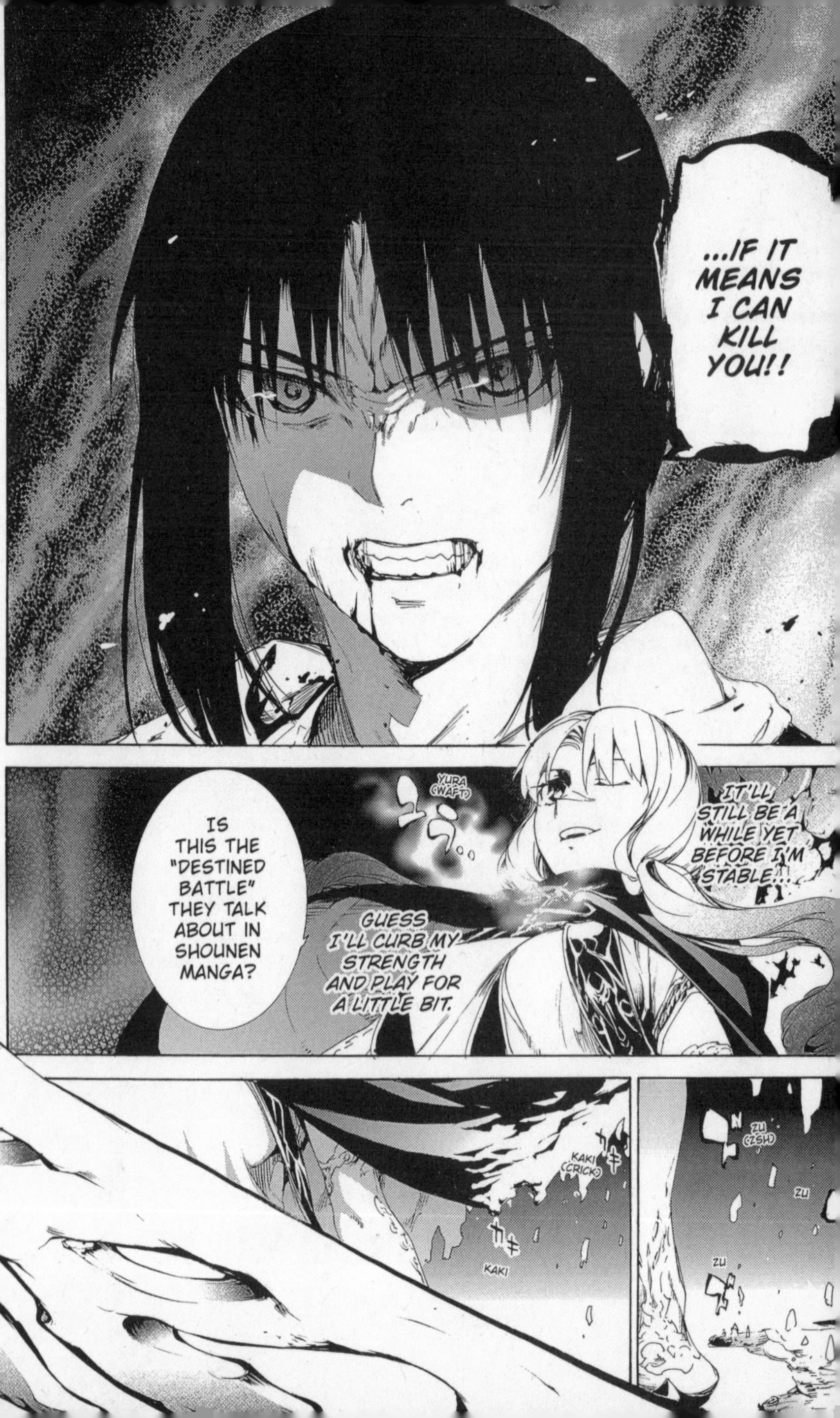
...IF IT MEANS I CAN KILL YOU!!
IT'LL STILL BE A WHILE YET BEFORE I'M STABLE...
YURA (WAFT)
GUESS I'LL CURB MY STRENGTH AND PLAY FOR A LITTLE BIT.
IS THIS THE "DESTINED BATTLE" THEY TALK ABOUT IN SHOUNEN MANGA?
ZU (ZSH)
ZU
ZU
KAKI (CRICK)
KAKI

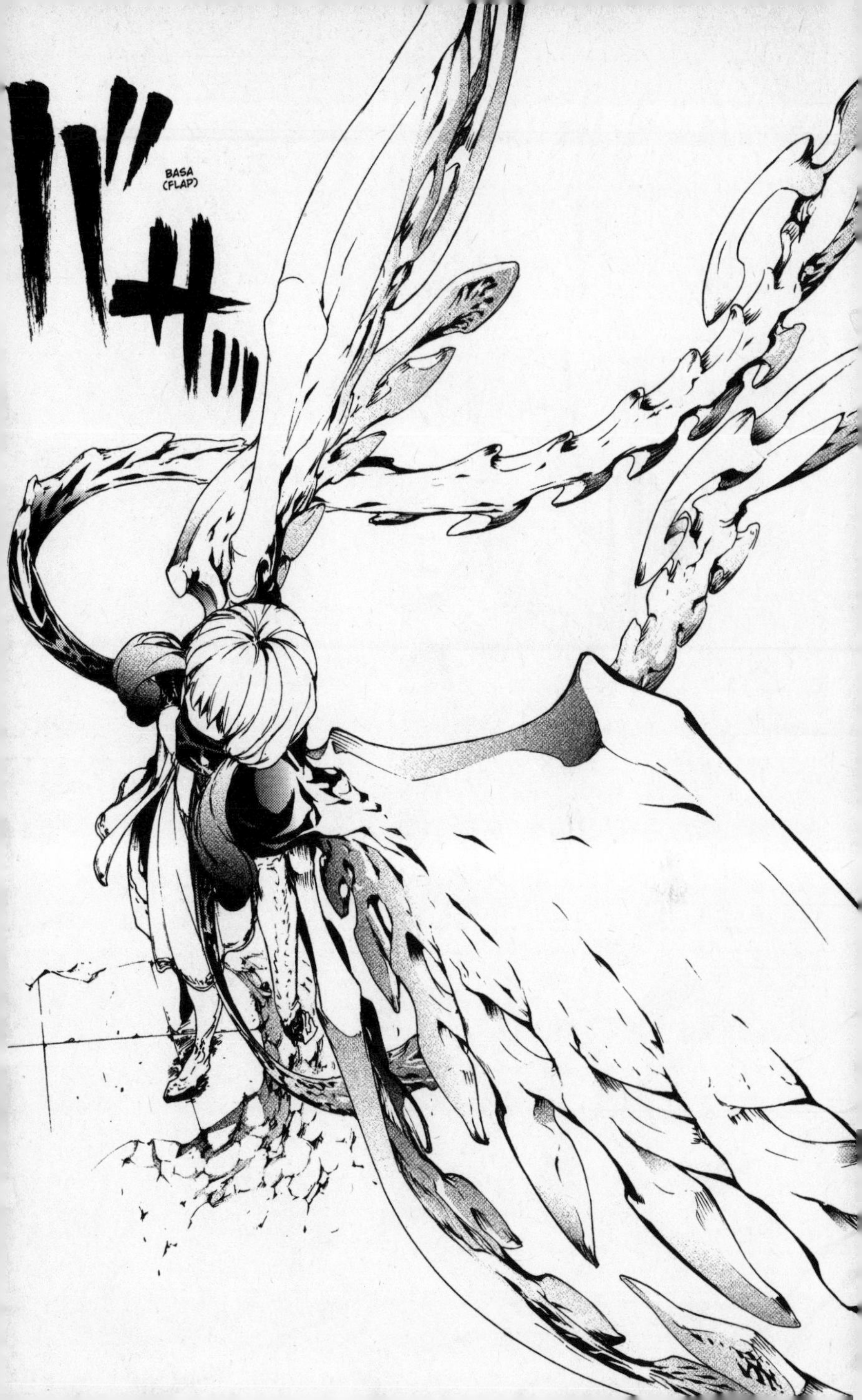
バサッ
BASA
(FLAP)

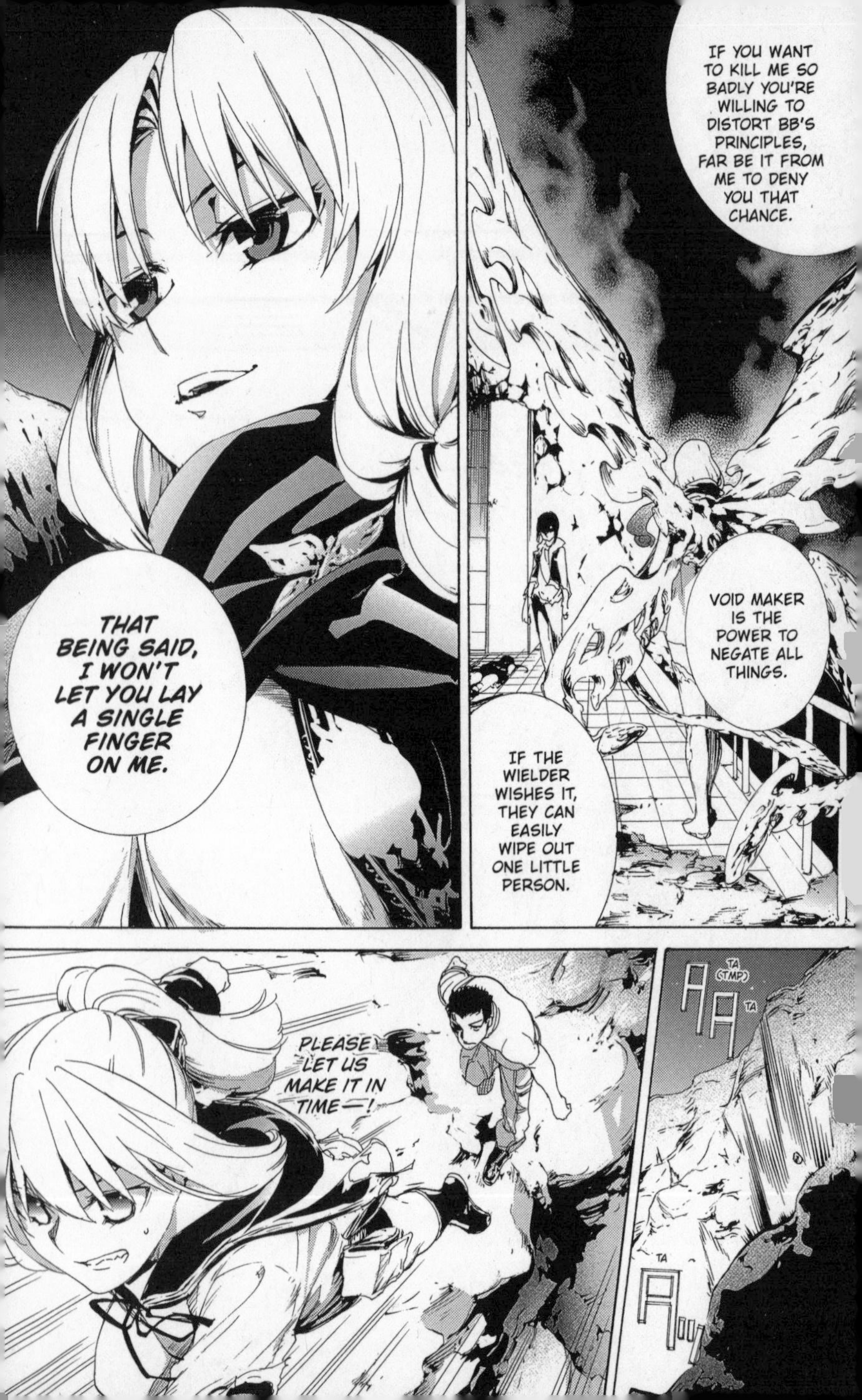
IF YOU WANT TO KILL ME SO BADLY YOU'RE WILLING TO DISTORT BB'S PRINCIPLES, FAR BE IT FROM ME TO DENY YOU THAT CHANCE.
VOID MAKER IS THE POWER TO NEGATE ALL THINGS.
IF THE WIELDER WISHES IT, THEY CAN EASILY WIPE OUT ONE LITTLE PERSON.
THAT BEING SAID, I WON'T LET YOU LAY A SINGLE FINGER ON ME.
TA (TMP)
TA
TA
PLEASE LET US MAKE IT IN TIME—!

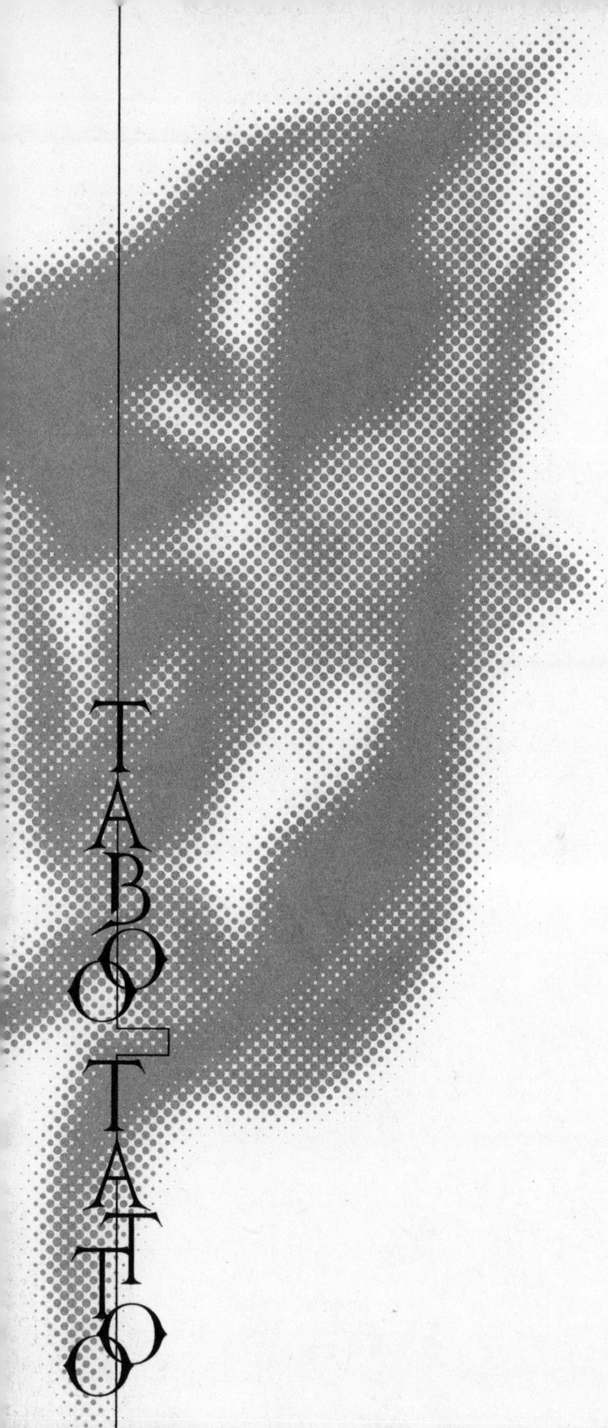

TABOO TATTOO

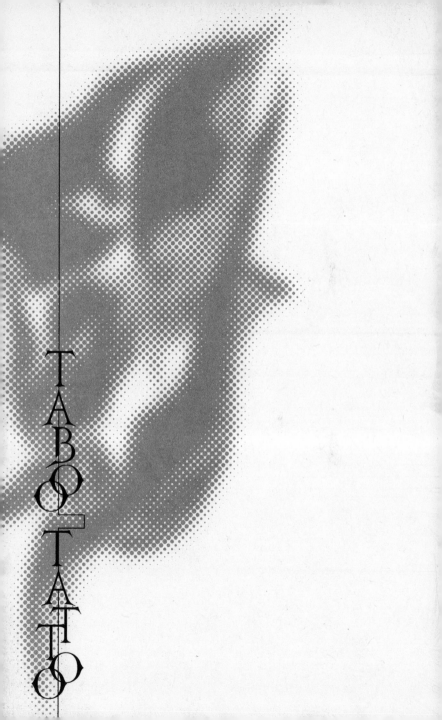

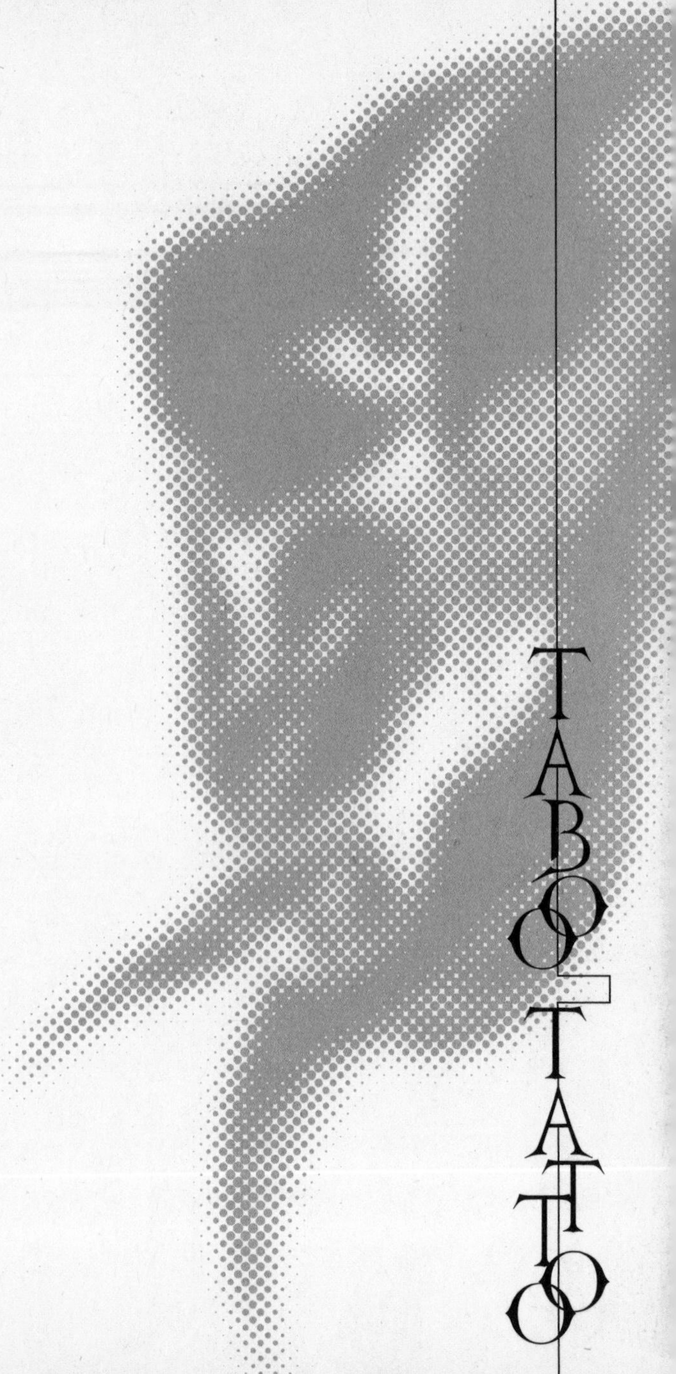

TABOO TATTOO

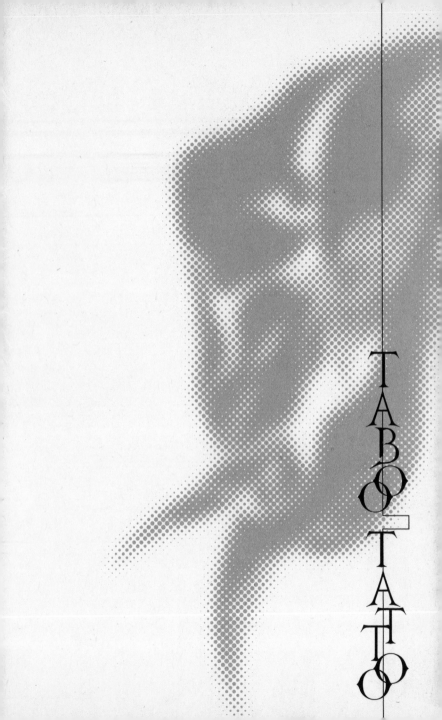

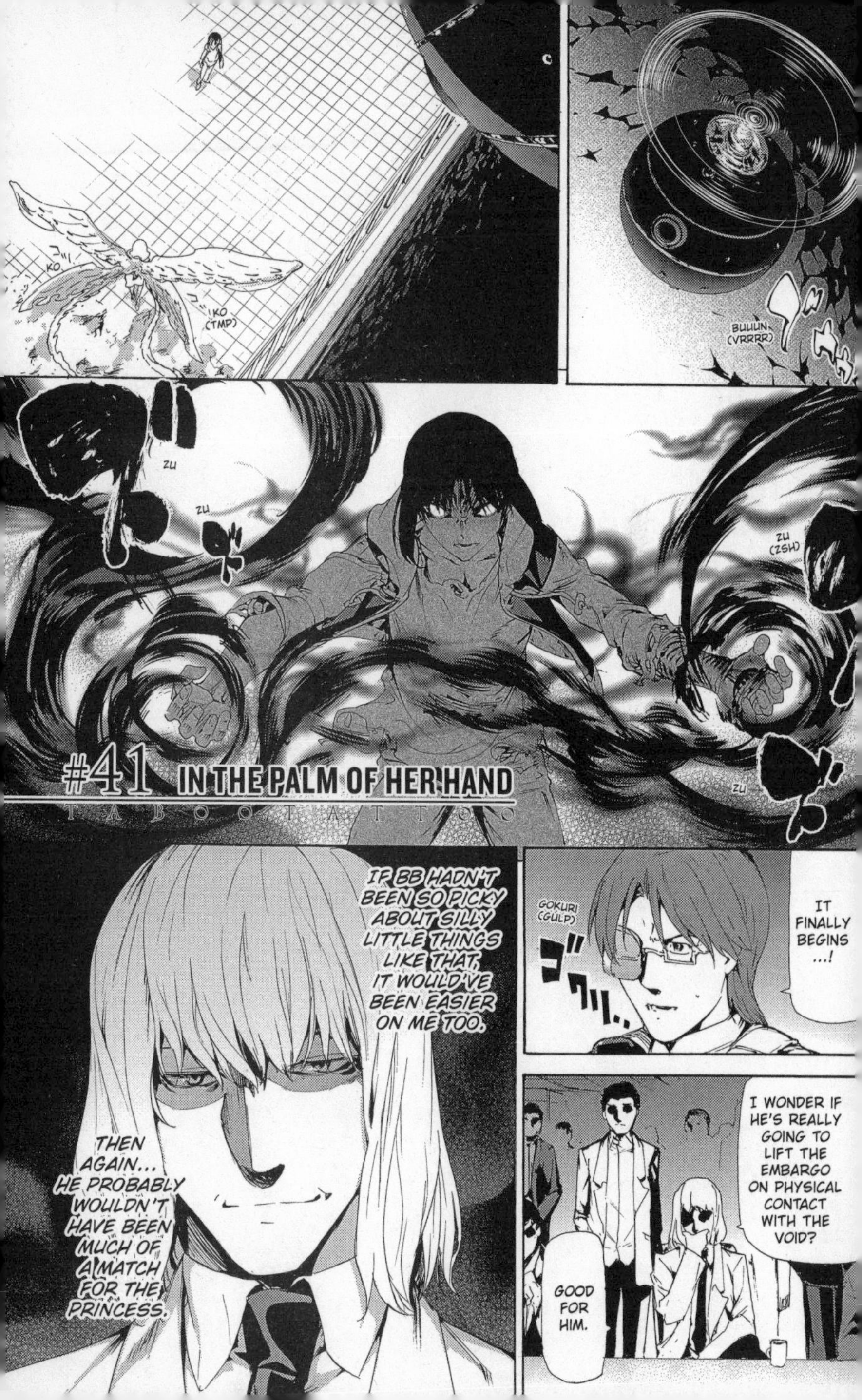
BUUUN (VRRRR)
KO
KO (TMP)
ZU (ZSH)
ZU
ZU
ZU
#41 IN THE PALM OF HER HAND
TABOO TATTOO
GOKURI (GULP)
IT FINALLY BEGINS ...!
I WONDER IF HE'S REALLY GOING TO LIFT THE EMBARGO ON PHYSICAL CONTACT WITH THE VOID?
GOOD FOR HIM.
IF BB HADN'T BEEN SO PICKY ABOUT SILLY LITTLE THINGS LIKE THAT, IT WOULD'VE BEEN EASIER ON ME TOO.
THEN AGAIN... HE PROBABLY WOULDN'T HAVE BEEN MUCH OF A MATCH FOR THE PRINCESS.

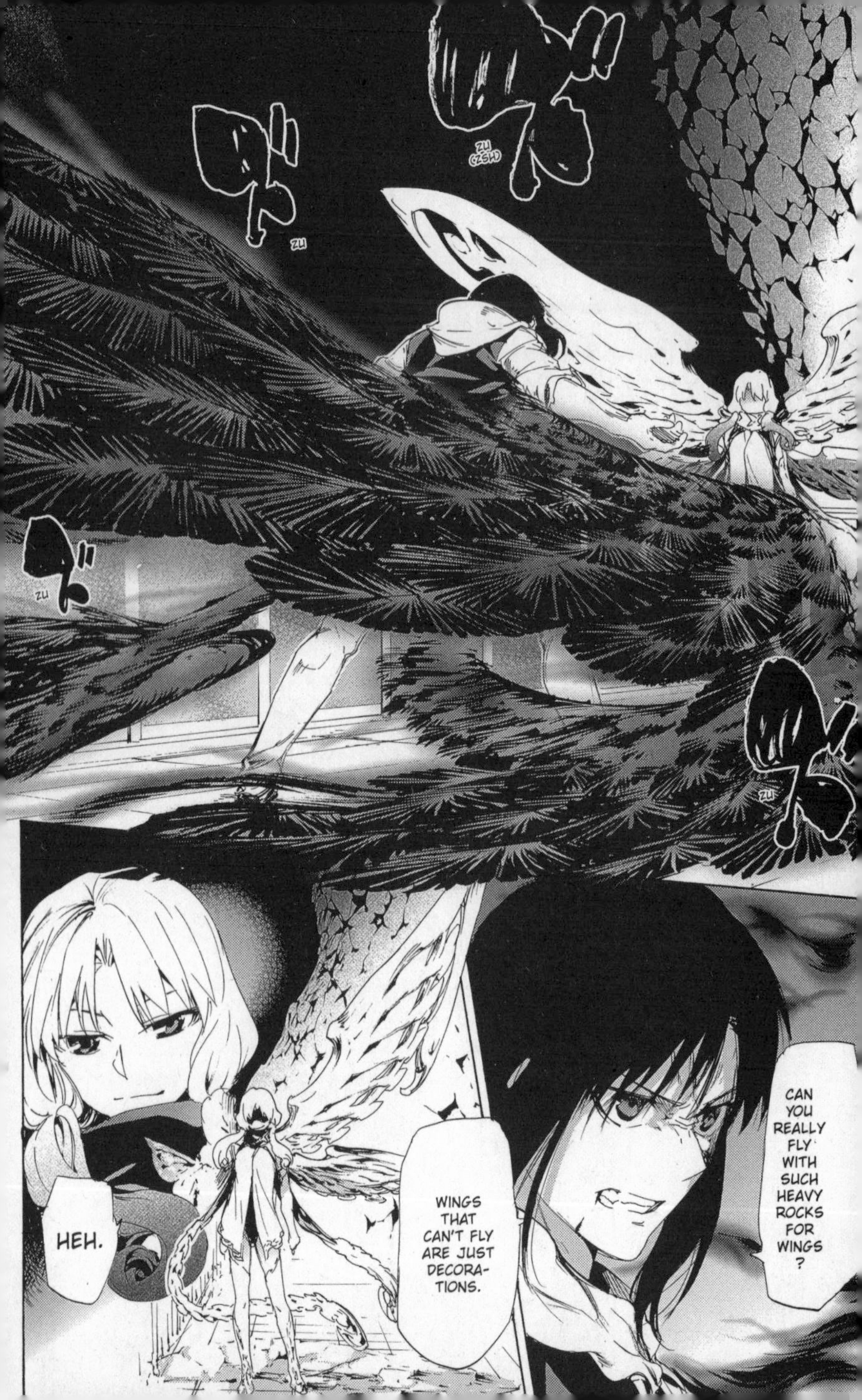
ZU (ZSH)
ZU
ZU
ZU
CAN YOU REALLY FLY WITH SUCH HEAVY ROCKS FOR WINGS?
WINGS THAT CAN'T FLY ARE JUST DECORATIONS.
HEH.

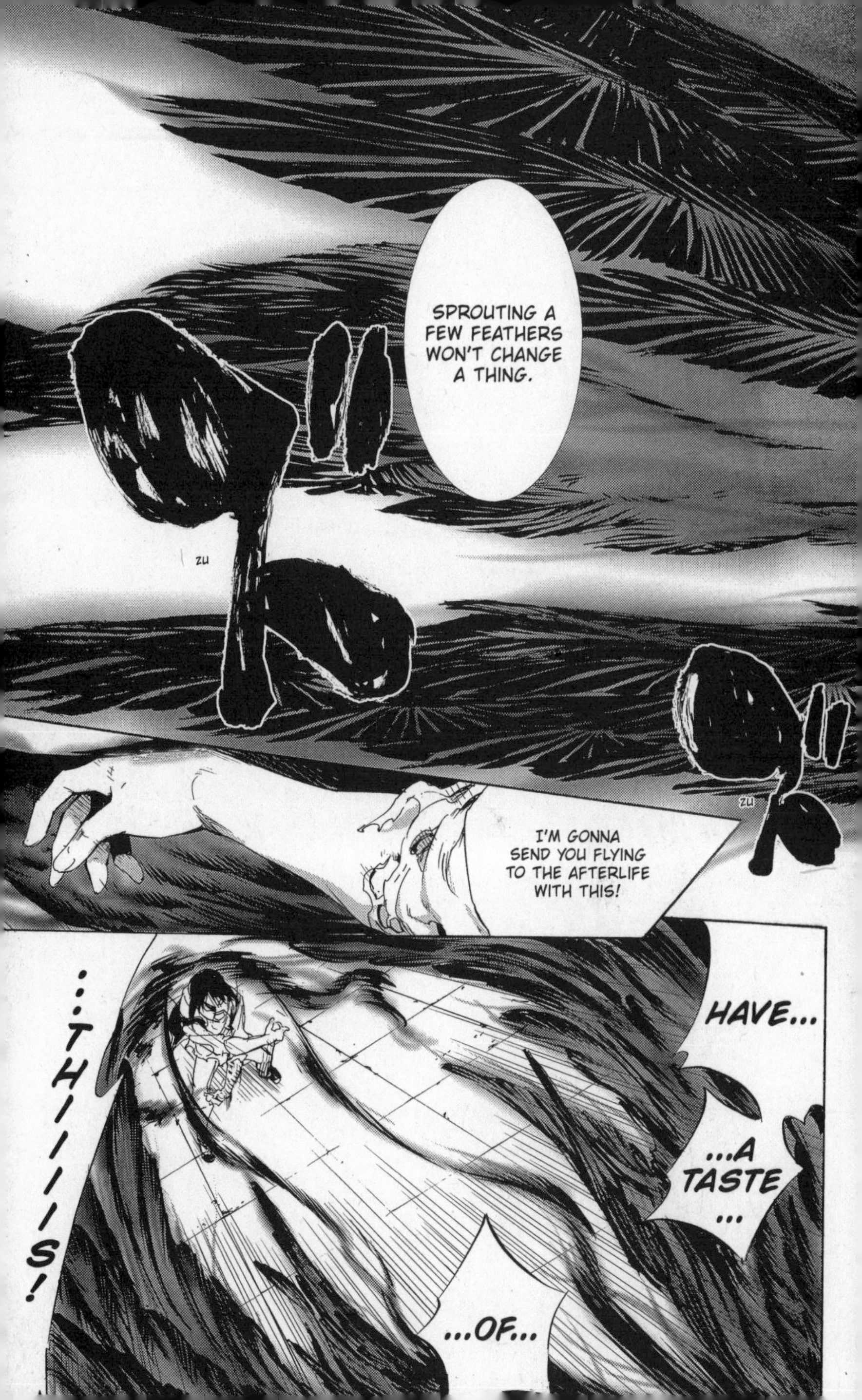
SPROUTING A FEW FEATHERS WON'T CHANGE A THING.
ZU
ZU
I'M GONNA SEND YOU FLYING TO THE AFTERLIFE WITH THIS!
HAVE...
...A TASTE ...
...OF...
...THIIIIS!

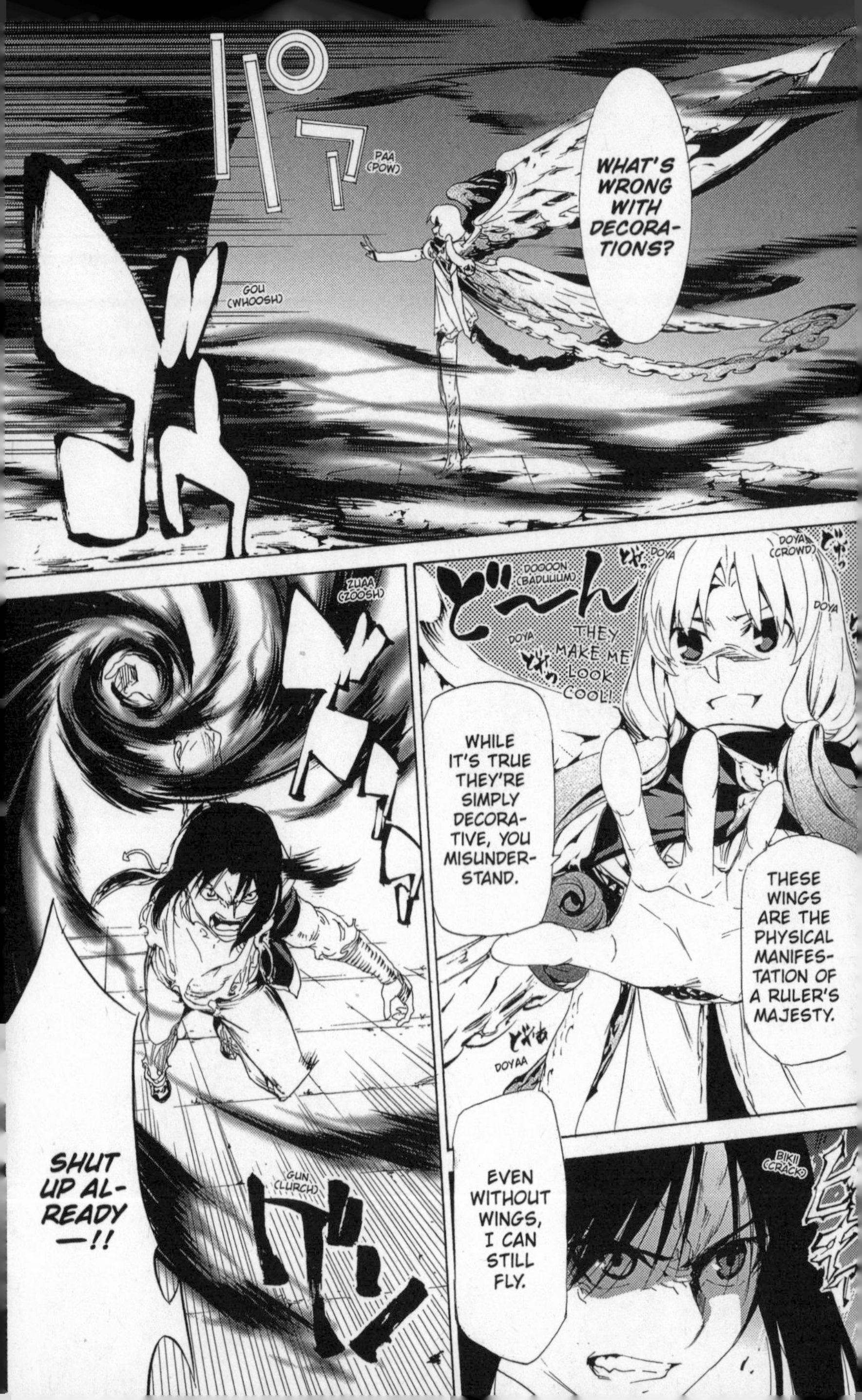

WHAT'S WRONG WITH DECORA- TIONS?
PAA (POW)
GOU (WHOOSH)
DOYA (CROWD)
DOYA
DOGOOON (BADUUUM)
DOYA
DOYA
THEY MAKE ME LOOK COOL!
WHILE IT'S TRUE THEY'RE SIMPLY DECORA- TIVE, YOU MISUNDER- STAND.
THESE WINGS ARE THE PHYSICAL MANIFES- TATION OF A RULER'S MAJESTY.
DOYAA
BIKII (CRACK)
EVEN WITHOUT WINGS, I CAN STILL FLY.
ZUAA (ZOOSH)
GUN (LURCH)
SHUT UP AL- READY —!!

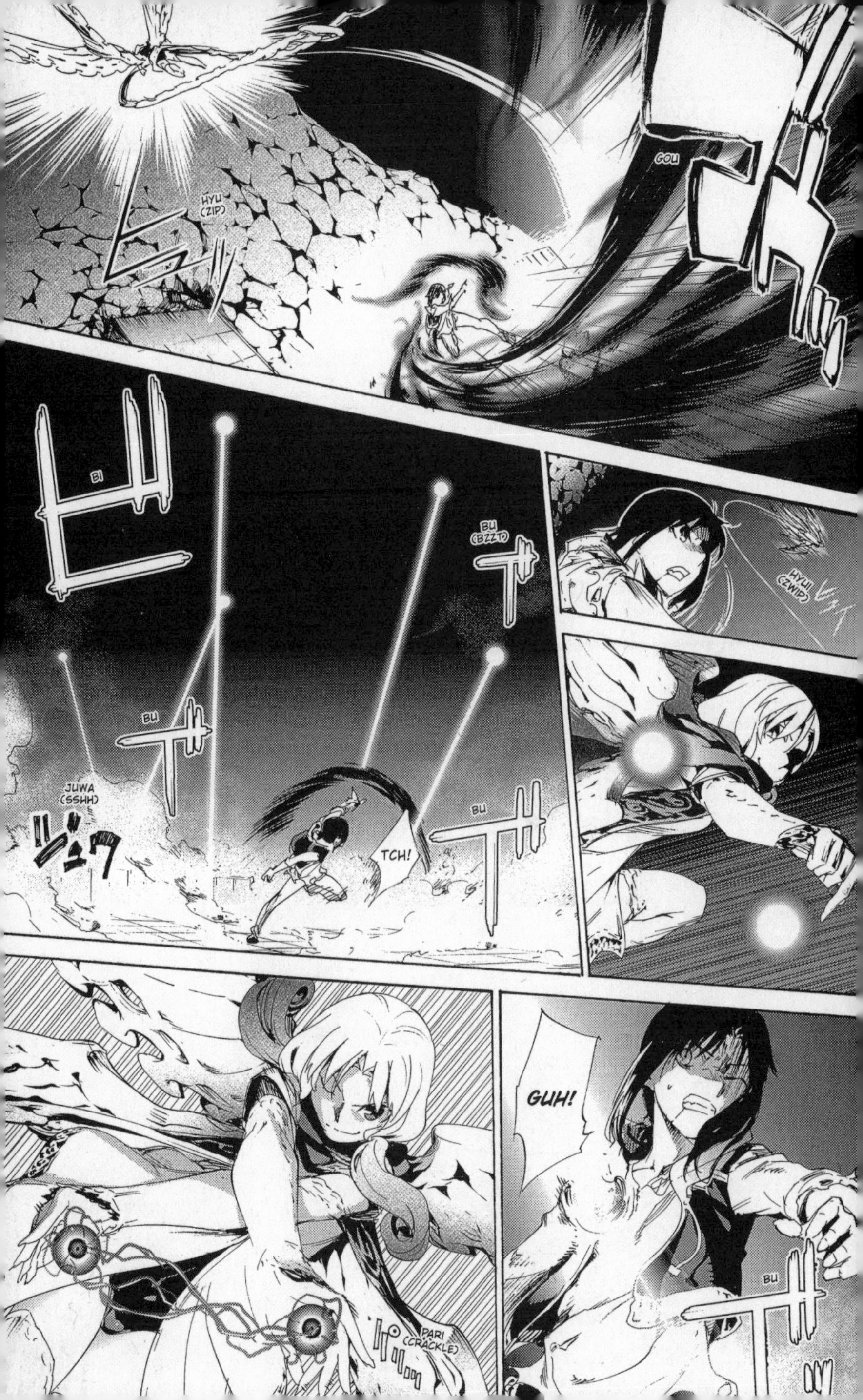
GOU
HYU (ZIP)
HYU! (ZWIP)
BU (BZZT)
BI
BU
BU
TCH!
JUWA (SSHH)
GUH!
BU
PARI (CRACKLE)

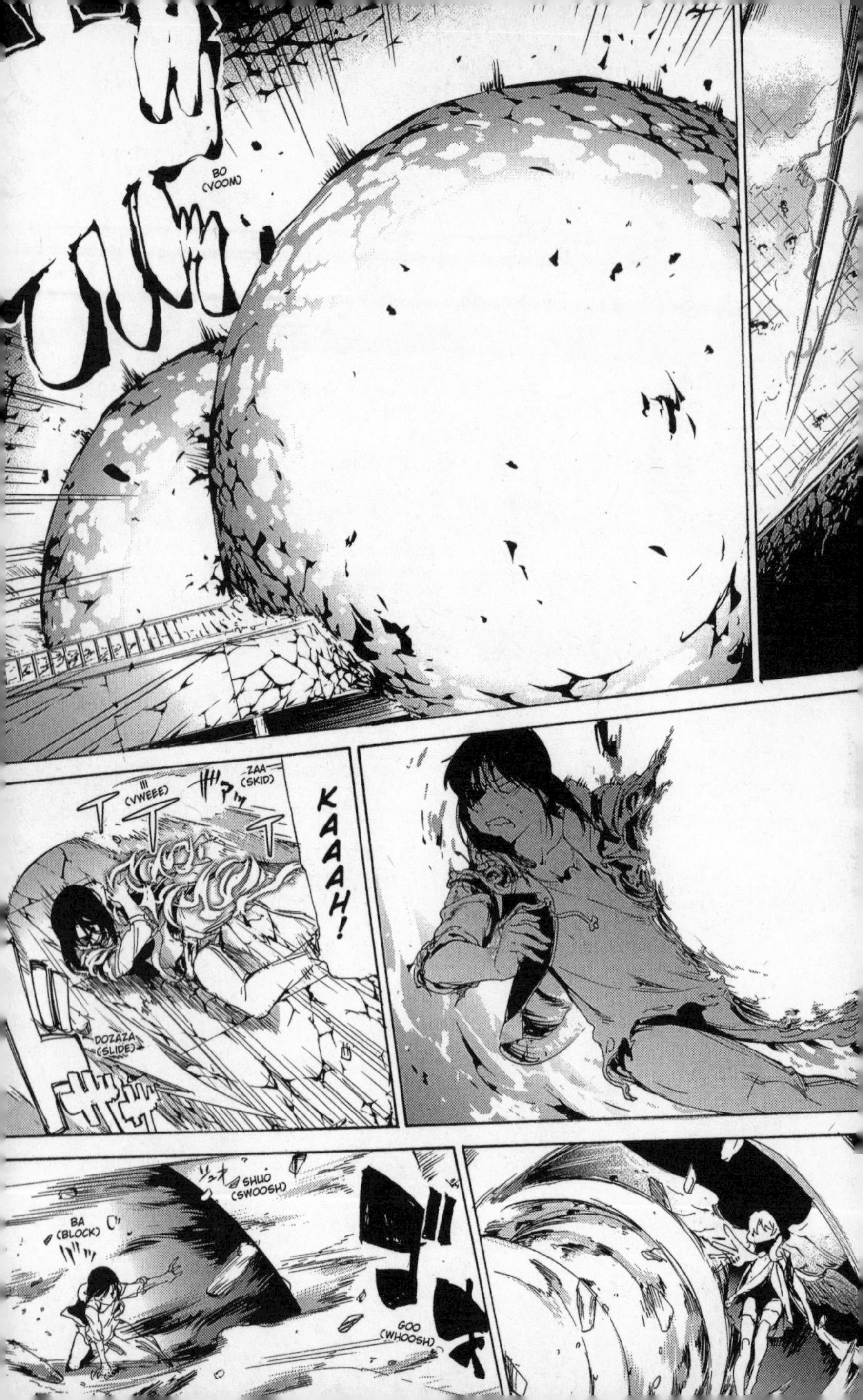
BO (VOOM)
KAAAAH!
ZAA (SKID)
III (VWEEE)
DOZAZA (SLIDE)
SHUO (SWOOSH)
BA (BLOCK)
GOO (WHOOSH)

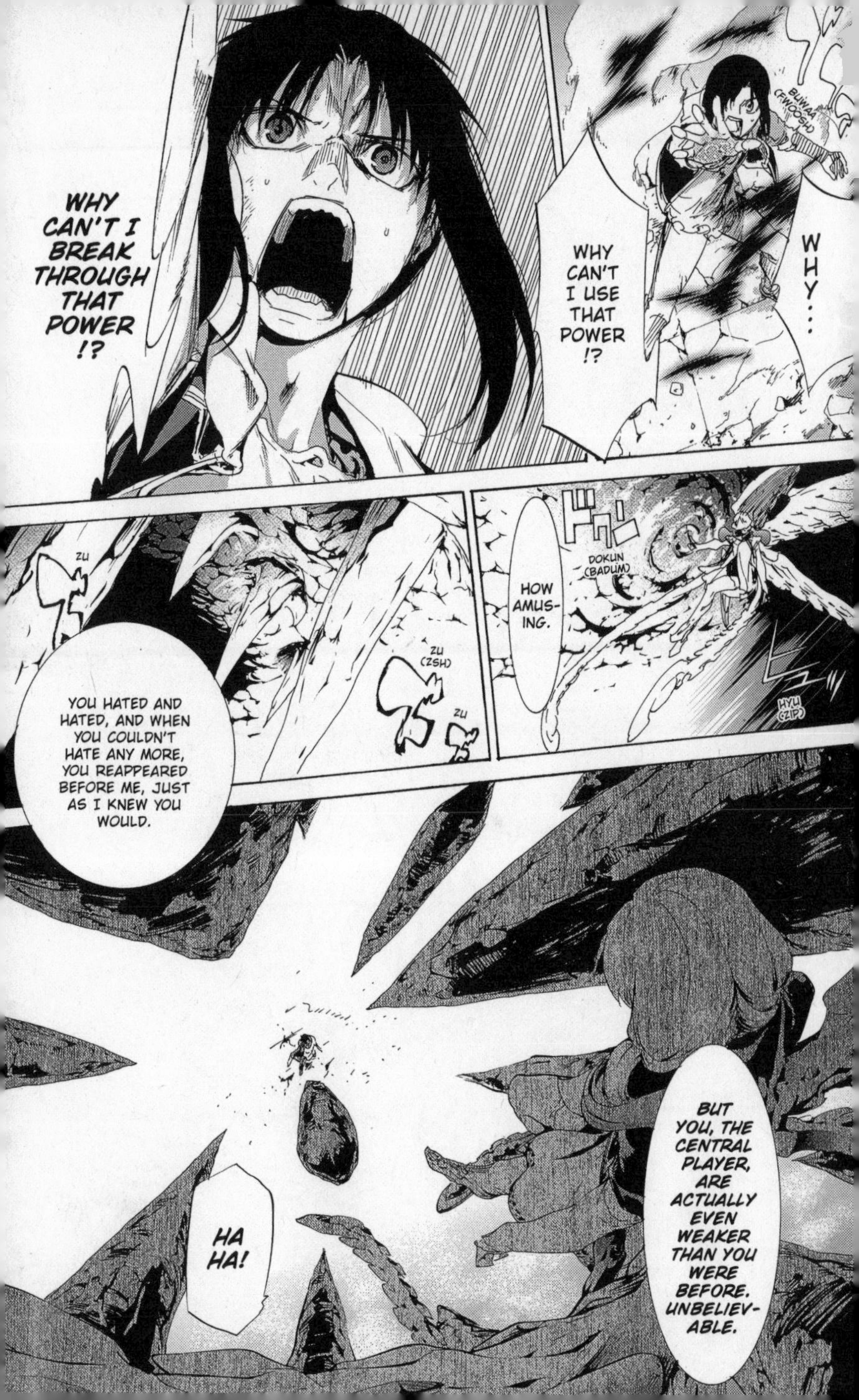

BUWAA (FWOOSH)
WHY...
WHY CAN'T I USE THAT POWER!?
WHY CAN'T I BREAK THROUGH THAT POWER!?
ドクン
DOKUN (BADUM)
HOW AMUSING.
HYU (ZIP)
ZU
ZU (ZSH)
ZU
YOU HATED AND HATED, AND WHEN YOU COULDN'T HATE ANY MORE, YOU REAPPEARED BEFORE ME, JUST AS I KNEW YOU WOULD.
BUT YOU, THE CENTRAL PLAYER, ARE ACTUALLY EVEN WEAKER THAN YOU WERE BEFORE. UNBELIEVABLE.
HA HA!

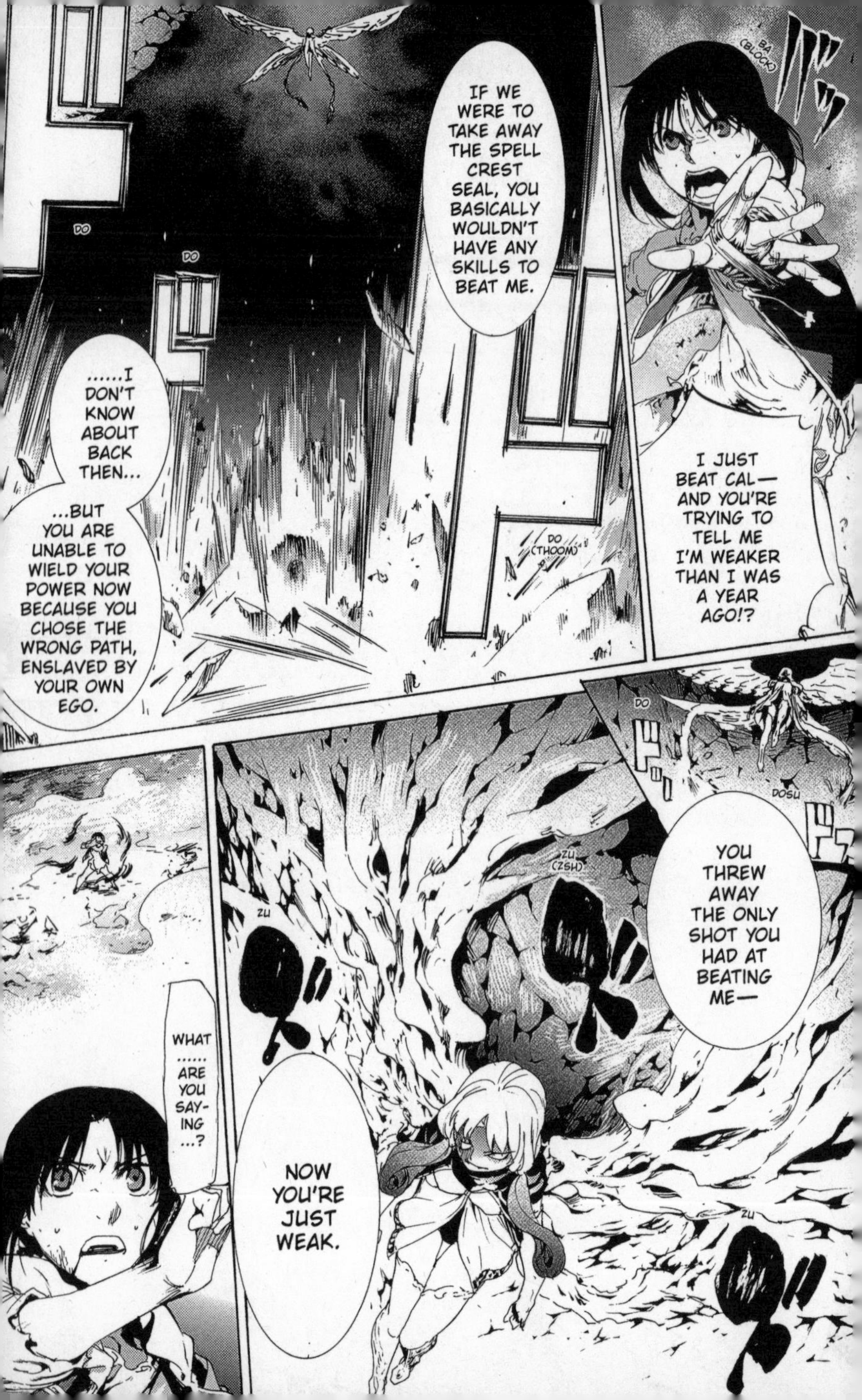
BA (BLOCK)
I JUST BEAT CAL— AND YOU'RE TRYING TO TELL ME I'M WEAKER THAN I WAS A YEAR AGO!?
IF WE WERE TO TAKE AWAY THE SPELL CREST SEAL, YOU BASICALLY WOULDN'T HAVE ANY SKILLS TO BEAT ME.
DO
DO
DO (THOOM)
......I DON'T KNOW ABOUT BACK THEN...
...BUT YOU ARE UNABLE TO WIELD YOUR POWER NOW BECAUSE YOU CHOSE THE WRONG PATH, ENSLAVED BY YOUR OWN EGO.
DO
DOSU
YOU THREW AWAY THE ONLY SHOT YOU HAD AT BEATING ME—
ZU (ZSH)
ZU
NOW YOU'RE JUST WEAK.
ZU
WHAT ...... ARE YOU SAY-ING ...?

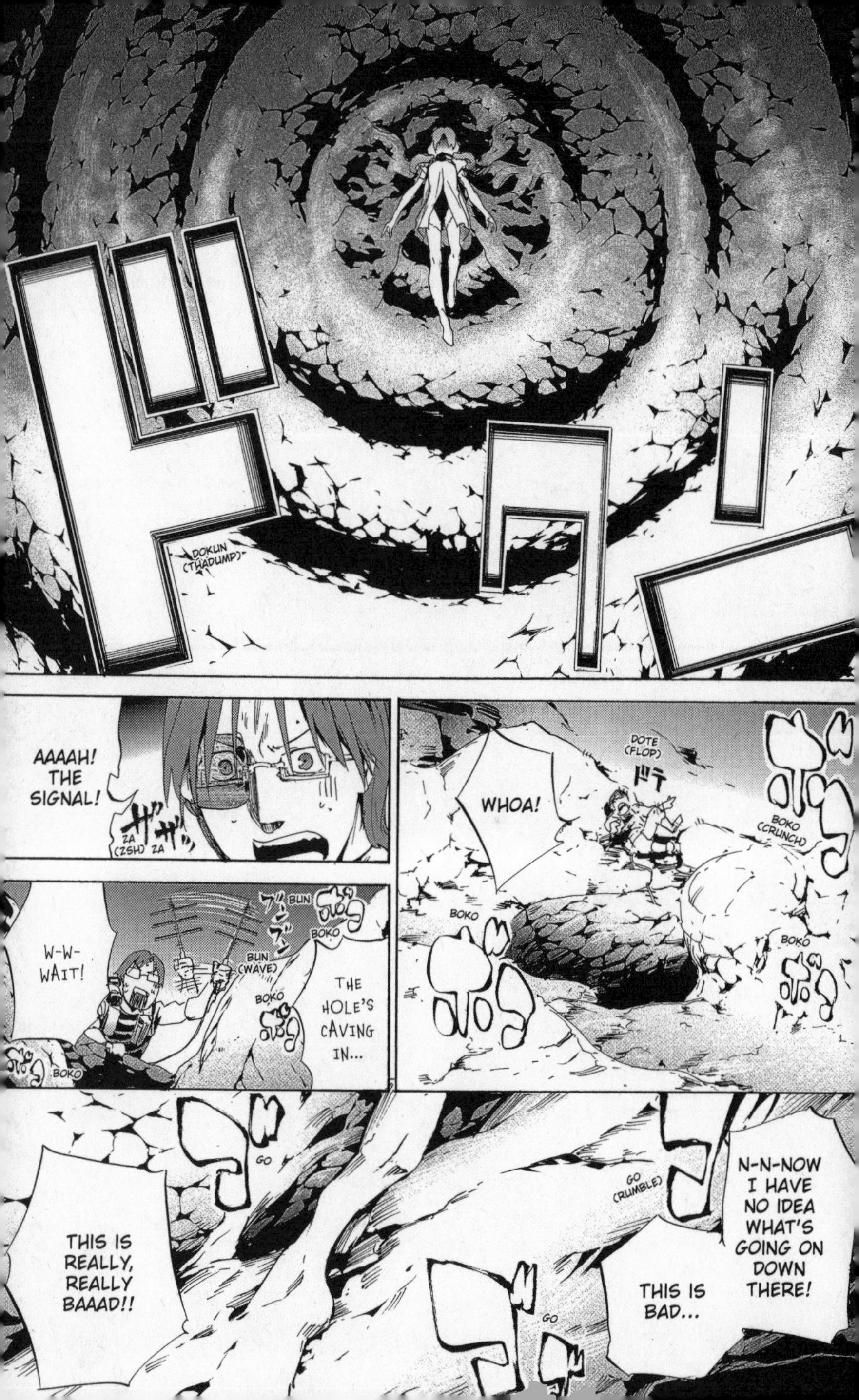
DOKUN (THADUMP)
DOTE (FLOP)
WHOA!
BOKO (CRUNCH)
BOKO
BOKO
AAAAH! THE SIGNAL!
ZA (ZSH) ZA
THE HOLE'S CAVING IN...
BUN
BOKO
BUN (WAVE)
BOKO
W-W-WAIT!
BOKO
N-N-NOW I HAVE NO IDEA WHAT'S GOING ON DOWN THERE!
GO (RUMBLE)
THIS IS BAD...
GO
GO
THIS IS REALLY, REALLY BAAAD!!

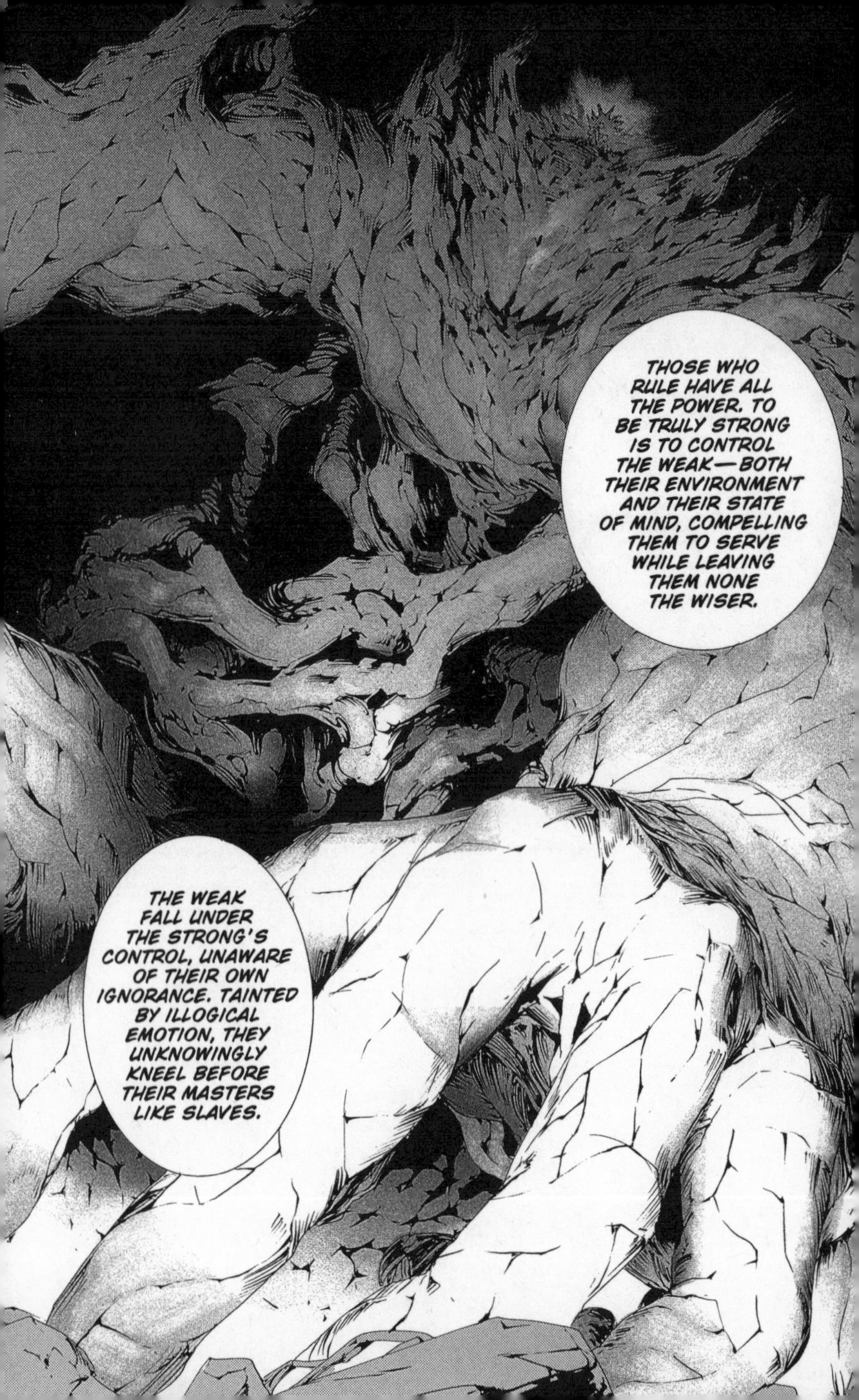
THOSE WHO RULE HAVE ALL THE POWER. TO BE TRULY STRONG IS TO CONTROL THE WEAK—BOTH THEIR ENVIRONMENT AND THEIR STATE OF MIND, COMPELLING THEM TO SERVE WHILE LEAVING THEM NONE THE WISER.
THE WEAK FALL UNDER THE STRONG'S CONTROL, UNAWARE OF THEIR OWN IGNORANCE. TAINTED BY ILLOGICAL EMOTION, THEY UNKNOWINGLY KNEEL BEFORE THEIR MASTERS LIKE SLAVES.

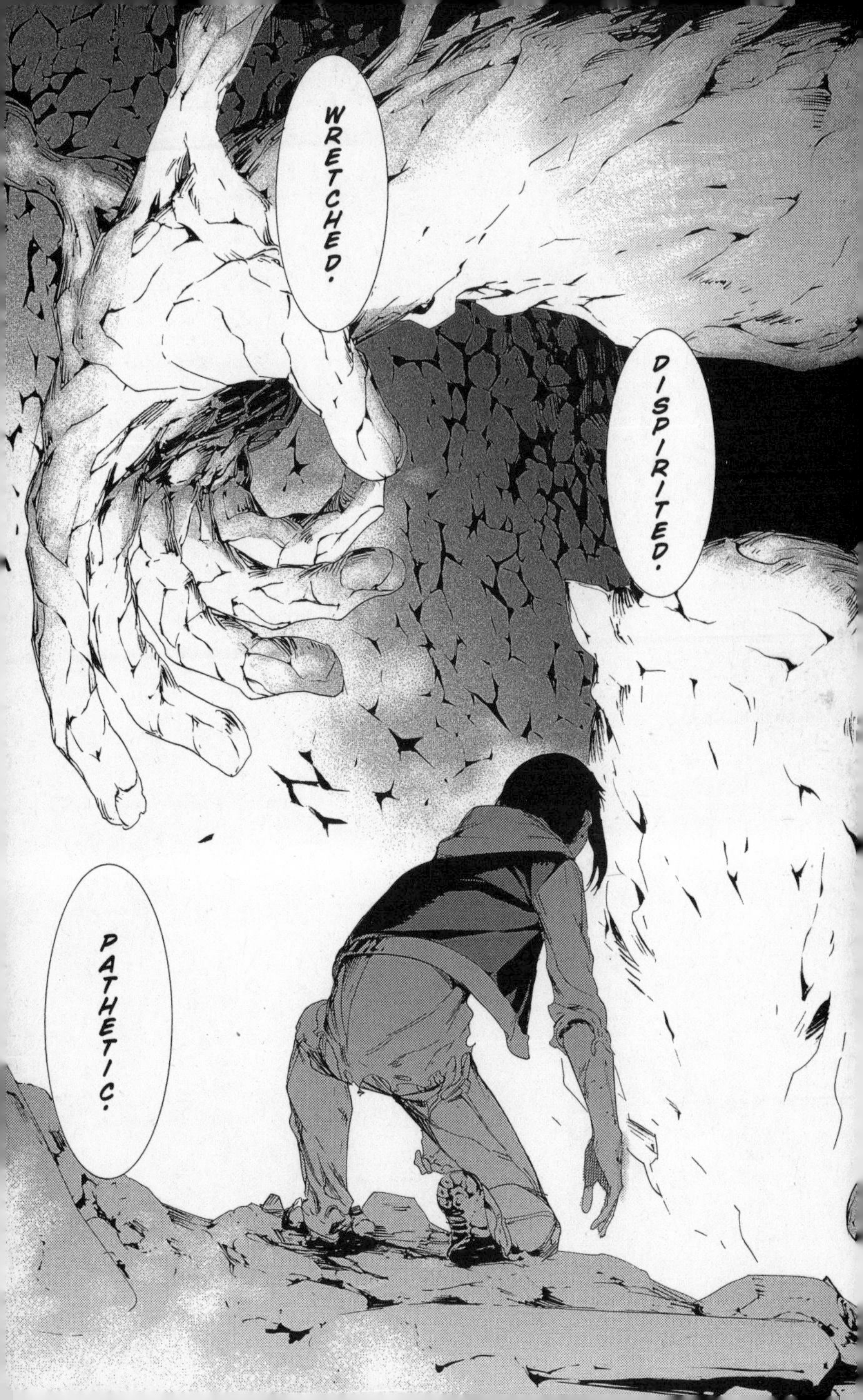
WRETCHED.
DISPIRITED.
PATHETIC.

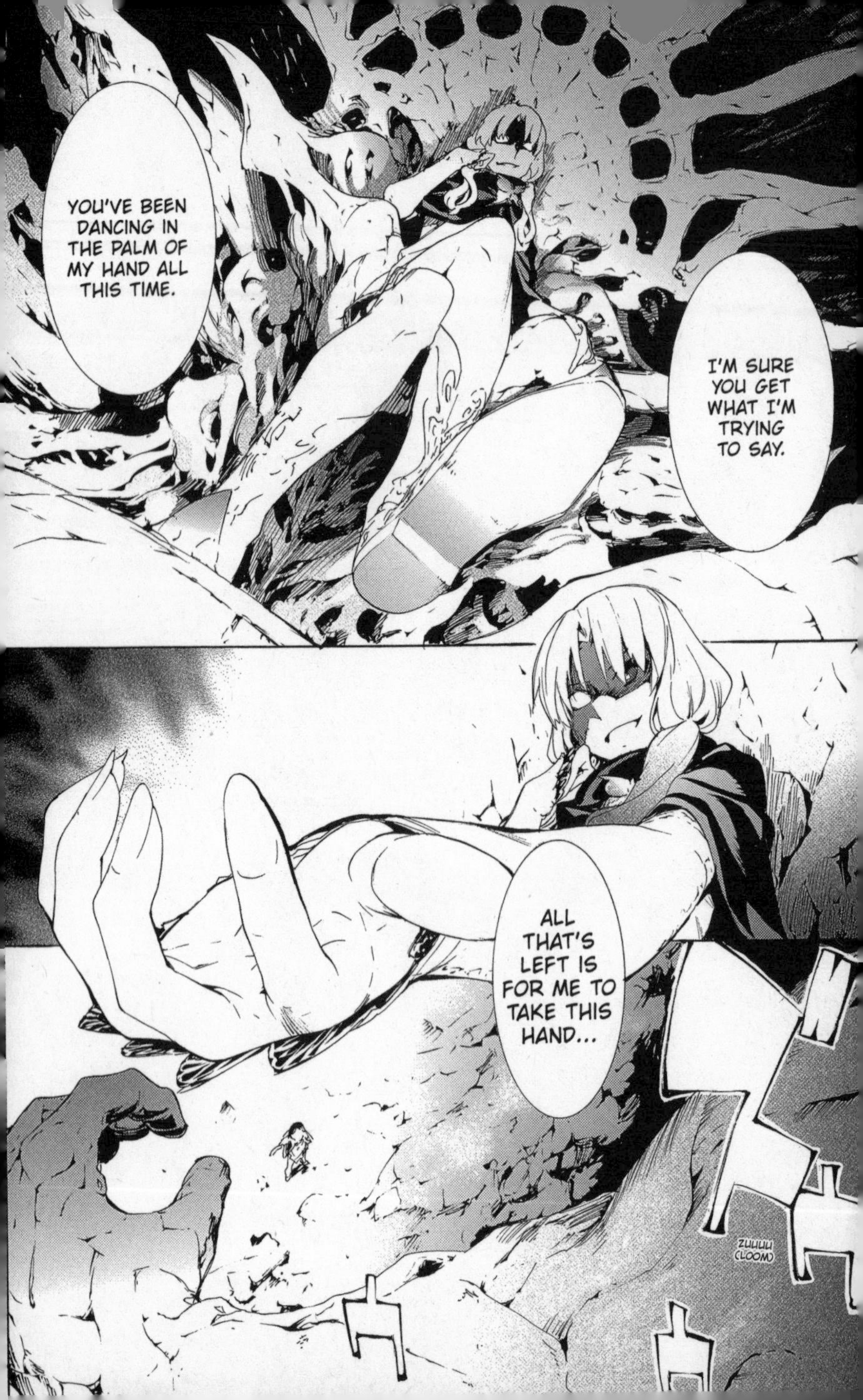
I'M SURE YOU GET WHAT I'M TRYING TO SAY.
YOU'VE BEEN DANCING IN THE PALM OF MY HAND ALL THIS TIME.
ALL THAT'S LEFT IS FOR ME TO TAKE THIS HAND...
ZUUUU (LOOM)

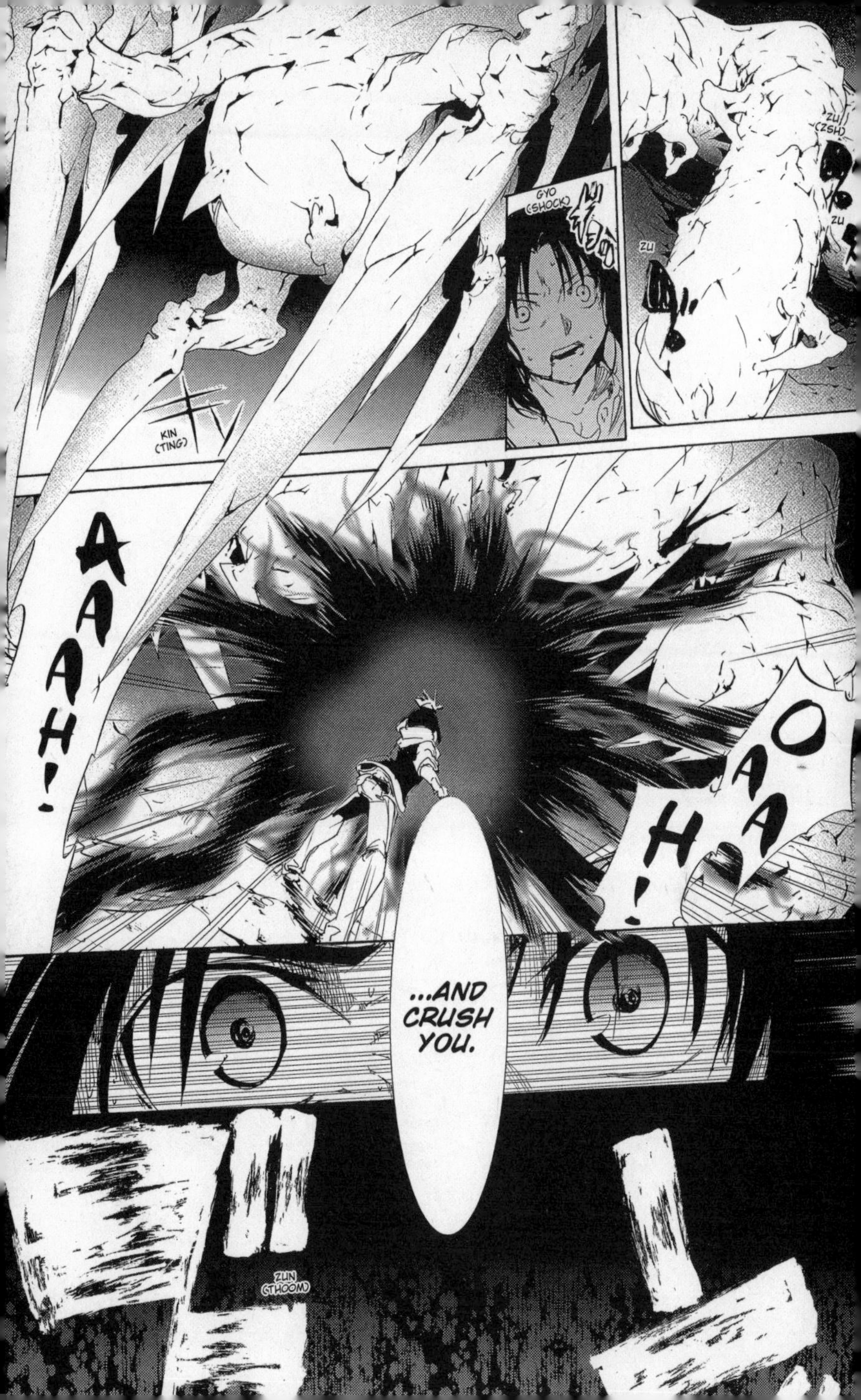
ZU (ZSH)
ZU
ZU
GYO (SHOCK)
KIN (TING)
OAAAH!
AAAH!
...AND CRUSH YOU.
ZUN (THOOM)

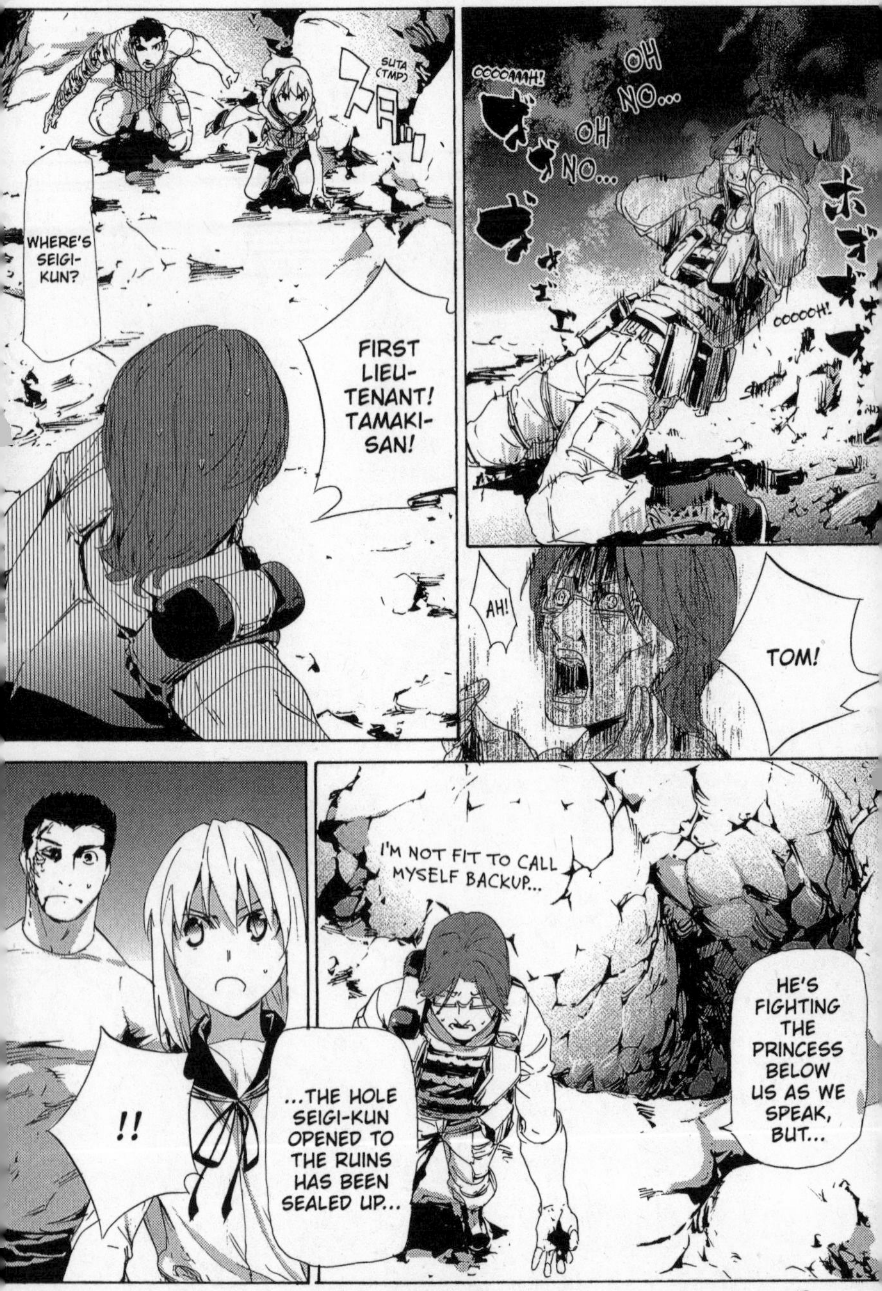
OH NO...
OH NO...
OOOOAAAH!
OOOOOH!
TOM!
AH!
SUTA (TMP)
FIRST LIEUTENANT! TAMAKI-SAN!
WHERE'S SEIGI-KUN?
HE'S FIGHTING THE PRINCESS BELOW US AS WE SPEAK, BUT...
I'M NOT FIT TO CALL MYSELF BACKUP...
...THE HOLE SEIGI-KUN OPENED TO THE RUINS HAS BEEN SEALED UP...
!!

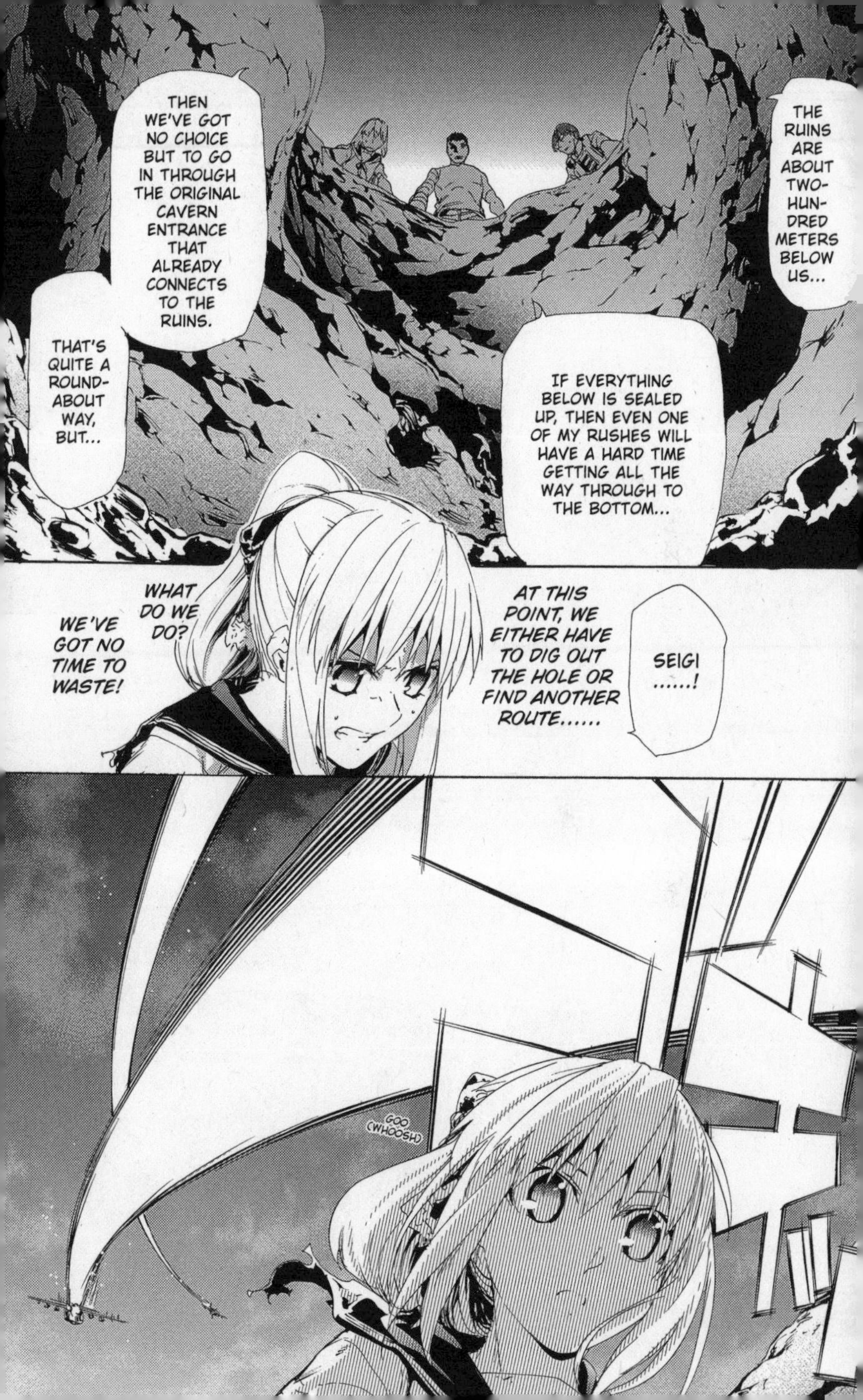
THE RUINS ARE ABOUT TWO-HUNDRED METERS BELOW US...
IF EVERYTHING BELOW IS SEALED UP, THEN EVEN ONE OF MY RUSHES WILL HAVE A HARD TIME GETTING ALL THE WAY THROUGH TO THE BOTTOM...
THEN WE'VE GOT NO CHOICE BUT TO GO IN THROUGH THE ORIGINAL CAVERN ENTRANCE THAT ALREADY CONNECTS TO THE RUINS.
THAT'S QUITE A ROUND-ABOUT WAY, BUT...
SEIGI ......!
AT THIS POINT, WE EITHER HAVE TO DIG OUT THE HOLE OR FIND ANOTHER ROUTE......
WHAT DO WE DO?
WE'VE GOT NO TIME TO WASTE!
GOO (WHOOSH)

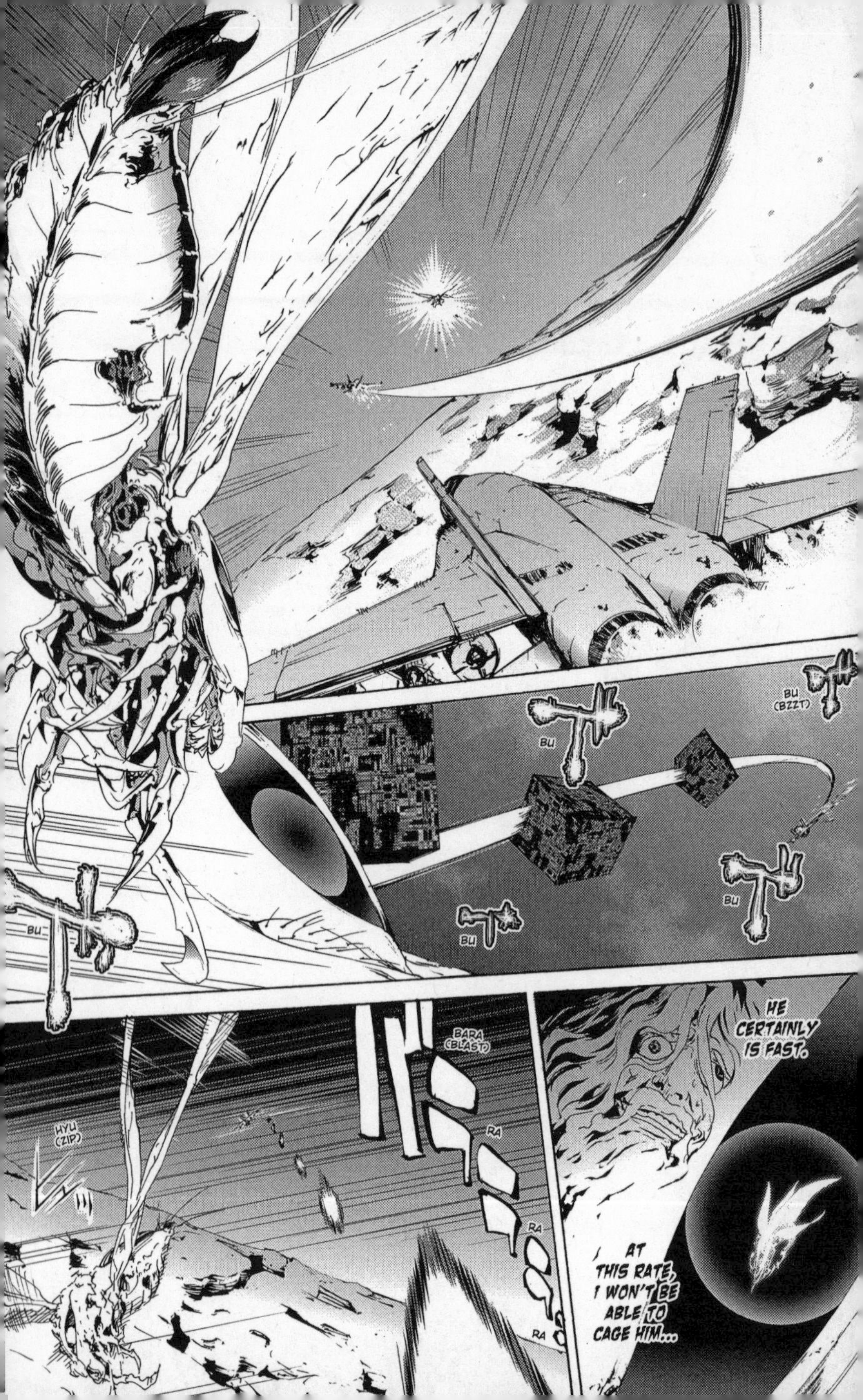
BU (BZZT)
BU
BU
BU
BU
HE CERTAINLY IS FAST.
AT THIS RATE, I WON'T BE ABLE TO CAGE HIM...
BARA (BLAST)
RA
RA
RA
HYU (ZIP)

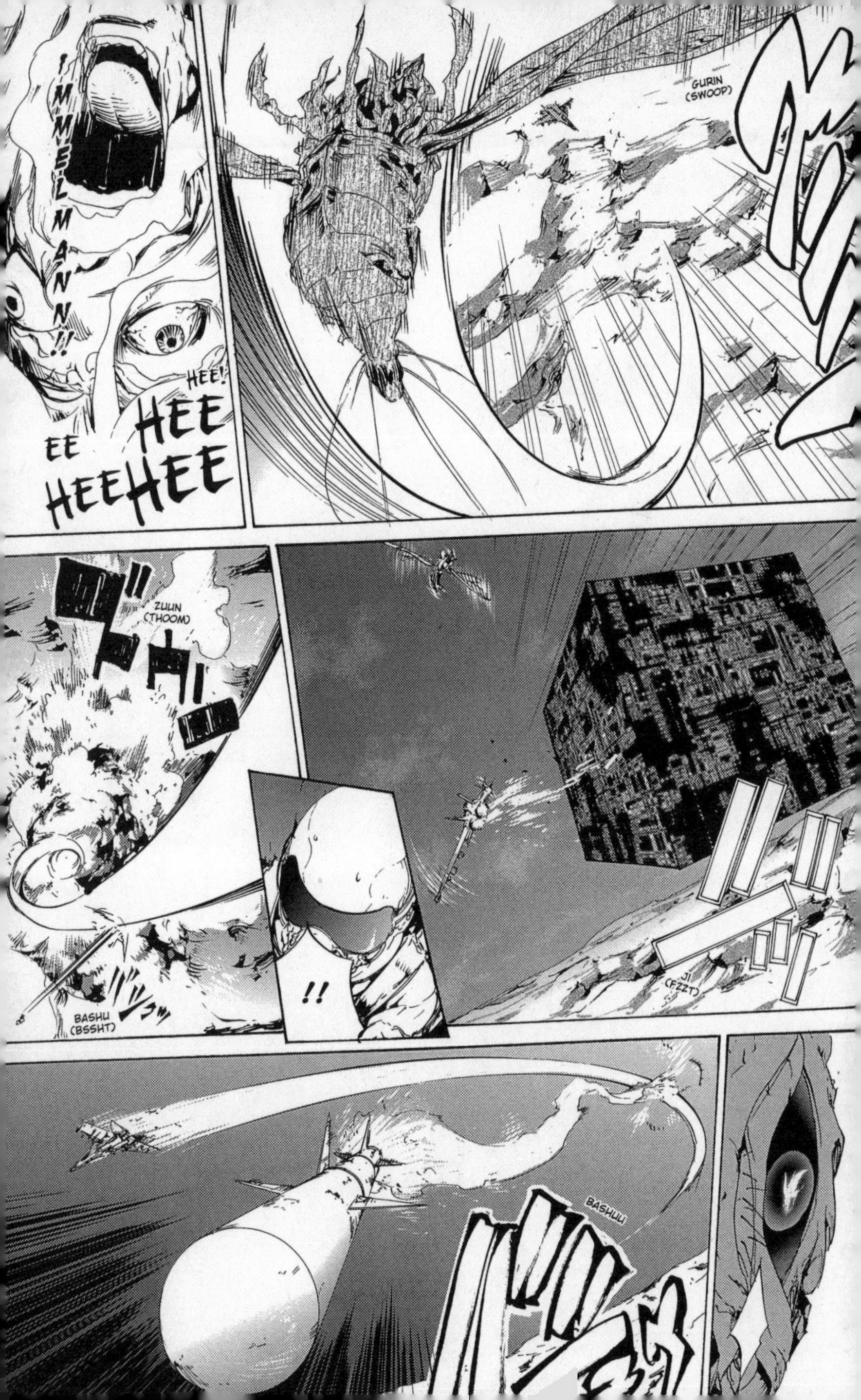
GURIN (SWOOP)
IMMELMANN!!
HEE!
HEE
EE
HEEHEE
JI (FZZT)
!!
ZUUN (THOOM)
BASHU (BSSHT)
BASHUU

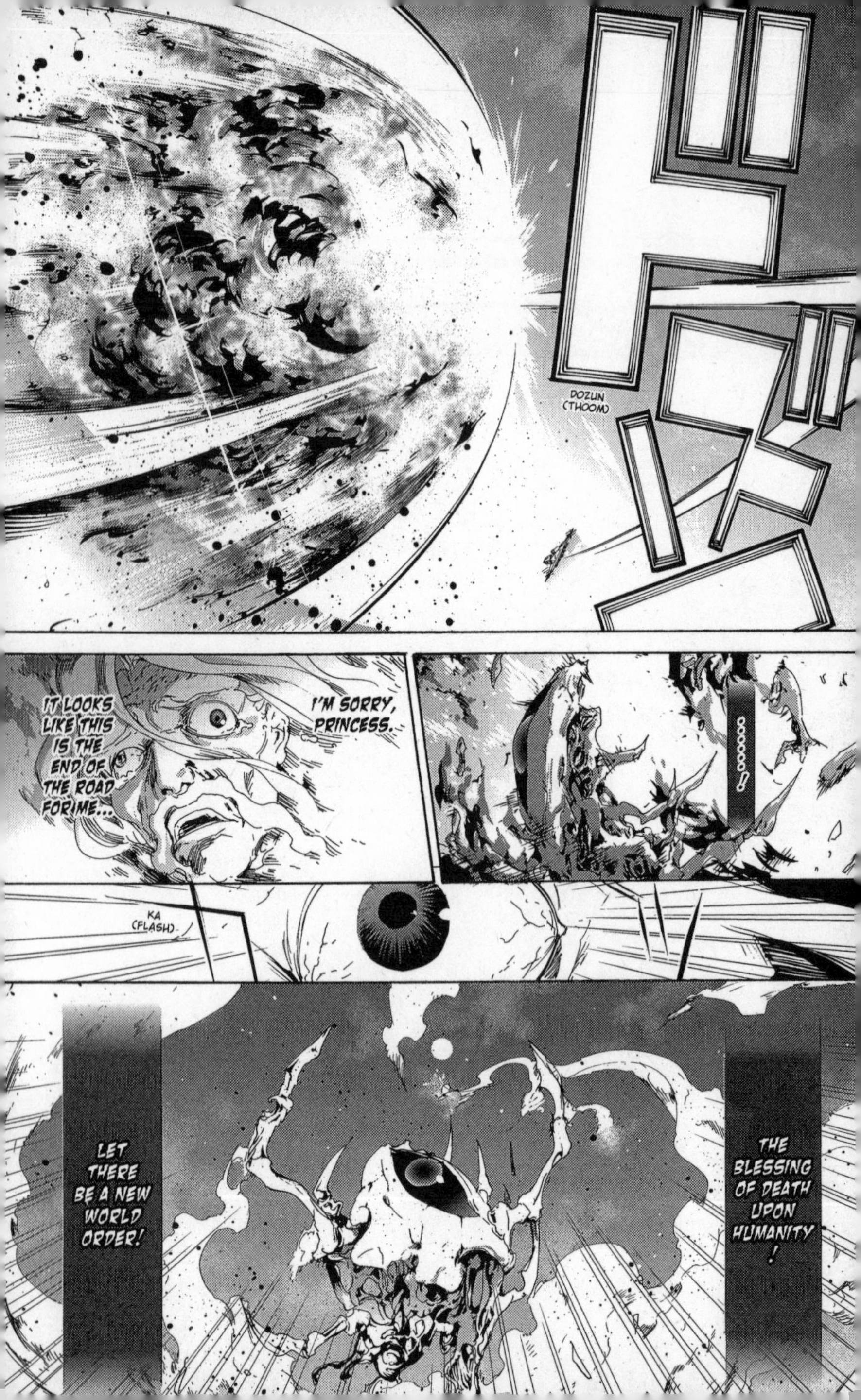
DOZUN
(THOOM)
OOOOOO!
I'M SORRY, PRINCESS.
IT LOOKS LIKE THIS IS THE END OF THE ROAD FOR ME...
KA
(FLASH)
THE BLESSING OF DEATH UPON HUMANITY!
LET THERE BE A NEW WORLD ORDER!

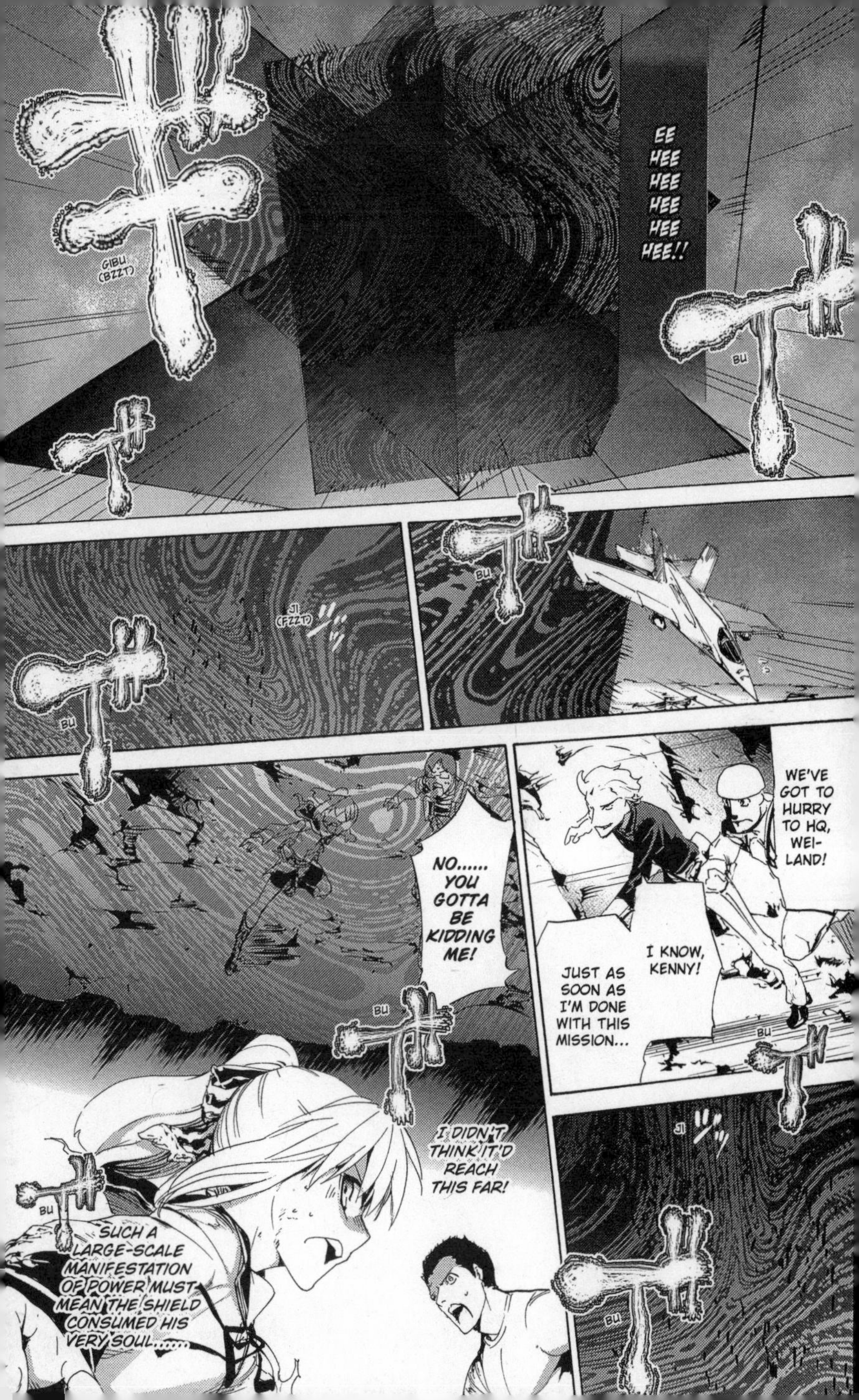
EE HEE HEE HEE HEE HEE!!
BU
GIBU (BZZT)
BU
BU
JI (PZZZT)
BU
WE'VE GOT TO HURRY TO HQ, WEI-LAND!
I KNOW, KENNY!
JUST AS SOON AS I'M DONE WITH THIS MISSION...
BU
NO...... YOU GOTTA BE KIDDING ME!
BU
JI
BU
I DIDN'T THINK IT'D REACH THIS FAR!
BU
SUCH A LARGE-SCALE MANIFESTATION OF POWER MUST MEAN THE SHIELD CONSUMED HIS VERY SOUL......

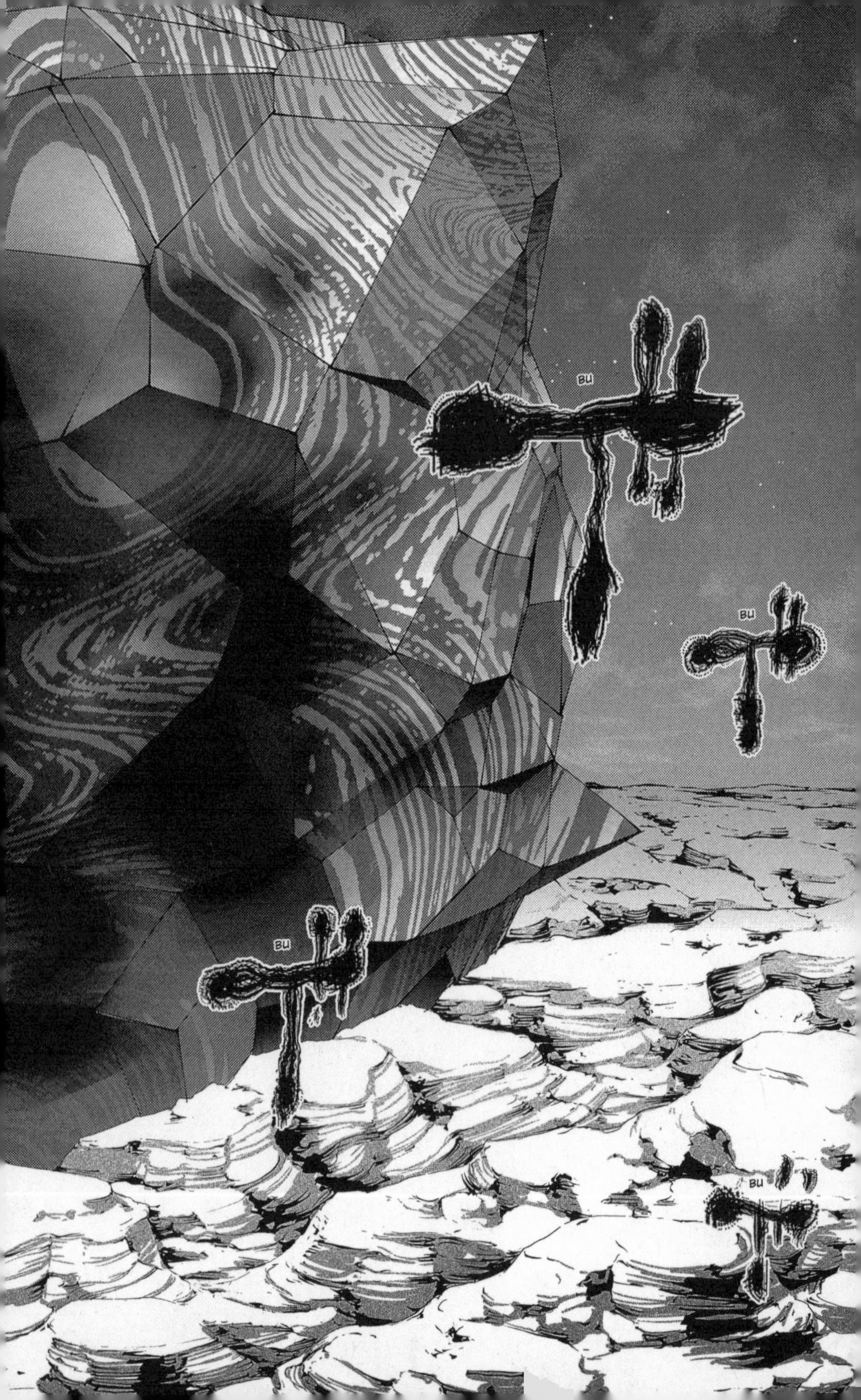
BU
BU
BU
BU

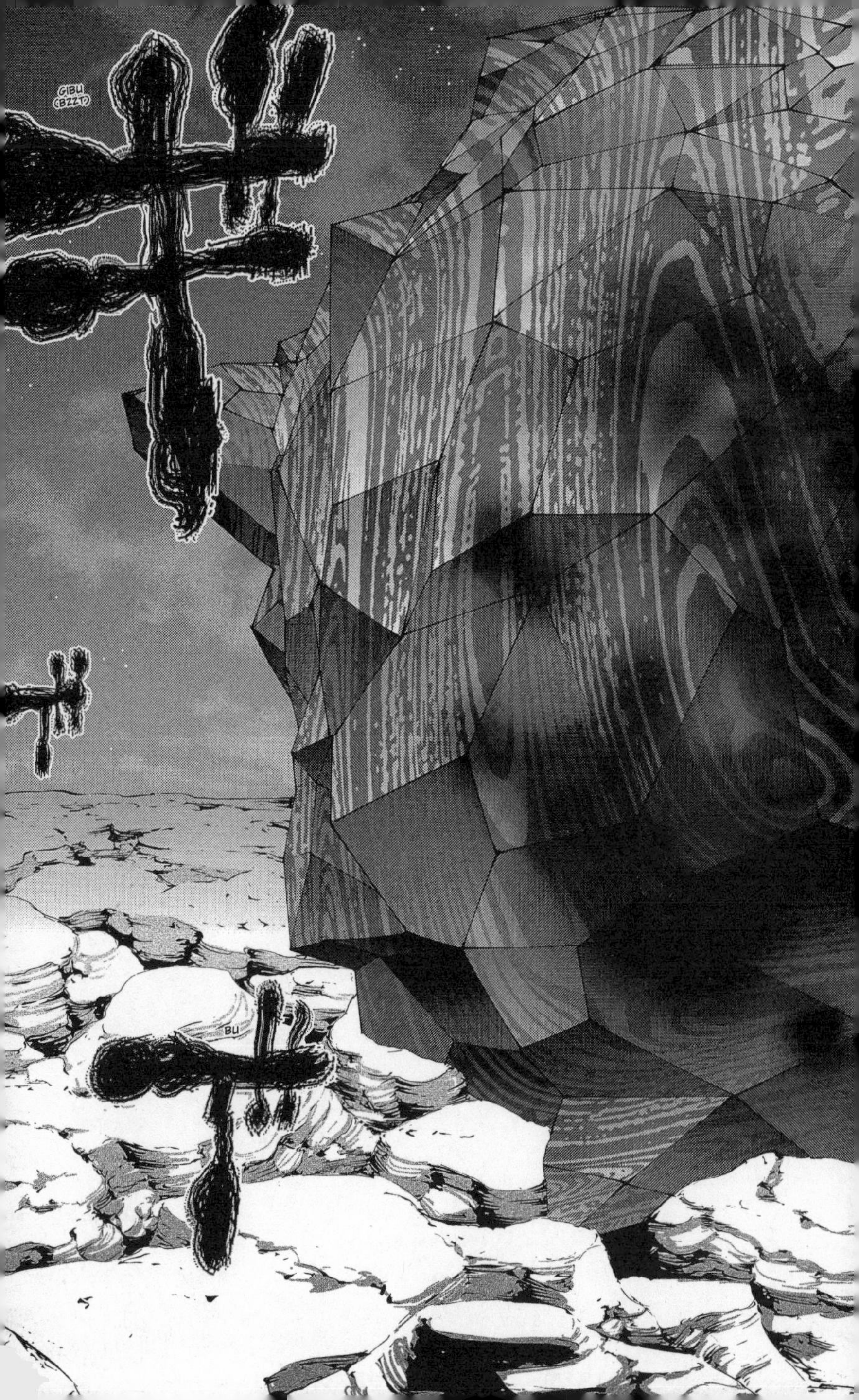
GIBU
(BZZT)
BU

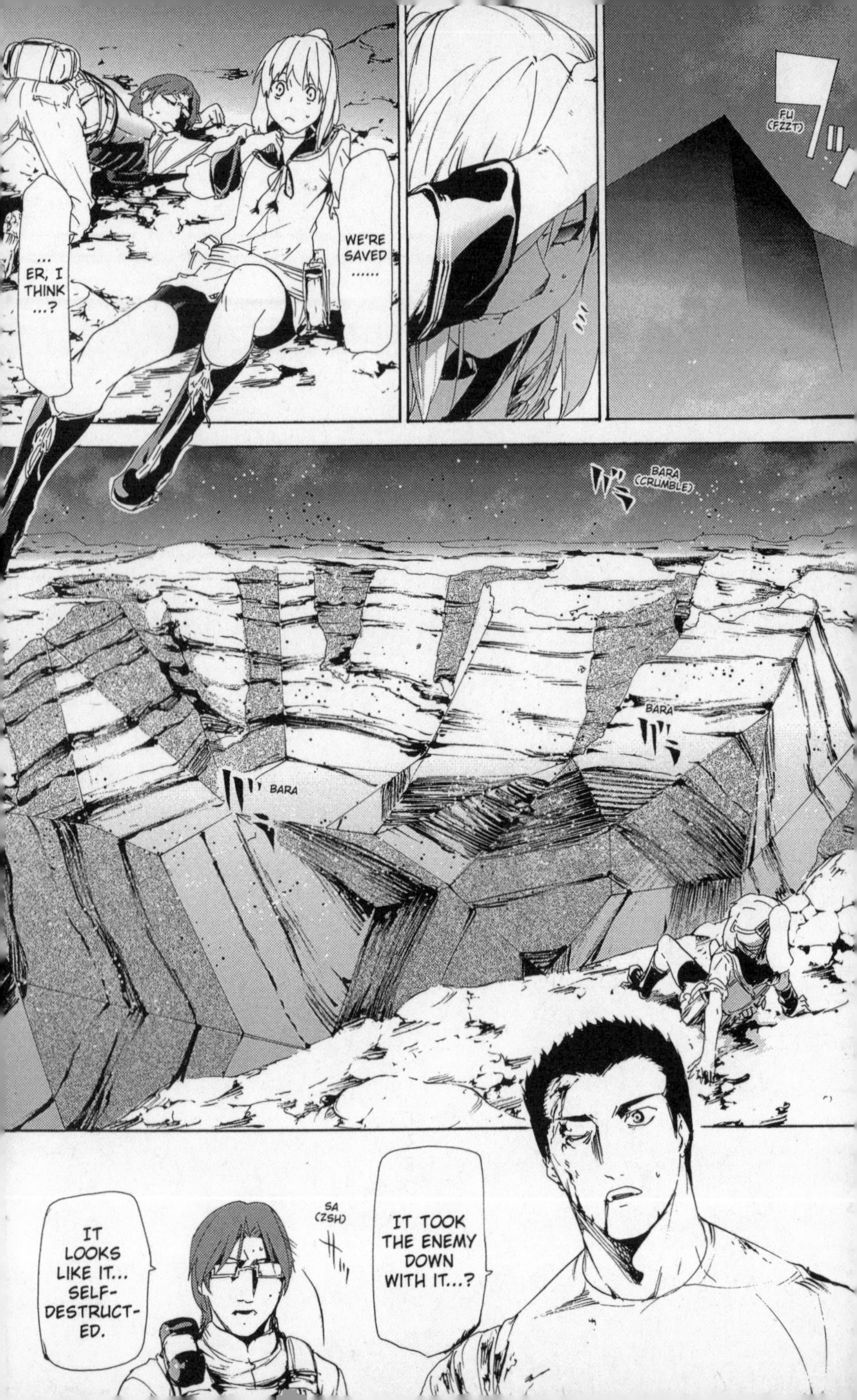
FU (FZZT)
WE'RE SAVED ......
... ER, I THINK ...?
BARA (CRUMBLE)
BARA
BARA
IT TOOK THE ENEMY DOWN WITH IT...?
SA (ZSH)
IT LOOKS LIKE IT... SELF-DESTRUCT-ED.

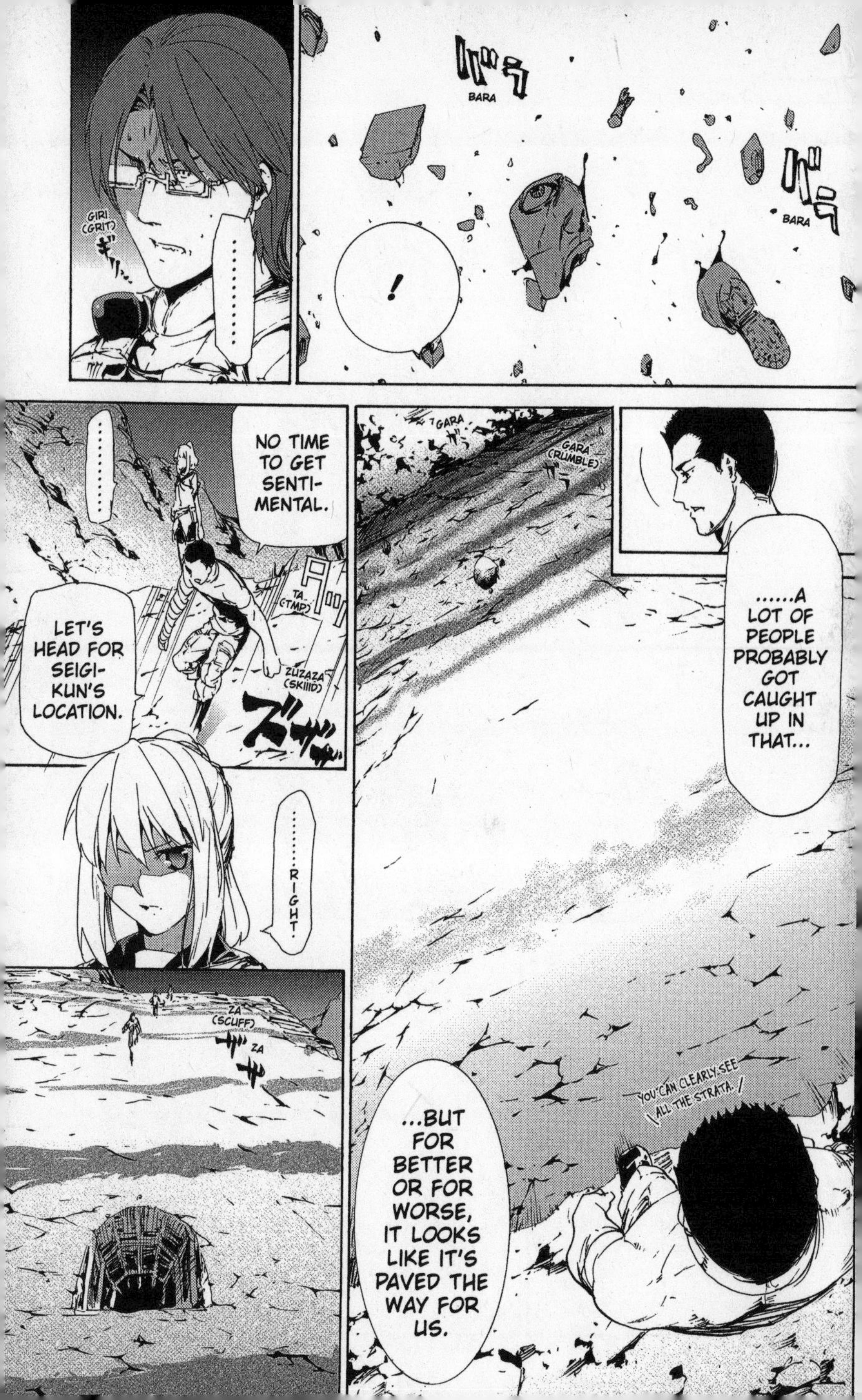
BARA
BARA
!
GIRI (GRIT)
......
GARA
GARA (RUMBLE)
......A LOT OF PEOPLE PROBABLY GOT CAUGHT UP IN THAT...
YOU CAN CLEARLY SEE ALL THE STRATA.
...BUT FOR BETTER OR FOR WORSE, IT LOOKS LIKE IT'S PAVED THE WAY FOR US.
NO TIME TO GET SENTI-MENTAL.
......
TA (TMP)
ZUZAZA (SKIIID)
LET'S HEAD FOR SEIGI-KUN'S LOCATION.
......RIGHT.
ZA (SCUFF)
ZA

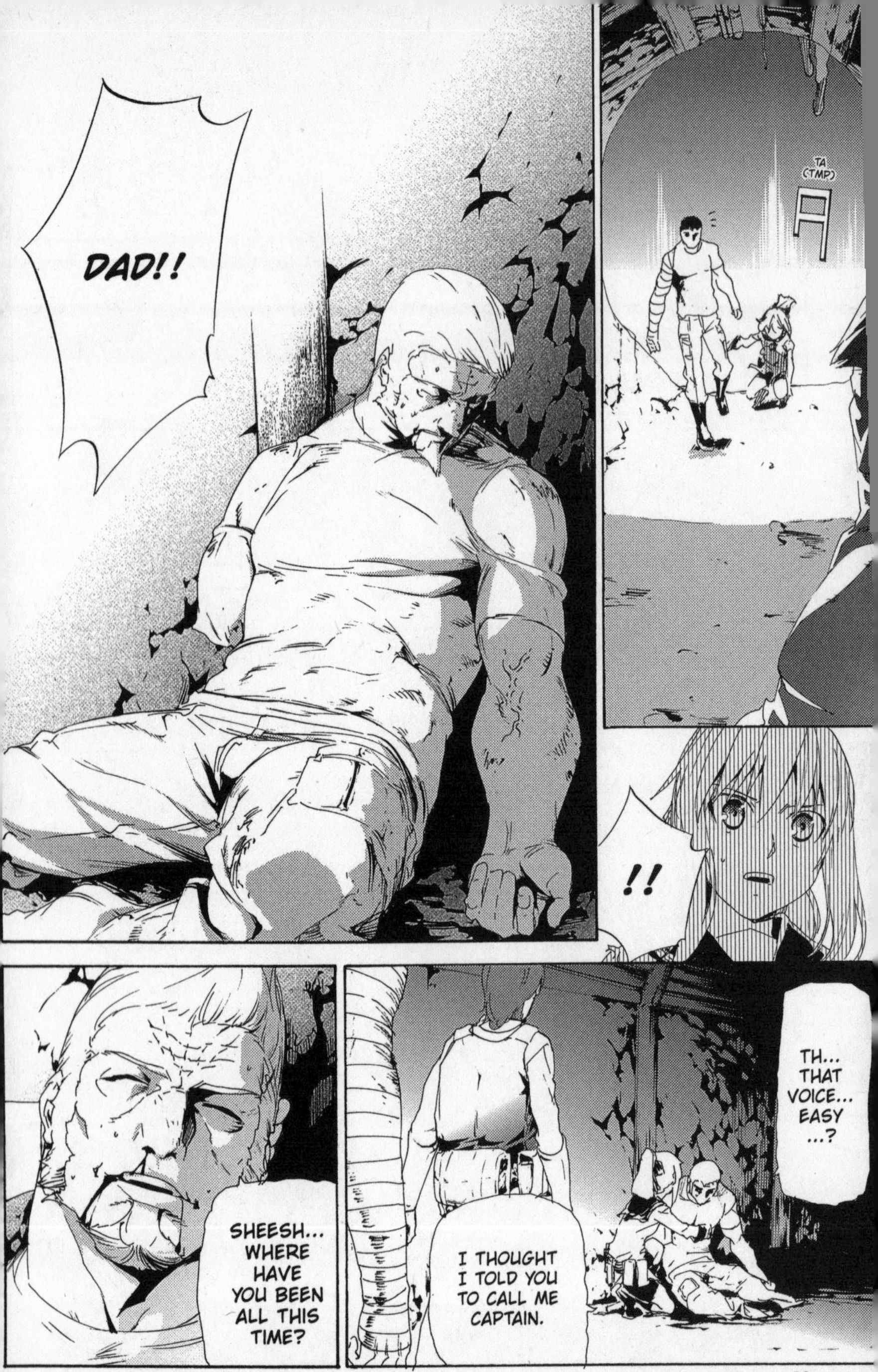
TA (TMP)
!!
DAD!!
TH... THAT VOICE... EASY ...?
I THOUGHT I TOLD YOU TO CALL ME CAPTAIN.
SHEESH... WHERE HAVE YOU BEEN ALL THIS TIME?

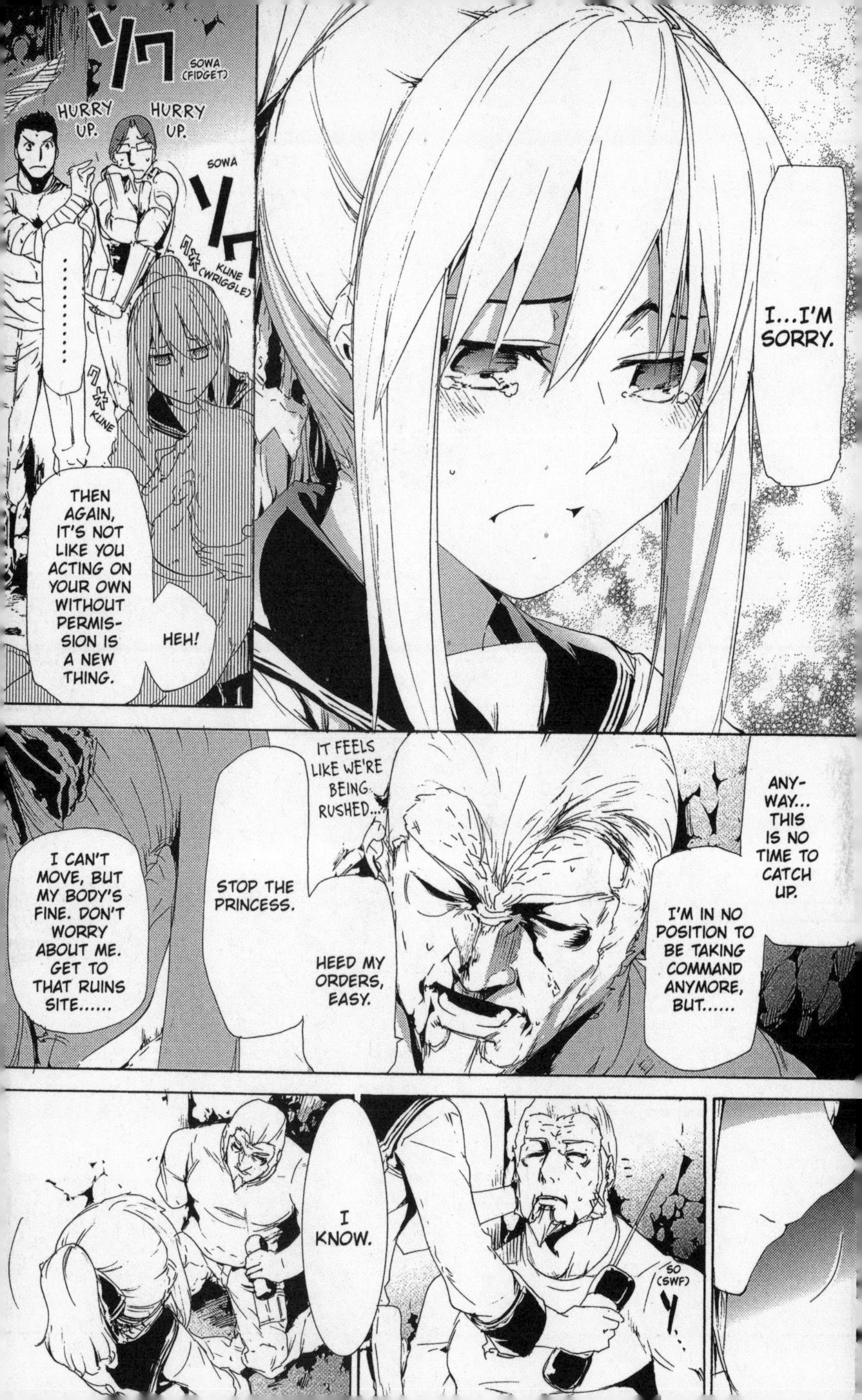
I...I'M SORRY.
SOWA (FIDGET)
HURRY UP.
HURRY UP.
SOWA
KUNE (WRIGGLE)
KUNE
......
THEN AGAIN, IT'S NOT LIKE YOU ACTING ON YOUR OWN WITHOUT PERMISSION IS A NEW THING.
HEH!
ANYWAY... THIS IS NO TIME TO CATCH UP.
I'M IN NO POSITION TO BE TAKING COMMAND ANYMORE, BUT......
IT FEELS LIKE WE'RE BEING RUSHED...
HEED MY ORDERS, EASY.
STOP THE PRINCESS.
I CAN'T MOVE, BUT MY BODY'S FINE. DON'T WORRY ABOUT ME. GET TO THAT RUINS SITE......
SO (SWF)
I KNOW.

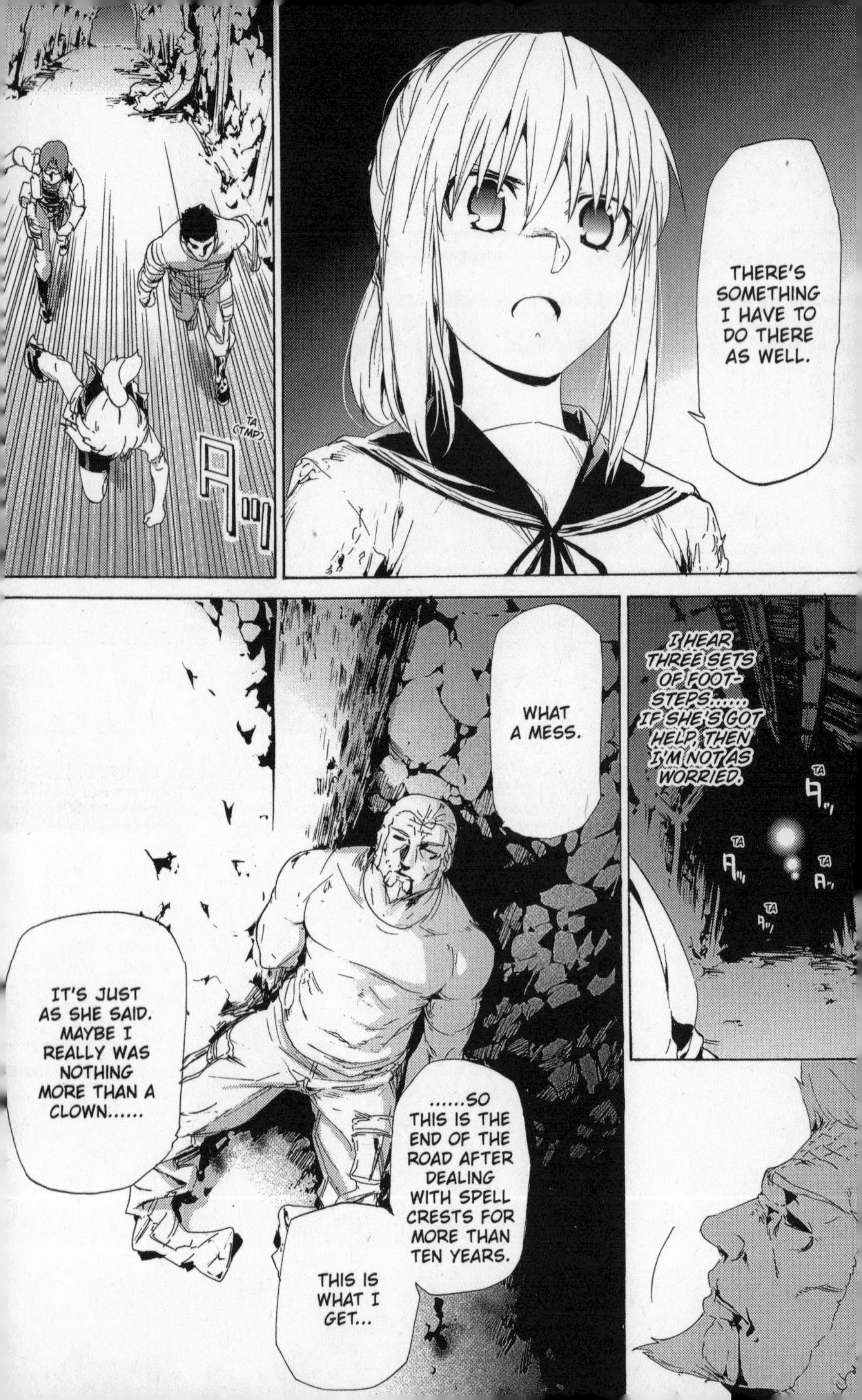
THERE'S SOMETHING I HAVE TO DO THERE AS WELL.
TA (TMP)
I HEAR THREE SETS OF FOOT-STEPS...... IF SHE'S GOT HELP, THEN I'M NOT AS WORRIED.
TA
TA
TA
TA
WHAT A MESS.
......SO THIS IS THE END OF THE ROAD AFTER DEALING WITH SPELL CRESTS FOR MORE THAN TEN YEARS.
THIS IS WHAT I GET...
IT'S JUST AS SHE SAID. MAYBE I REALLY WAS NOTHING MORE THAN A CLOWN......

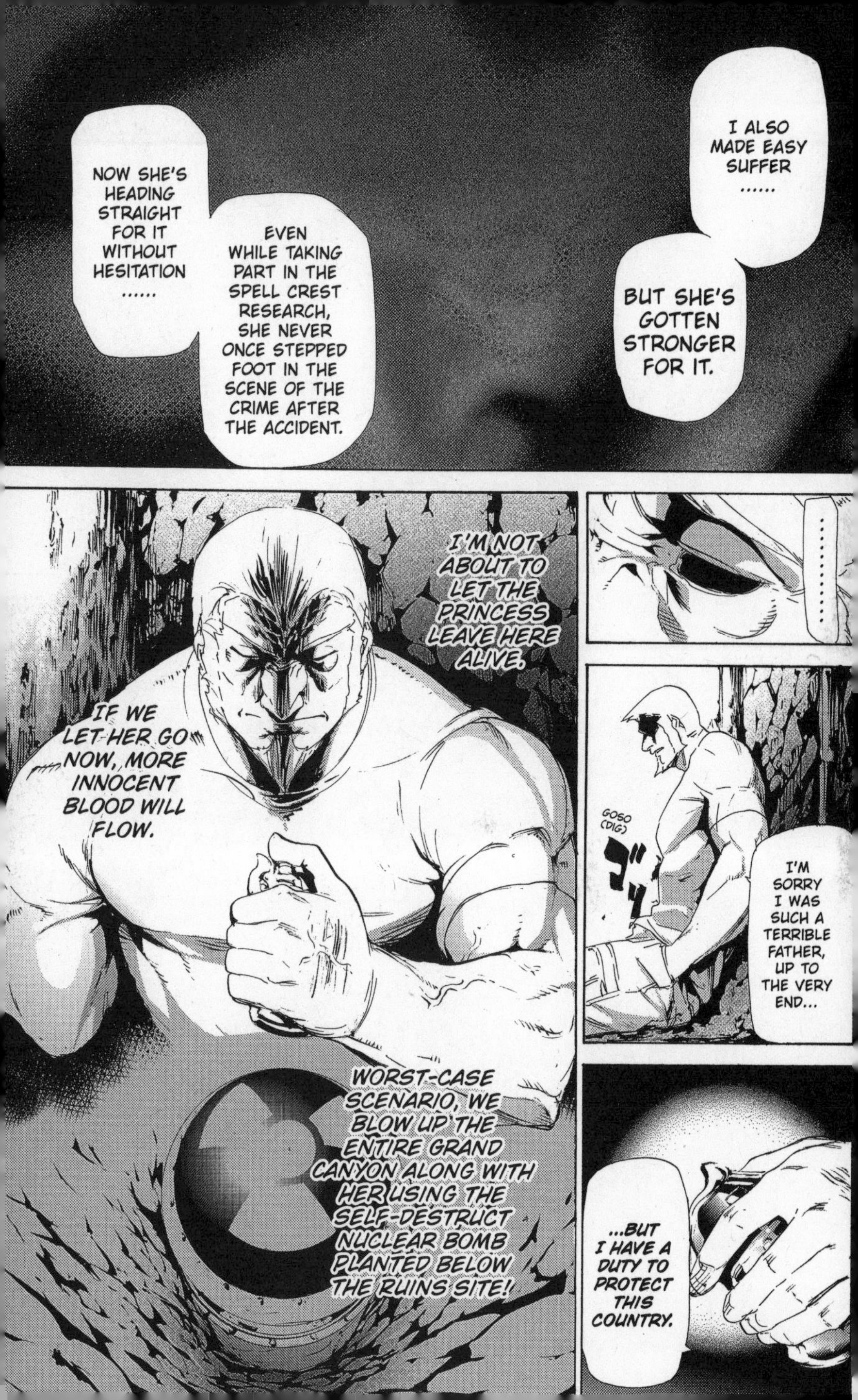
I ALSO MADE EASY SUFFER ......
BUT SHE'S GOTTEN STRONGER FOR IT.
EVEN WHILE TAKING PART IN THE SPELL CREST RESEARCH, SHE NEVER ONCE STEPPED FOOT IN THE SCENE OF THE CRIME AFTER THE ACCIDENT.
NOW SHE'S HEADING STRAIGHT FOR IT WITHOUT HESITATION ......
......
ゴッ
GOSO (DIG)
I'M SORRY I WAS SUCH A TERRIBLE FATHER, UP TO THE VERY END...
...BUT I HAVE A DUTY TO PROTECT THIS COUNTRY.
I'M NOT ABOUT TO LET THE PRINCESS LEAVE HERE ALIVE.
IF WE LET HER GO NOW, MORE INNOCENT BLOOD WILL FLOW.
WORST-CASE SCENARIO, WE BLOW UP THE ENTIRE GRAND CANYON ALONG WITH HER USING THE SELF-DESTRUCT NUCLEAR BOMB PLANTED BELOW THE RUINS SITE!

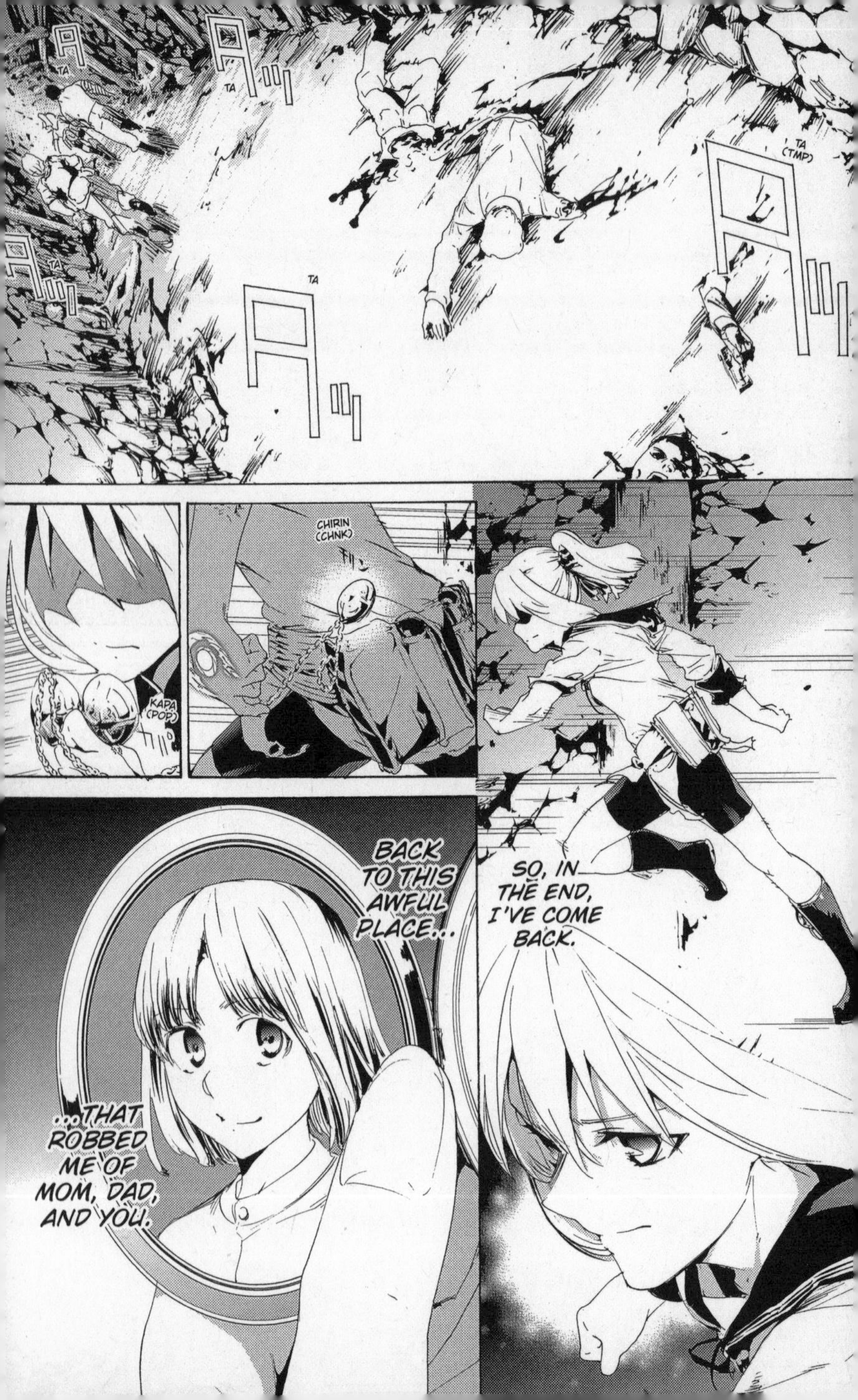
TA (TMP)
TA
TA
TA
TA
CHIRIN (CHNK)
KAPA (POP)
SO, IN THE END, I'VE COME BACK.
BACK TO THIS AWFUL PLACE...
...THAT ROBBED ME OF MOM, DAD, AND YOU.

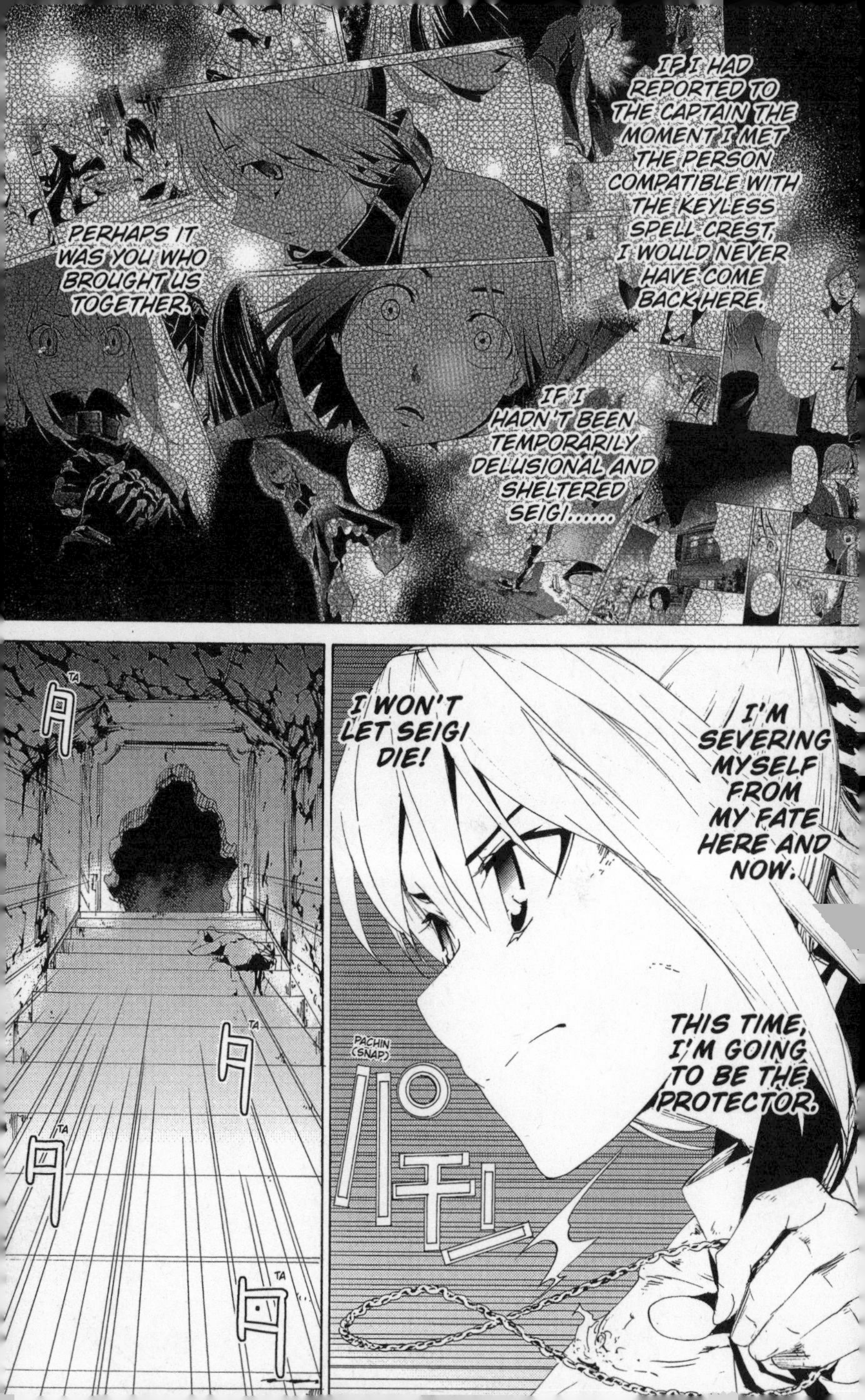
IF I HAD REPORTED TO THE CAPTAIN THE MOMENT I MET THE PERSON COMPATIBLE WITH THE KEYLESS SPELL CREST, I WOULD NEVER HAVE COME BACK HERE.
IF I HADN'T BEEN TEMPORARILY DELUSIONAL AND SHELTERED SEIGI......
PERHAPS IT WAS YOU WHO BROUGHT US TOGETHER.
I'M SEVERING MYSELF FROM MY FATE HERE AND NOW.
I WON'T LET SEIGI DIE!
PACHIN (SNAP)
THIS TIME, I'M GOING TO BE THE PROTECTOR.
TA
TA
TA
TA

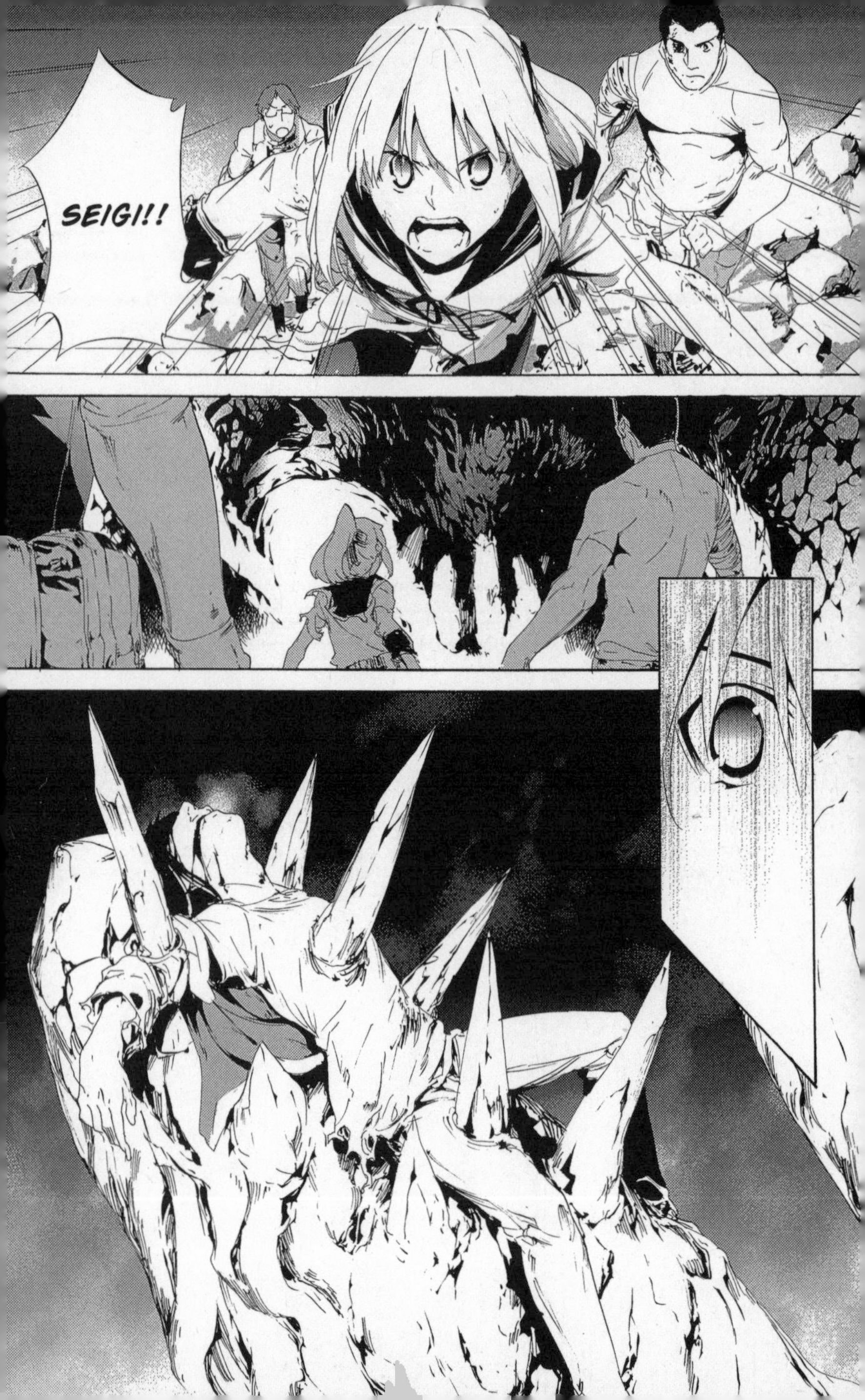
SEIGI!!

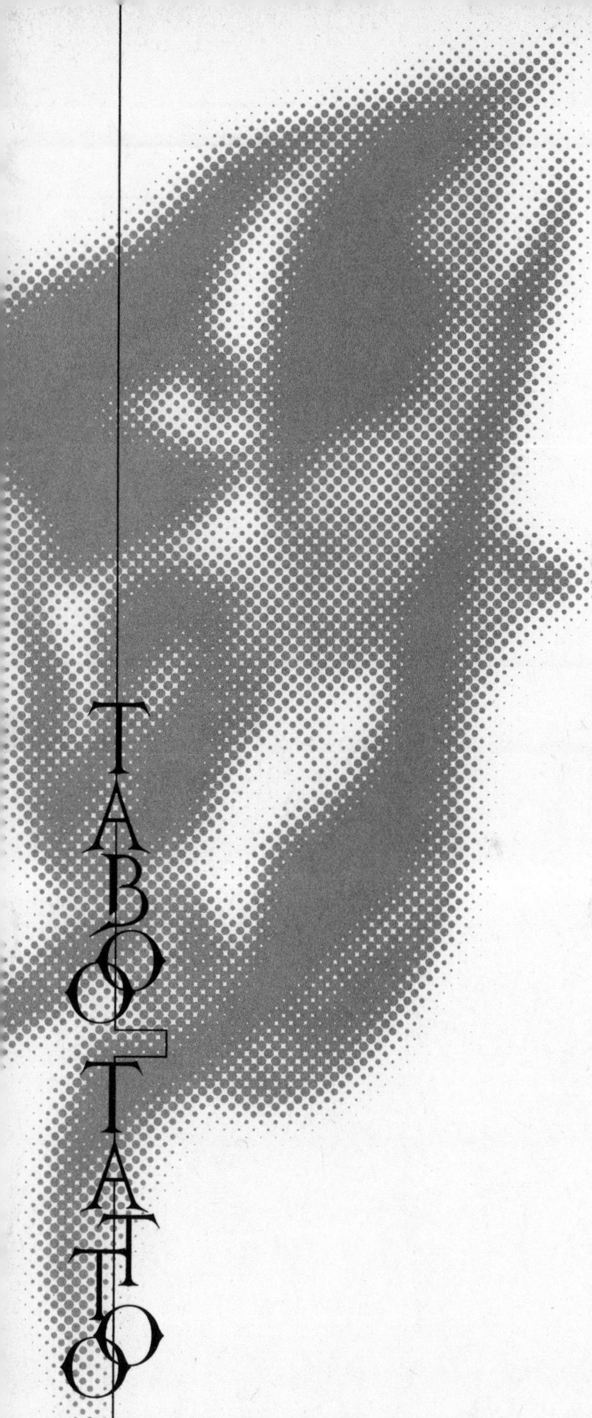

TABOO TATTOO

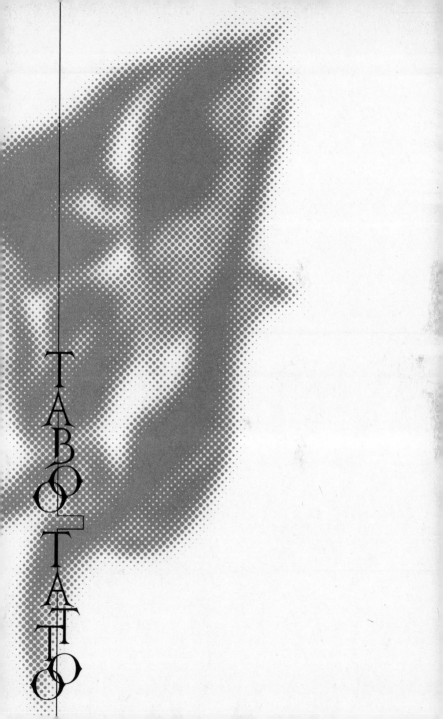

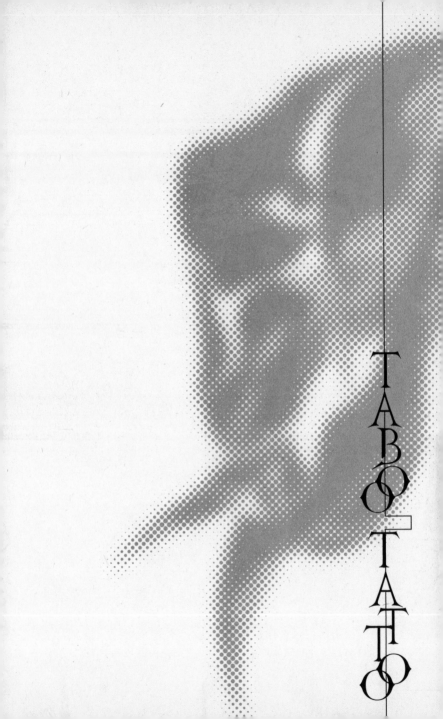

TABOO TATTOO

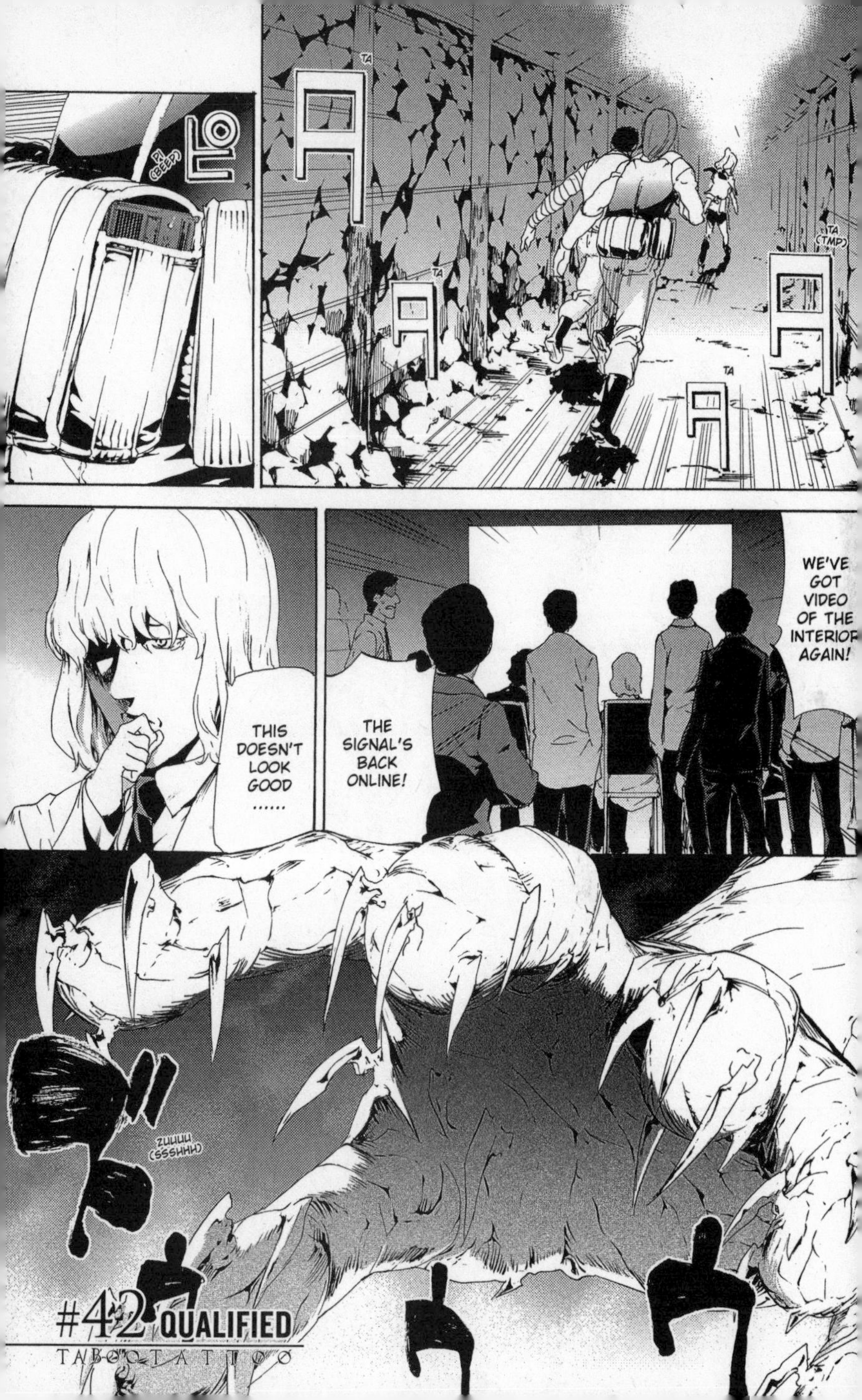
TA
TA
TA (TMP)
TA
PI (BEEP)
WE'VE GOT VIDEO OF THE INTERIOR AGAIN!
THE SIGNAL'S BACK ONLINE!
THIS DOESN'T LOOK GOOD ......
ZUUUU (SSSHHH)
#42 QUALIFIED
TABOO TATTOO

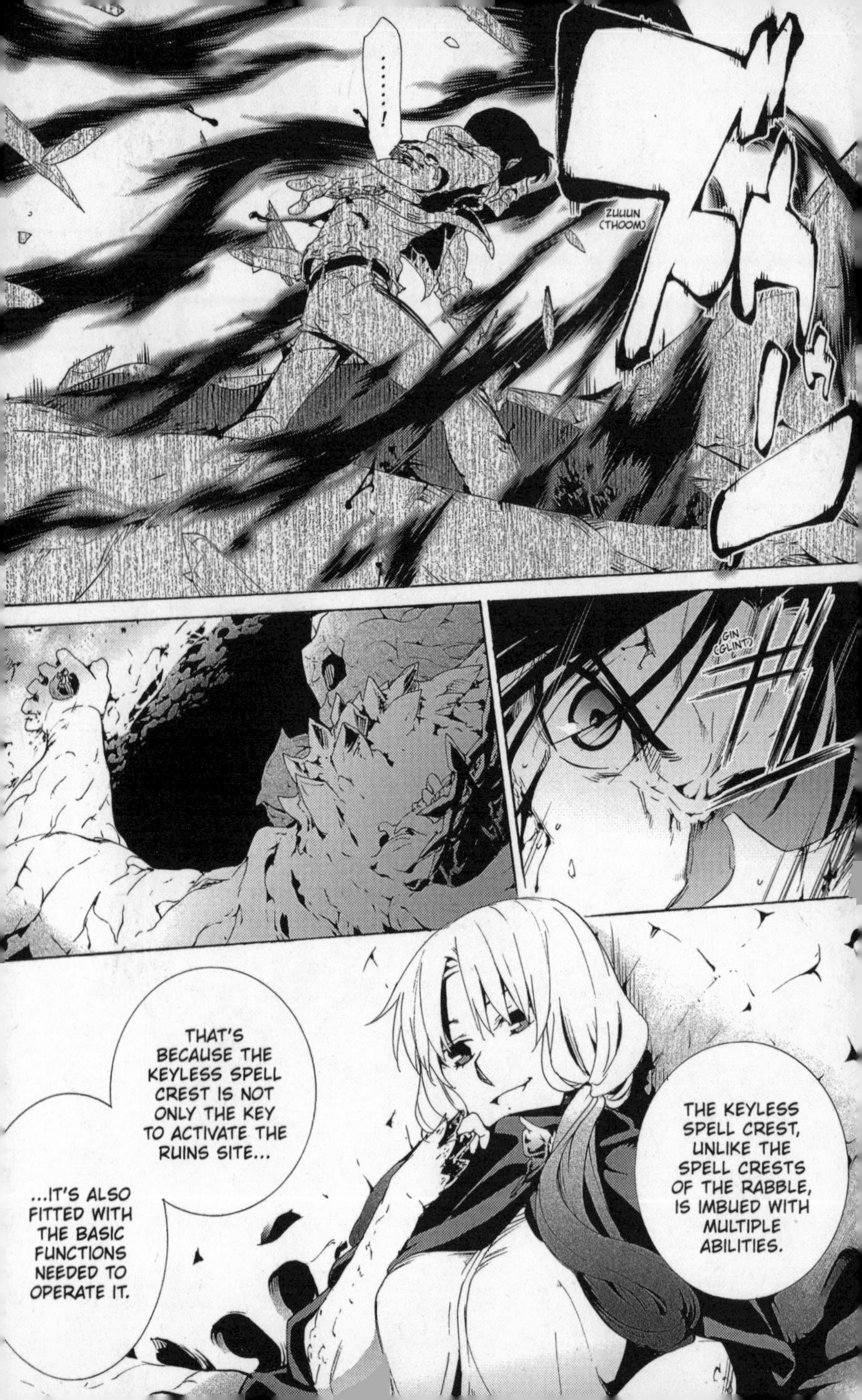
……!
ZUUUN (THOOM)
GIN (GLINT)
THE KEYLESS SPELL CREST, UNLIKE THE SPELL CRESTS OF THE RABBLE, IS IMBUED WITH MULTIPLE ABILITIES.
THAT'S BECAUSE THE KEYLESS SPELL CREST IS NOT ONLY THE KEY TO ACTIVATE THE RUINS SITE…
…IT'S ALSO FITTED WITH THE BASIC FUNCTIONS NEEDED TO OPERATE IT.

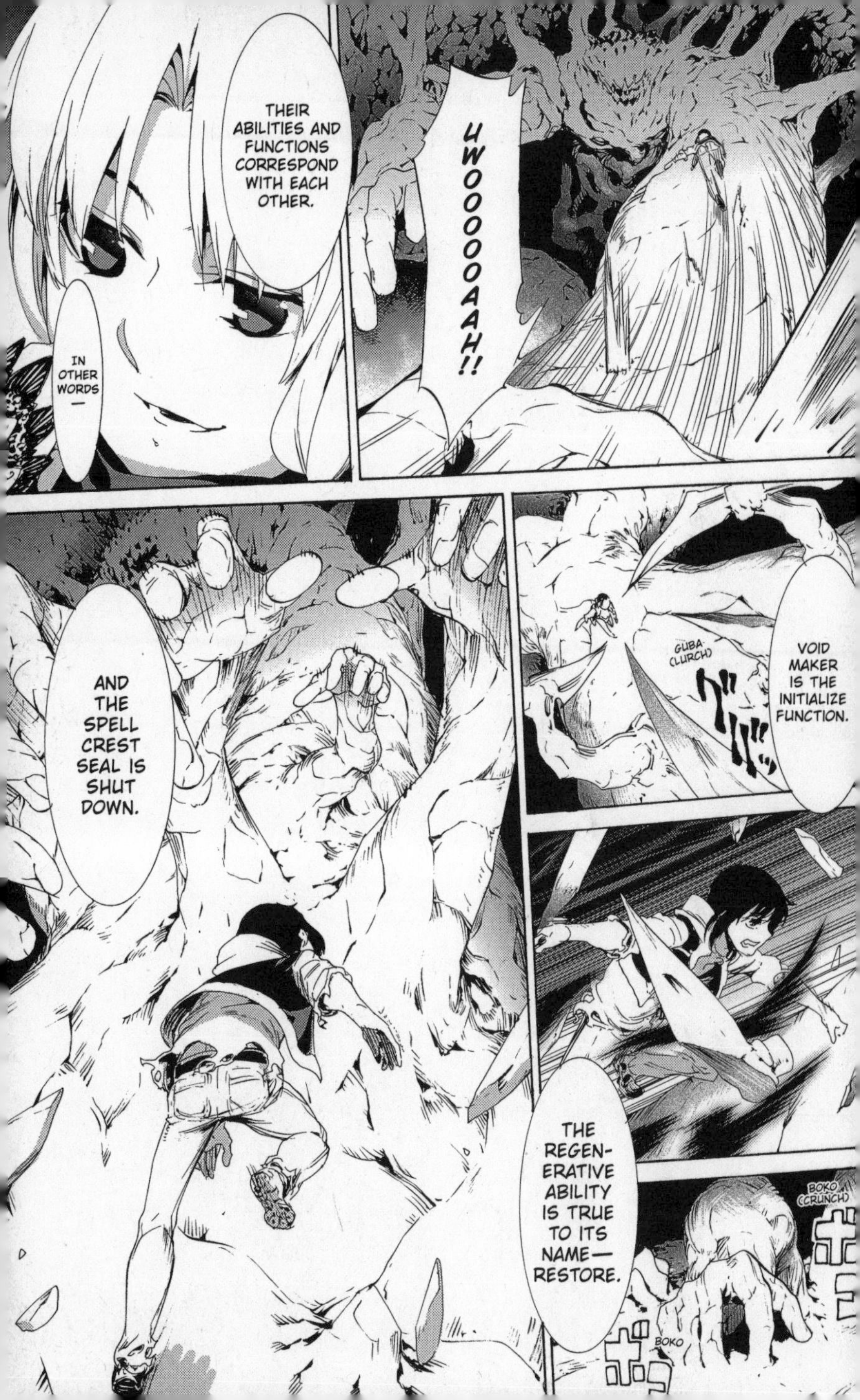

UWOOOOOAAH!!
THEIR ABILITIES AND FUNCTIONS CORRESPOND WITH EACH OTHER.
IN OTHER WORDS —
VOID MAKER IS THE INITIALIZE FUNCTION.
GUBA (LURCH)
THE REGENERATIVE ABILITY IS TRUE TO ITS NAME—RESTORE.
BOKO (CRUNCH)
BOKO
AND THE SPELL CREST SEAL IS SHUT DOWN.

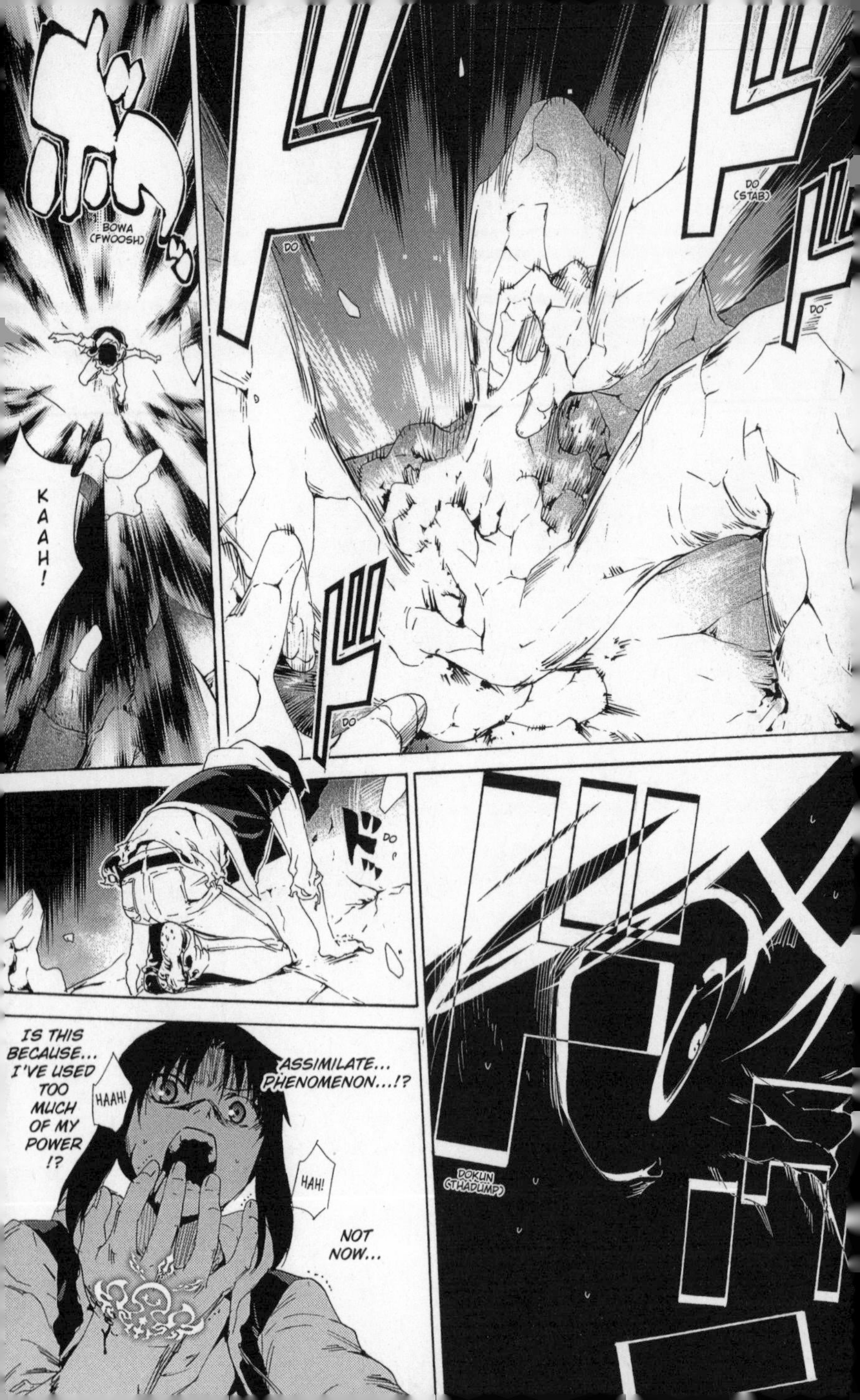
DO
(STAB)
DO
DO
DO
BOWA
(FWOOSH)
KAAAH!
DOKUN
(THADUMP)
DO
ASSIMILATE... PHENOMENON...!?
HAAH!
IS THIS BECAUSE... I'VE USED TOO MUCH OF MY POWER!?
HAH!
NOT NOW...

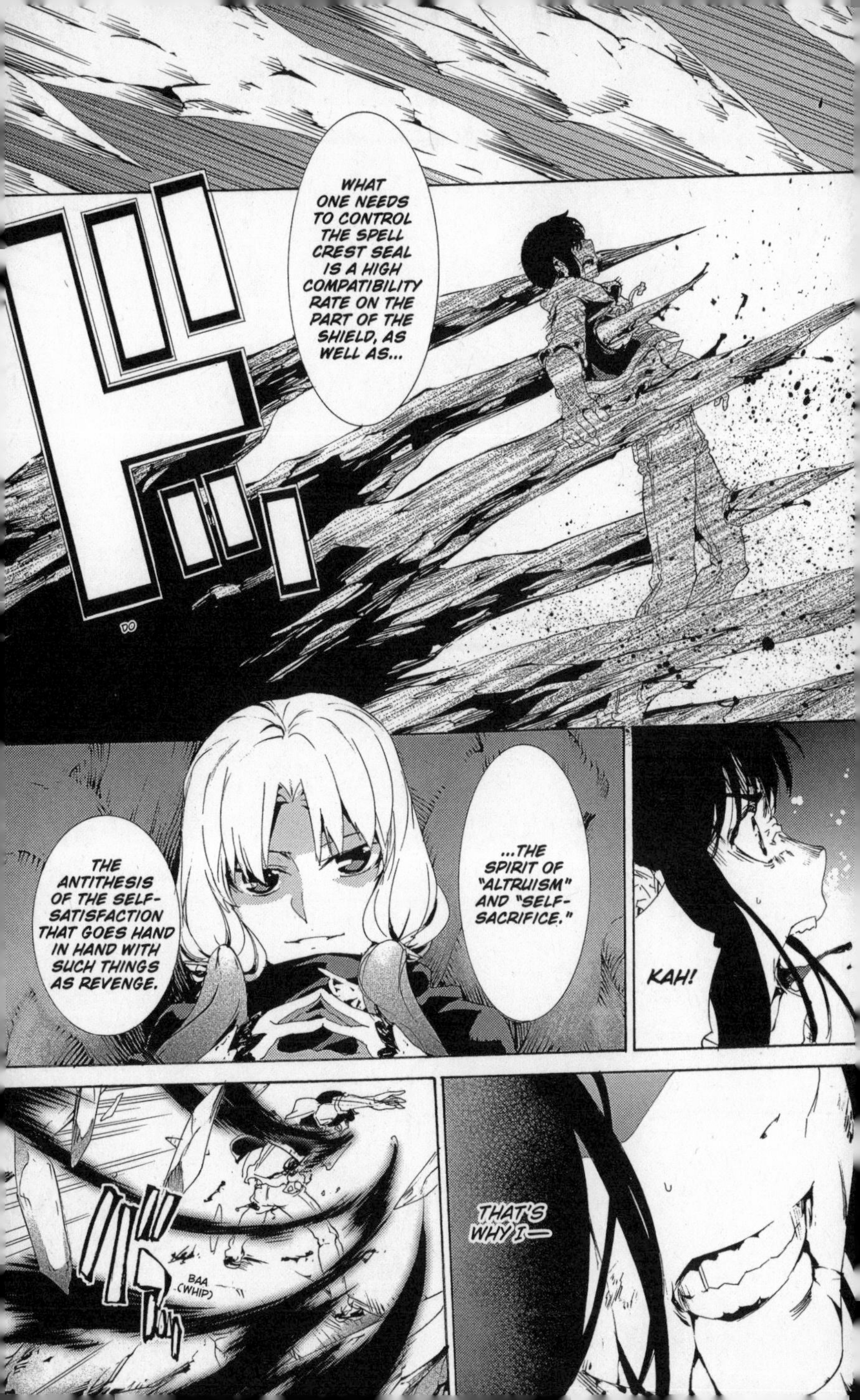
WHAT ONE NEEDS TO CONTROL THE SPELL CREST SEAL IS A HIGH COMPATIBILITY RATE ON THE PART OF THE SHIELD, AS WELL AS...
DO
KAH!
...THE SPIRIT OF "ALTRUISM" AND "SELF-SACRIFICE."
THE ANTITHESIS OF THE SELF-SATISFACTION THAT GOES HAND IN HAND WITH SUCH THINGS AS REVENGE.
THAT'S WHY I—
BAA (WHIP)

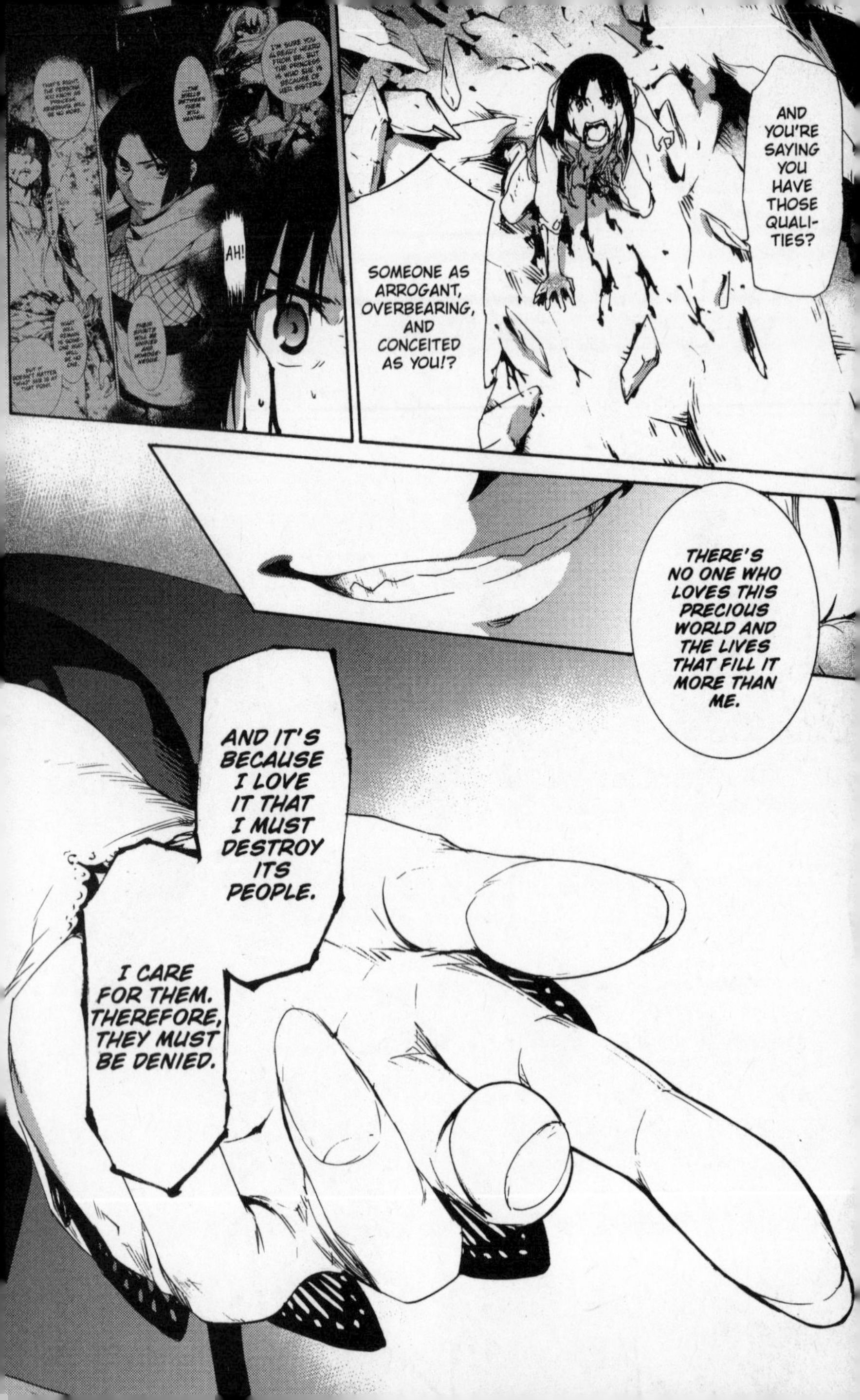
AND YOU'RE SAYING YOU HAVE THOSE QUALI-TIES?
SOMEONE AS ARROGANT, OVERBEARING, AND CONCEITED AS YOU!?
AH!
THERE'S NO ONE WHO LOVES THIS PRECIOUS WORLD AND THE LIVES THAT FILL IT MORE THAN ME.
AND IT'S BECAUSE I LOVE IT THAT I MUST DESTROY ITS PEOPLE.
I CARE FOR THEM. THEREFORE, THEY MUST BE DENIED.

THE OLD GODS ARE SIMPLY FICTIONAL CREATIONS. MERE CONCEPTS.
THEY WERE NOTHING MORE THAN CORROSIVE IDEAS THAT KINDLED THE FIRES OF WAR AND LOCKED THE LIGHT OF INTELLIGENCE INTO A DARK CAGE.
THE GOD I WILL CRAFT WILL BE A CREATION OF POSSI-BILITIES DEVOTED TO THIS WORLD AND ALL LIFE.
AND FOR THAT...I WILL GLADLY OFFER UP MY LIFE AS A SACRIFICE TO THIS NEWBORN GOD.

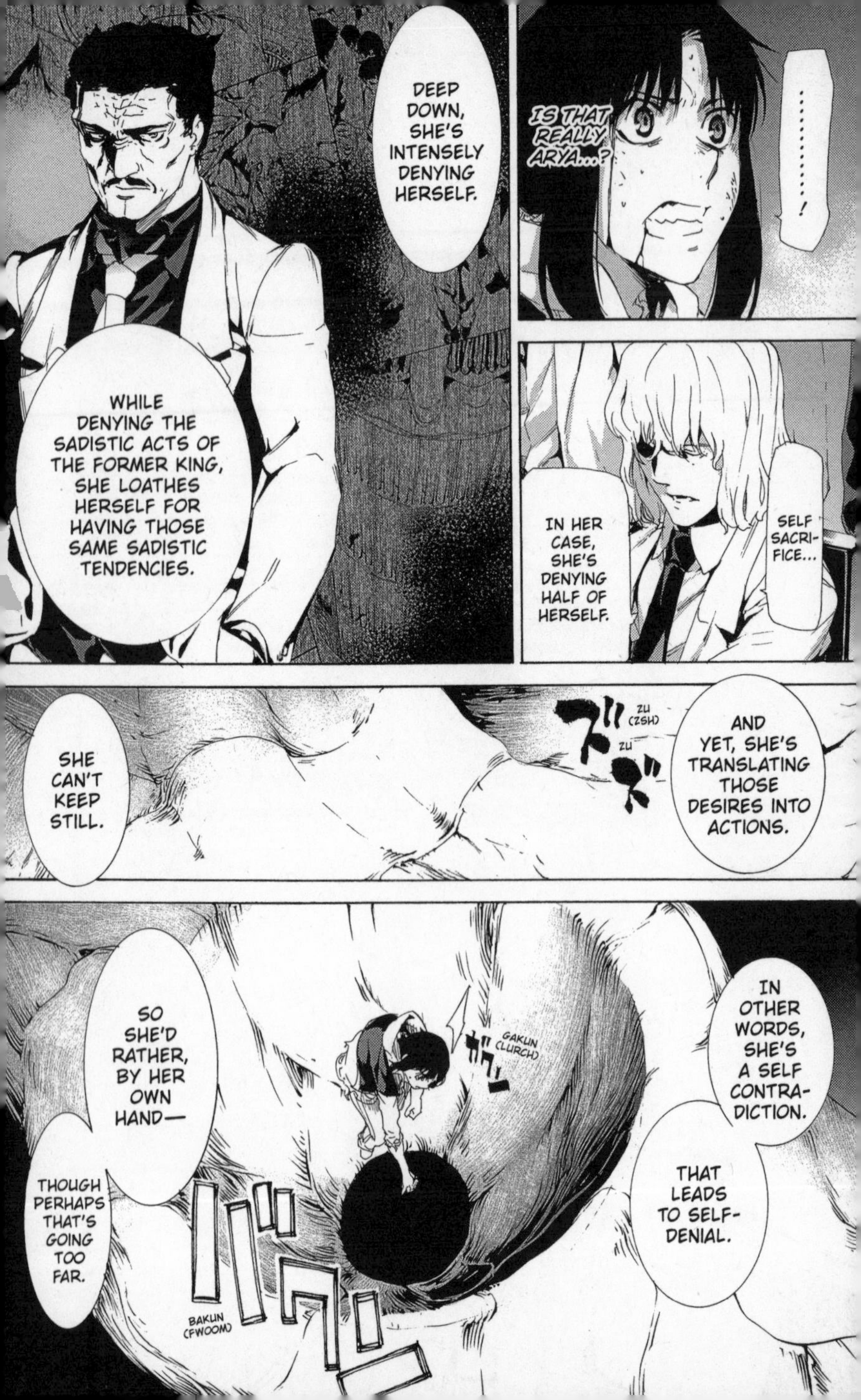
......!
IS THAT REALLY ARYA...?
SELF SACRI-FICE...
IN HER CASE, SHE'S DENYING HALF OF HERSELF.
DEEP DOWN, SHE'S INTENSELY DENYING HERSELF.
WHILE DENYING THE SADISTIC ACTS OF THE FORMER KING, SHE LOATHES HERSELF FOR HAVING THOSE SAME SADISTIC TENDENCIES.
AND YET, SHE'S TRANSLATING THOSE DESIRES INTO ACTIONS.
ZU (ZSH)
ZU
SHE CAN'T KEEP STILL.
IN OTHER WORDS, SHE'S A SELF CONTRA-DICTION.
THAT LEADS TO SELF-DENIAL.
GAKUN (LURCH)
SO SHE'D RATHER, BY HER OWN HAND—
THOUGH PERHAPS THAT'S GOING TOO FAR.
BAKUN (FWOOM)

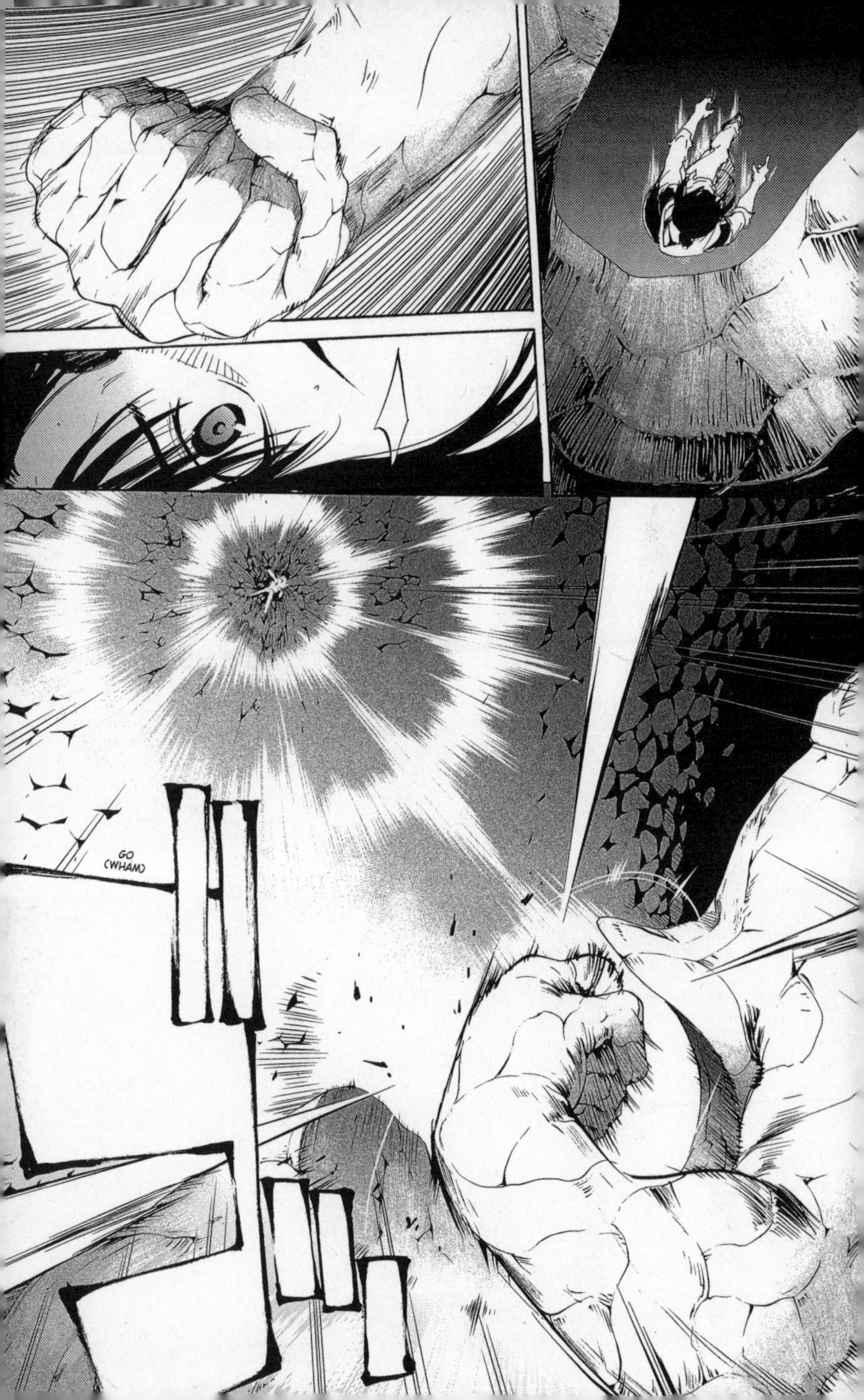
GO
(WHAM)

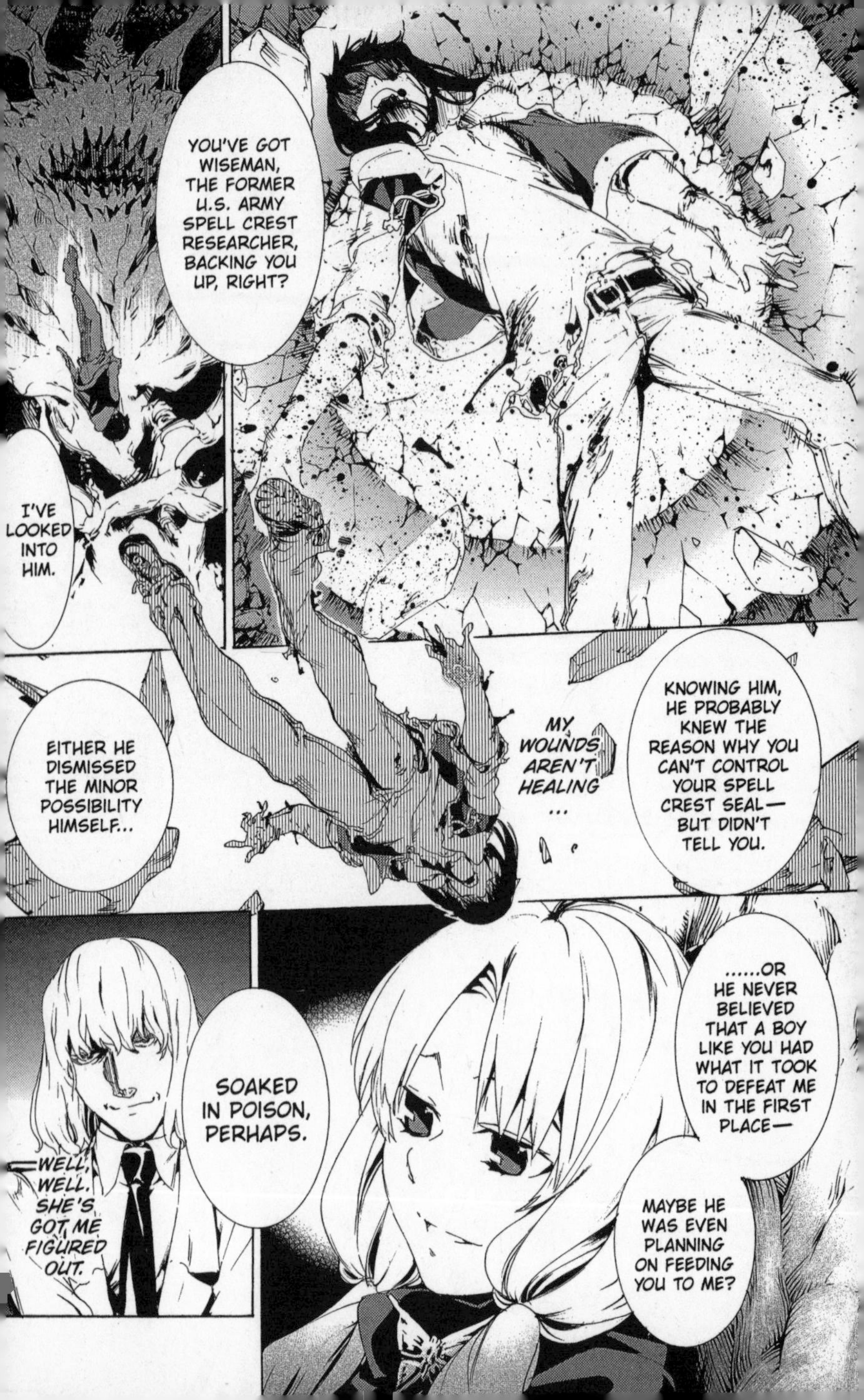

YOU'VE GOT WISEMAN, THE FORMER U.S. ARMY SPELL CREST RESEARCHER, BACKING YOU UP, RIGHT?
I'VE LOOKED INTO HIM.
KNOWING HIM, HE PROBABLY KNEW THE REASON WHY YOU CAN'T CONTROL YOUR SPELL CREST SEAL— BUT DIDN'T TELL YOU.
MY WOUNDS AREN'T HEALING...
EITHER HE DISMISSED THE MINOR POSSIBILITY HIMSELF...
......OR HE NEVER BELIEVED THAT A BOY LIKE YOU HAD WHAT IT TOOK TO DEFEAT ME IN THE FIRST PLACE—
MAYBE HE WAS EVEN PLANNING ON FEEDING YOU TO ME?
SOAKED IN POISON, PERHAPS.
—WELL, WELL. SHE'S GOT ME FIGURED OUT.

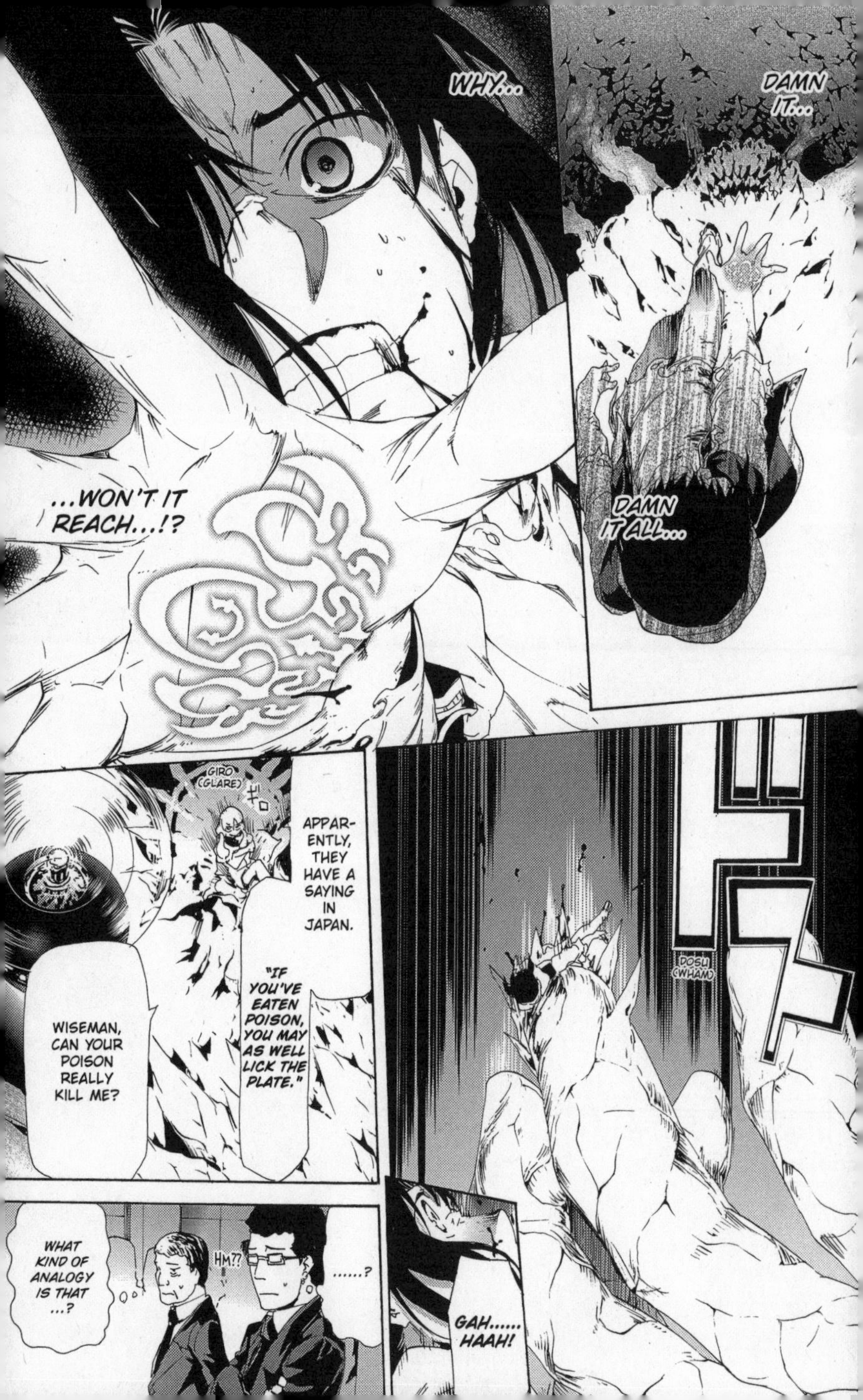
DAMN IT...
DAMN IT ALL...
WHY...
...WON'T IT REACH...!?
DOSU (WHAM)
GIRO (GLARE)
APPARENTLY, THEY HAVE A SAYING IN JAPAN.
"IF YOU'VE EATEN POISON, YOU MAY AS WELL LICK THE PLATE."
WISEMAN, CAN YOUR POISON REALLY KILL ME?
GAH...... HAAH!
HM??
......?
WHAT KIND OF ANALOGY IS THAT ...?

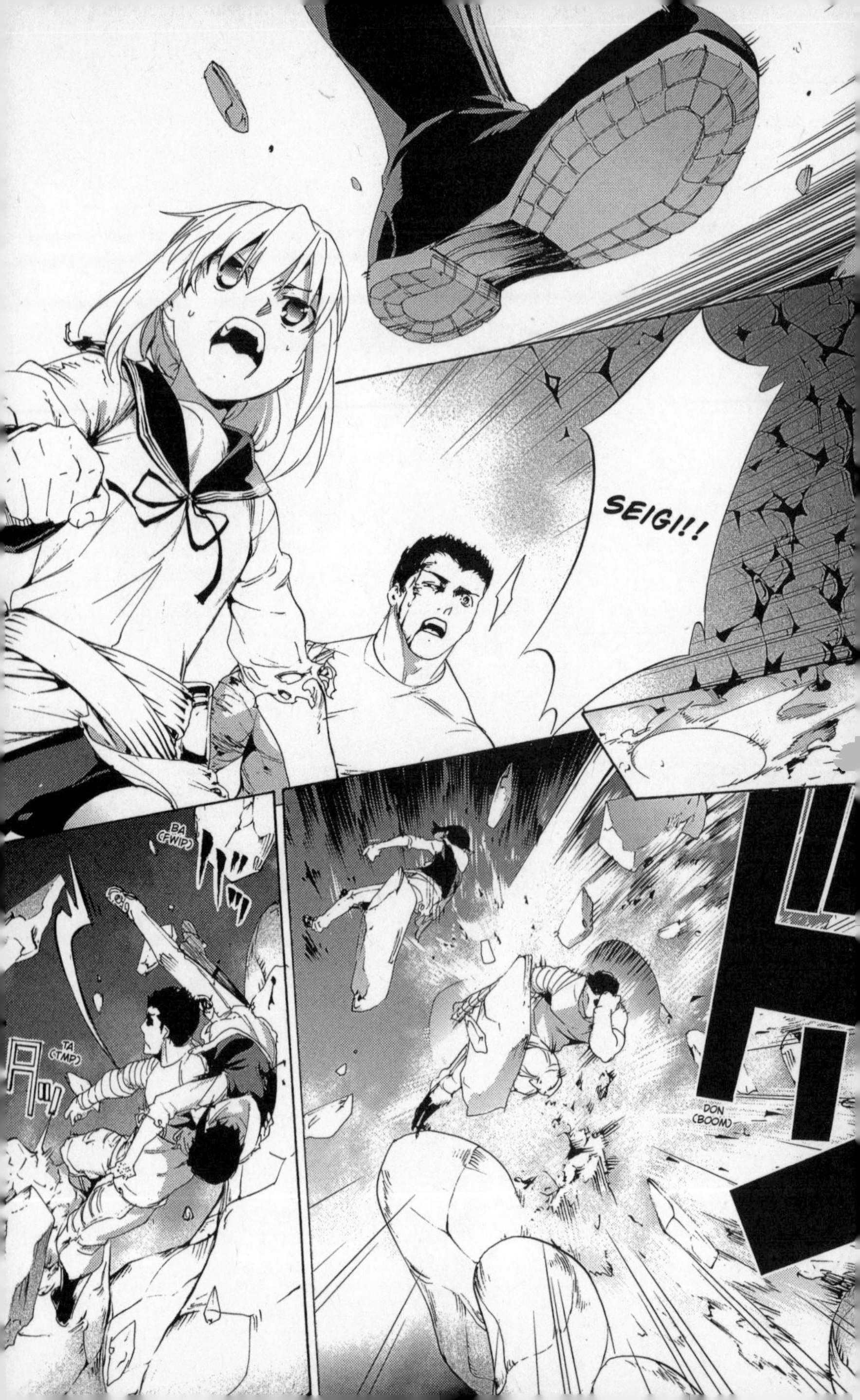
SEIGI!!
DON (BOOM)
BA (FWIP)
TA (TMP)

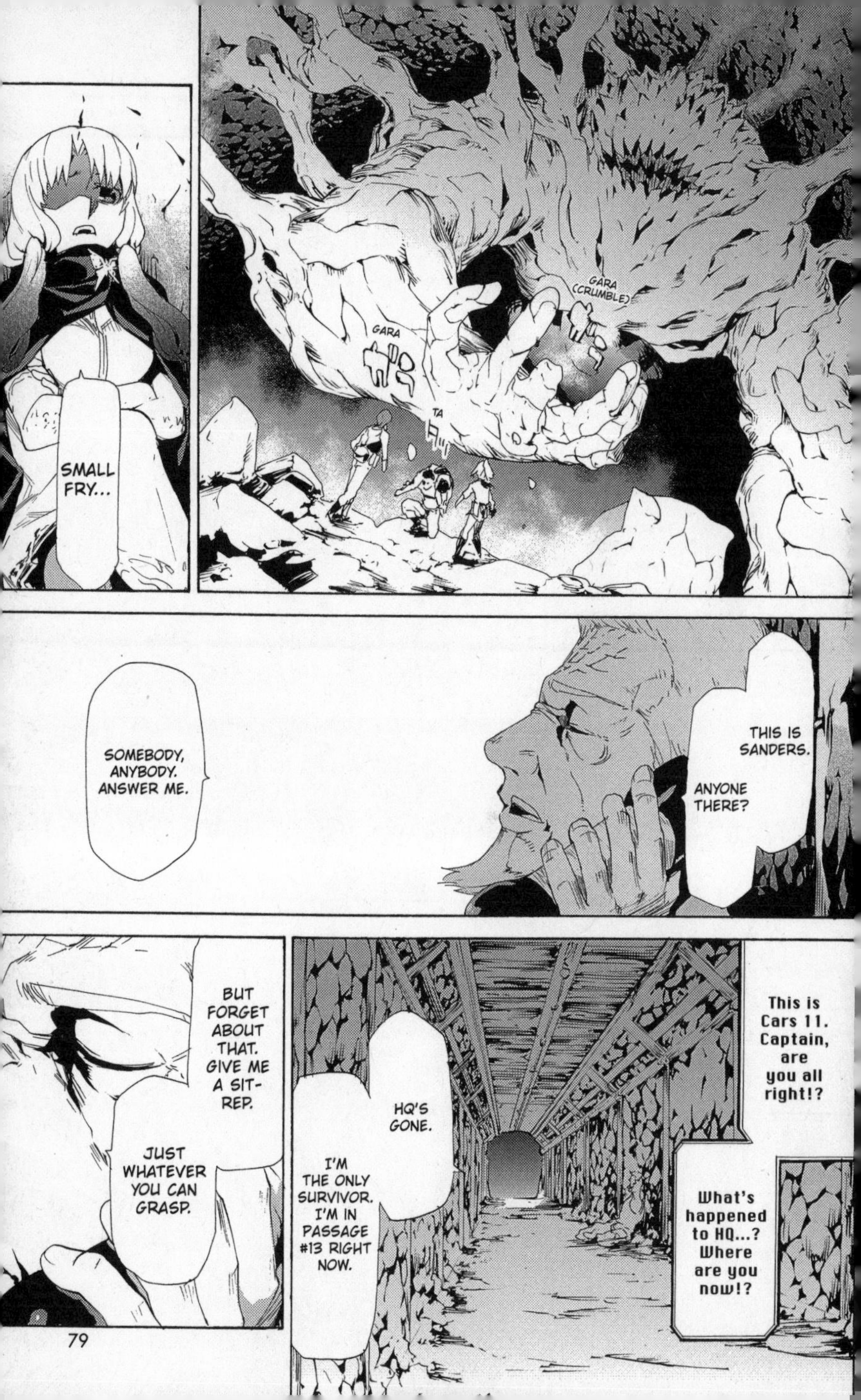
GARA (CRUMBLE)
GARA
TA
SMALL FRY...
THIS IS SANDERS.
ANYONE THERE?
SOMEBODY, ANYBODY. ANSWER ME.
This is Cars 11. Captain, are you all right!?
What's happened to HQ...? Where are you now!?
HQ'S GONE.
I'M THE ONLY SURVIVOR. I'M IN PASSAGE #13 RIGHT NOW.
BUT FORGET ABOUT THAT. GIVE ME A SIT-REP.
JUST WHATEVER YOU CAN GRASP.

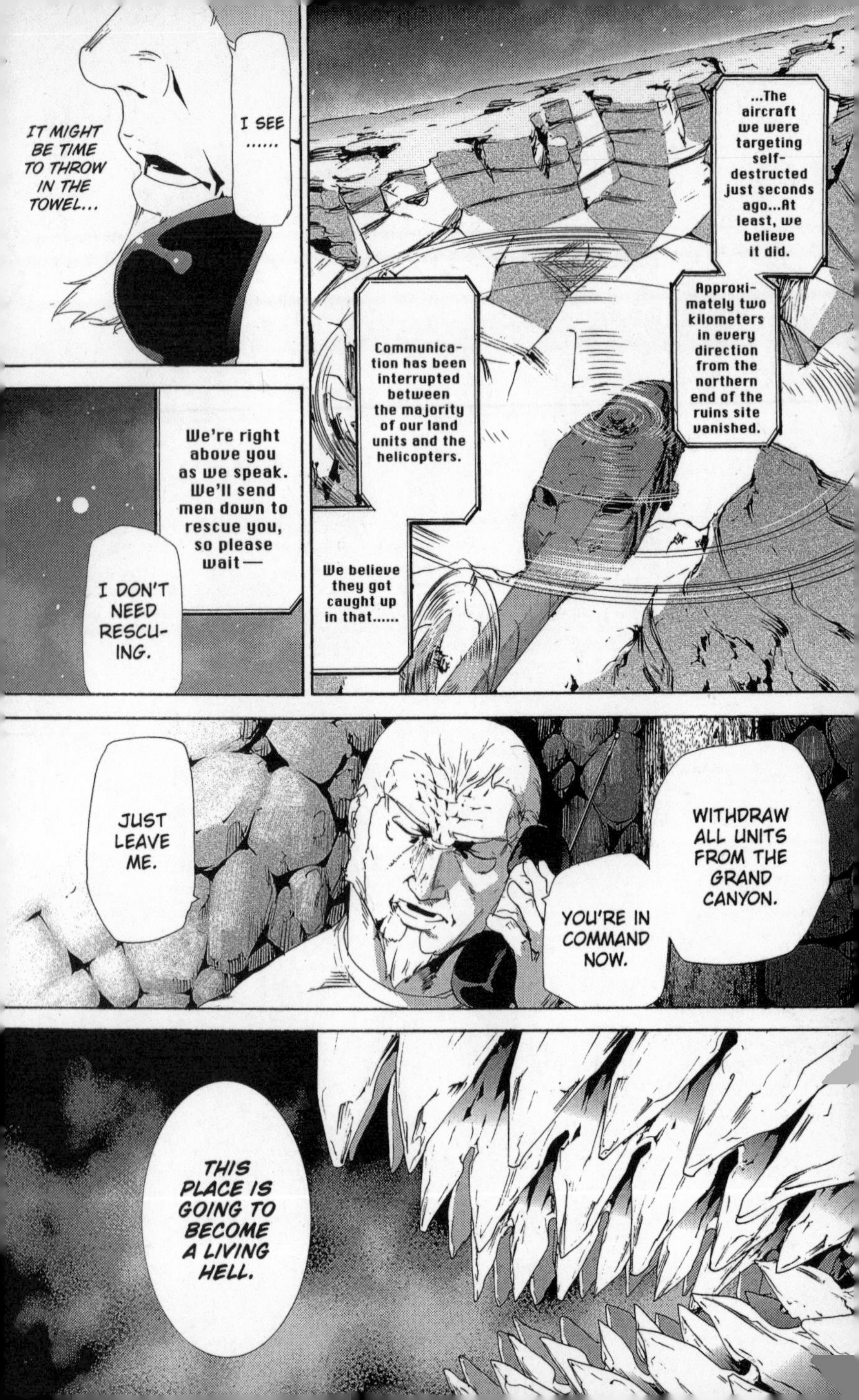
...The aircraft we were targeting self-destructed just seconds ago...At least, we believe it did.
Approximately two kilometers in every direction from the northern end of the ruins site vanished.
Communication has been interrupted between the majority of our land units and the helicopters.
We believe they got caught up in that......
I SEE ......
IT MIGHT BE TIME TO THROW IN THE TOWEL...
We're right above you as we speak. We'll send men down to rescue you, so please wait—
I DON'T NEED RESCUING.
WITHDRAW ALL UNITS FROM THE GRAND CANYON.
YOU'RE IN COMMAND NOW.
JUST LEAVE ME.
THIS PLACE IS GOING TO BECOME A LIVING HELL.

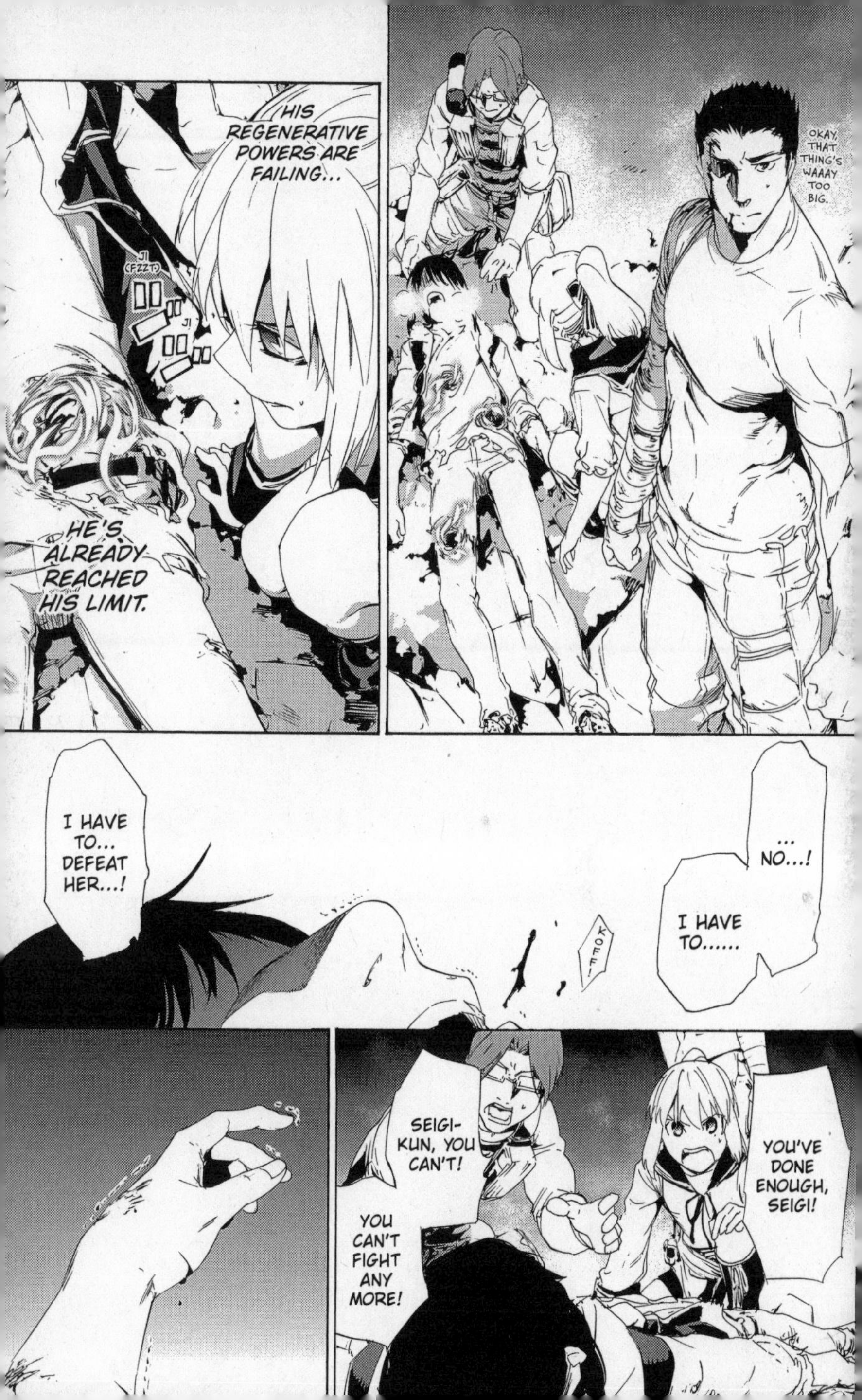
OKAY, THAT THING'S WAAAY TOO BIG.
HIS REGENERATIVE POWERS ARE FAILING...
JI (FZZT)
JI
HE'S ALREADY REACHED HIS LIMIT.
... NO...!
I HAVE TO......
KOFF!
I HAVE TO... DEFEAT HER...!
YOU'VE DONE ENOUGH, SEIGI!
SEIGI-KUN, YOU CAN'T!
YOU CAN'T FIGHT ANY MORE!

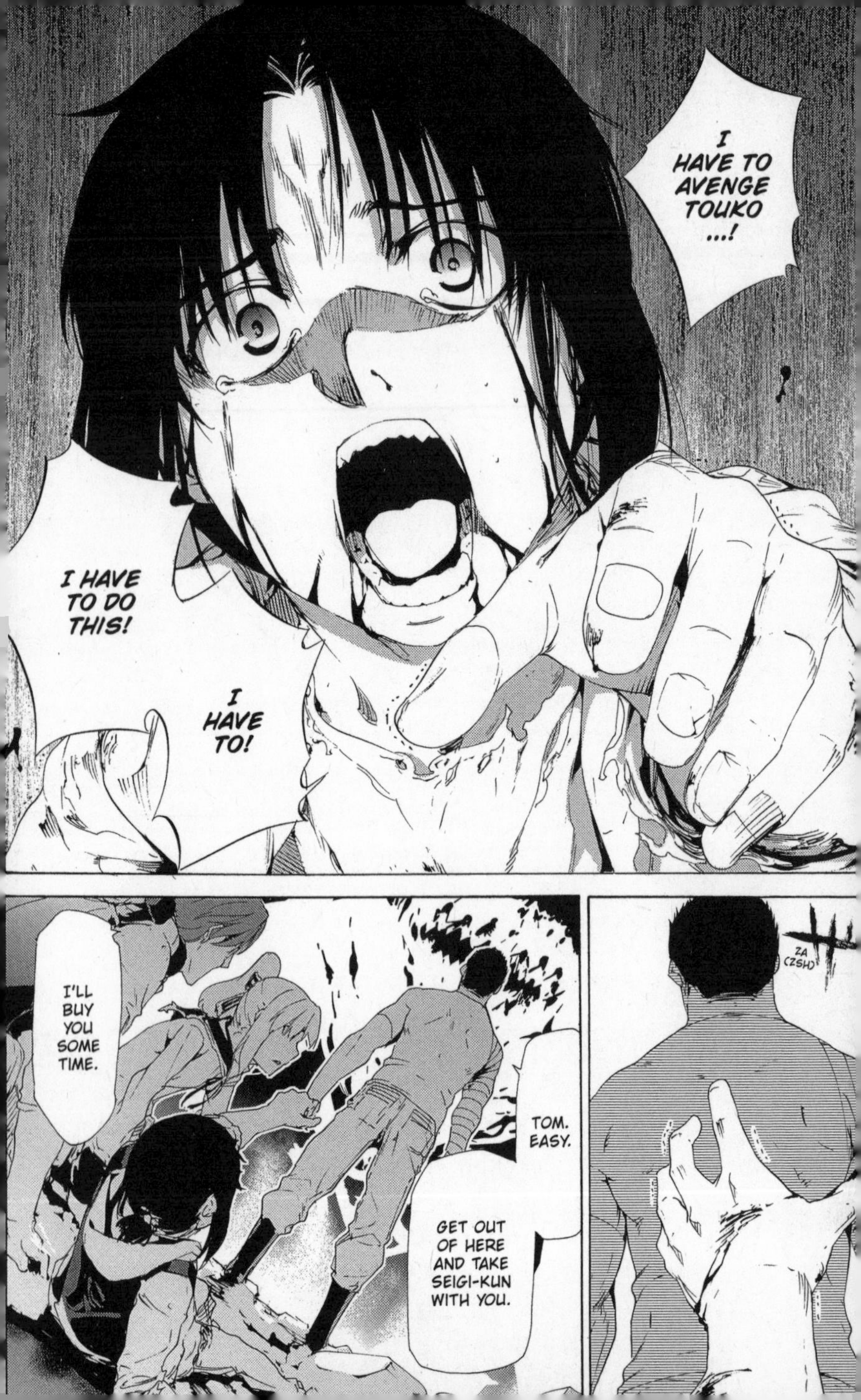
I HAVE TO AVENGE TOUKO ...!
I HAVE TO DO THIS!
I HAVE TO!
ZA (ZSH)
TOM. EASY.
GET OUT OF HERE AND TAKE SEIGI-KUN WITH YOU.
I'LL BUY YOU SOME TIME.

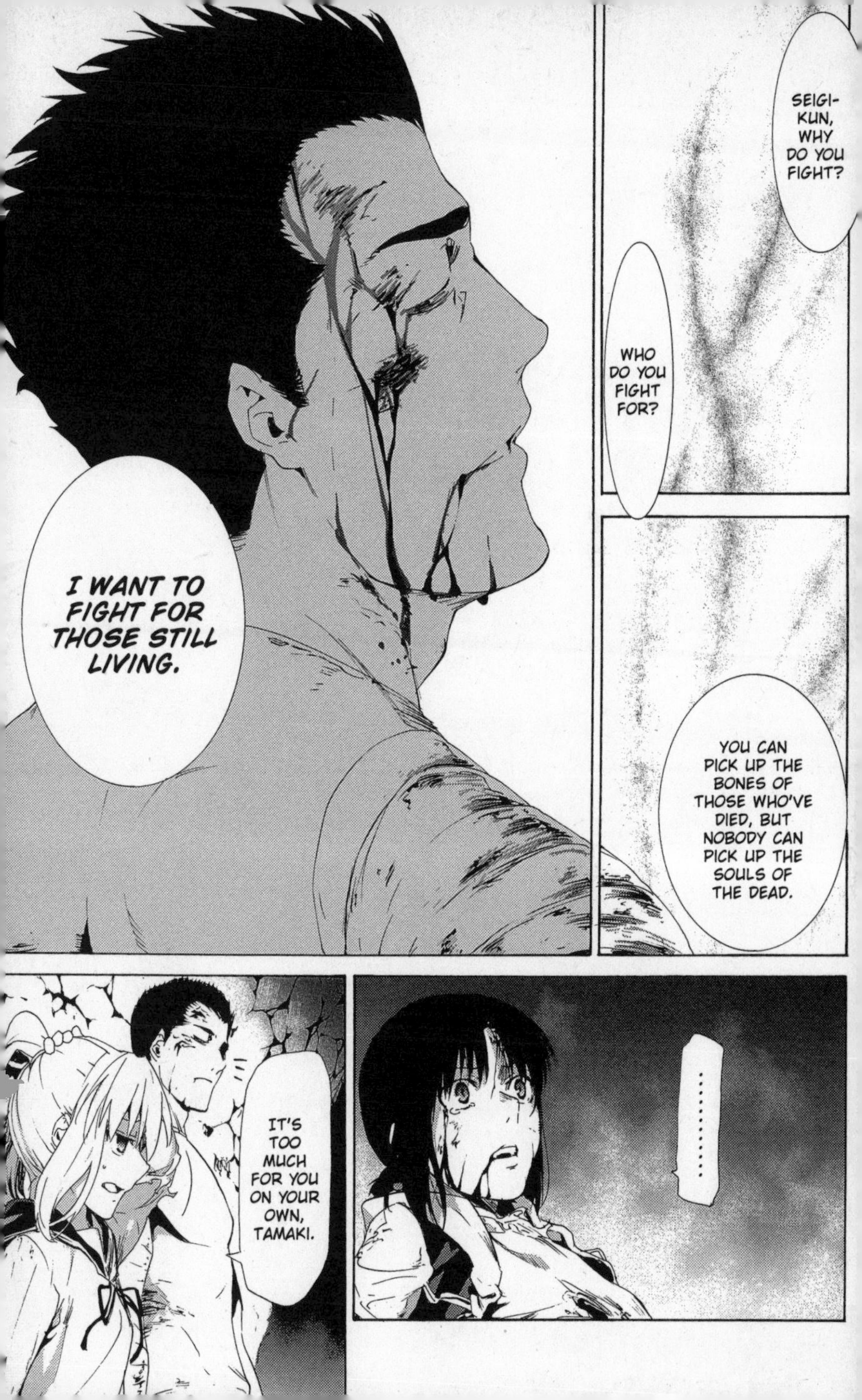
SEIGI-KUN, WHY DO YOU FIGHT?
WHO DO YOU FIGHT FOR?
YOU CAN PICK UP THE BONES OF THOSE WHO'VE DIED, BUT NOBODY CAN PICK UP THE SOULS OF THE DEAD.
I WANT TO FIGHT FOR THOSE STILL LIVING.
......
IT'S TOO MUCH FOR YOU ON YOUR OWN, TAMAKI.

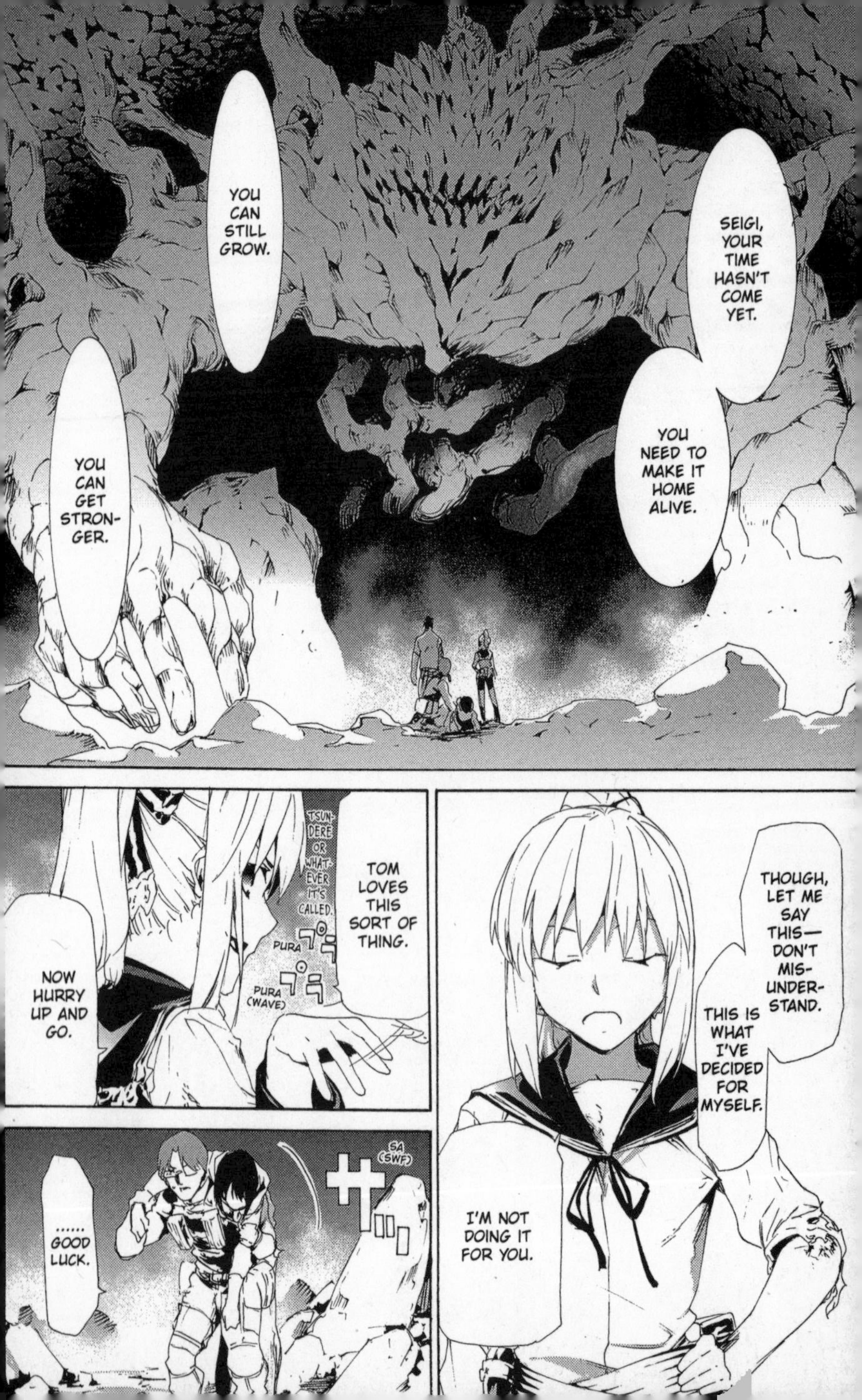
SEIGI, YOUR TIME HASN'T COME YET.
YOU NEED TO MAKE IT HOME ALIVE.
YOU CAN STILL GROW.
YOU CAN GET STRON-GER.
THOUGH, LET ME SAY THIS— DON'T MIS-UNDER-STAND.
THIS IS WHAT I'VE DECIDED FOR MYSELF.
I'M NOT DOING IT FOR YOU.
TOM LOVES THIS SORT OF THING.
TSUN-DERE OR WHAT-EVER IT'S CALLED.
PURA
PURA (WAVE)
NOW HURRY UP AND GO.
SA (SWF)
...... GOOD LUCK.

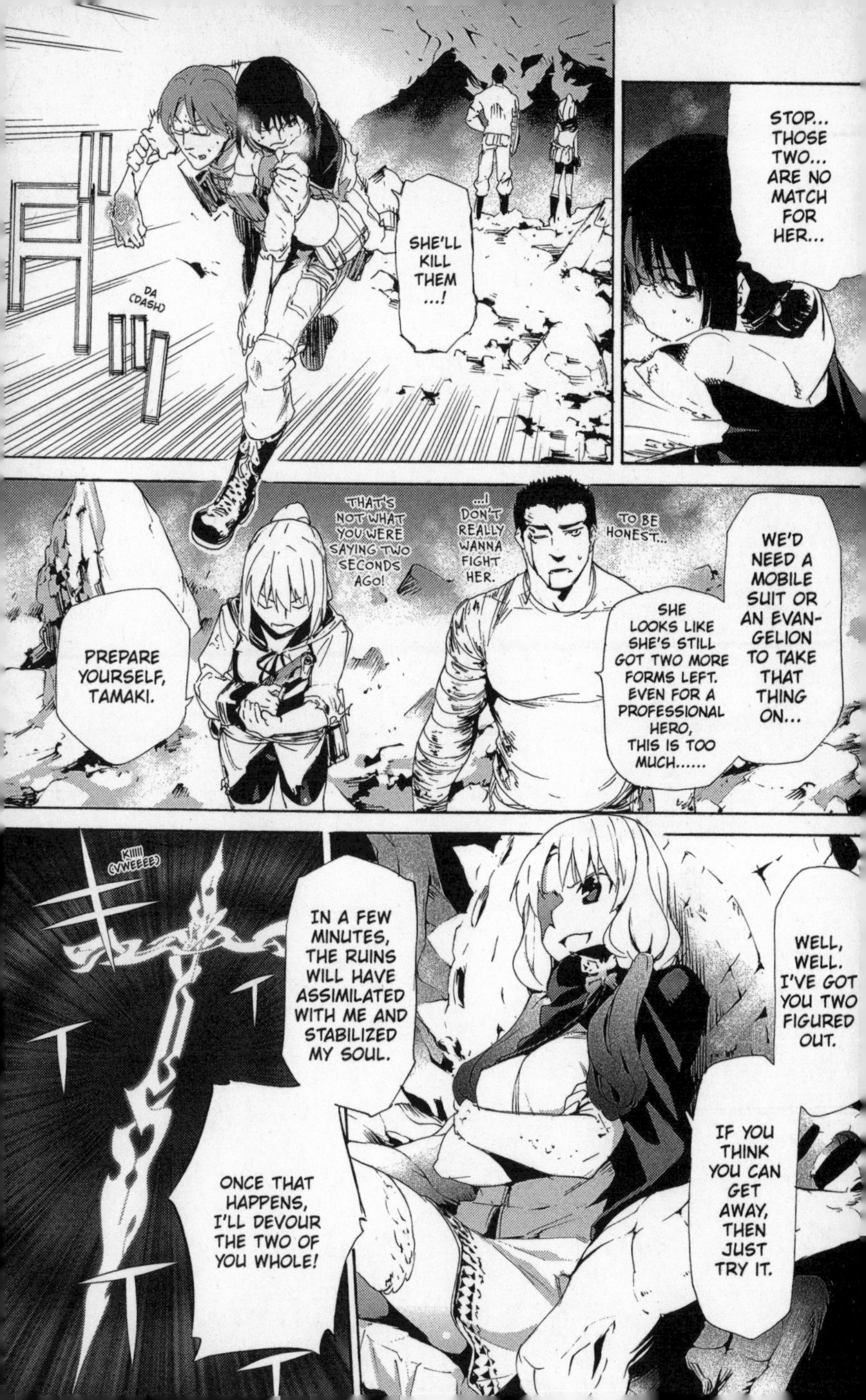
STOP... THOSE TWO... ARE NO MATCH FOR HER...
SHE'LL KILL THEM ...!
DA (DASH)
WE'D NEED A MOBILE SUIT OR AN EVANGELION TO TAKE THAT THING ON...
TO BE HONEST...
SHE LOOKS LIKE SHE'S STILL GOT TWO MORE FORMS LEFT. EVEN FOR A PROFESSIONAL HERO, THIS IS TOO MUCH......
...I DON'T REALLY WANNA FIGHT HER.
THAT'S NOT WHAT YOU WERE SAYING TWO SECONDS AGO!
PREPARE YOURSELF, TAMAKI.
WELL, WELL. I'VE GOT YOU TWO FIGURED OUT.
IF YOU THINK YOU CAN GET AWAY, THEN JUST TRY IT.
IN A FEW MINUTES, THE RUINS WILL HAVE ASSIMILATED WITH ME AND STABILIZED MY SOUL.
ONCE THAT HAPPENS, I'LL DEVOUR THE TWO OF YOU WHOLE!
KIIIII (VWEEEE)

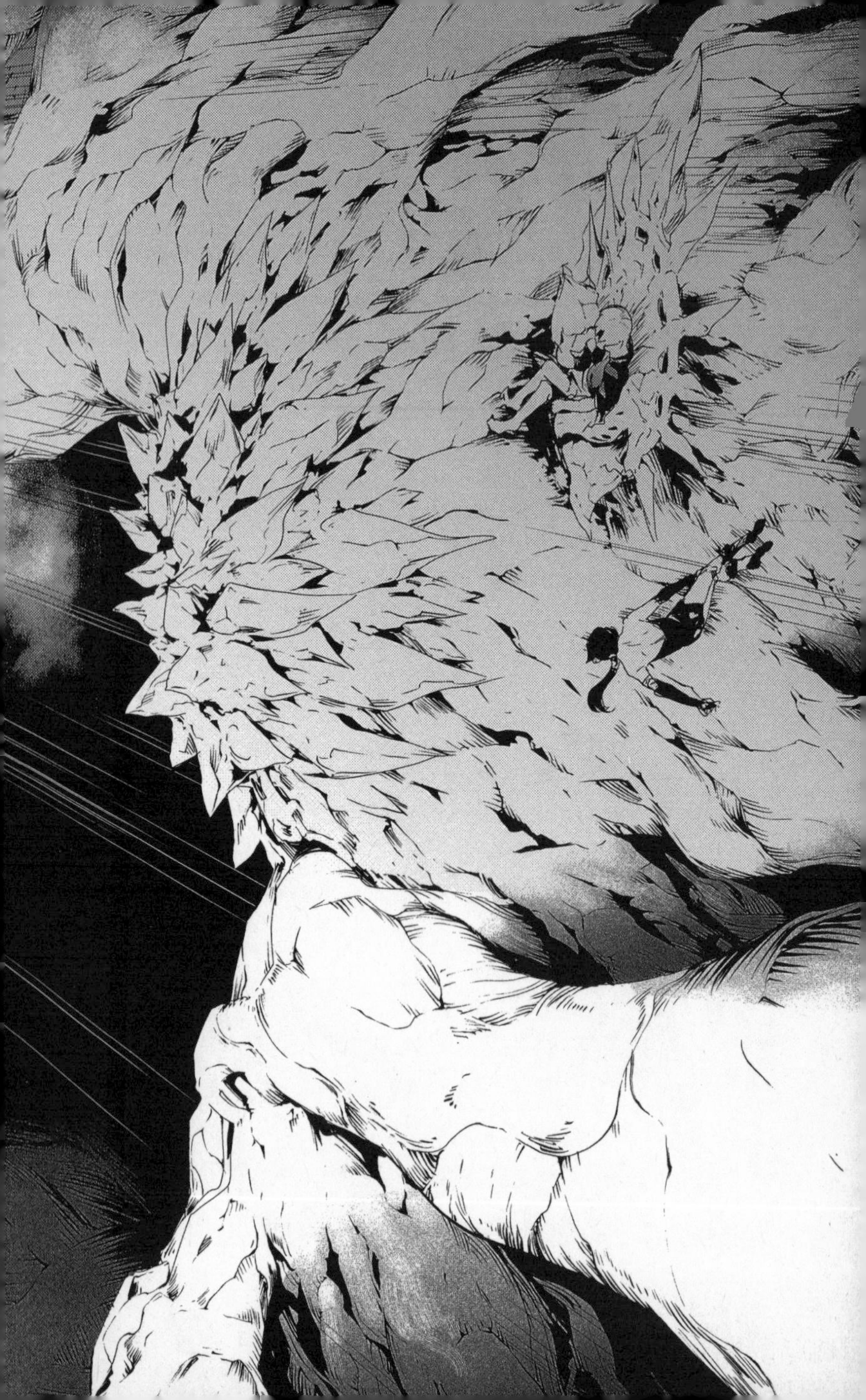

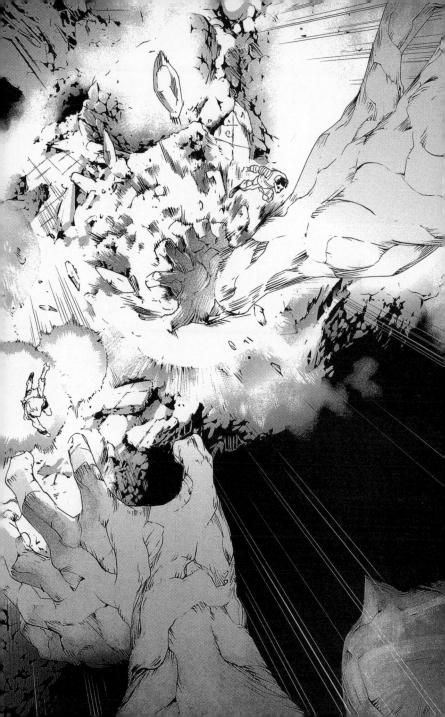

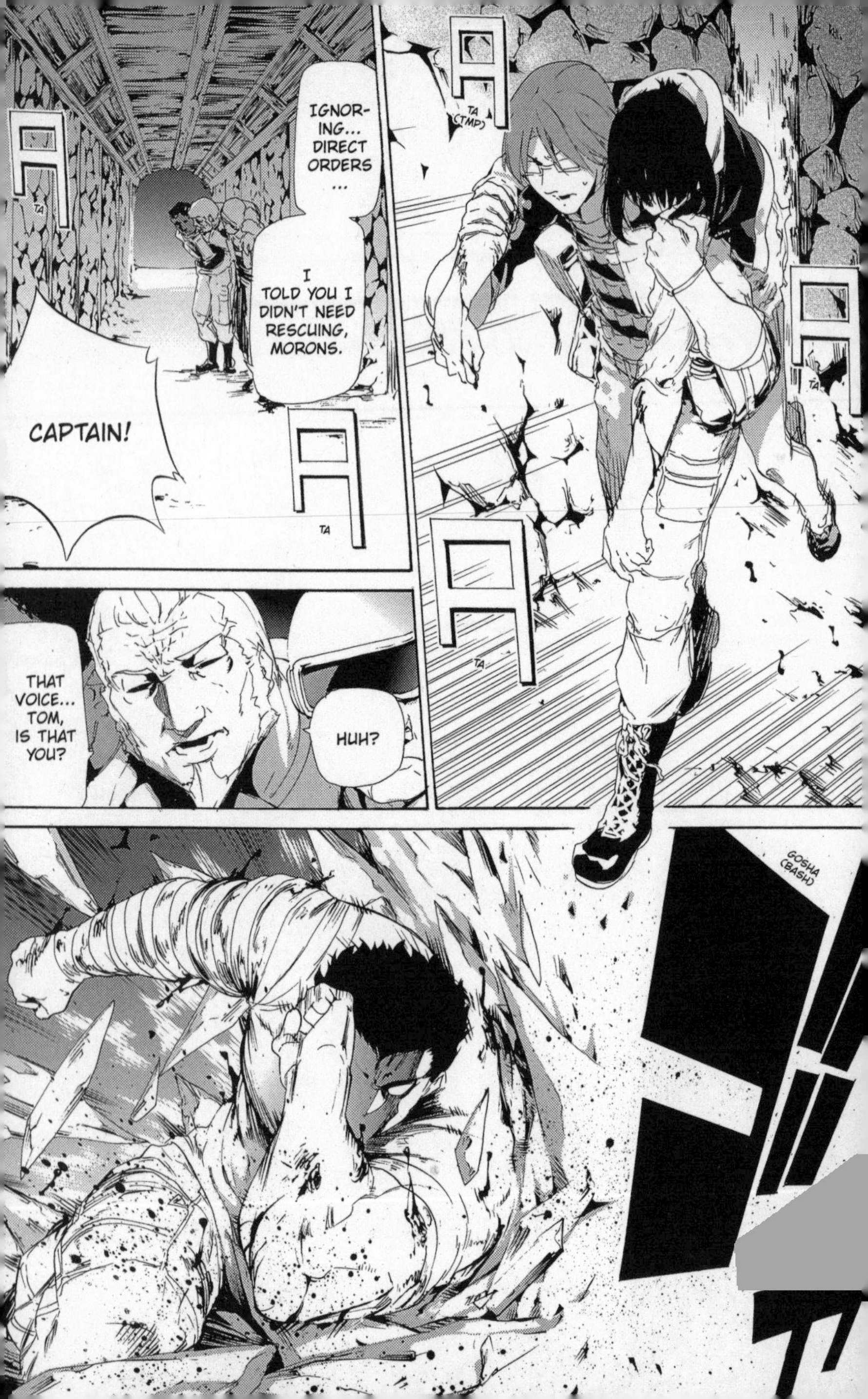
TA (TMP)
TA
TA
IGNORING... DIRECT ORDERS ...
I TOLD YOU I DIDN'T NEED RESCUING, MORONS.
TA
CAPTAIN!
TA
THAT VOICE... TOM, IS THAT YOU?
HUH?
GOSHA (BASH)

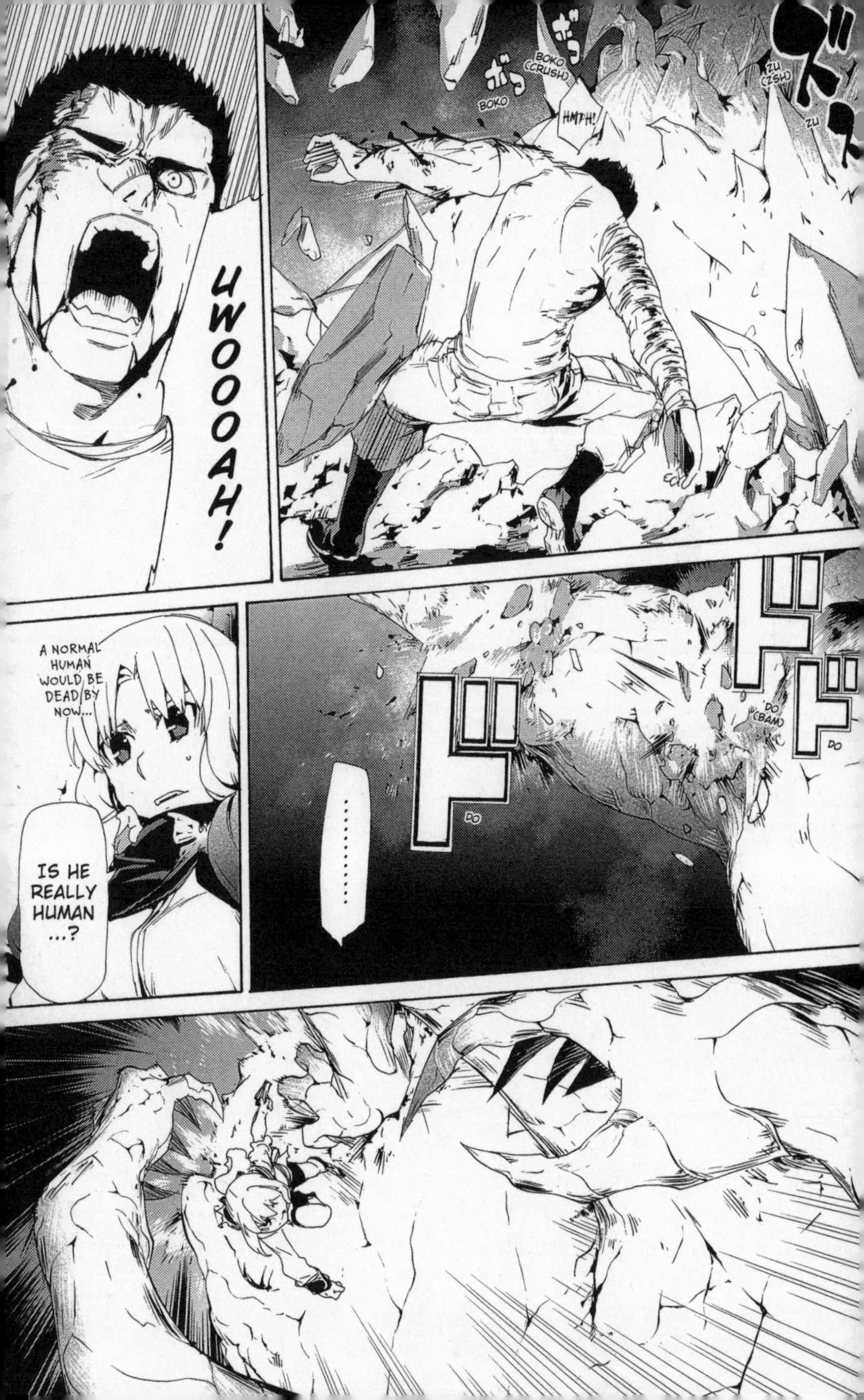
ZU (ZSH)
ZU
BOKO (CRUSH)
BOKO
HMPH!
UWOOOOAH!
DO (BAM)
DO
DO
......
A NORMAL HUMAN WOULD BE DEAD BY NOW...
IS HE REALLY HUMAN ...?

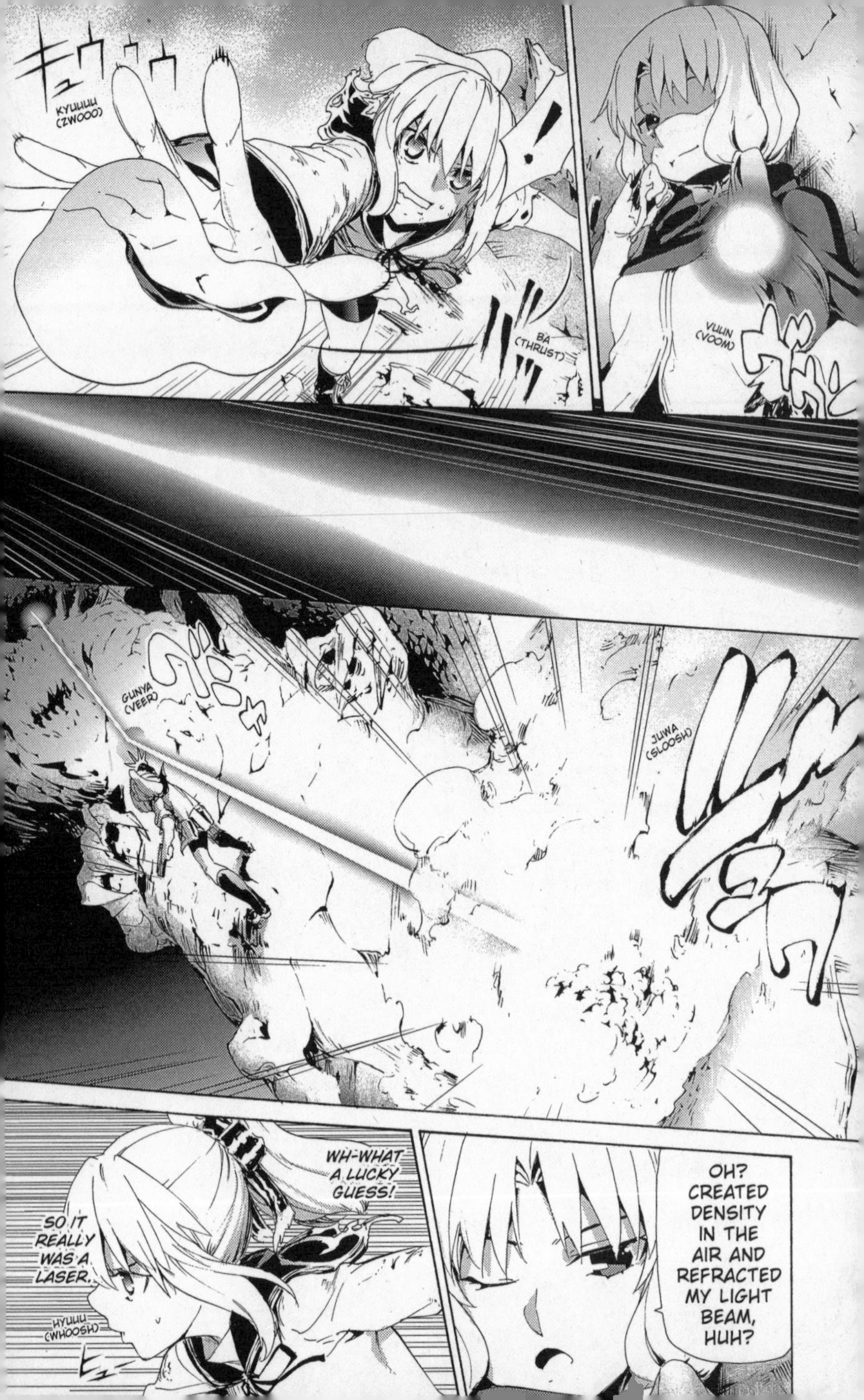
VUUN (VOOM)
KYUUUU (ZWOOO)
BA (THRUST)
JUWA (SLOOSH)
GUNYA (VEER)
OH? CREATED DENSITY IN THE AIR AND REFRACTED MY LIGHT BEAM, HUH?
WH-WHAT A LUCKY GUESS!
SO IT REALLY WAS A LASER...
HYUUU (WHOOSH)

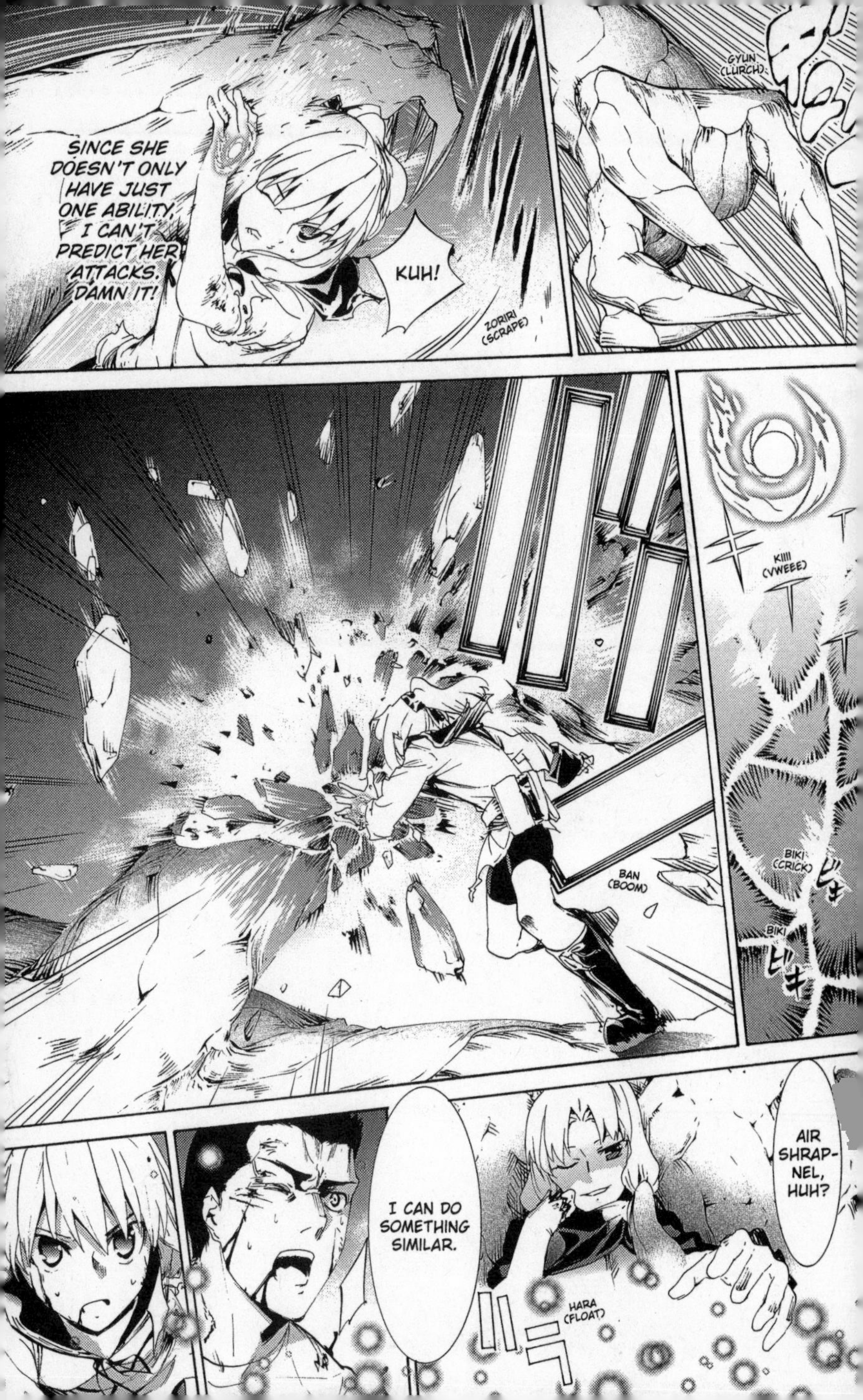
GYUN (LURCH)
SINCE SHE DOESN'T ONLY HAVE JUST ONE ABILITY, I CAN'T PREDICT HER ATTACKS. DAMN IT!
KUH!
ZORIRI (SCRAPE)
KIII (VWEEE)
BIKI (CRICK)
BIKI
BAN (BOOM)
AIR SHRAP-NEL, HUH?
I CAN DO SOMETHING SIMILAR.
HARA (FLOAT)

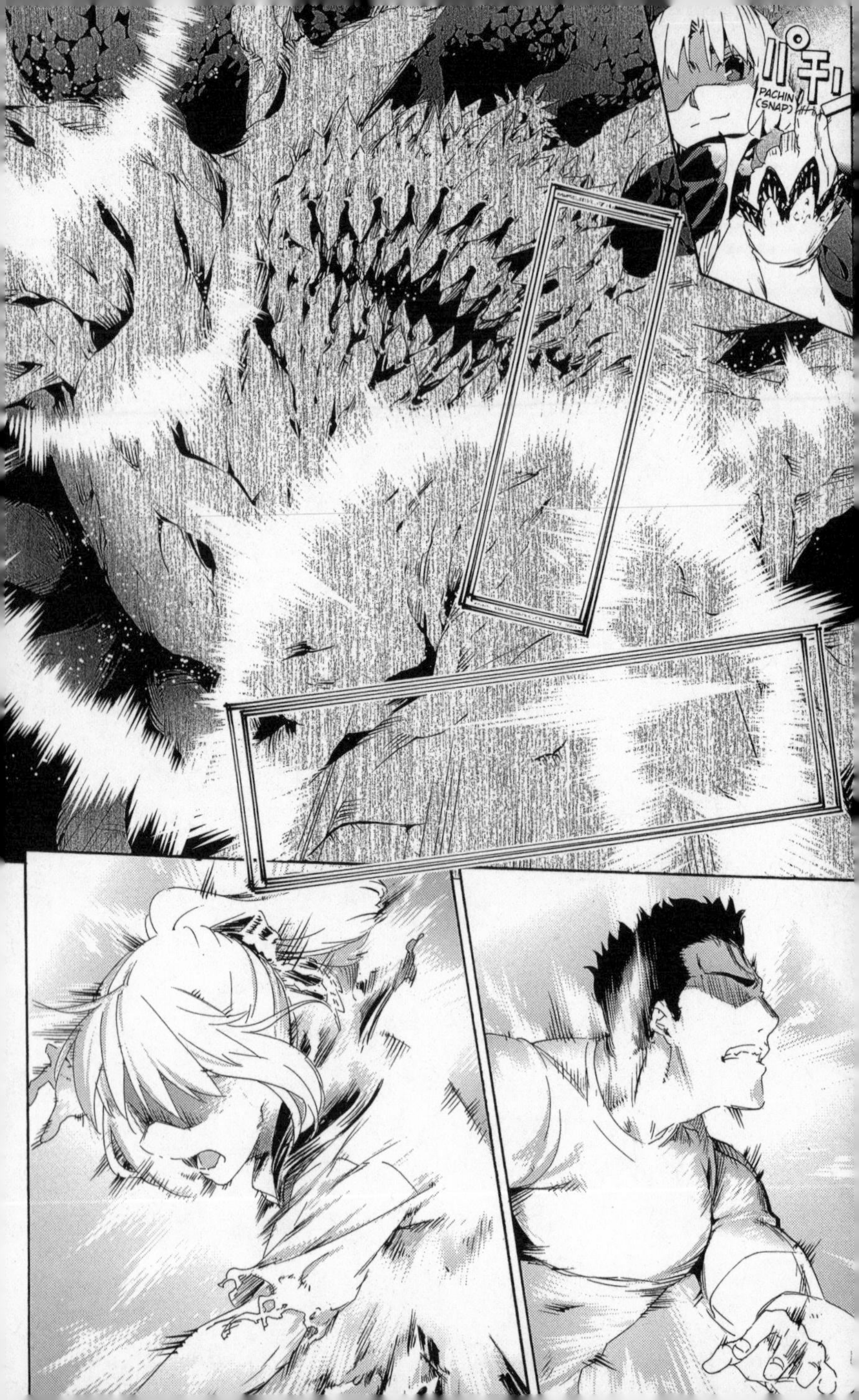

パチ
PACHIN
(SNAP)

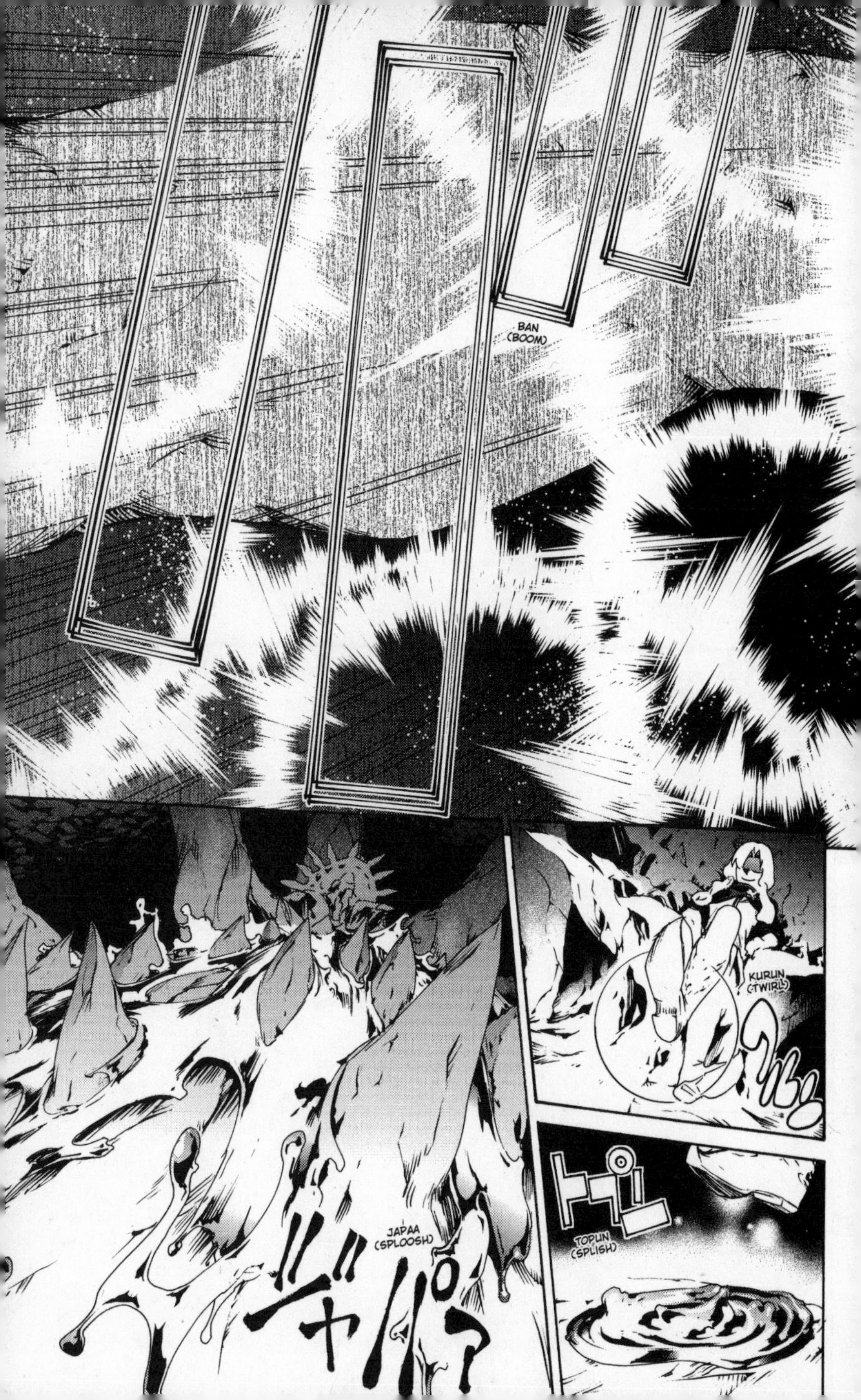
BAN (BOOM)
KURUN (TWIRL)
TOPUN (SPLISH)
JAPAA (SPLOOSH)

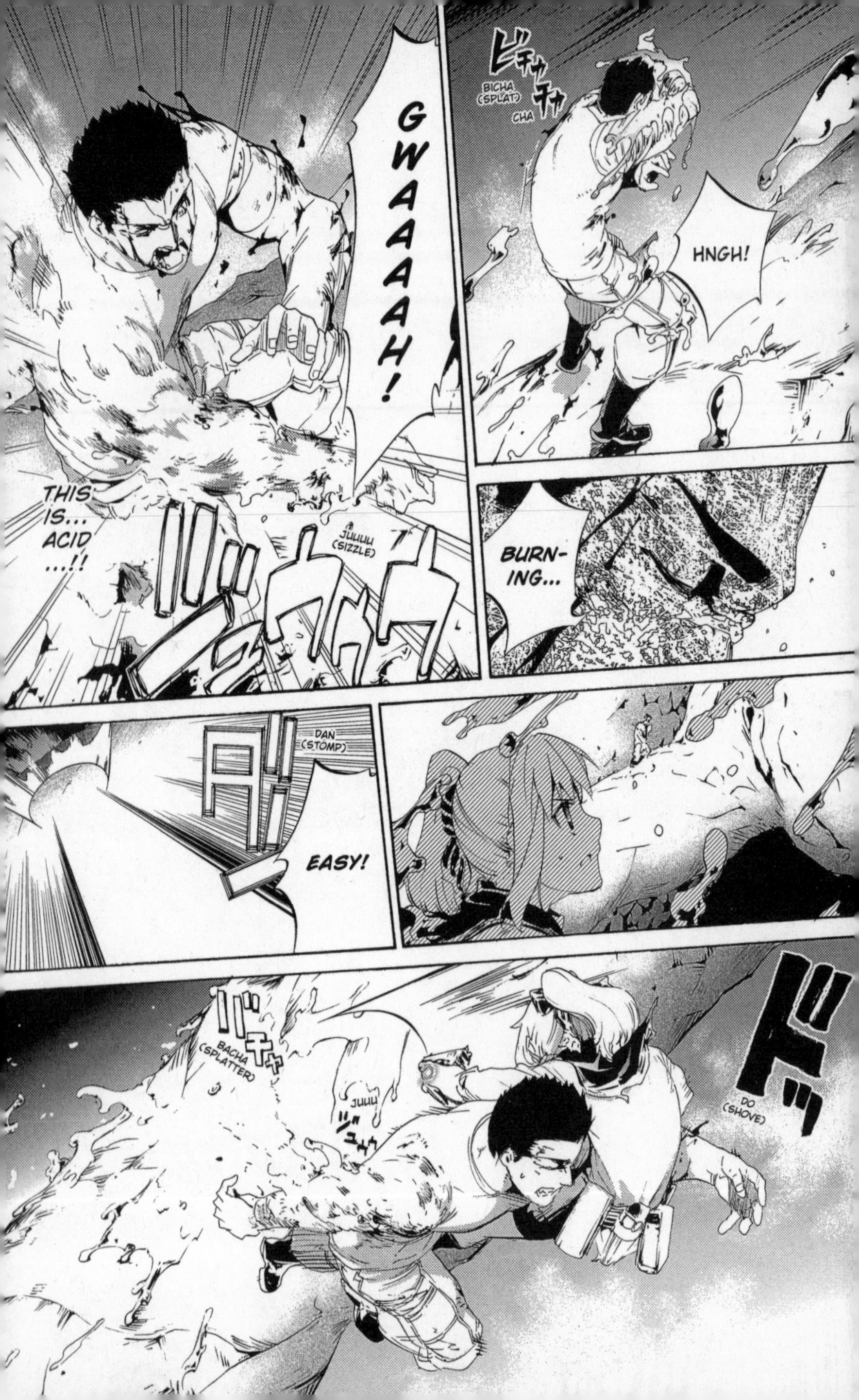
BICHA (SPLAT) CHA
HNGH!
BURNING...
GWAAAAAH!
JUUUU (SIZZLE)
THIS IS... ACID ...!!
DAN (STOMP)
EASY!
DO (SHOVE)
BACHA (SPLATTER)
JUUU

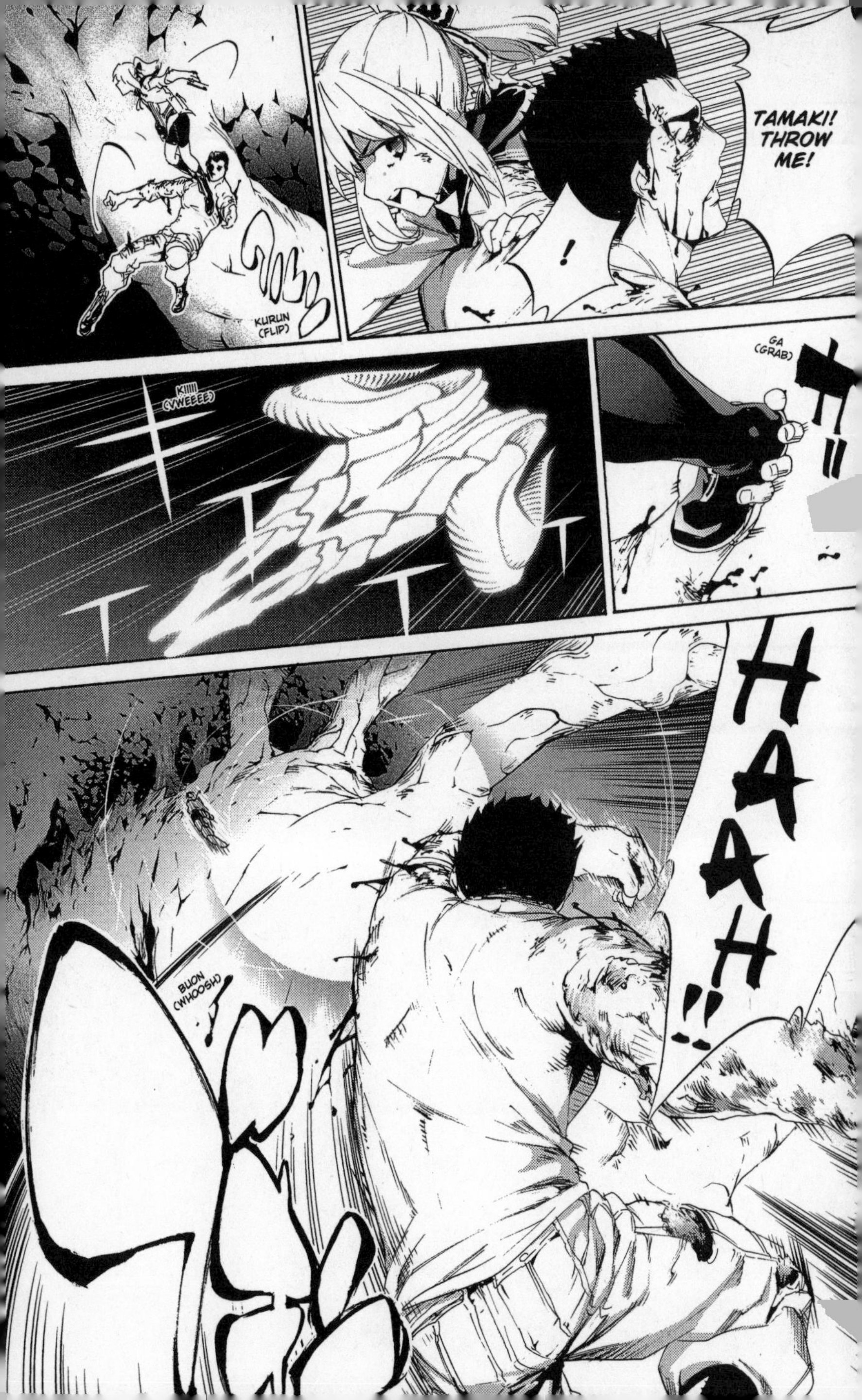
TAMAKI! THROW ME!
!
KURUN (FLIP)
GA (GRAB)
KIIII (VWEEEE)
HAAAH!!
BUON (WHOOSH)

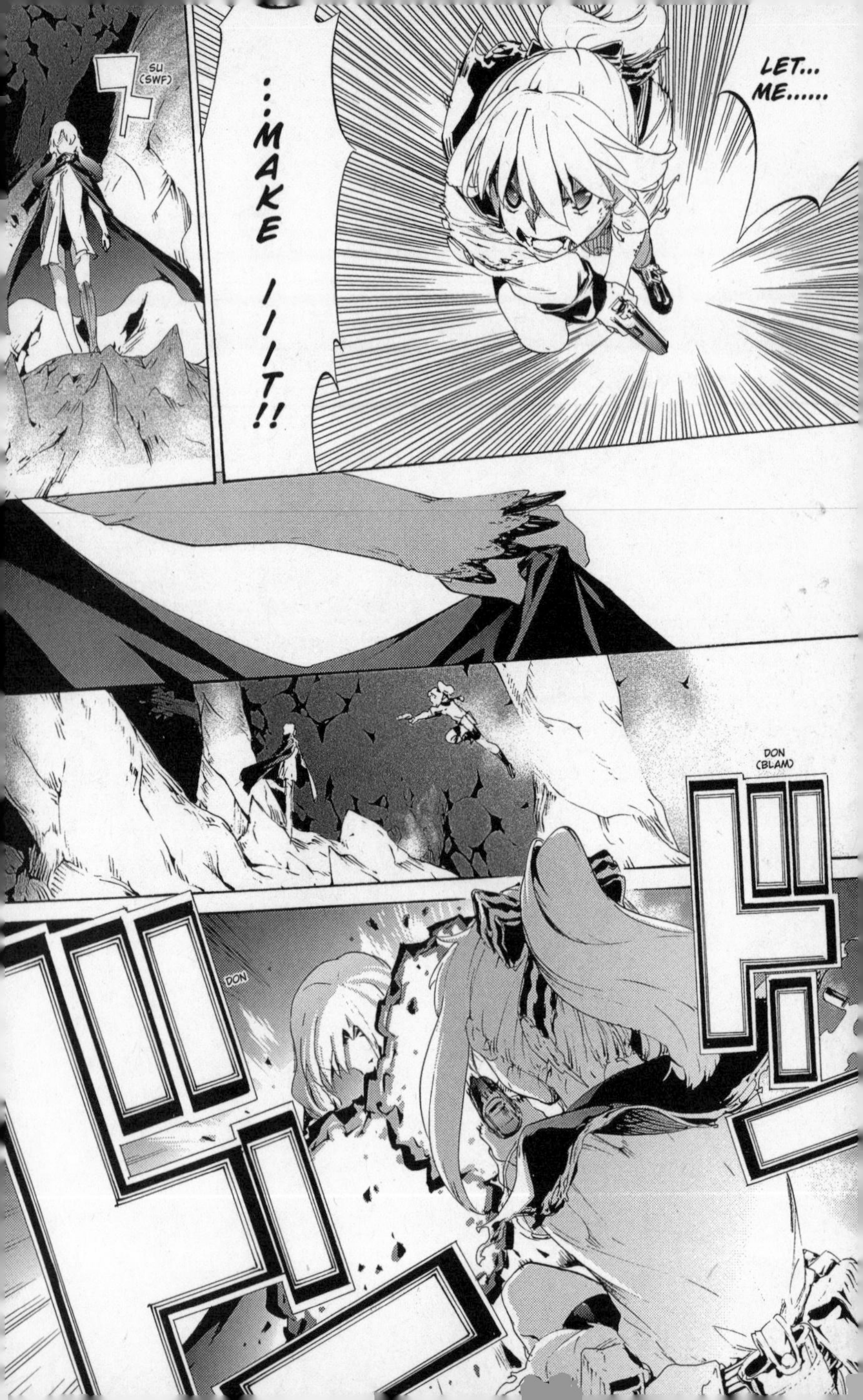
LET... ME......
...MAKE IIIIT!!
SU (SWF)
DON (BLAM)
DON

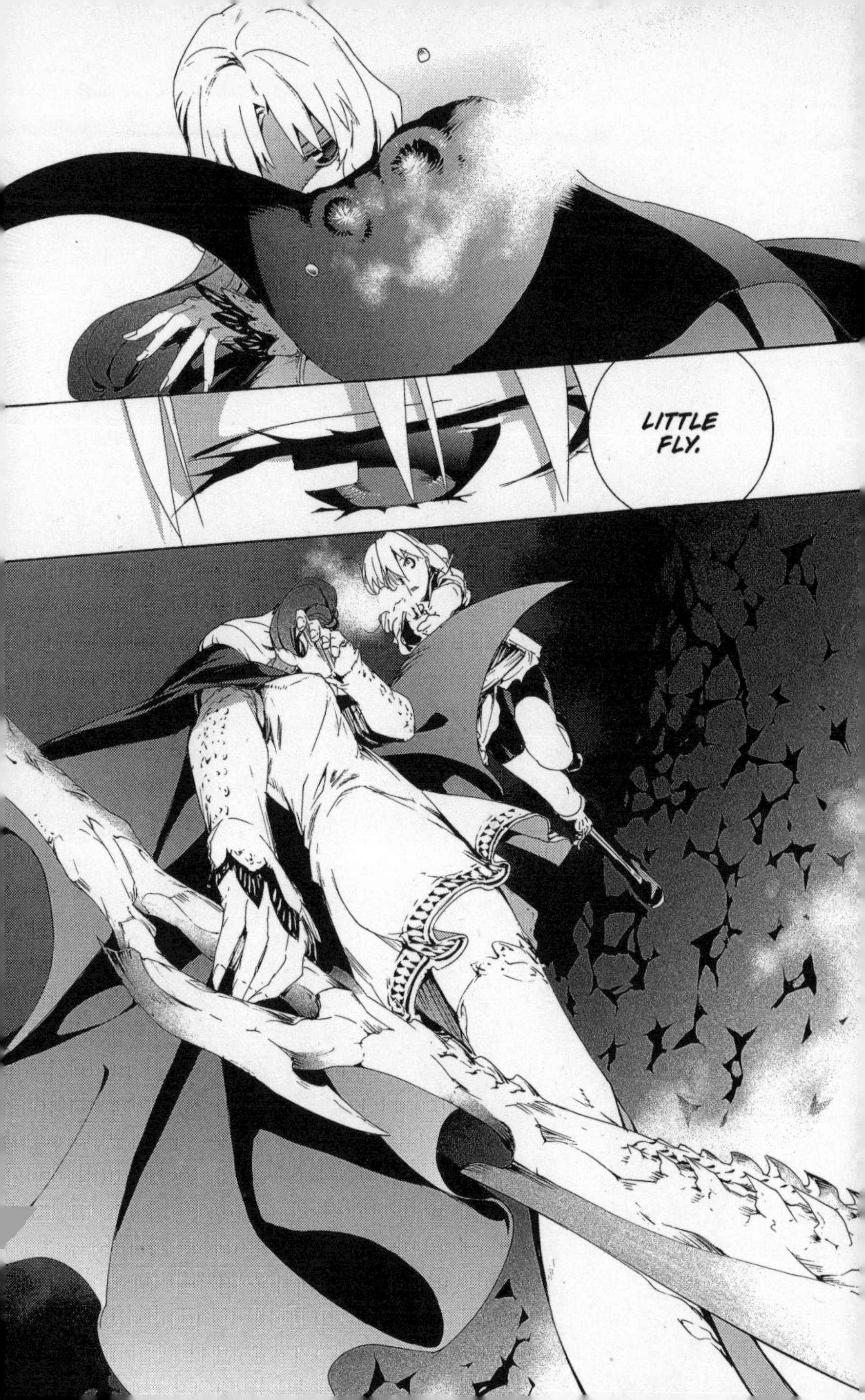
LITTLE FLY.

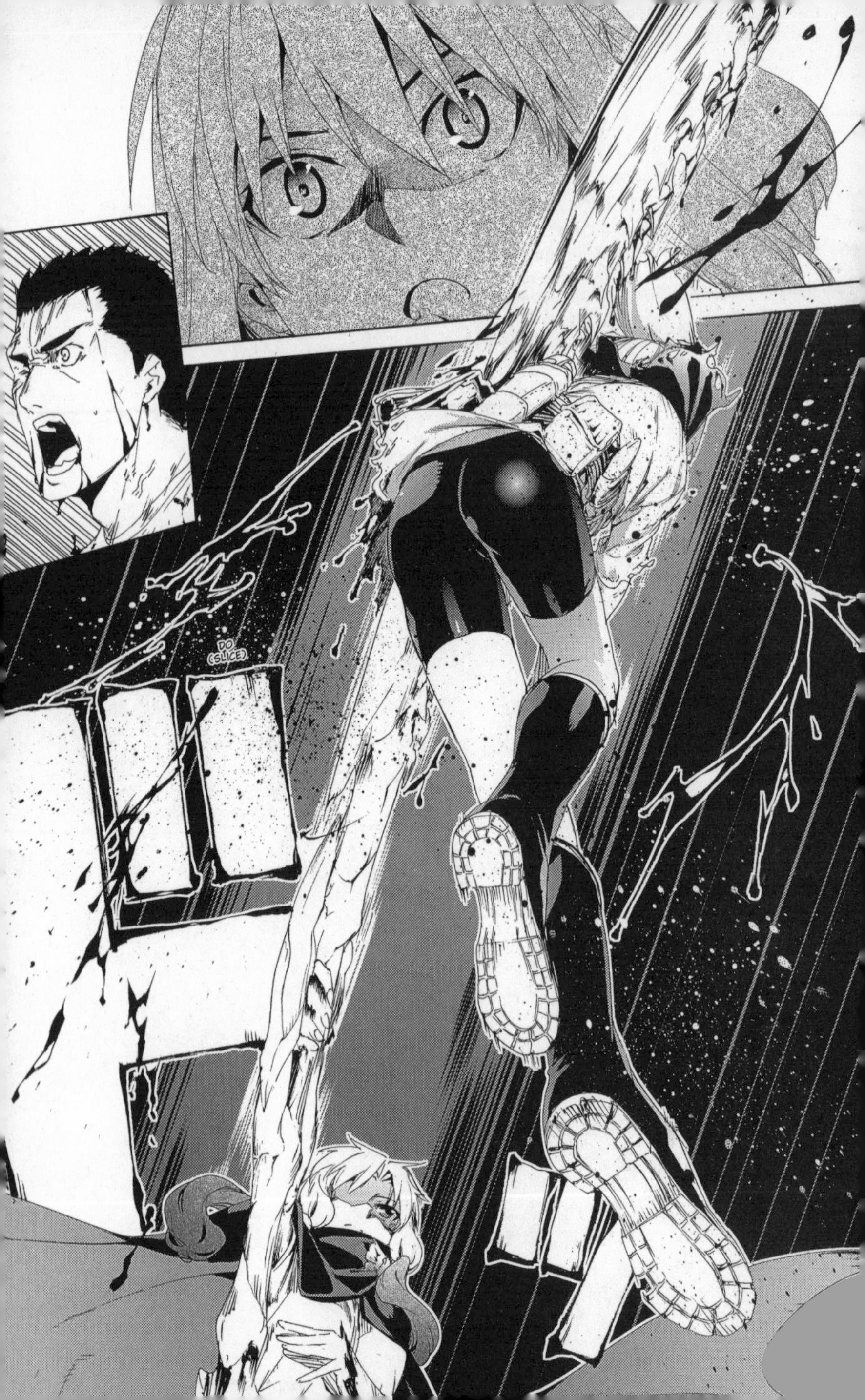
DO
(SLICE)

#43 VIRUS
TABOOTATTOO

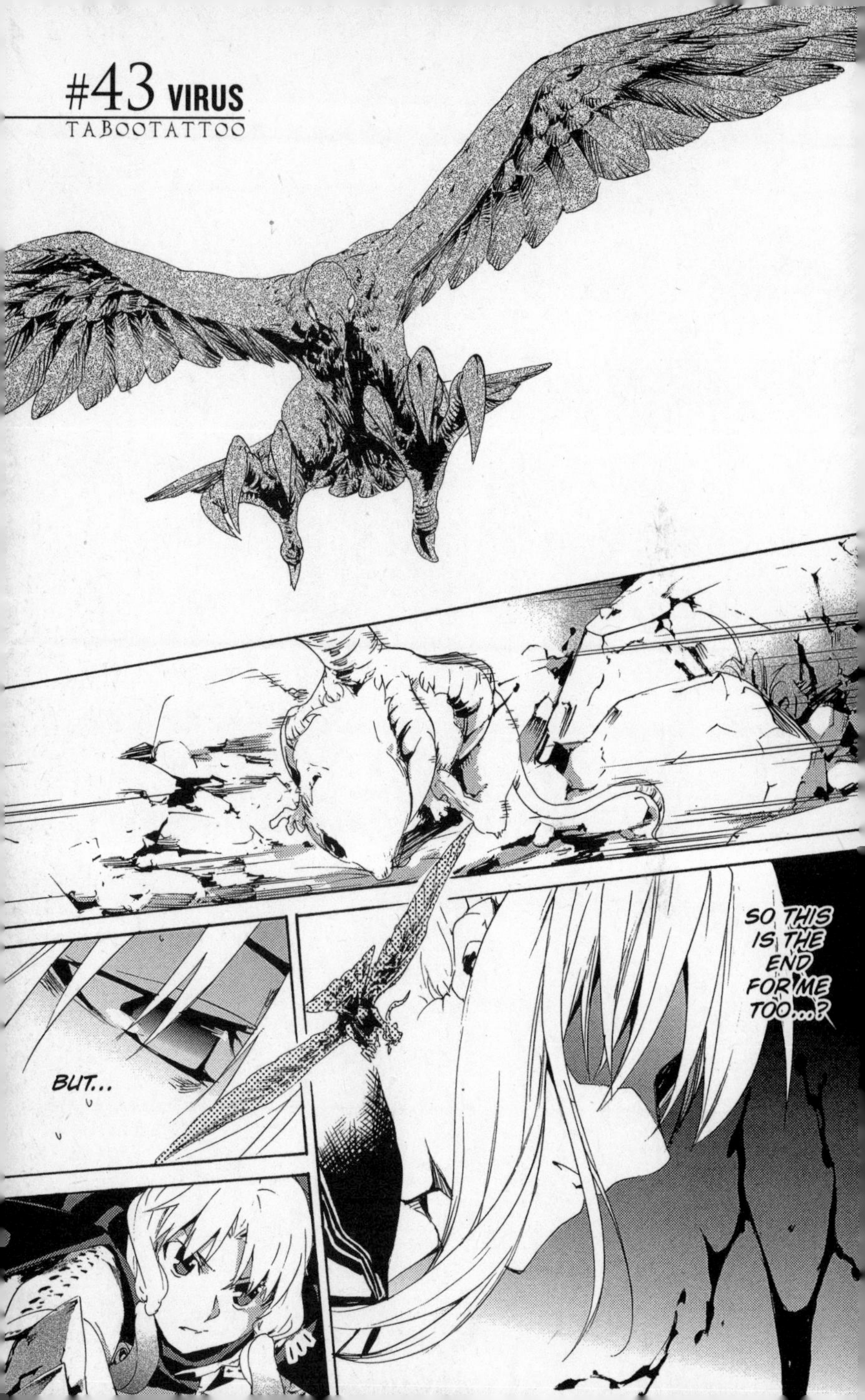
SO THIS IS THE END FOR ME TOO...?
BUT...

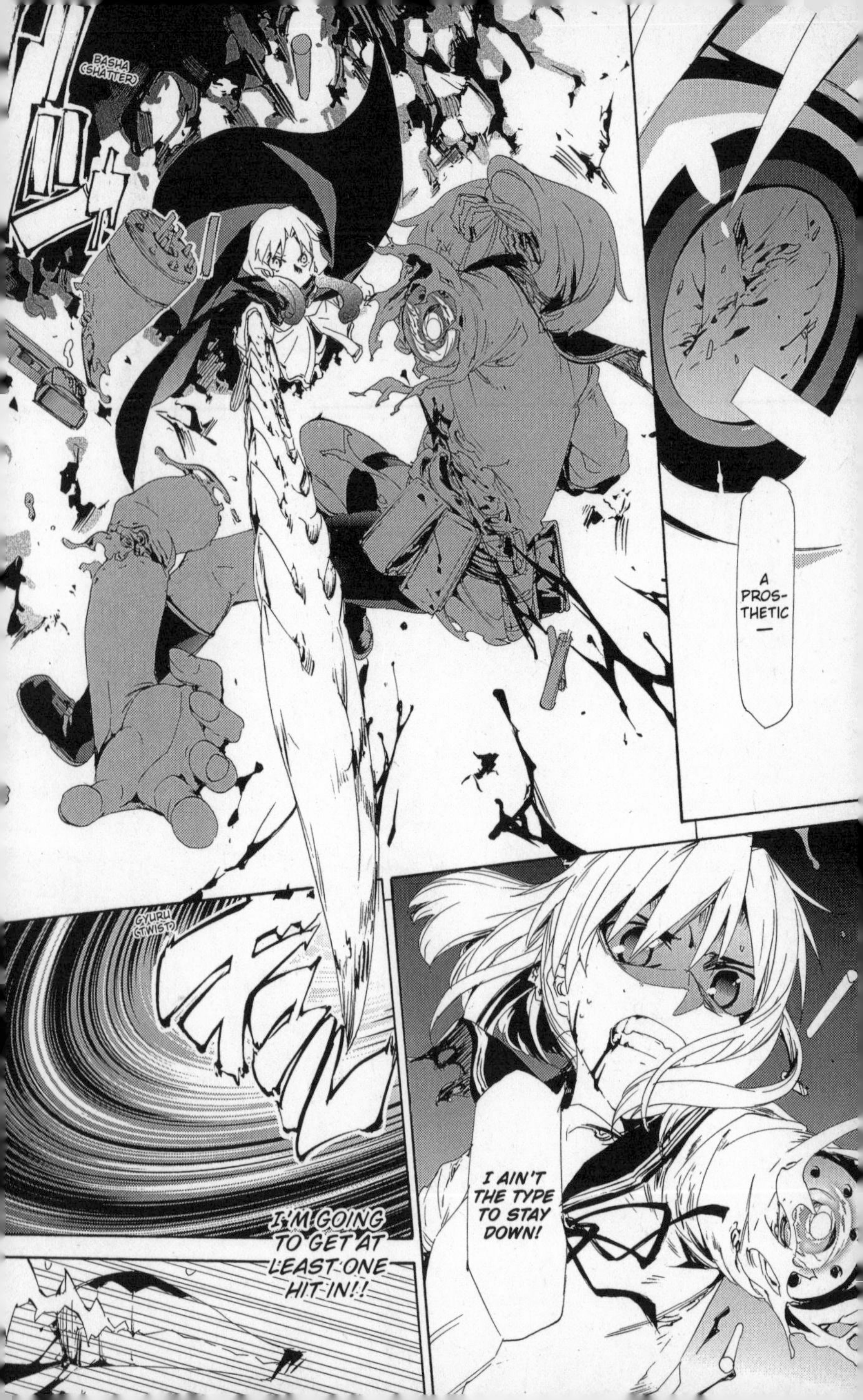
A PROS-THETIC—
BASHA (SHATTER)
I AIN'T THE TYPE TO STAY DOWN!
GYURU (TWIST)
I'M GOING TO GET AT LEAST ONE HIT IN!!

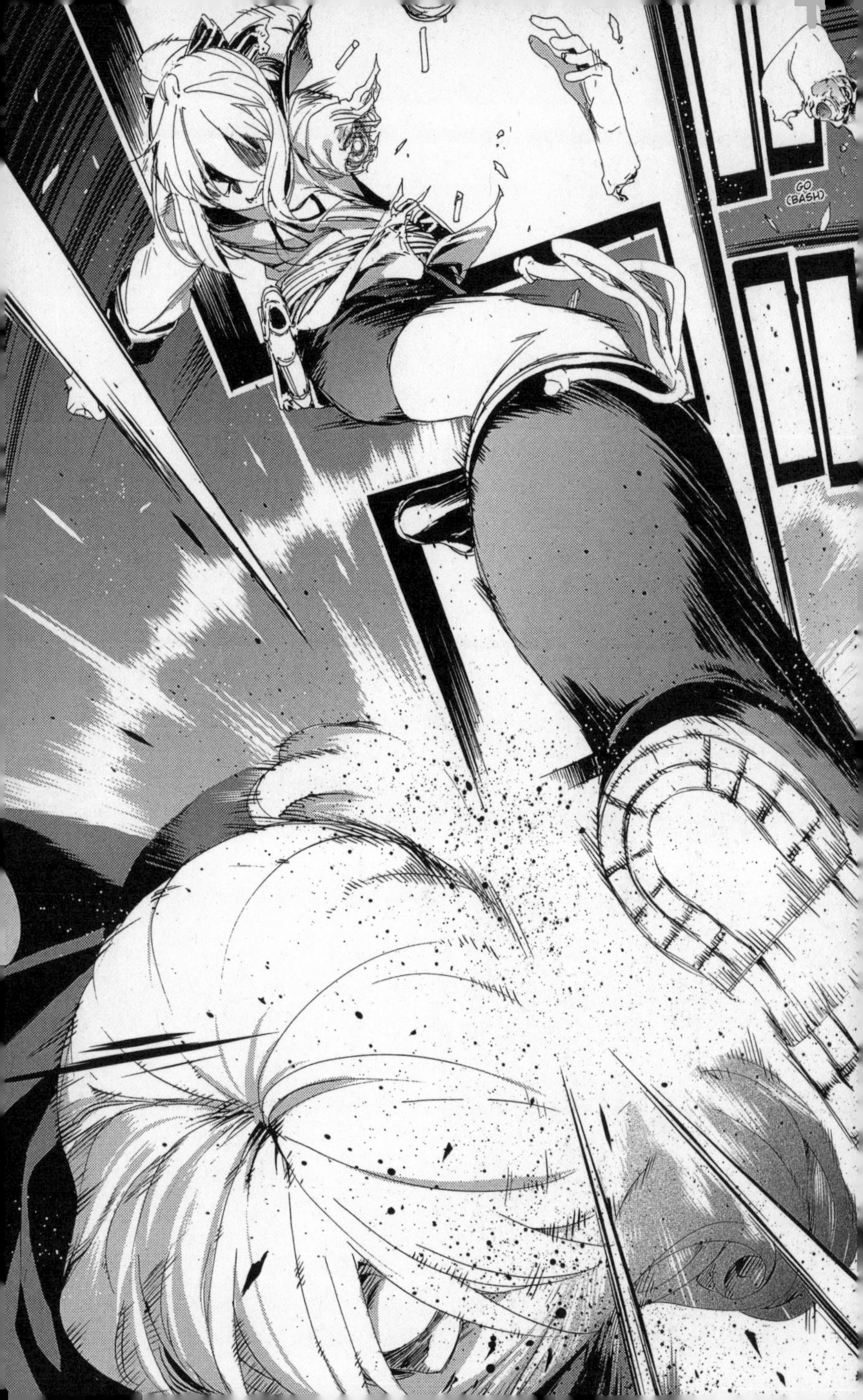
GO
(BASH)

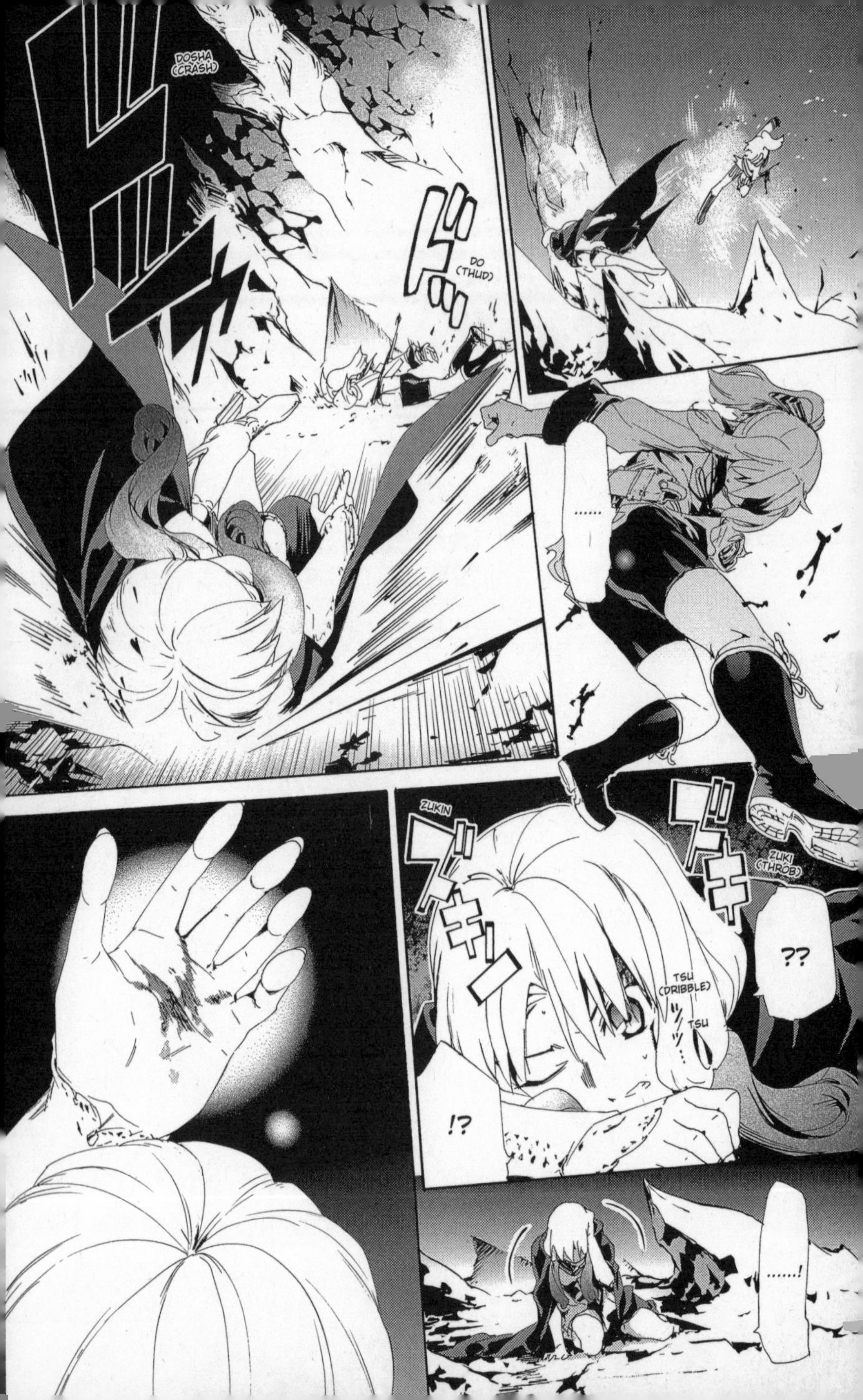
......
DO
(THUD)
DOSHA
(CRASH)
ZUKI
(THROB)
??
ZUKIN
TSU
(DRIBBLE)
TSU
!?
......!

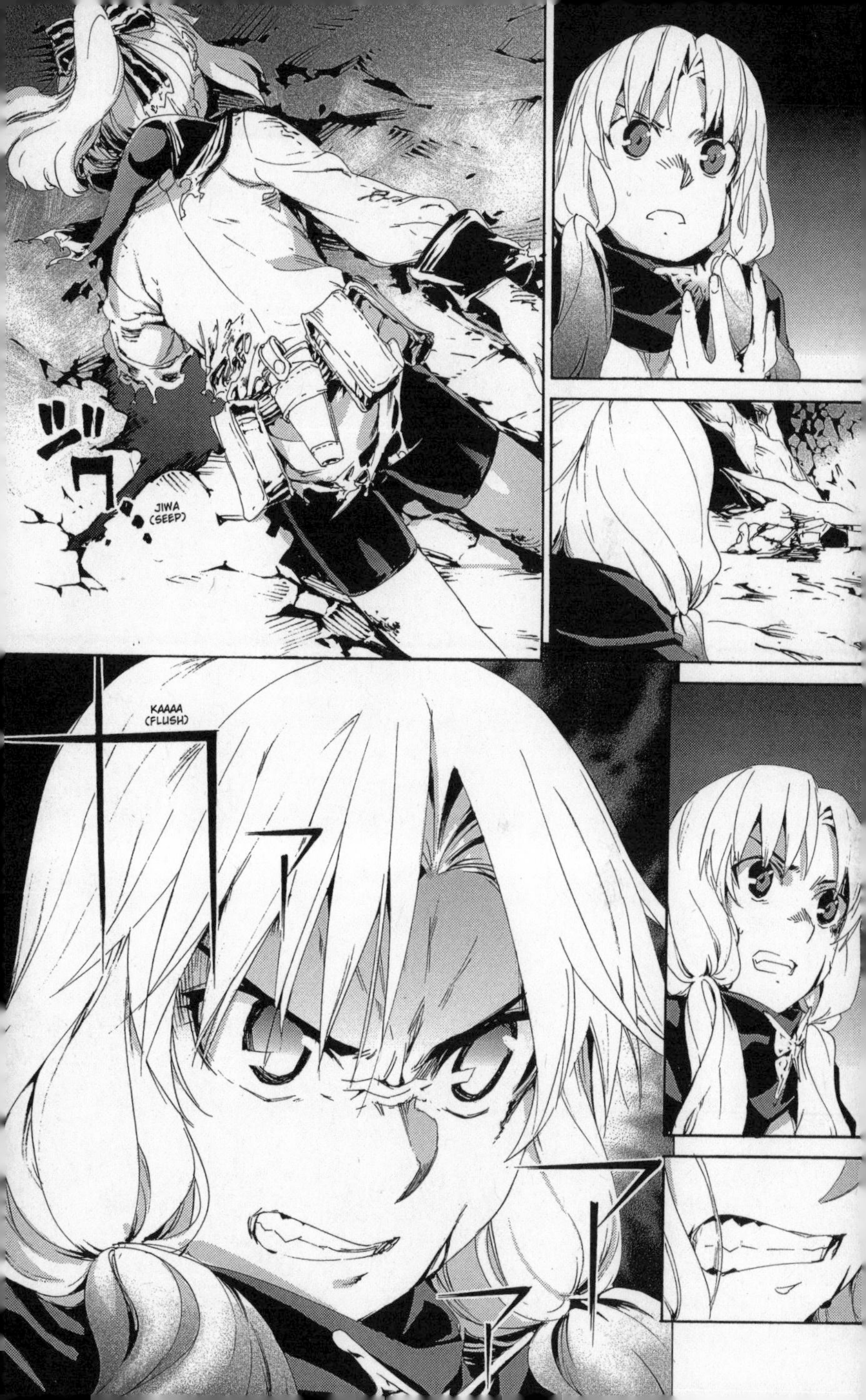
JIWA
(SEEP)
KAAAA
(FLUSH)

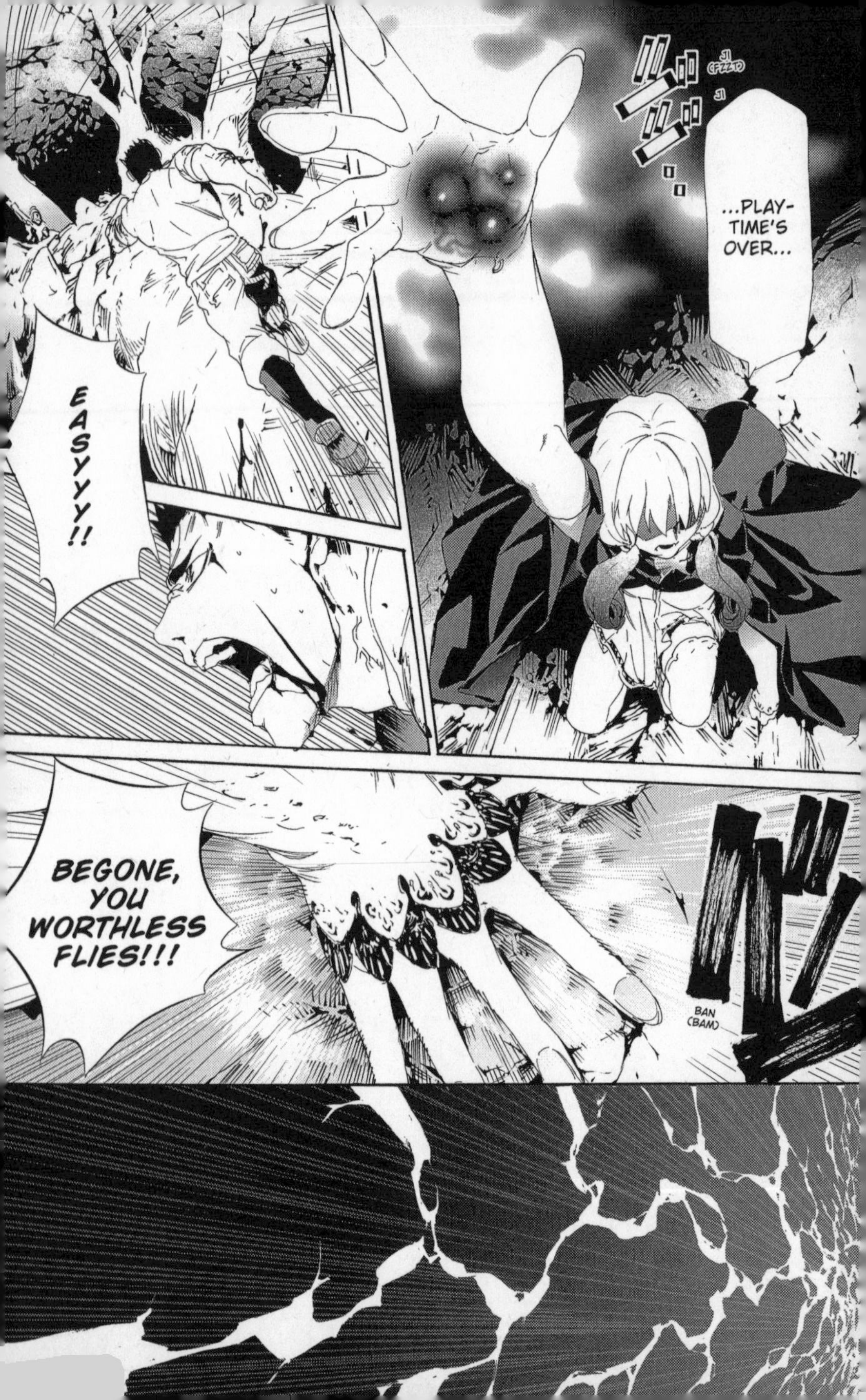
JI (FZZT)
JI
...PLAY-TIME'S OVER...
EASYYY!!
BAN (BAM)
BEGONE, YOU WORTHLESS FLIES!!!

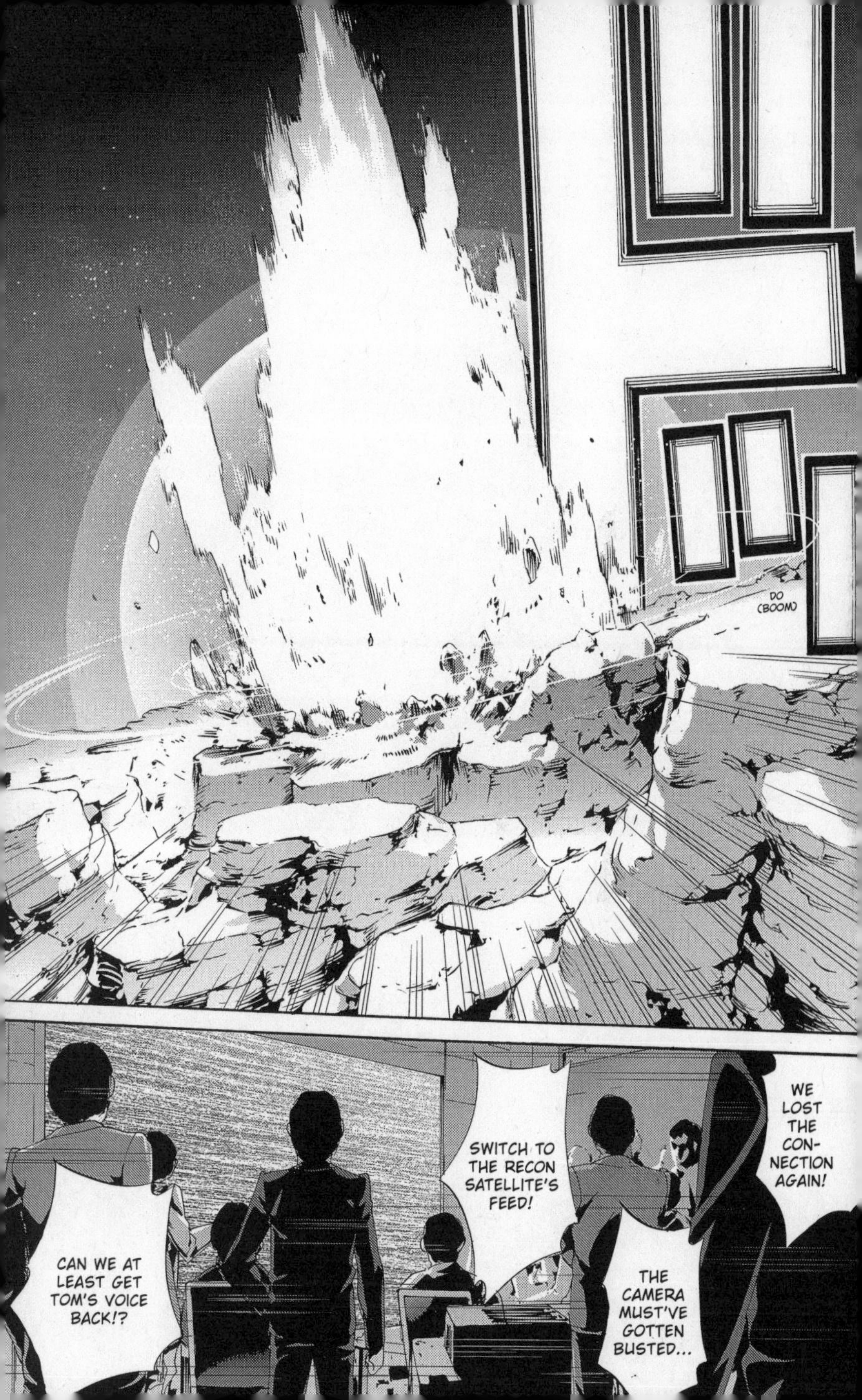
DO (BOOM)
WE LOST THE CON-NECTION AGAIN!
SWITCH TO THE RECON SATELLITE'S FEED!
THE CAMERA MUST'VE GOTTEN BUSTED...
CAN WE AT LEAST GET TOM'S VOICE BACK!?

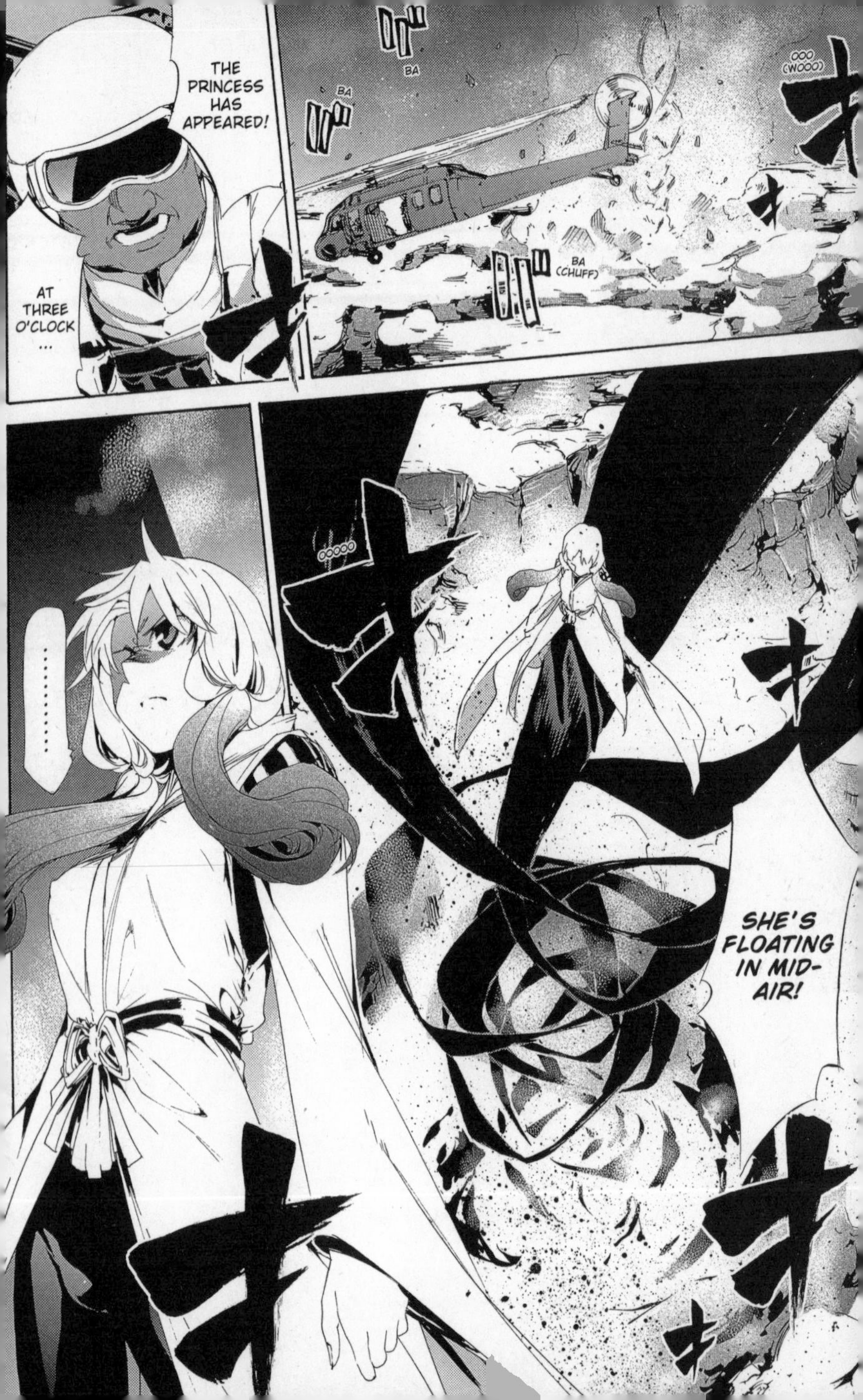
OOO (WOOO)
BA
BA
BA (CHUFF)
THE PRINCESS HAS APPEARED!
AT THREE O'CLOCK ...
OOOOO
SHE'S FLOATING IN MID-AIR!
......

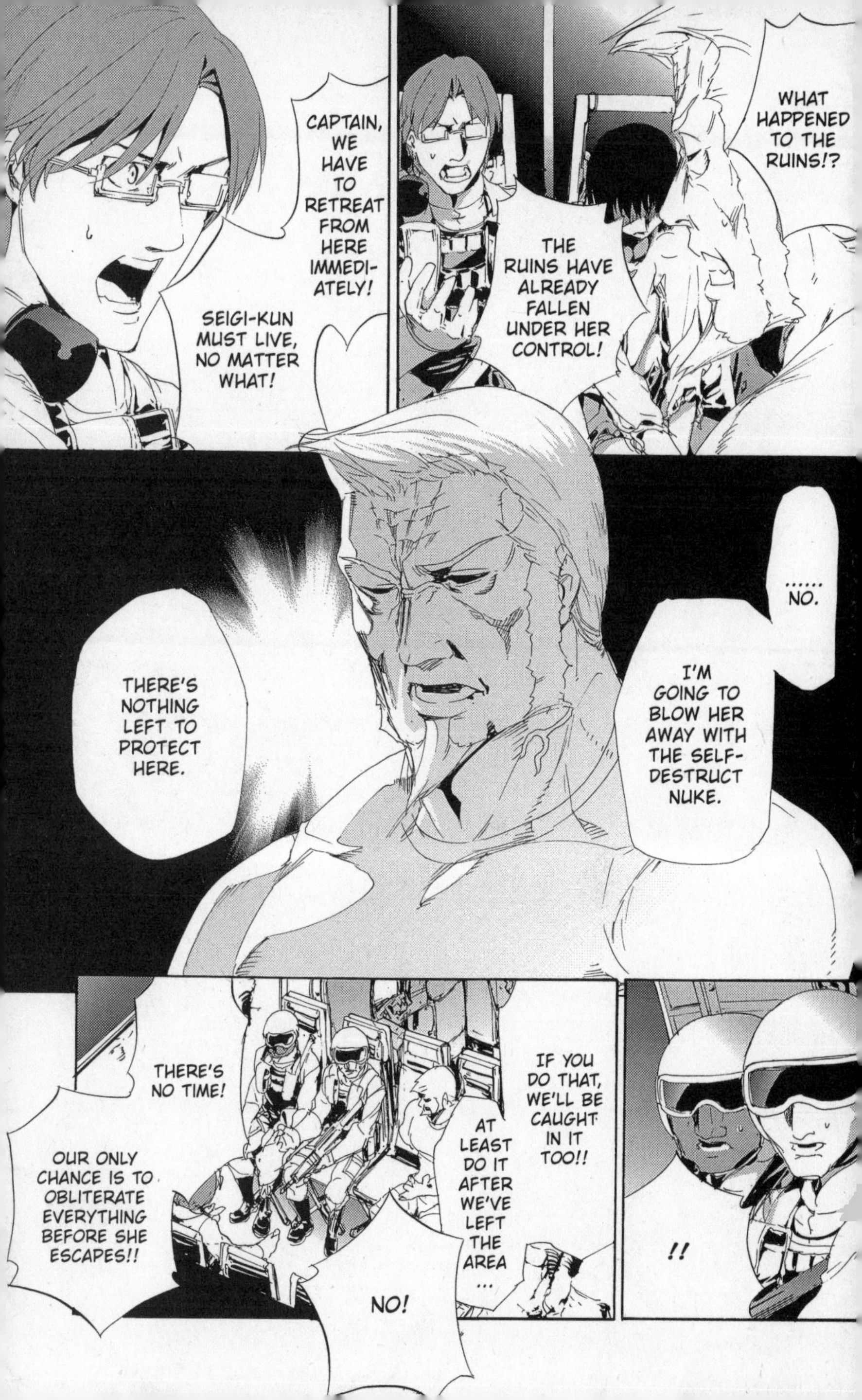
WHAT HAPPENED TO THE RUINS!?
THE RUINS HAVE ALREADY FALLEN UNDER HER CONTROL!
CAPTAIN, WE HAVE TO RETREAT FROM HERE IMMEDIATELY!
SEIGI-KUN MUST LIVE, NO MATTER WHAT!
...... NO.
I'M GOING TO BLOW HER AWAY WITH THE SELF-DESTRUCT NUKE.
THERE'S NOTHING LEFT TO PROTECT HERE.
!!
IF YOU DO THAT, WE'LL BE CAUGHT IN IT TOO!!
AT LEAST DO IT AFTER WE'VE LEFT THE AREA...
NO!
THERE'S NO TIME!
OUR ONLY CHANCE IS TO OBLITERATE EVERYTHING BEFORE SHE ESCAPES!!

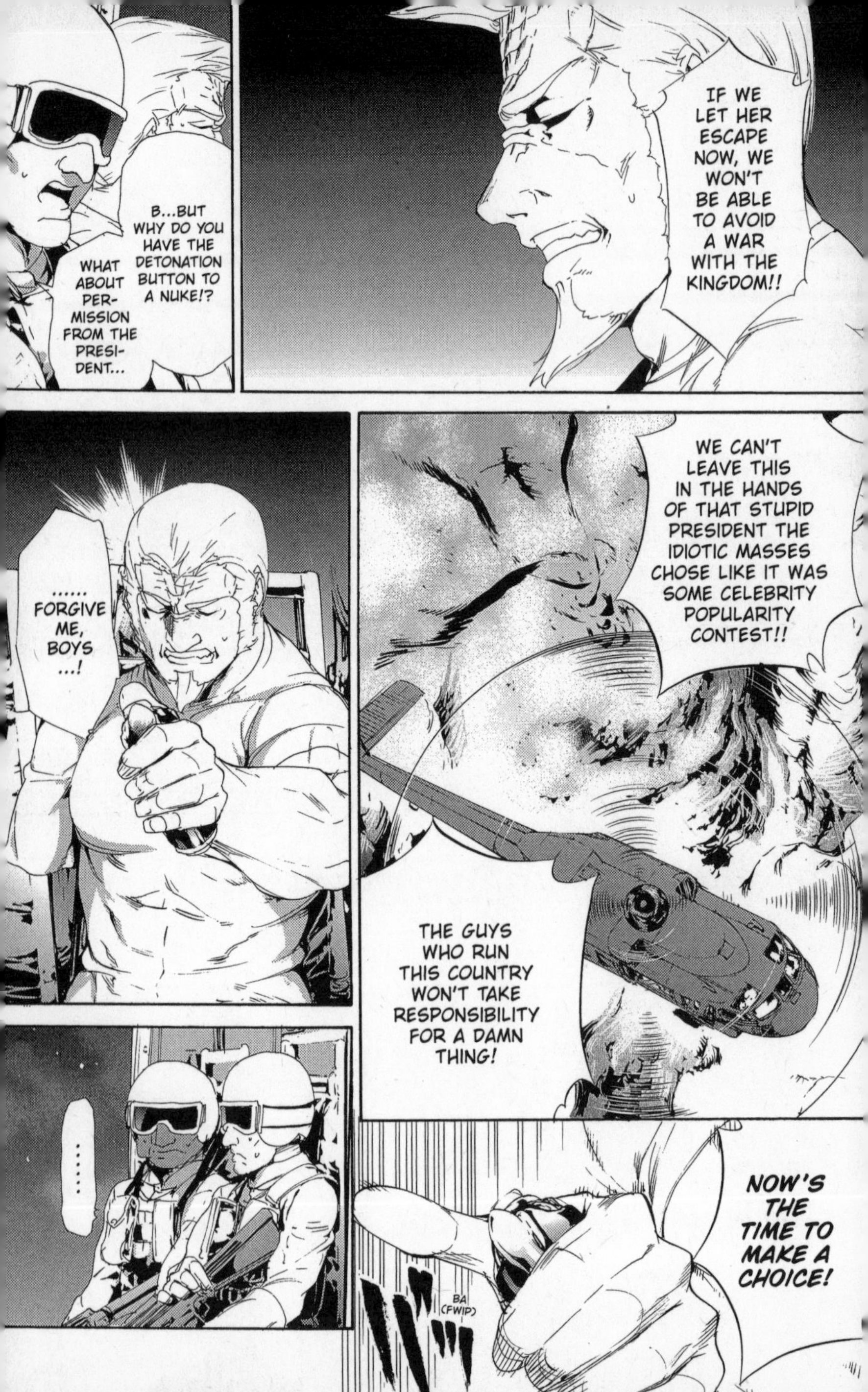
IF WE LET HER ESCAPE NOW, WE WON'T BE ABLE TO AVOID A WAR WITH THE KINGDOM!!
B...BUT WHY DO YOU HAVE THE DETONATION BUTTON TO A NUKE!?
WHAT ABOUT PER-MISSION FROM THE PRESI-DENT...
WE CAN'T LEAVE THIS IN THE HANDS OF THAT STUPID PRESIDENT THE IDIOTIC MASSES CHOSE LIKE IT WAS SOME CELEBRITY POPULARITY CONTEST!!
THE GUYS WHO RUN THIS COUNTRY WON'T TAKE RESPONSIBILITY FOR A DAMN THING!
......FORGIVE ME, BOYS...!
NOW'S THE TIME TO MAKE A CHOICE!
BA (FWIP)
......

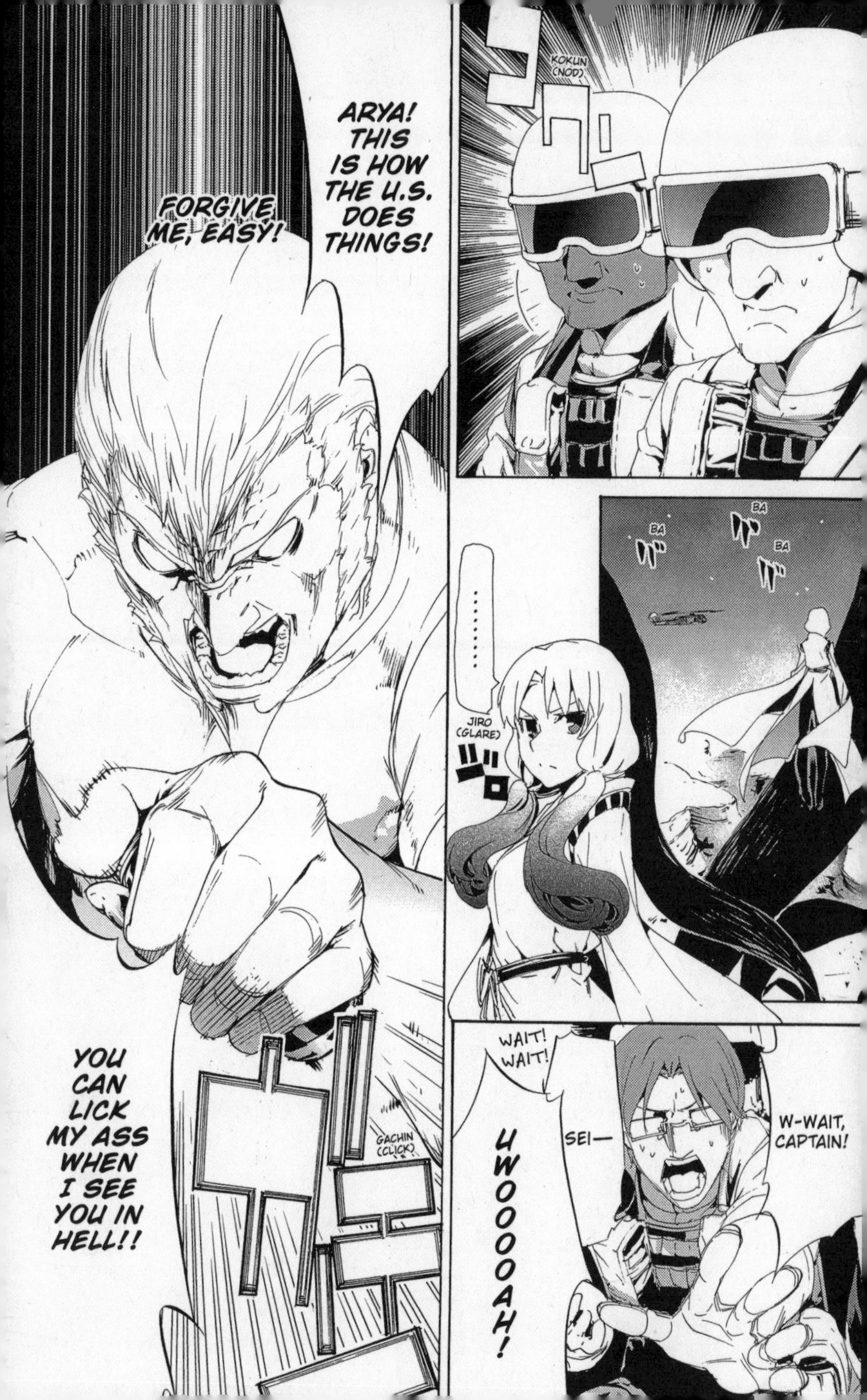
KOKUN (NOD)
BA
BA
BA
......
JIRO (GLARE)
WAIT! WAIT!
W-WAIT, CAPTAIN!
SEI—
UWOOOOOAH!
ARYA! THIS IS HOW THE U.S. DOES THINGS!
FORGIVE ME, EASY!
GACHIN (CLICK)
YOU CAN LICK MY ASS WHEN I SEE YOU IN HELL!!

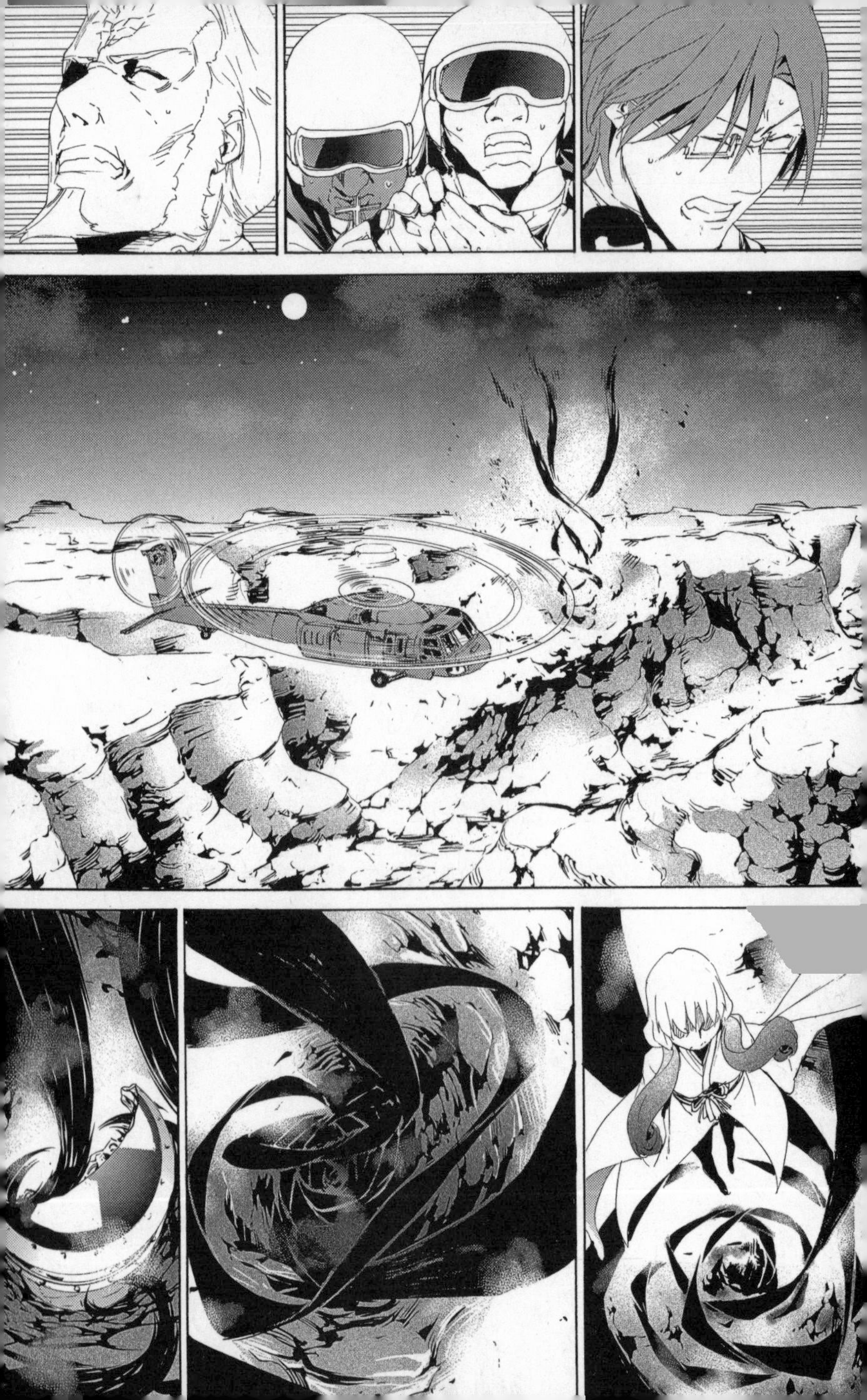

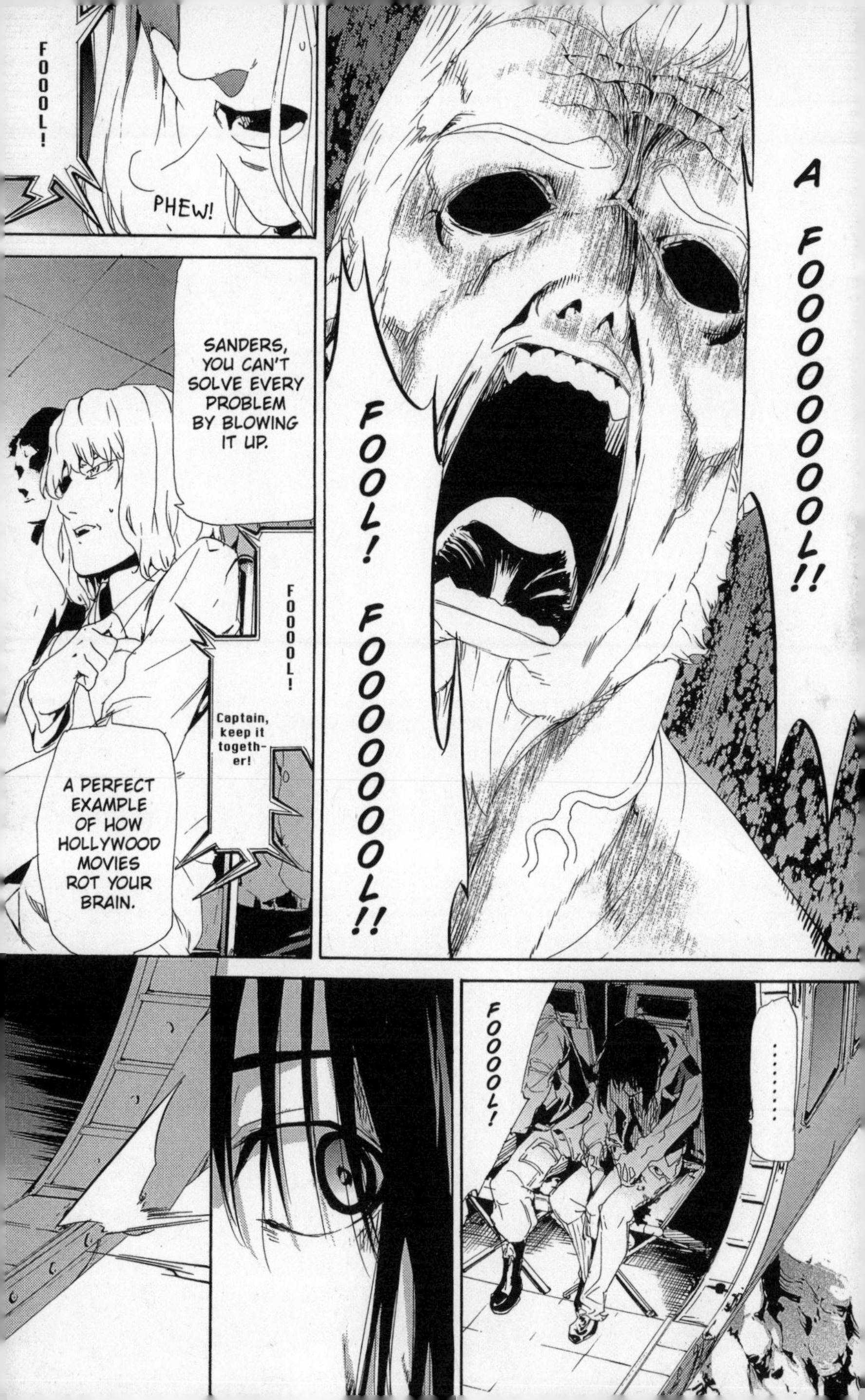
A FOOOOOOOOOL!!
FOOL! FOOOOOOOOL!!
FOOOL!
PHEW!
SANDERS, YOU CAN'T SOLVE EVERY PROBLEM BY BLOWING IT UP.
FOOOOOL!
Captain, keep it togeth-er!
A PERFECT EXAMPLE OF HOW HOLLYWOOD MOVIES ROT YOUR BRAIN.
......
FOOOOOL!

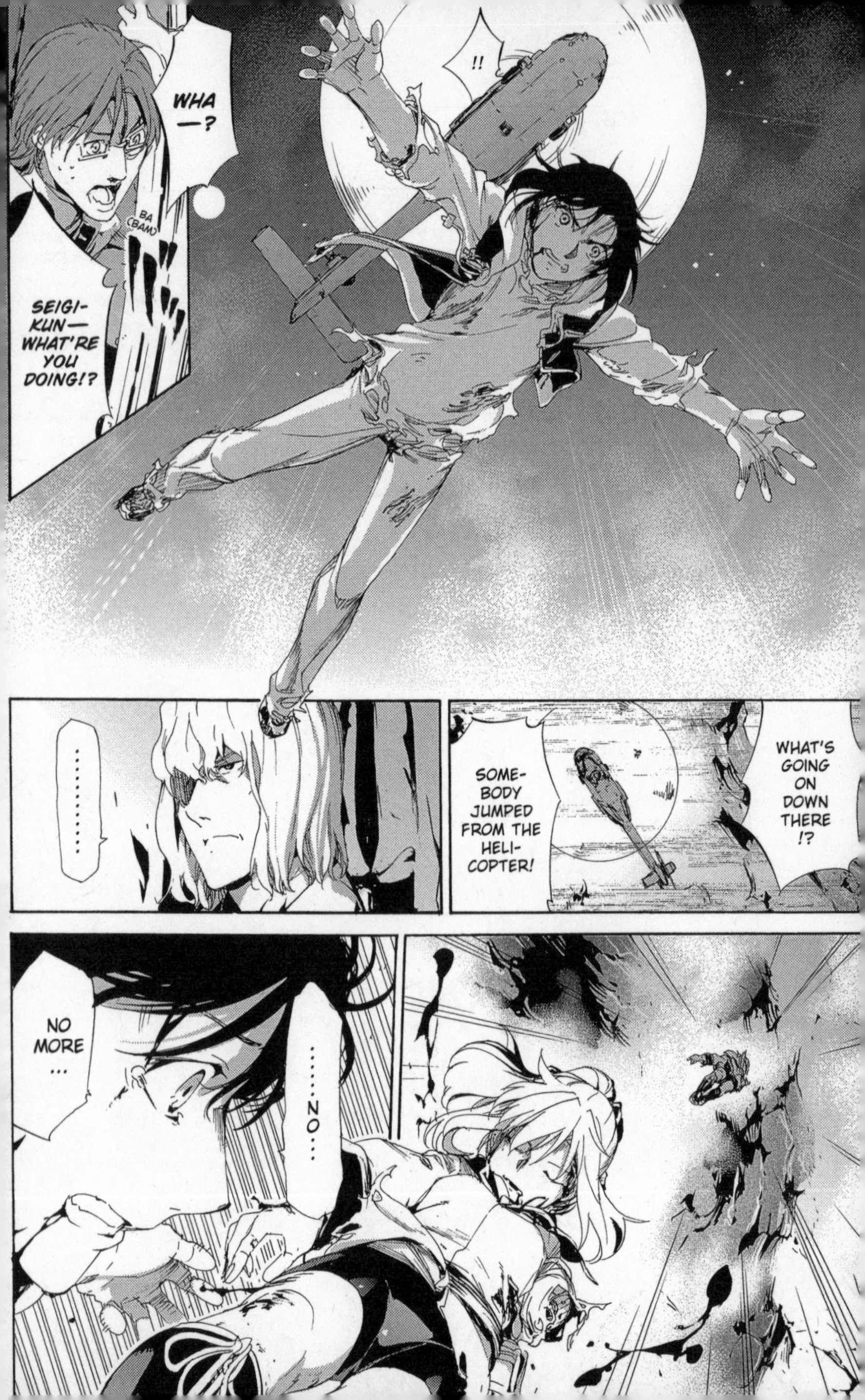
!!
WHA—?
BA (BAM)
SEIGI-KUN—WHAT'RE YOU DOING!?
WHAT'S GOING ON DOWN THERE!?
SOMEBODY JUMPED FROM THE HELICOPTER!
......
....NO....
NO MORE ...

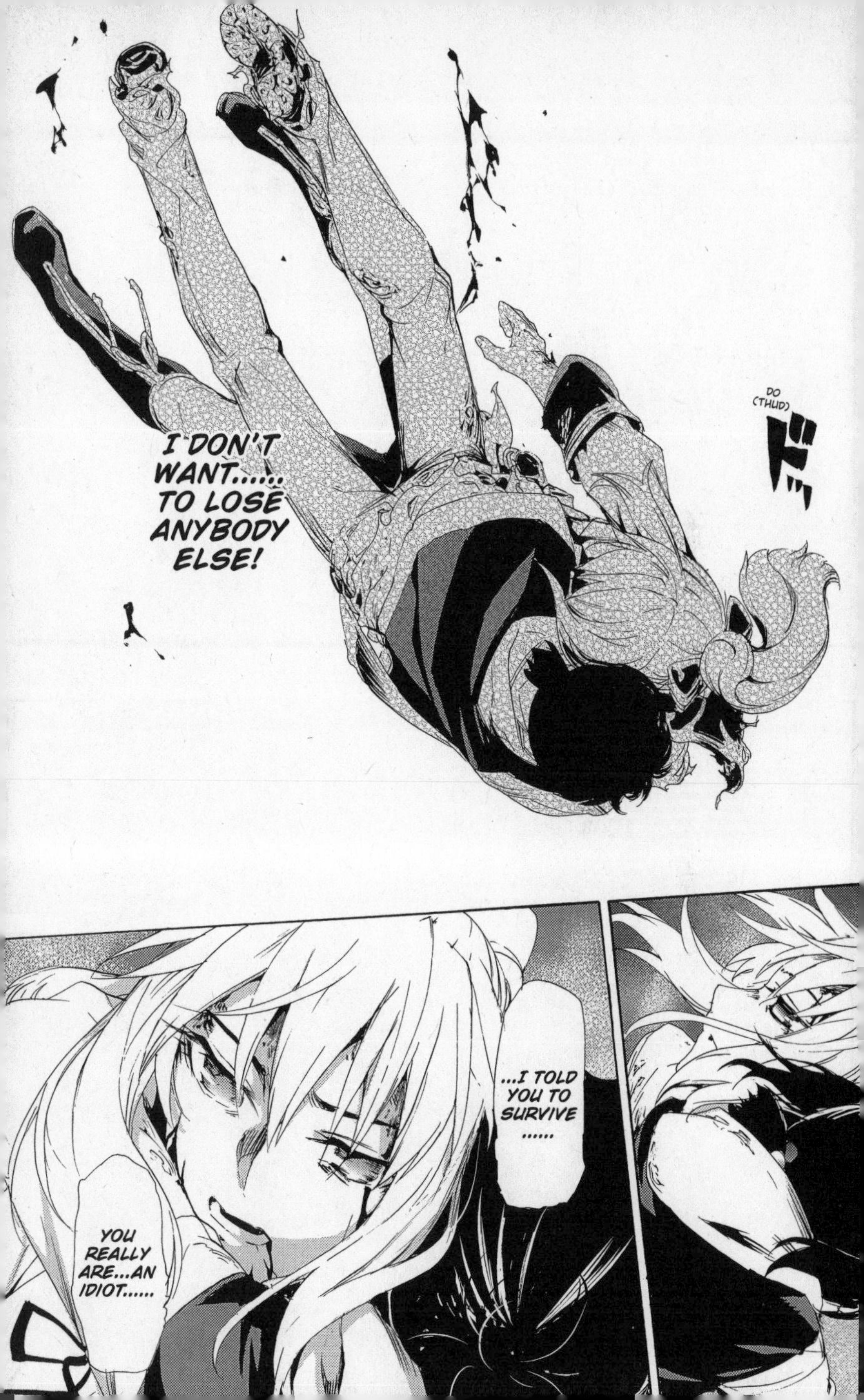
DO (THUD)
ド
I DON'T WANT...... TO LOSE ANYBODY ELSE!
...I TOLD YOU TO SURVIVE ......
YOU REALLY ARE...AN IDIOT......

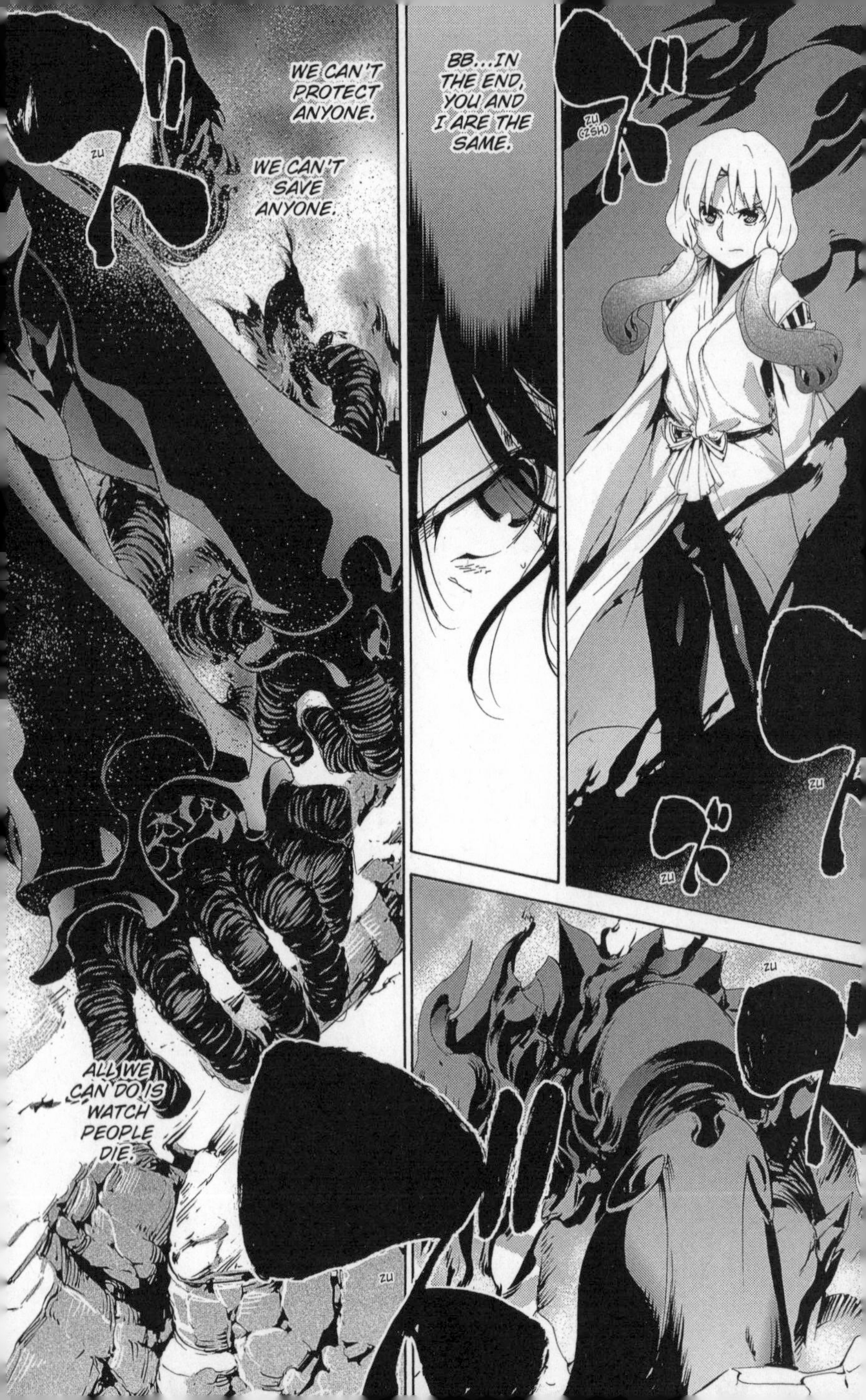

ZU (ZSH)
ZU
ZU
BB...IN THE END, YOU AND I ARE THE SAME.
ZU
ZU
WE CAN'T PROTECT ANYONE.
WE CAN'T SAVE ANYONE.
ALL WE CAN DO IS WATCH PEOPLE DIE.
ZU

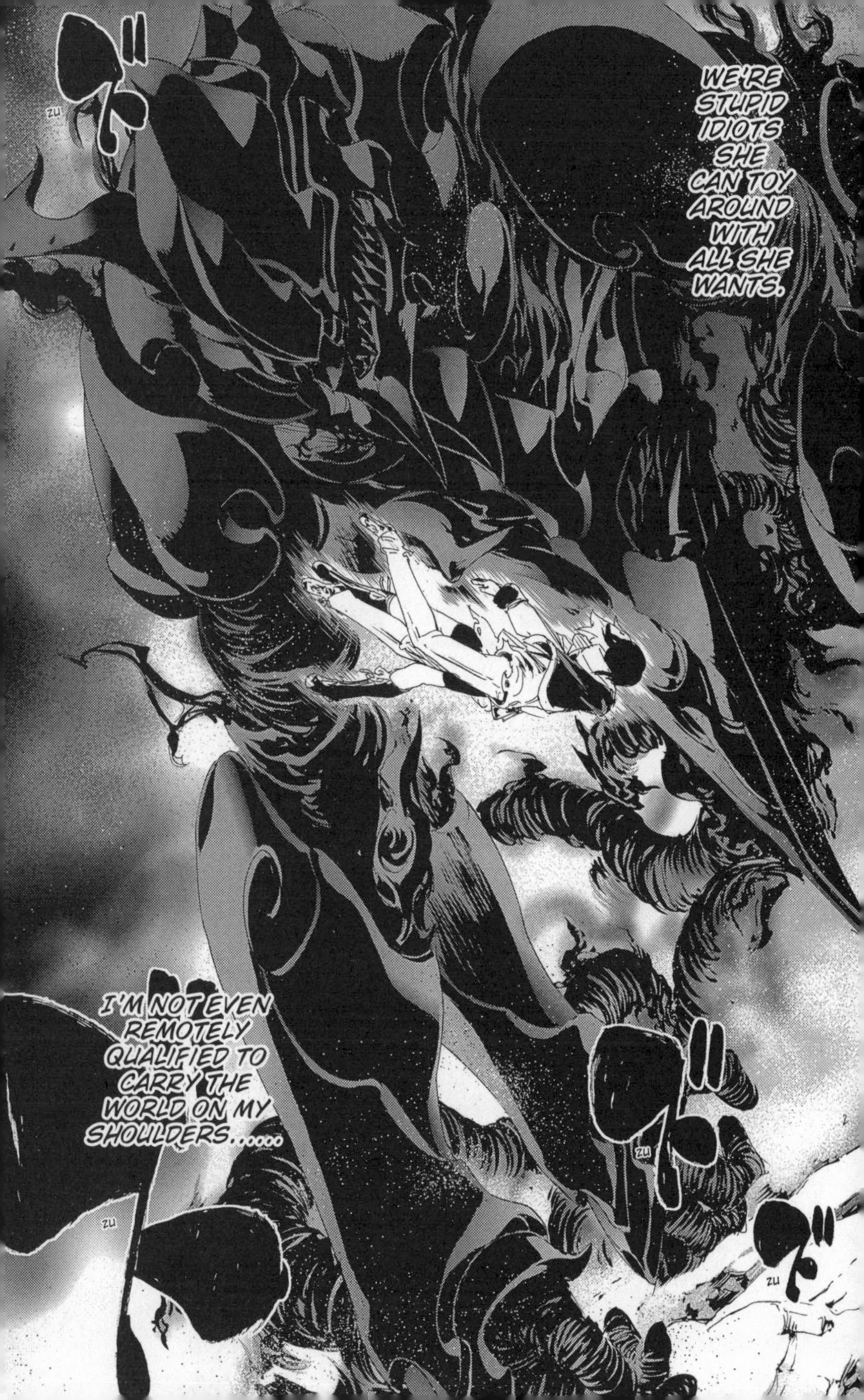
WE'RE STUPID IDIOTS SHE CAN TOY AROUND WITH ALL SHE WANTS.
ZU
I'M NOT EVEN REMOTELY QUALIFIED TO CARRY THE WORLD ON MY SHOULDERS......
ZU
ZU
ZU

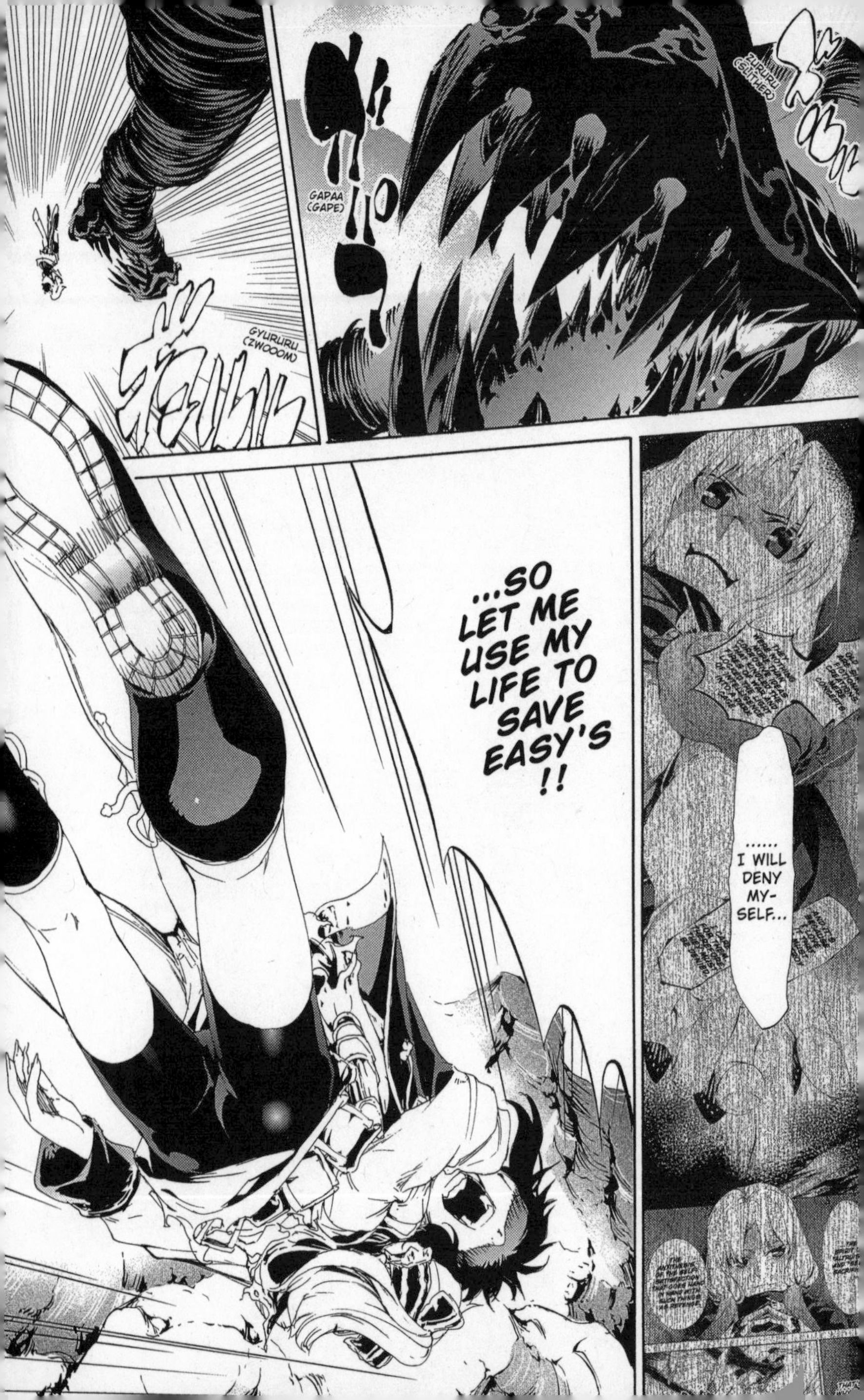
ZURURU (SLITHER)
GAPAA (GAPE)
GYURURU (ZWOOOM)
...... I WILL DENY MY-SELF...
...SO LET ME USE MY LIFE TO SAVE EASY'S !!

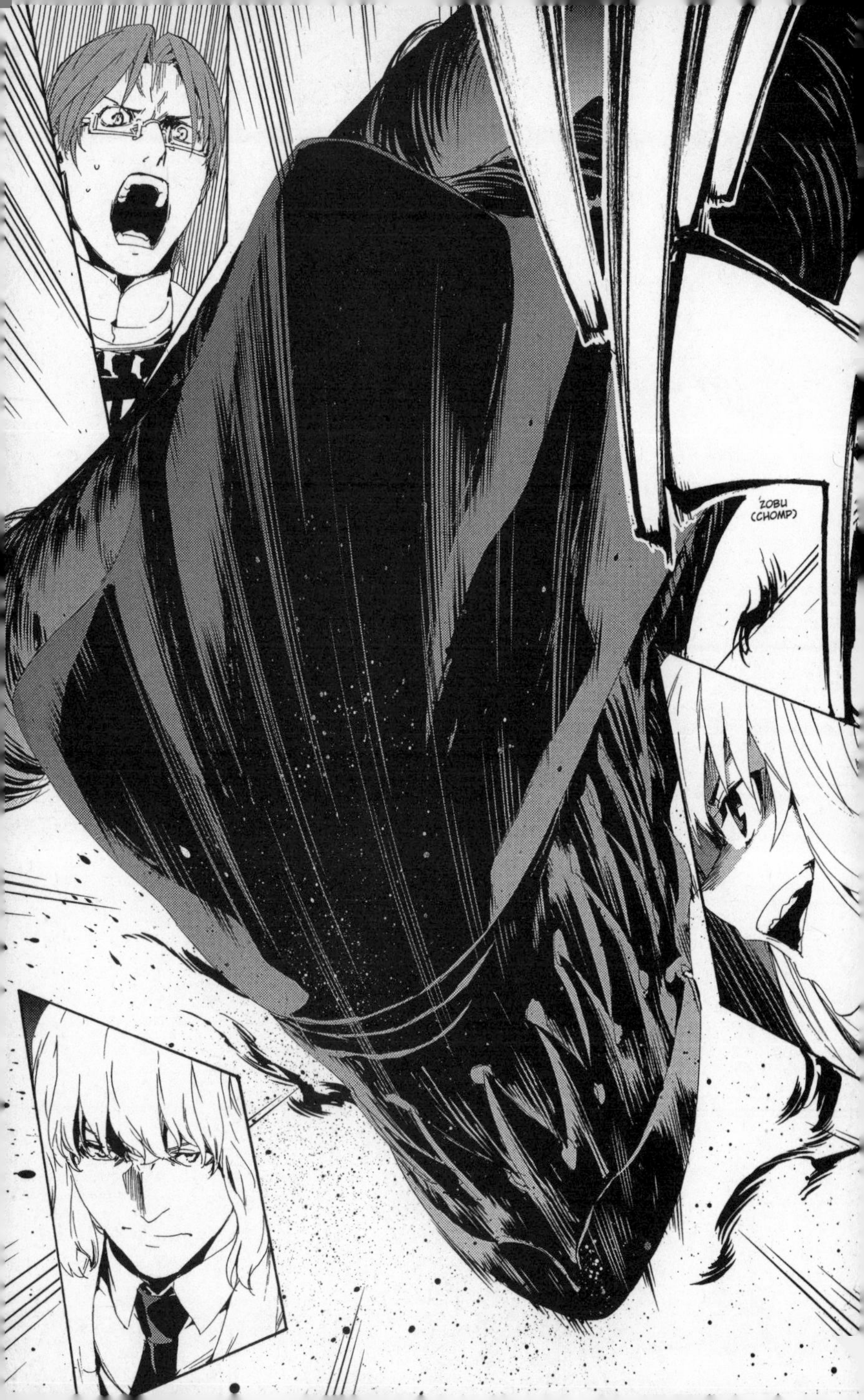
ZOBU
(CHOMP)

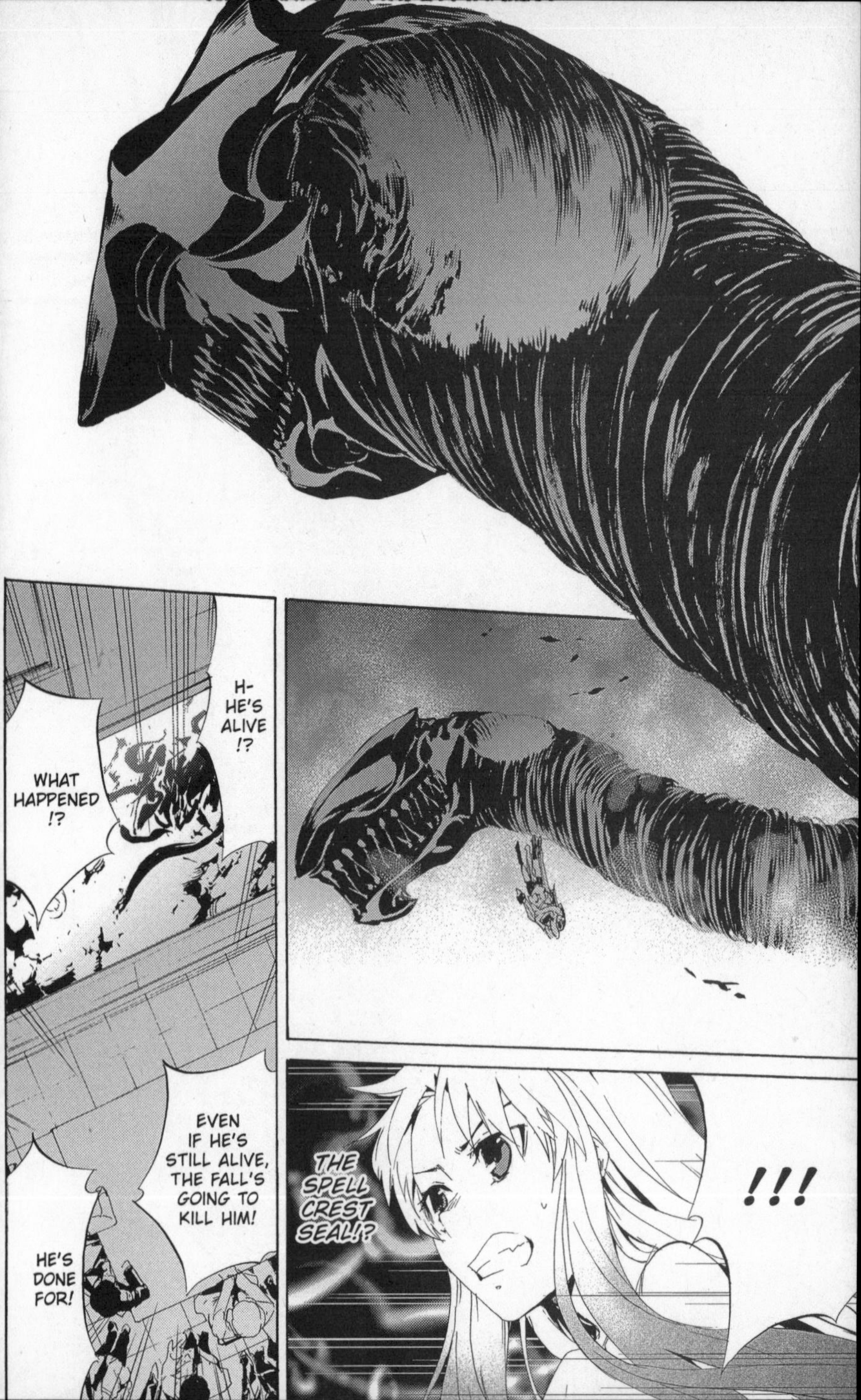
H-HE'S ALIVE!?
WHAT HAPPENED!?
!!!
THE SPELL CREST SEAL!?
EVEN IF HE'S STILL ALIVE, THE FALL'S GOING TO KILL HIM!
HE'S DONE FOR!

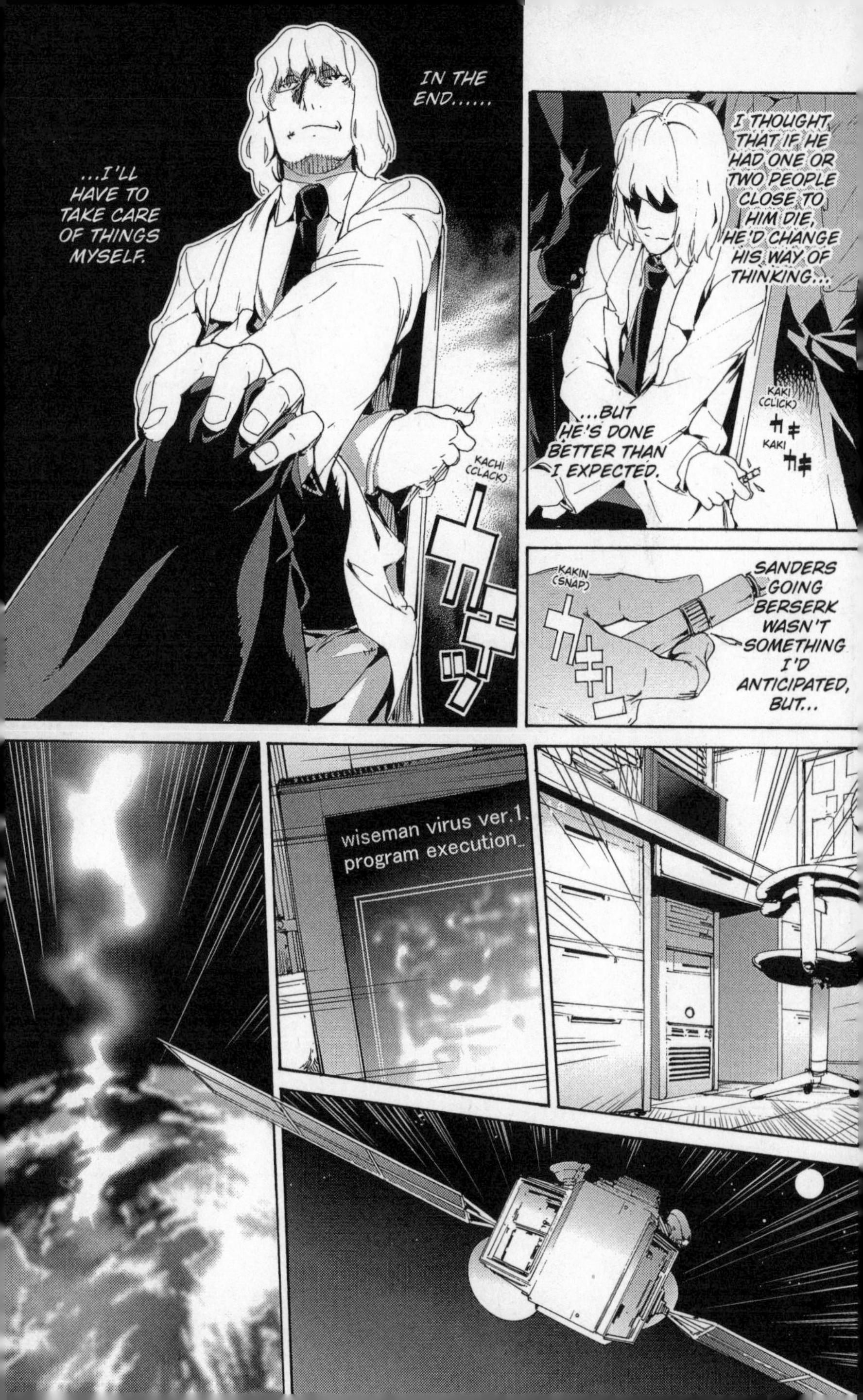
I THOUGHT THAT IF HE HAD ONE OR TWO PEOPLE CLOSE TO HIM DIE, HE'D CHANGE HIS WAY OF THINKING...
KAKI (CLICK)
KAKI
...BUT HE'S DONE BETTER THAN I EXPECTED.
SANDERS GOING BERSERK WASN'T SOMETHING I'D ANTICIPATED, BUT...
KAKIN (SNAP)
IN THE END......
...I'LL HAVE TO TAKE CARE OF THINGS MYSELF.
KACHI (CLACK)
wiseman virus ver.1.
program execution_

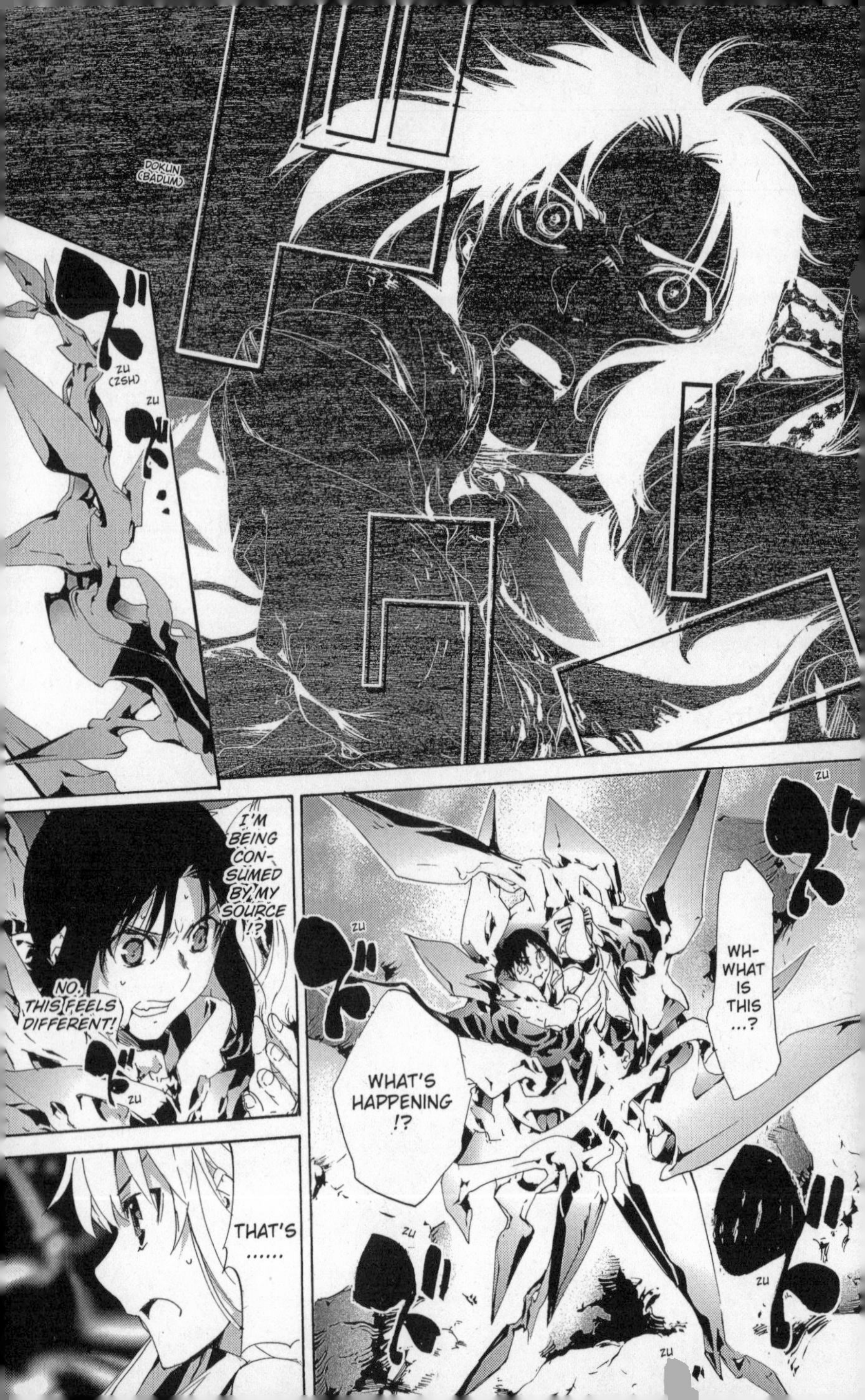
DOKUN (BADUM)
ZU (ZSH)
ZU
ZU
WH-WHAT IS THIS ...?
ZU
WHAT'S HAPPENING !?
ZU
ZU
ZU
I'M BEING CON-SUMED BY MY SOURCE !?
NO, THIS FEELS DIFFERENT!
ZU
THAT'S ......

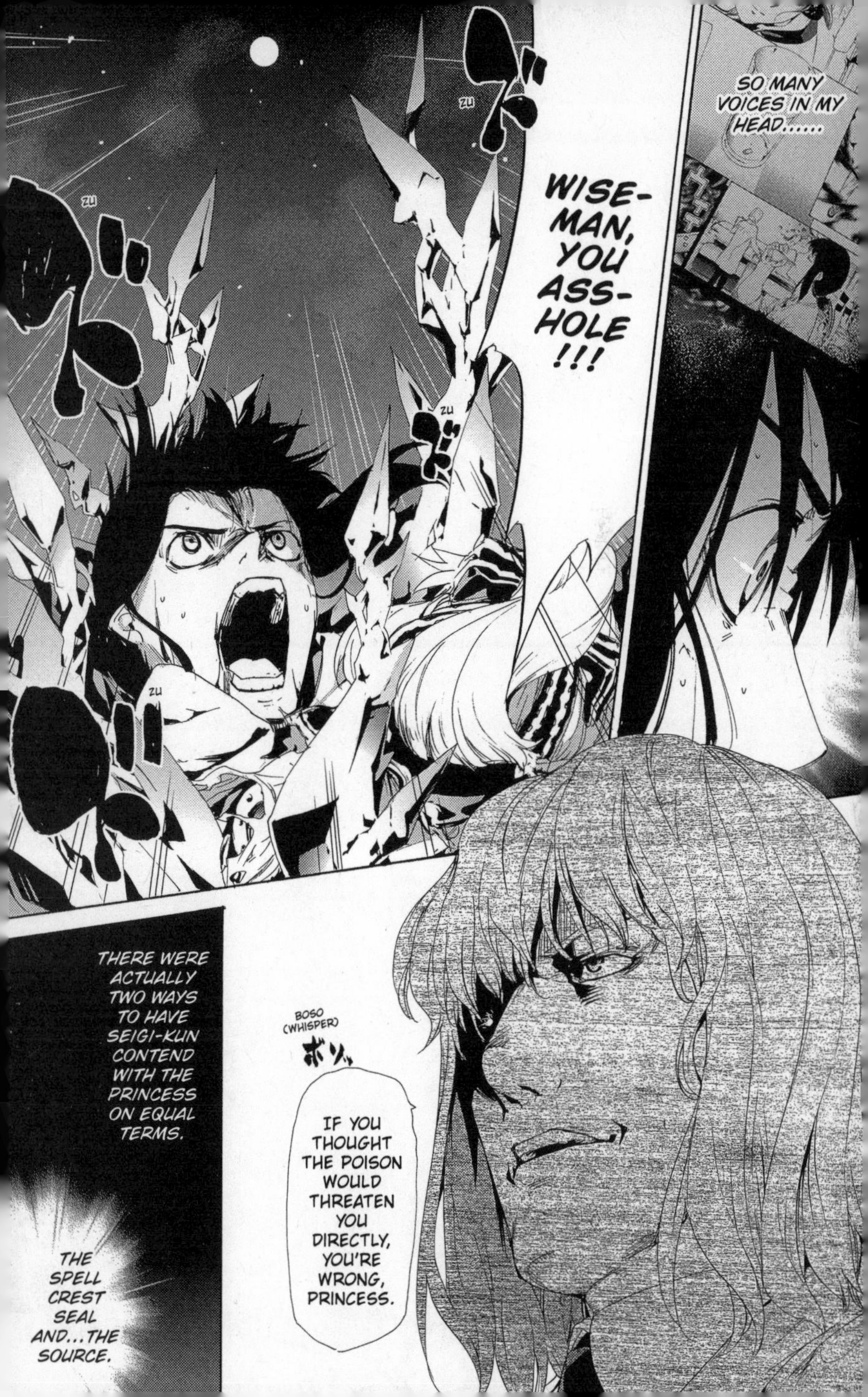

SO MANY VOICES IN MY HEAD......
WISE-MAN, YOU ASS-HOLE!!!
ZU
ZU
ZU
ZU
BOSO (WHISPER)
ボソッ
IF YOU THOUGHT THE POISON WOULD THREATEN YOU DIRECTLY, YOU'RE WRONG, PRINCESS.
THERE WERE ACTUALLY TWO WAYS TO HAVE SEIGI-KUN CONTEND WITH THE PRINCESS ON EQUAL TERMS.
THE SPELL CREST SEAL AND...THE SOURCE.

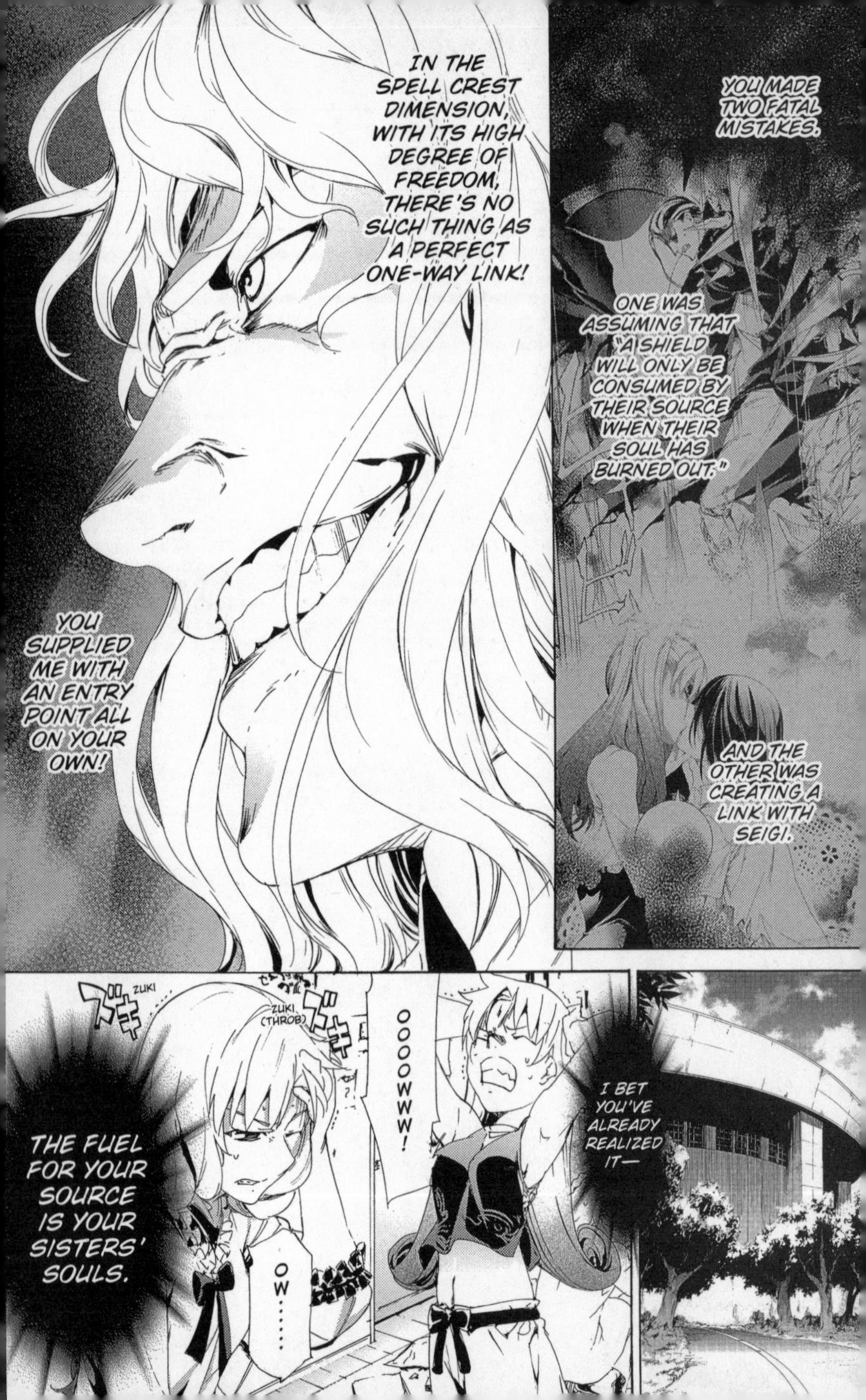
YOU MADE TWO FATAL MISTAKES.
ONE WAS ASSUMING THAT "A SHIELD WILL ONLY BE CONSUMED BY THEIR SOURCE WHEN THEIR SOUL HAS BURNED OUT."
AND THE OTHER WAS CREATING A LINK WITH SEIGI.
IN THE SPELL CREST DIMENSION, WITH ITS HIGH DEGREE OF FREEDOM, THERE'S NO SUCH THING AS A PERFECT ONE-WAY LINK!
YOU SUPPLIED ME WITH AN ENTRY POINT ALL ON YOUR OWN!
I BET YOU'VE ALREADY REALIZED IT—
OOOOOWWW!
ZUKI (THROB)
ZUKI
OW......
THE FUEL FOR YOUR SOURCE IS YOUR SISTERS' SOULS.

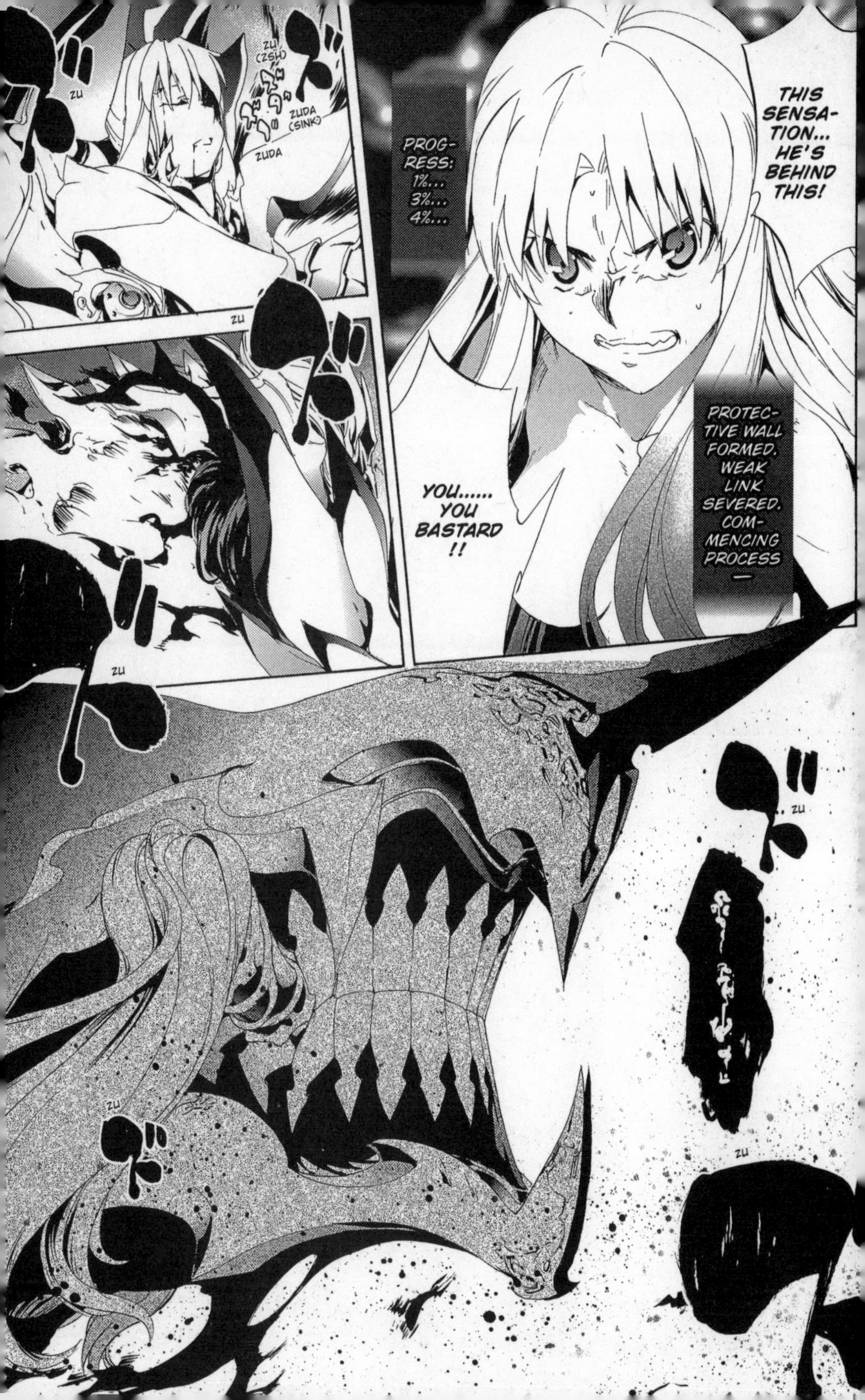
THIS SENSATION... HE'S BEHIND THIS!
PROGRESS: 1%... 3%... 4%...
PROTECTIVE WALL FORMED. WEAK LINK SEVERED. COMMENCING PROCESS —
YOU...... YOU BASTARD !!
ZU (ZSH)
ZU
ZUDA (SINK)
ZUDA
ZU
ZU
ZU
ZU
ZU

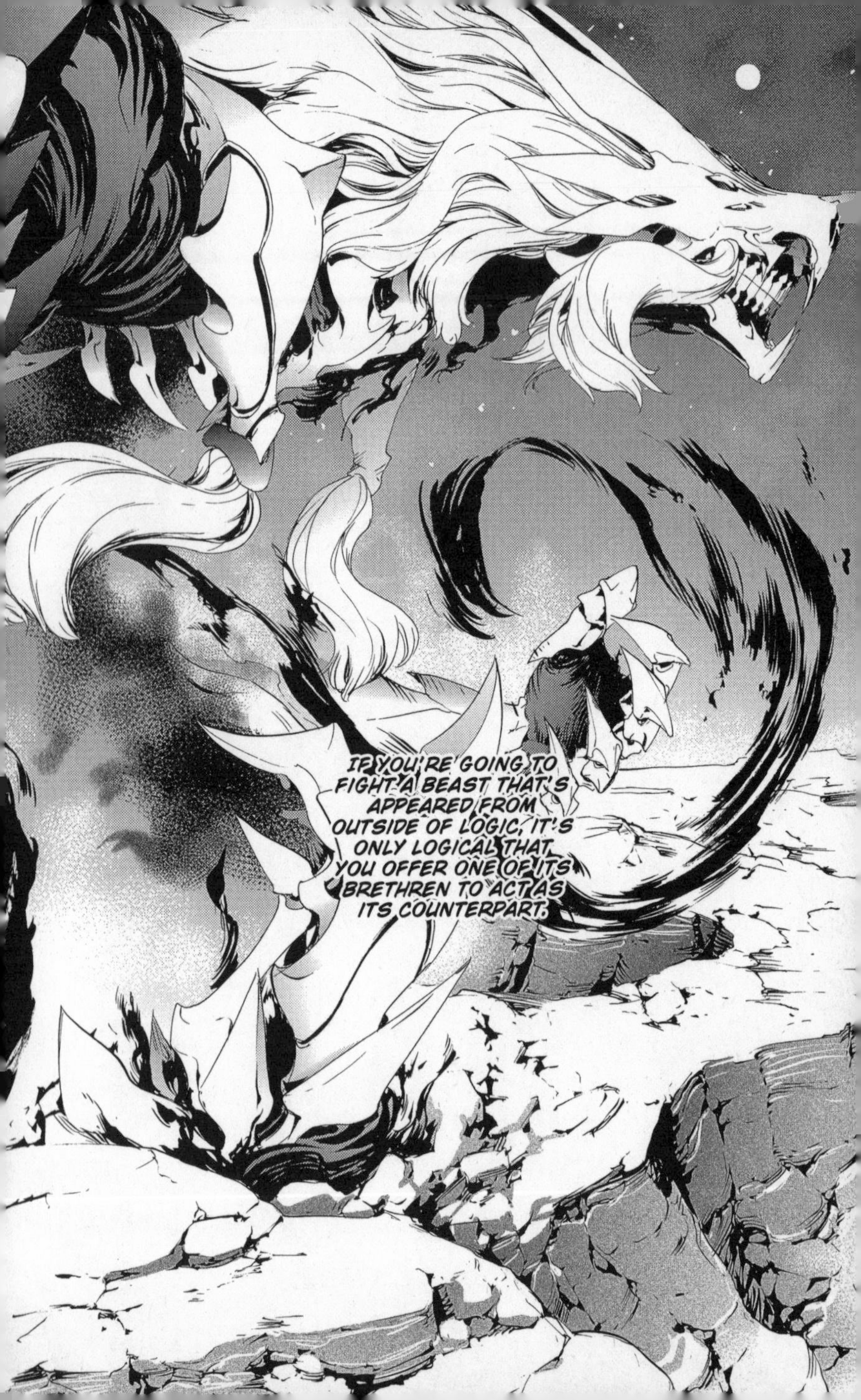
IF YOU'RE GOING TO FIGHT A BEAST THAT'S APPEARED FROM OUTSIDE OF LOGIC, IT'S ONLY LOGICAL THAT YOU OFFER ONE OF ITS BRETHREN TO ACT AS ITS COUNTERPART.

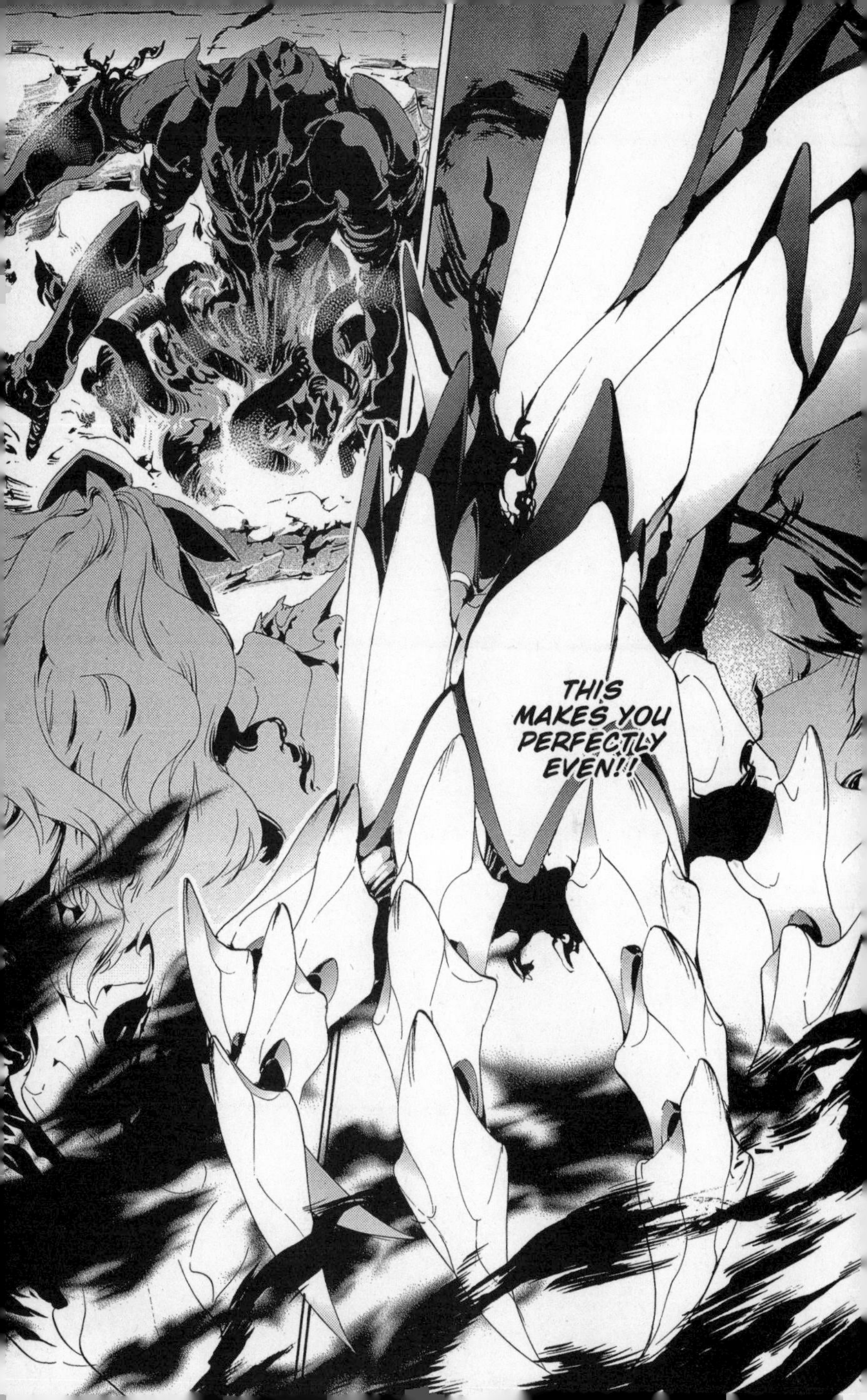
THIS MAKES YOU PERFECTLY EVEN!!

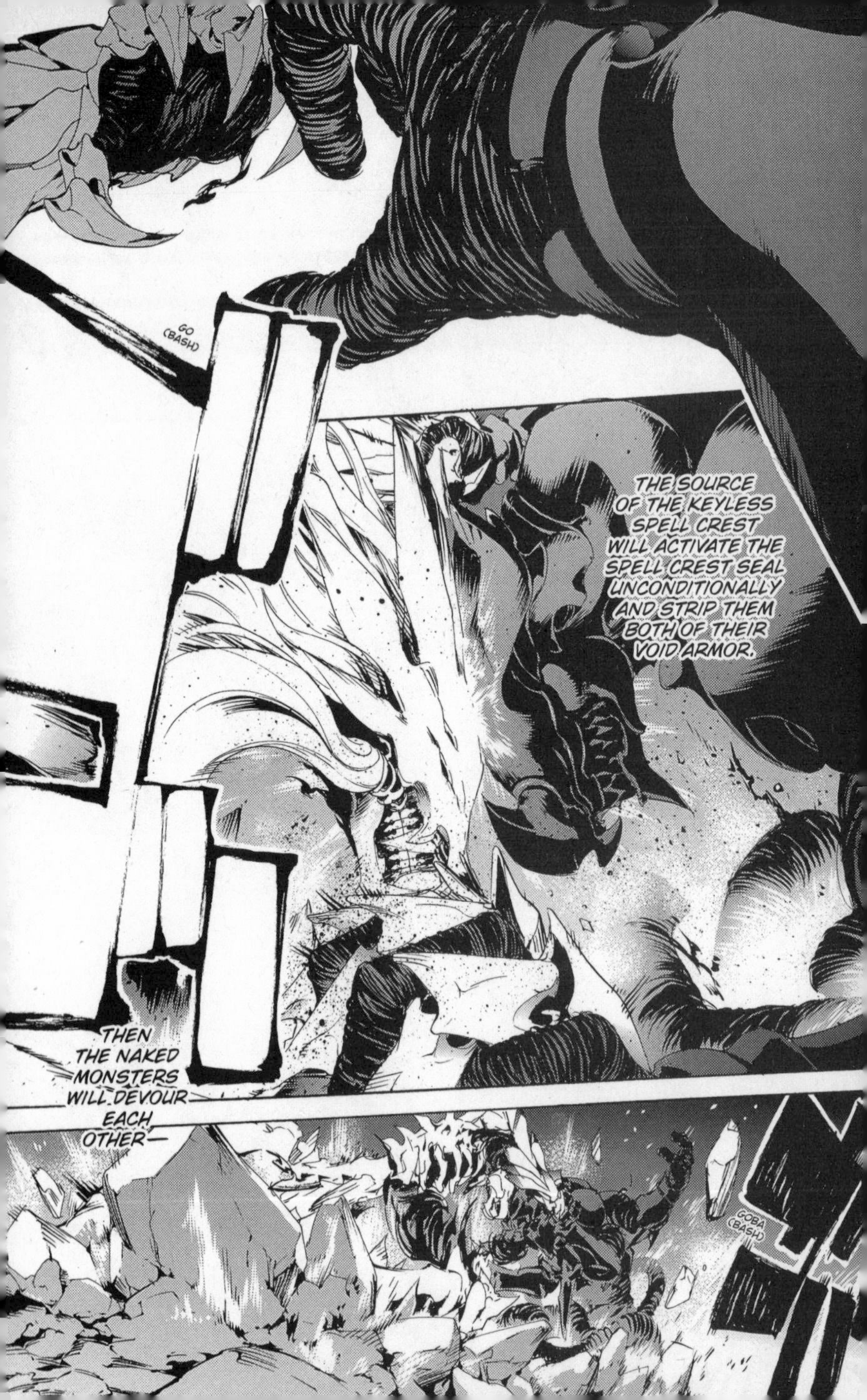
GO (BASH)
THE SOURCE OF THE KEYLESS SPELL CREST WILL ACTIVATE THE SPELL CREST SEAL UNCONDITIONALLY AND STRIP THEM BOTH OF THEIR VOID ARMOR.
THEN THE NAKED MONSTERS WILL DEVOUR EACH OTHER—
GOBA (BASH)

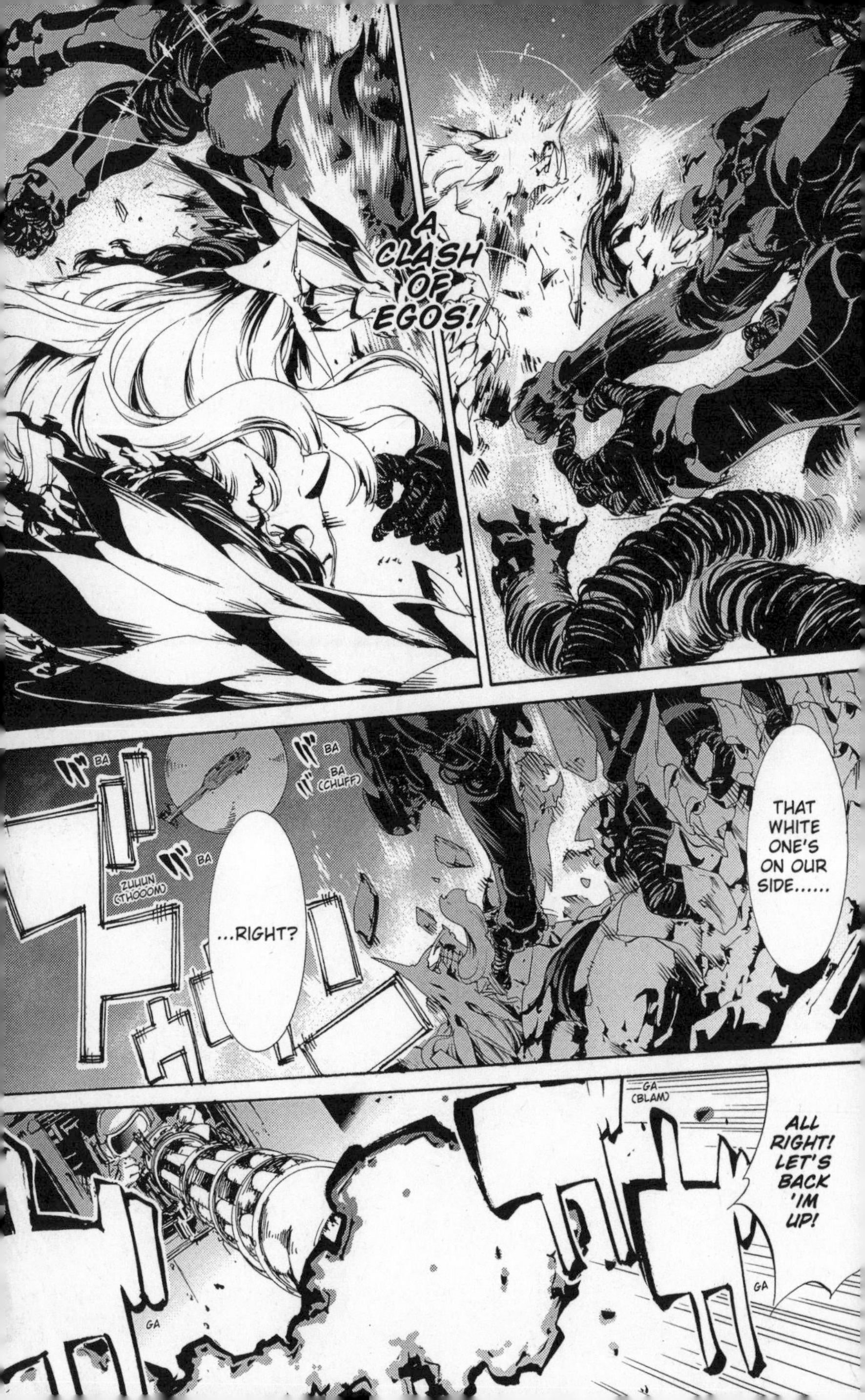
A CLASH OF EGOS!
THAT WHITE ONE'S ON OUR SIDE......
...RIGHT?
BA
BA
BA (CHUFF)
BA
ZUUUN (THOOOM)
GA (BLAM)
ALL RIGHT! LET'S BACK 'IM UP!
GA
GA

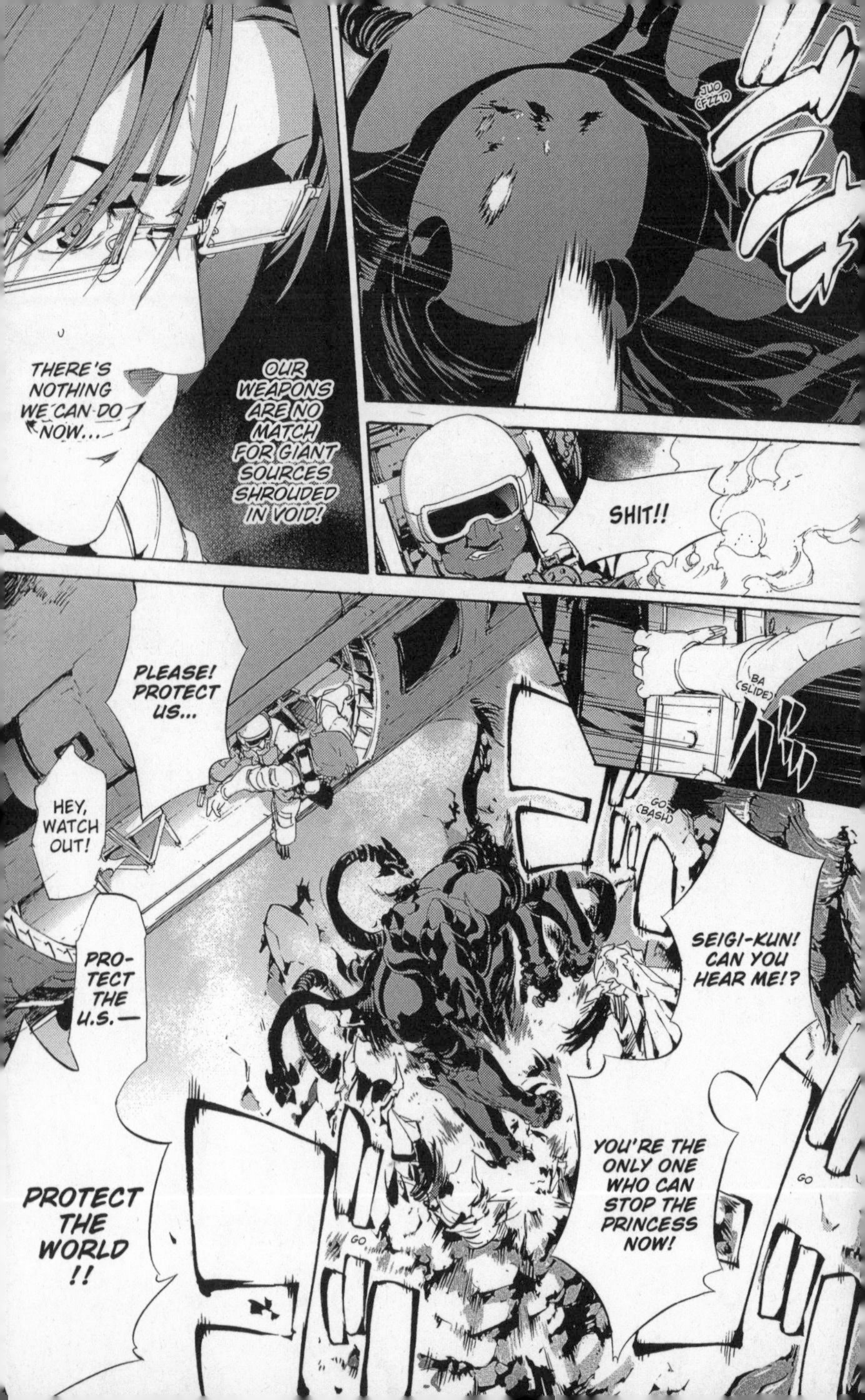
JUO (FZZT)
SHIT!!
OUR WEAPONS ARE NO MATCH FOR GIANT SOURCES SHROUDED IN VOID!
THERE'S NOTHING WE CAN DO NOW...
BA (SLIDE)
GO (BASH)
PLEASE! PROTECT US...
HEY, WATCH OUT!
SEIGI-KUN! CAN YOU HEAR ME!?
PRO-TECT THE U.S.—
GO
YOU'RE THE ONLY ONE WHO CAN STOP THE PRINCESS NOW!
GO
PROTECT THE WORLD!!

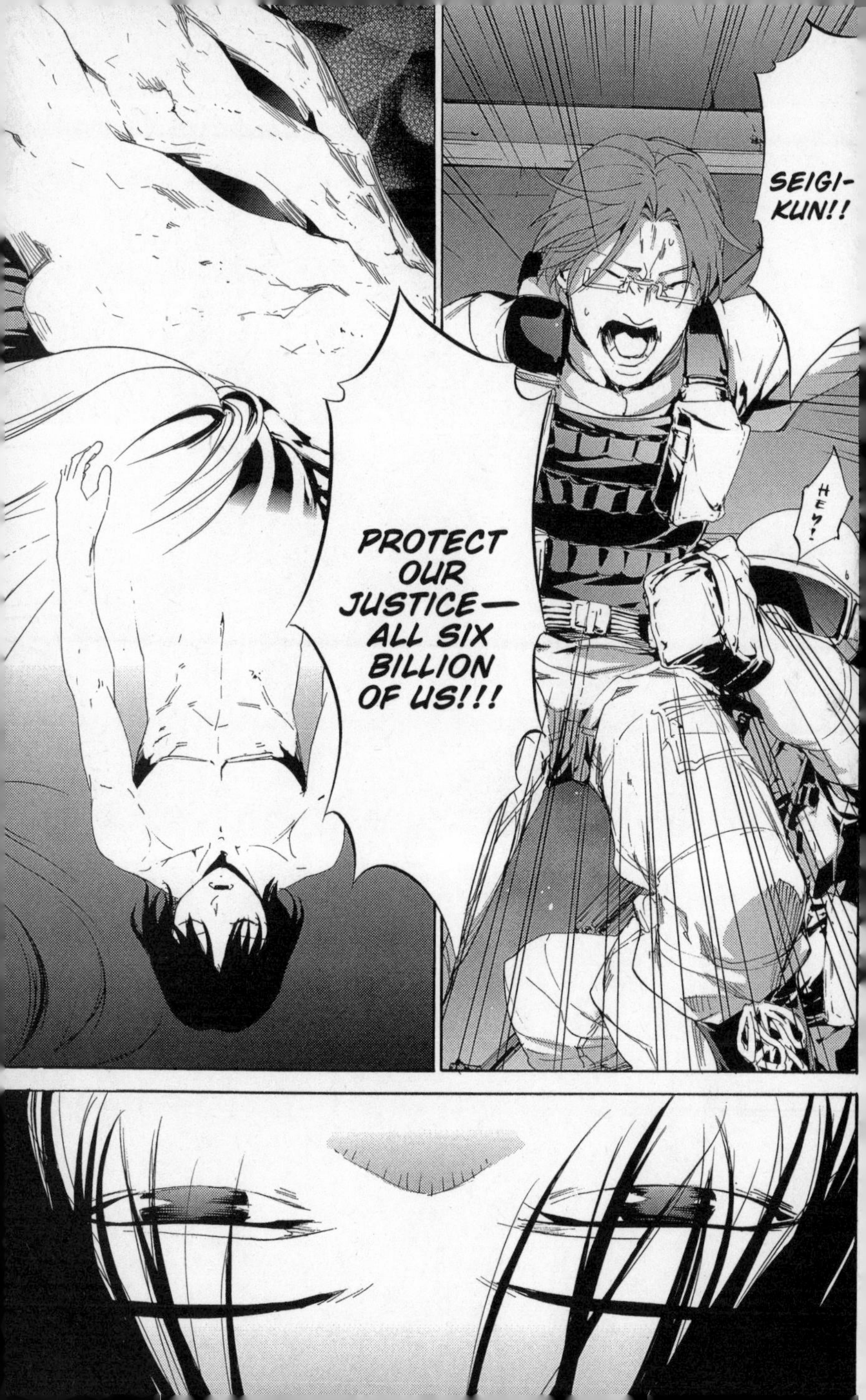
SEIGI-KUN!!
HEY!
PROTECT OUR JUSTICE—ALL SIX BILLION OF US!!!

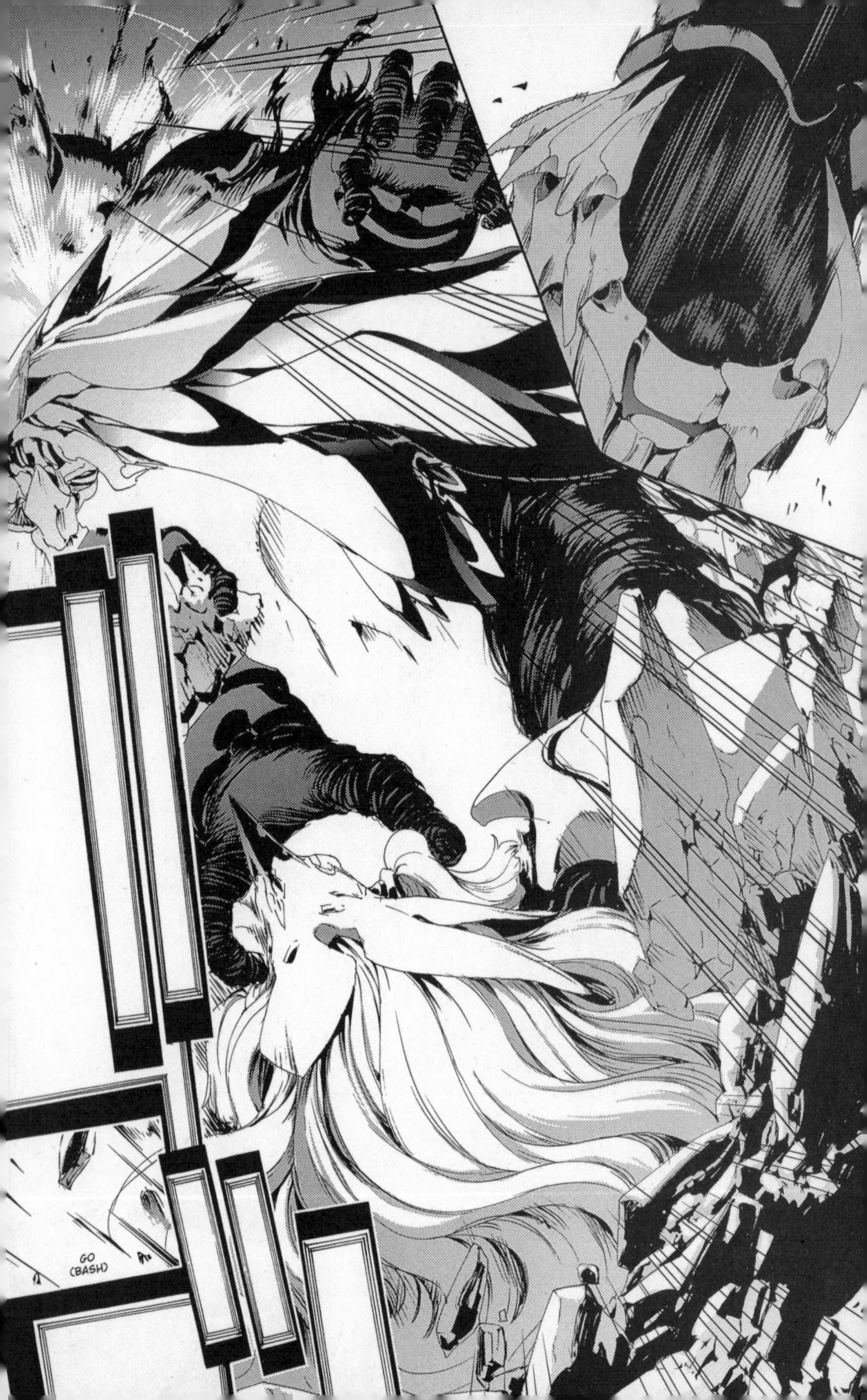
GO
(BASH)

#44 DECISIVE BATTLE

TABOOTATTOO

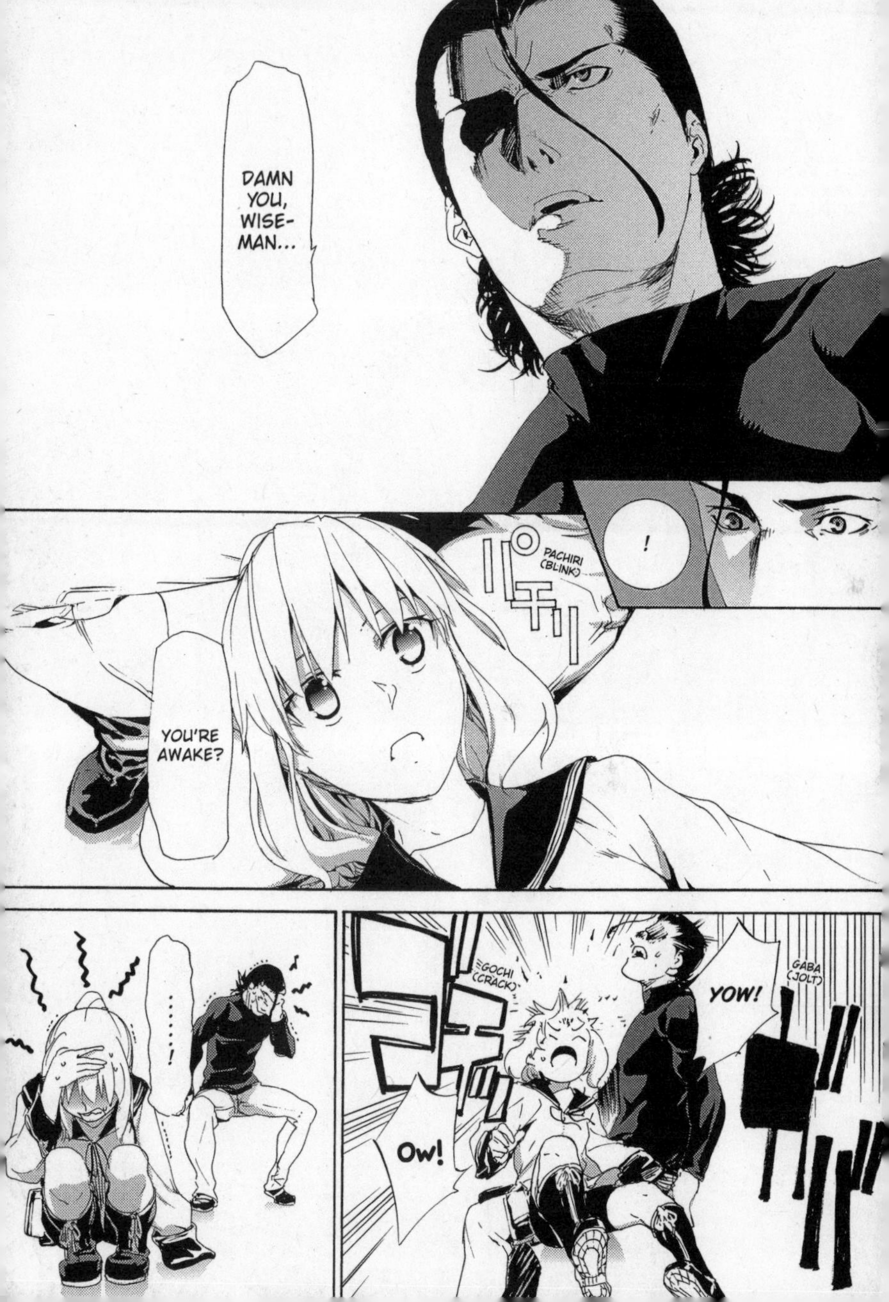
DAMN YOU, WISE-MAN...
!
PACHIRI (BLINK)
YOU'RE AWAKE?
GABA (JOLT)
YOW!
GOCHI (CRACK)
OW!
......!

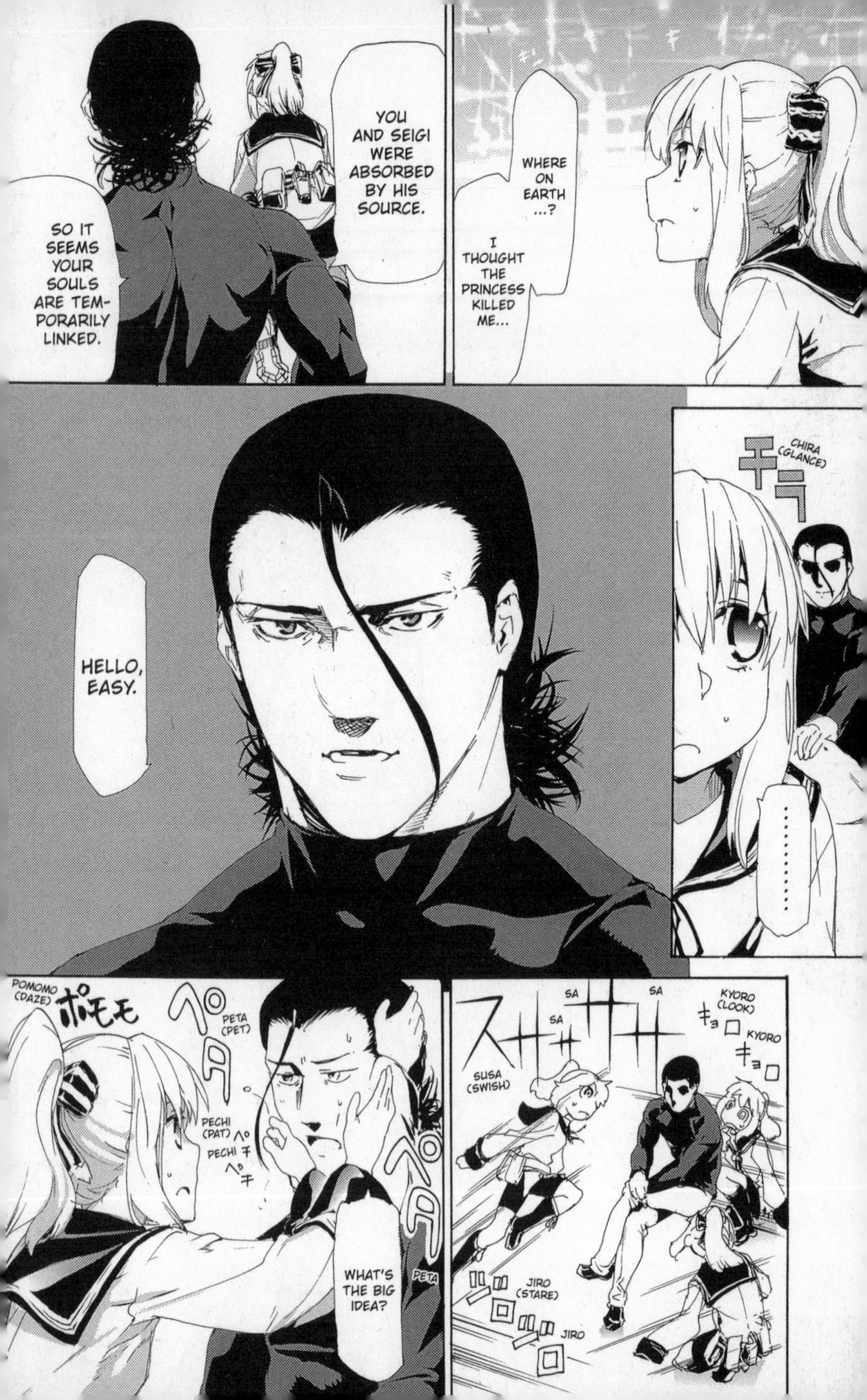

WHERE ON EARTH ...?
I THOUGHT THE PRINCESS KILLED ME...
YOU AND SEIGI WERE ABSORBED BY HIS SOURCE.
SO IT SEEMS YOUR SOULS ARE TEMPORARILY LINKED.
CHIRA (GLANCE)
......
HELLO, EASY.
SA
SA
SA
SUSA (SWISH)
KYORO (LOOK)
KYORO
JIRO (STARE)
JIRO
POMOMO (DAZE)
PETA (PET)
PECHI (PAT)
PECHI
PETA
WHAT'S THE BIG IDEA?

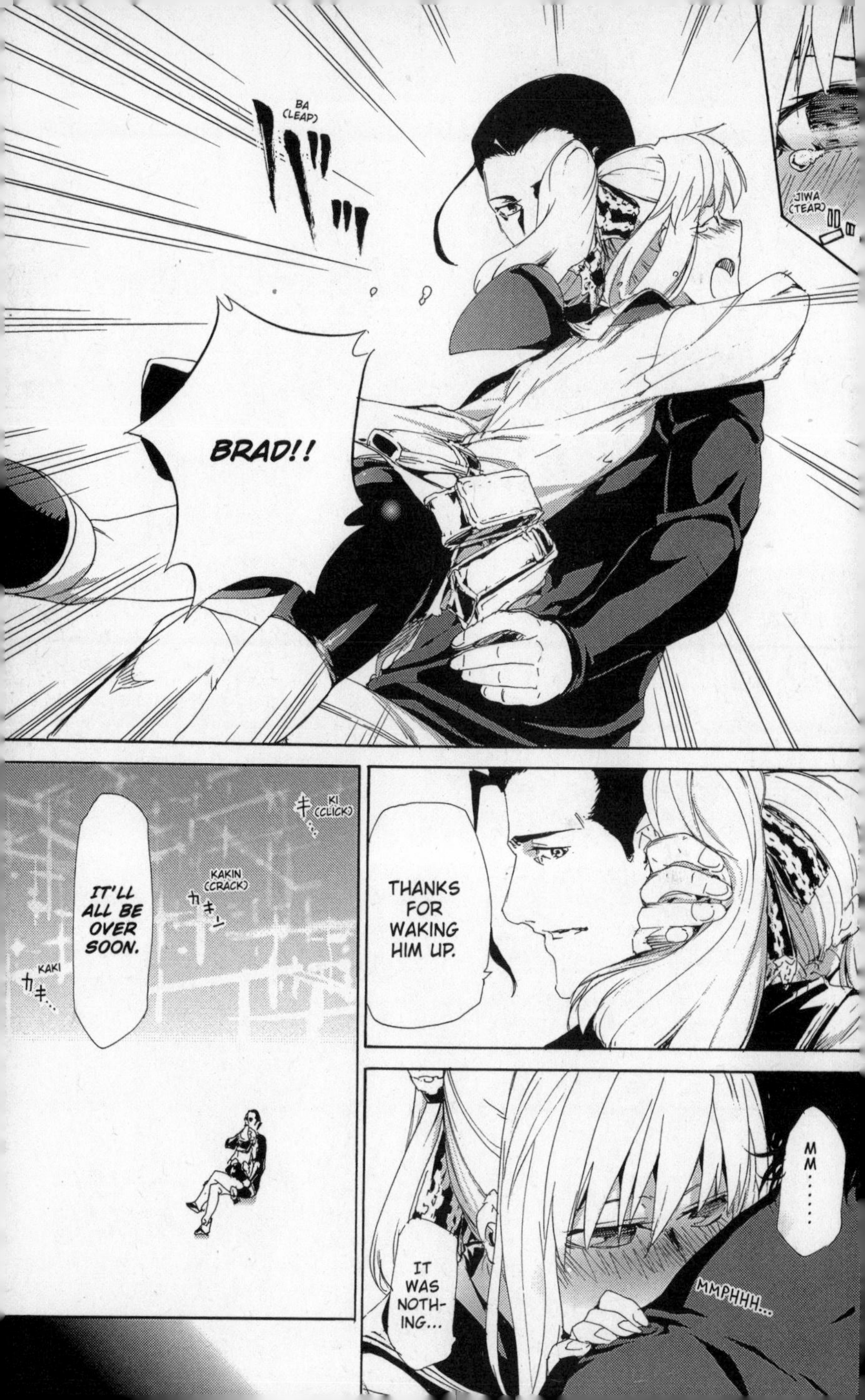
JIWA (TEAR)
BA (LEAP)
BRAD!!
THANKS FOR WAKING HIM UP.
MM......
IT WAS NOTHING...
MMPHHH...
キ... KI (CLICK)
カキーン KAKIN (CRACK)
IT'LL ALL BE OVER SOON.
カキ... KAKI

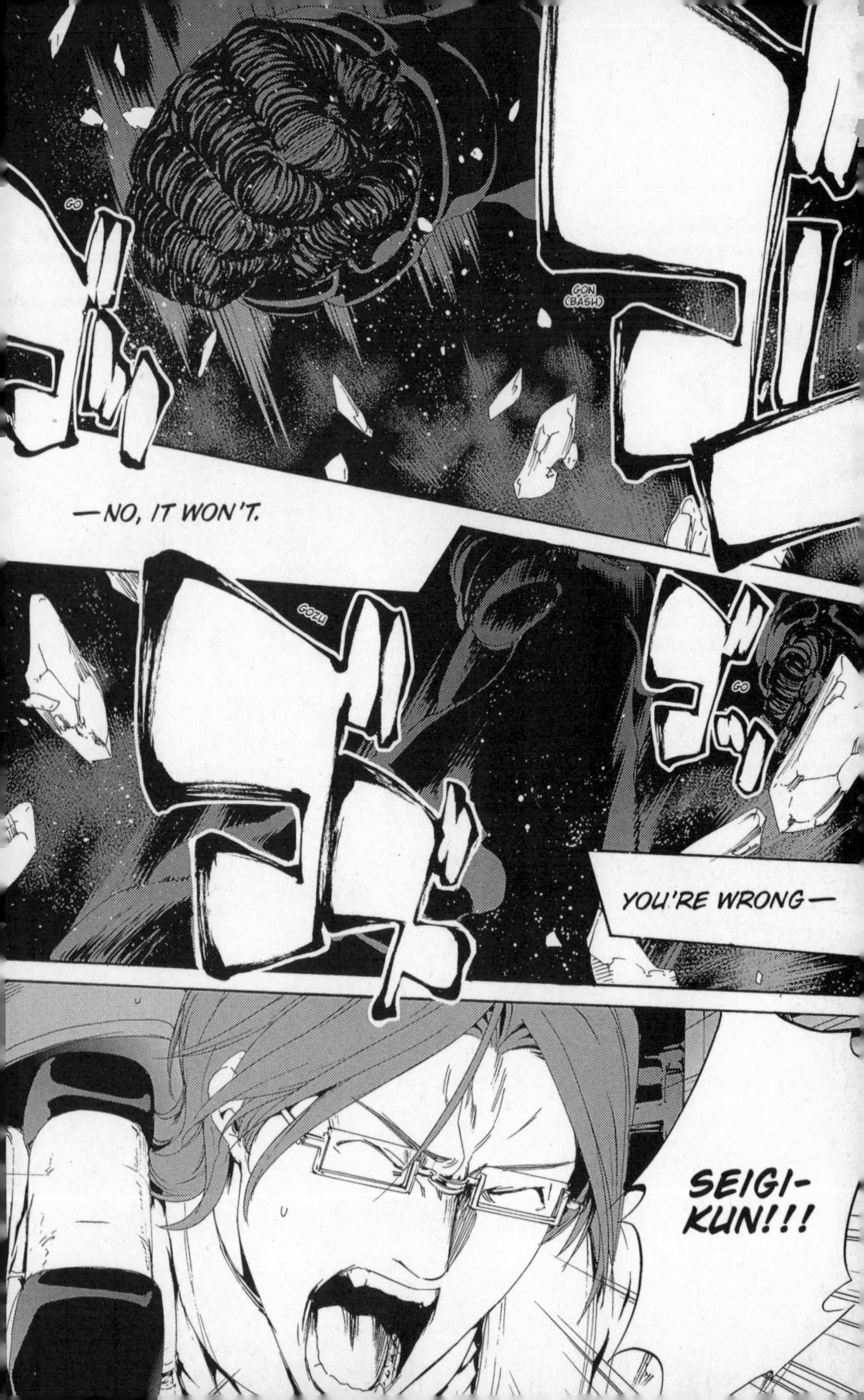
GON (BASH)
GO
—NO, IT WON'T.
GO
GOZU
YOU'RE WRONG—
SEIGI-KUN!!!

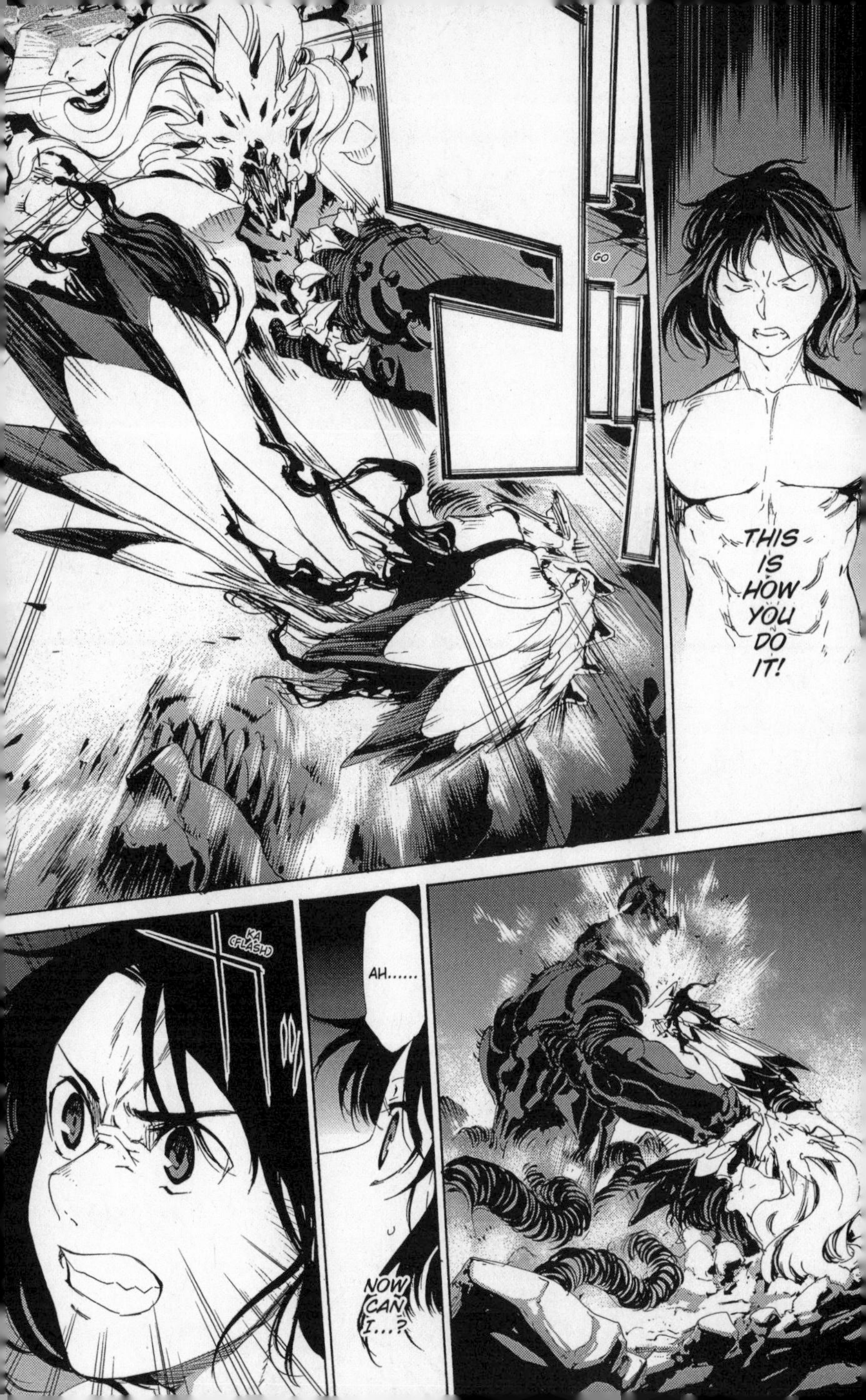
THIS IS HOW YOU DO IT!
GO
AH......
NOW CAN I...?
KA (FLASH)

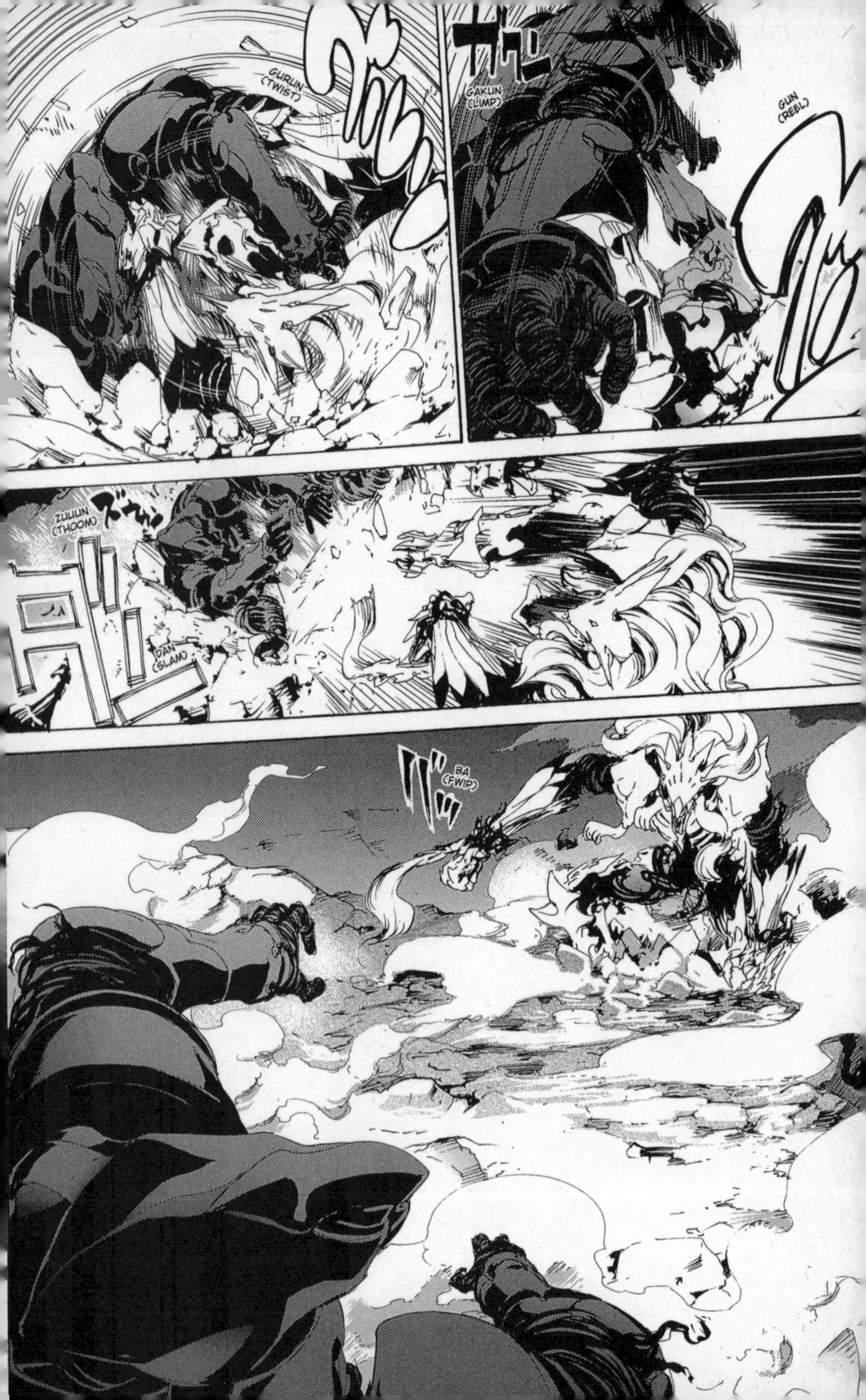
GAKUN (LIMP)
GUN (REEL)
GURUN (TWIST)
ZUUUN (THOOM)
DAN (SLAM)
BA (FWIP)

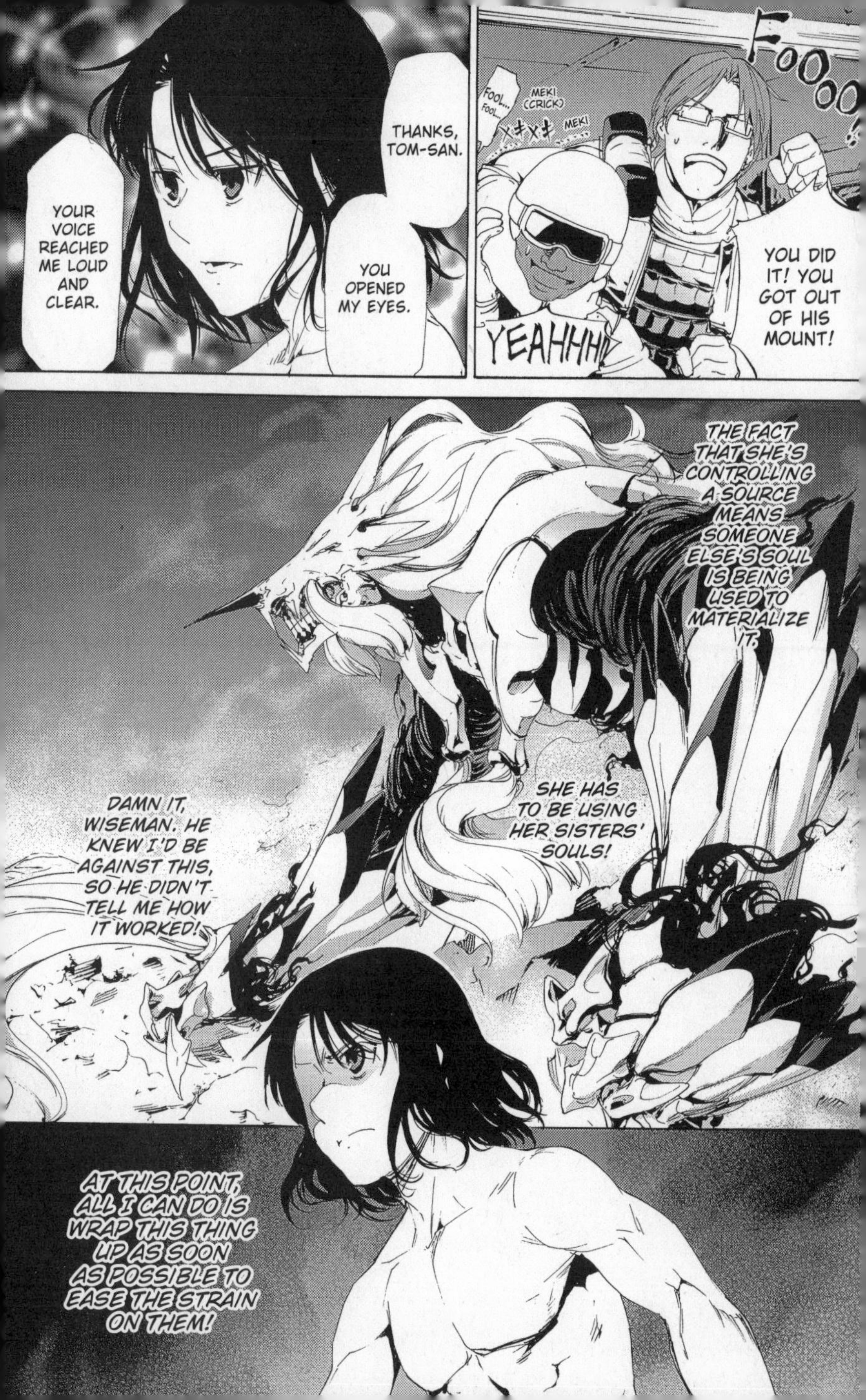
FOOOO
YOU DID IT! YOU GOT OUT OF HIS MOUNT!
MEKI (CRICK)
FOOL... FOOL...
メキメキ
MEKI
YEAHHH!
THANKS, TOM-SAN.
YOU OPENED MY EYES.
YOUR VOICE REACHED ME LOUD AND CLEAR.
THE FACT THAT SHE'S CONTROLLING A SOURCE MEANS SOMEONE ELSE'S SOUL IS BEING USED TO MATERIALIZE IT.
SHE HAS TO BE USING HER SISTERS' SOULS!
DAMN IT, WISEMAN. HE KNEW I'D BE AGAINST THIS, SO HE DIDN'T TELL ME HOW IT WORKED!
AT THIS POINT, ALL I CAN DO IS WRAP THIS THING UP AS SOON AS POSSIBLE TO EASE THE STRAIN ON THEM!

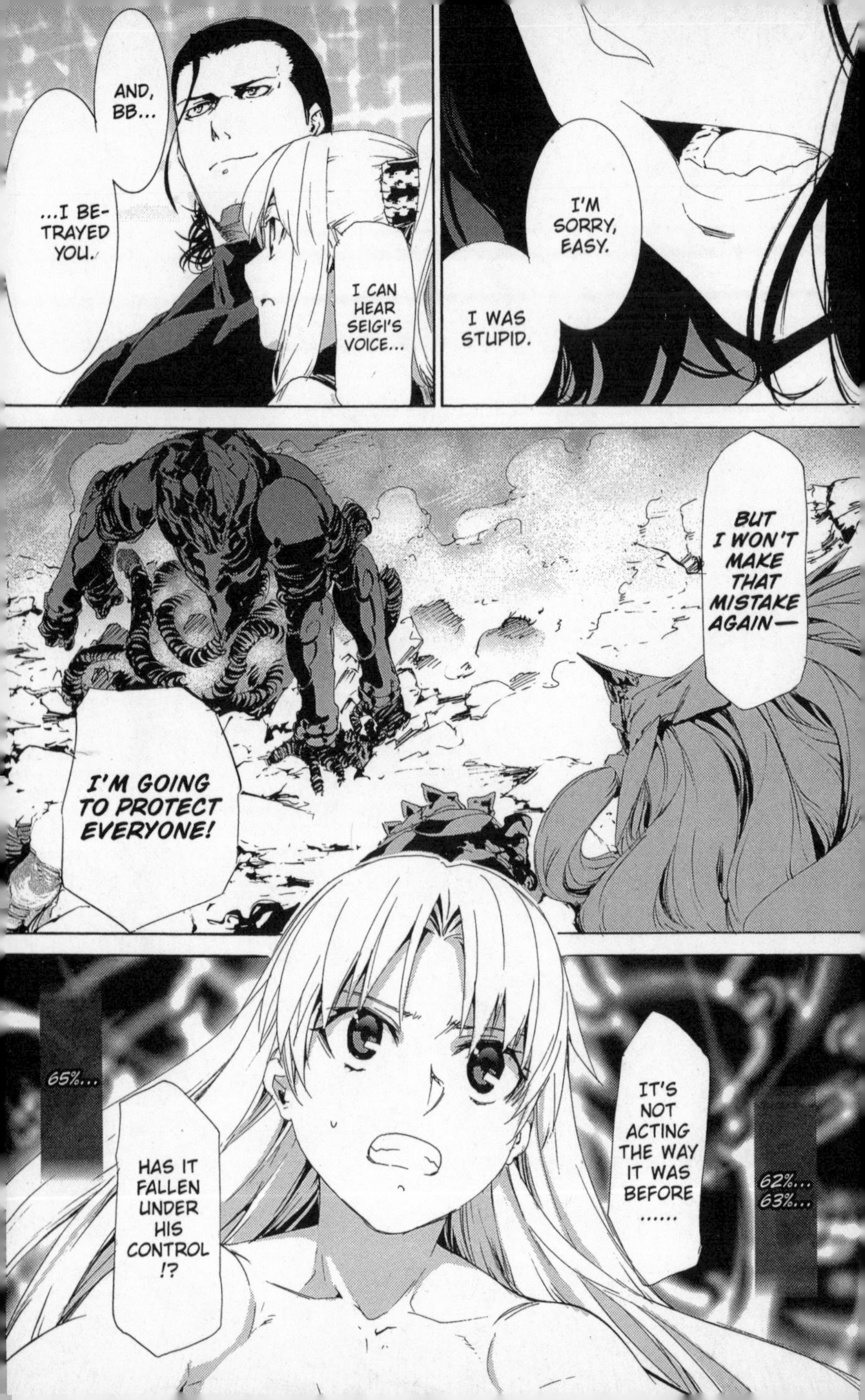
I'M SORRY, EASY.
I WAS STUPID.
AND, BB...
...I BETRAYED YOU.
I CAN HEAR SEIGI'S VOICE...
BUT I WON'T MAKE THAT MISTAKE AGAIN—
I'M GOING TO PROTECT EVERYONE!
62%... 63%...
IT'S NOT ACTING THE WAY IT WAS BEFORE ......
HAS IT FALLEN UNDER HIS CONTROL !?
65%...

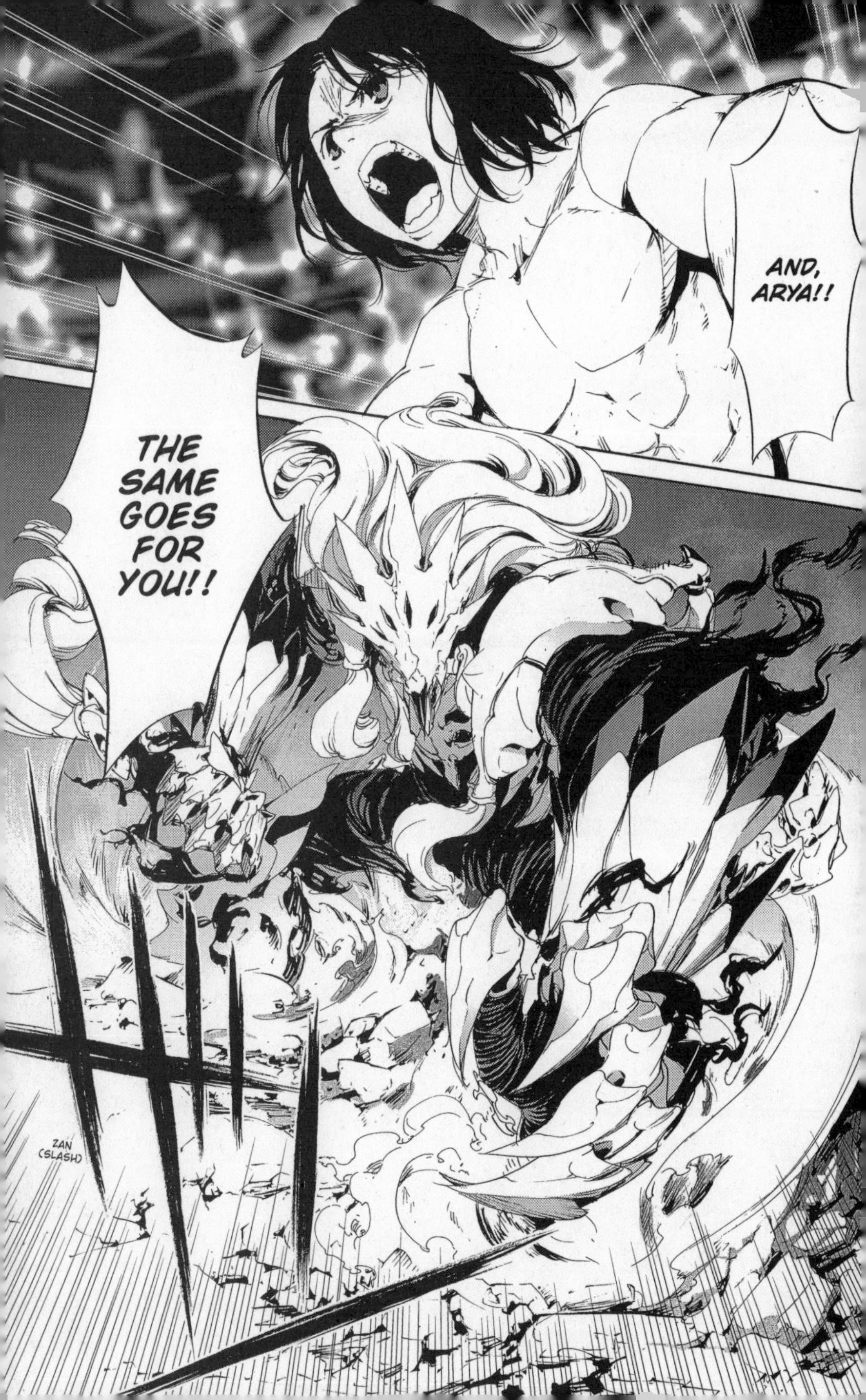
AND, ARYA!!
THE SAME GOES FOR YOU!!
ZAN (SLASH)

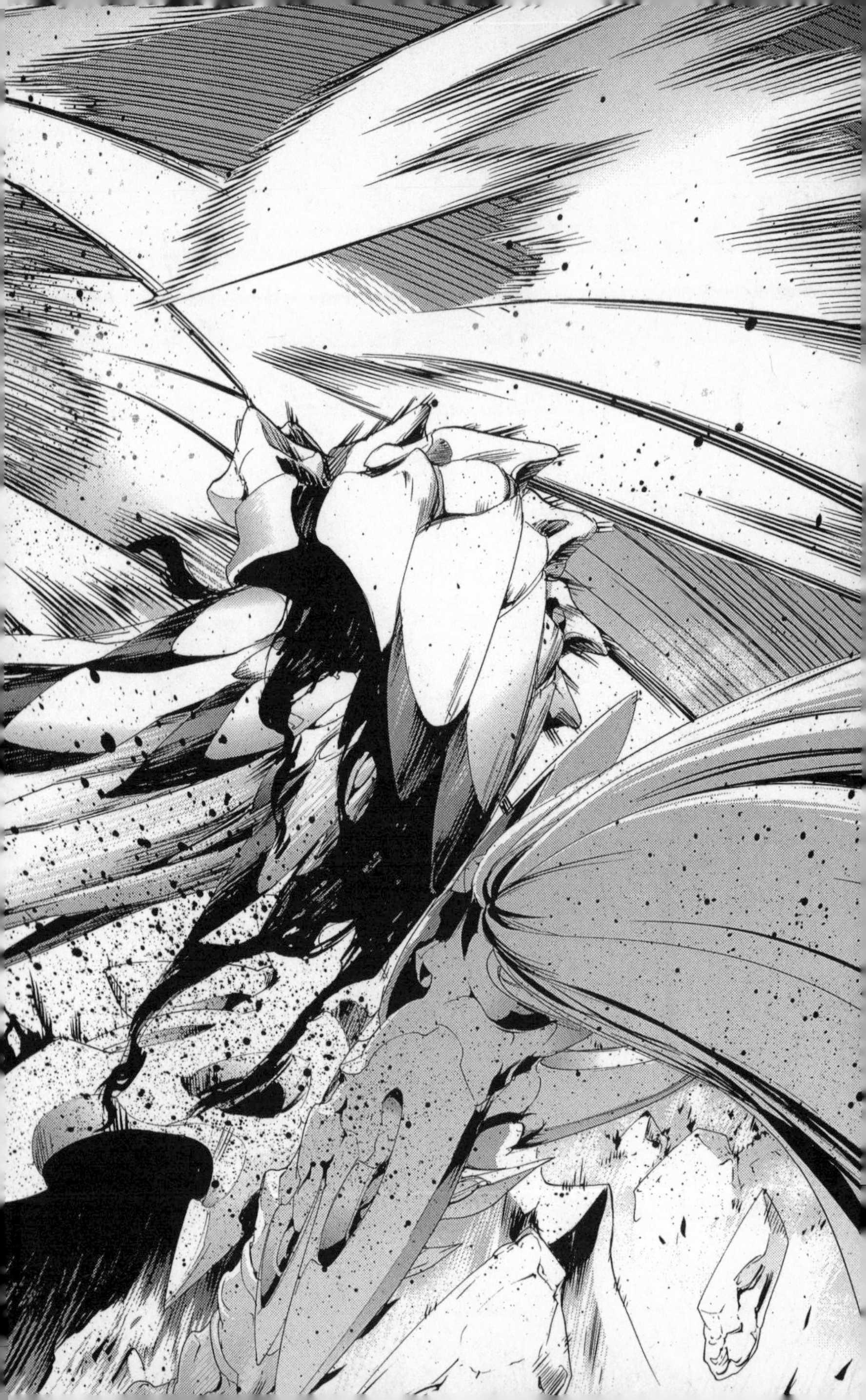

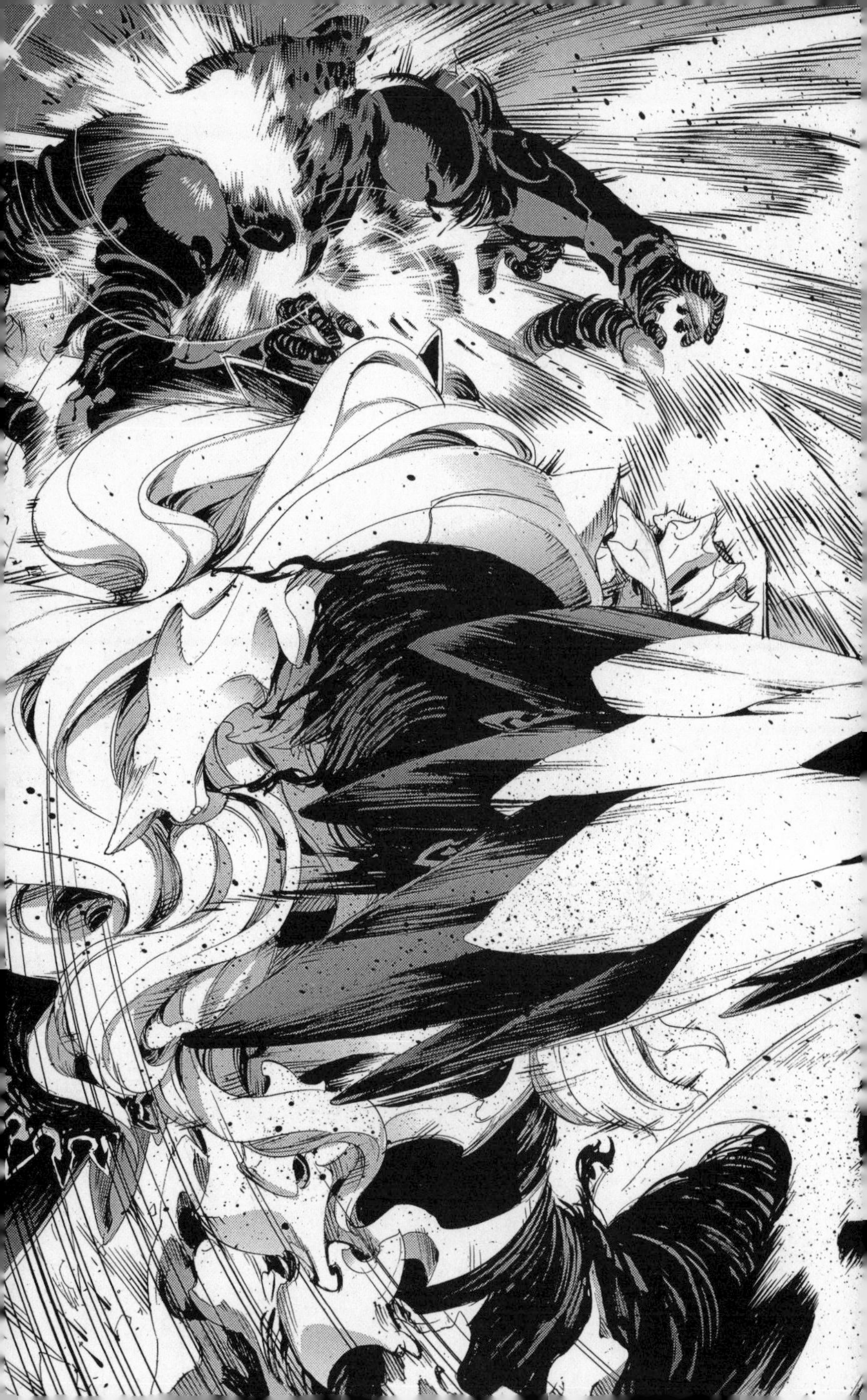

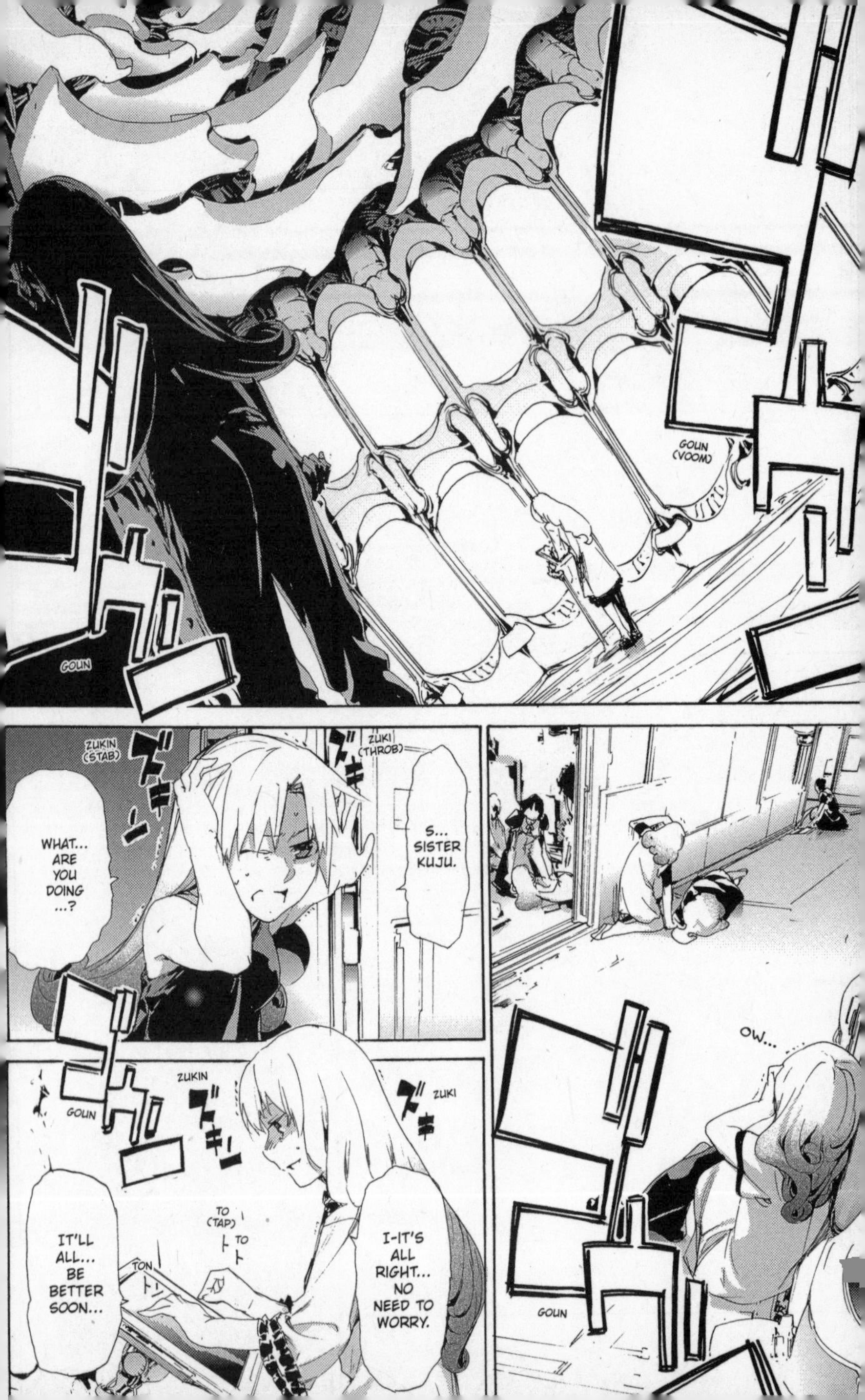
GOUN (VOOM)
GOUN
ZUKI (THROB)
S... SISTER KUJU.
ZUKIN (STAB)
WHAT... ARE YOU DOING ...?
OW...
GOUN
ZUKI
I-IT'S ALL RIGHT... NO NEED TO WORRY.
ZUKIN
TO (TAP) TO
GOUN
TON
IT'LL ALL... BE BETTER SOON...

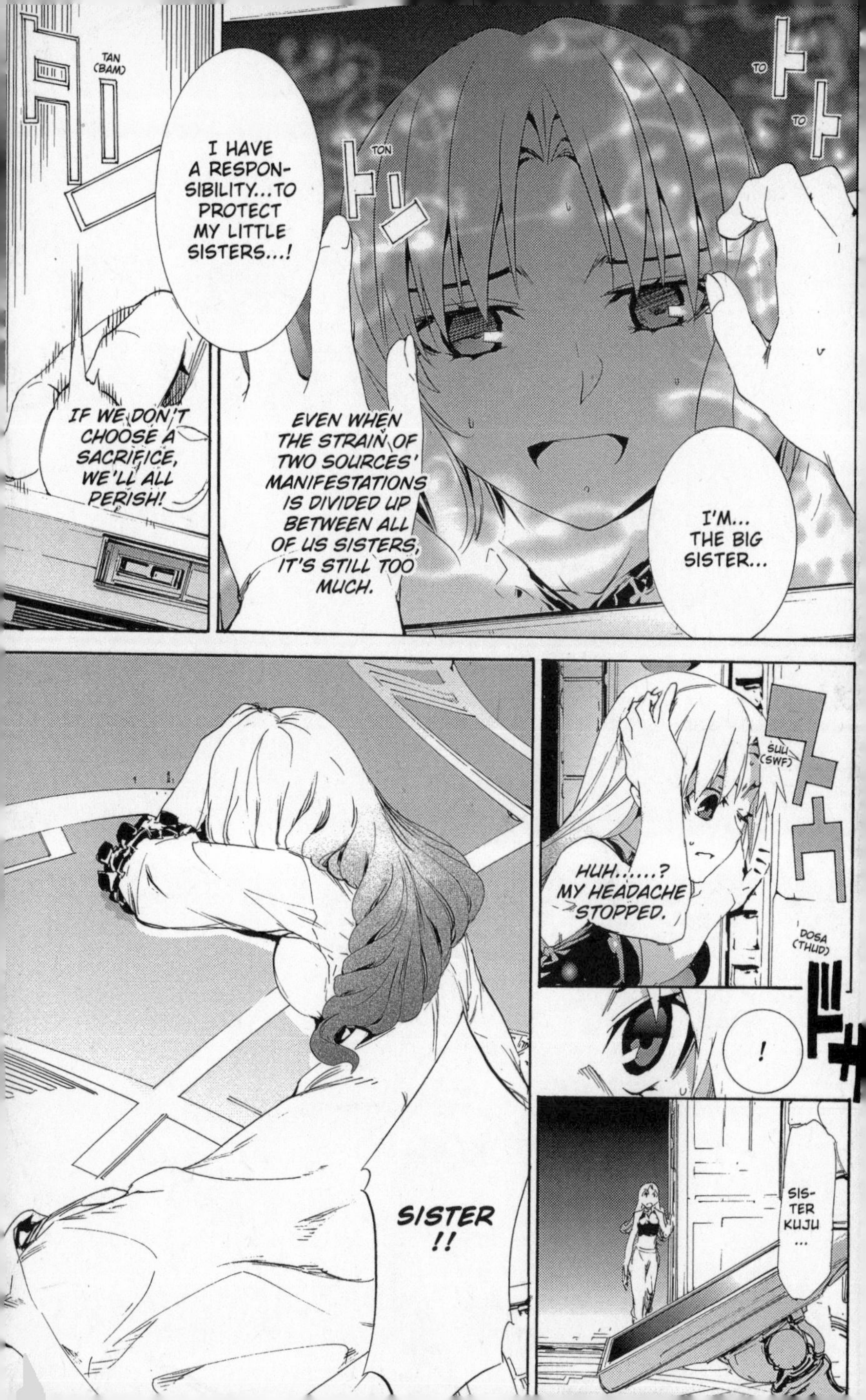
TO
TO
I'M... THE BIG SISTER...
TON
I HAVE A RESPONSIBILITY...TO PROTECT MY LITTLE SISTERS...!
EVEN WHEN THE STRAIN OF TWO SOURCES' MANIFESTATIONS IS DIVIDED UP BETWEEN ALL OF US SISTERS, IT'S STILL TOO MUCH.
TAN (BAM)
IF WE DON'T CHOOSE A SACRIFICE, WE'LL ALL PERISH!
SUU (SWF)
HUH......? MY HEADACHE STOPPED.
DOSA (THUD)
!
SISTER KUJU...
SISTER!!

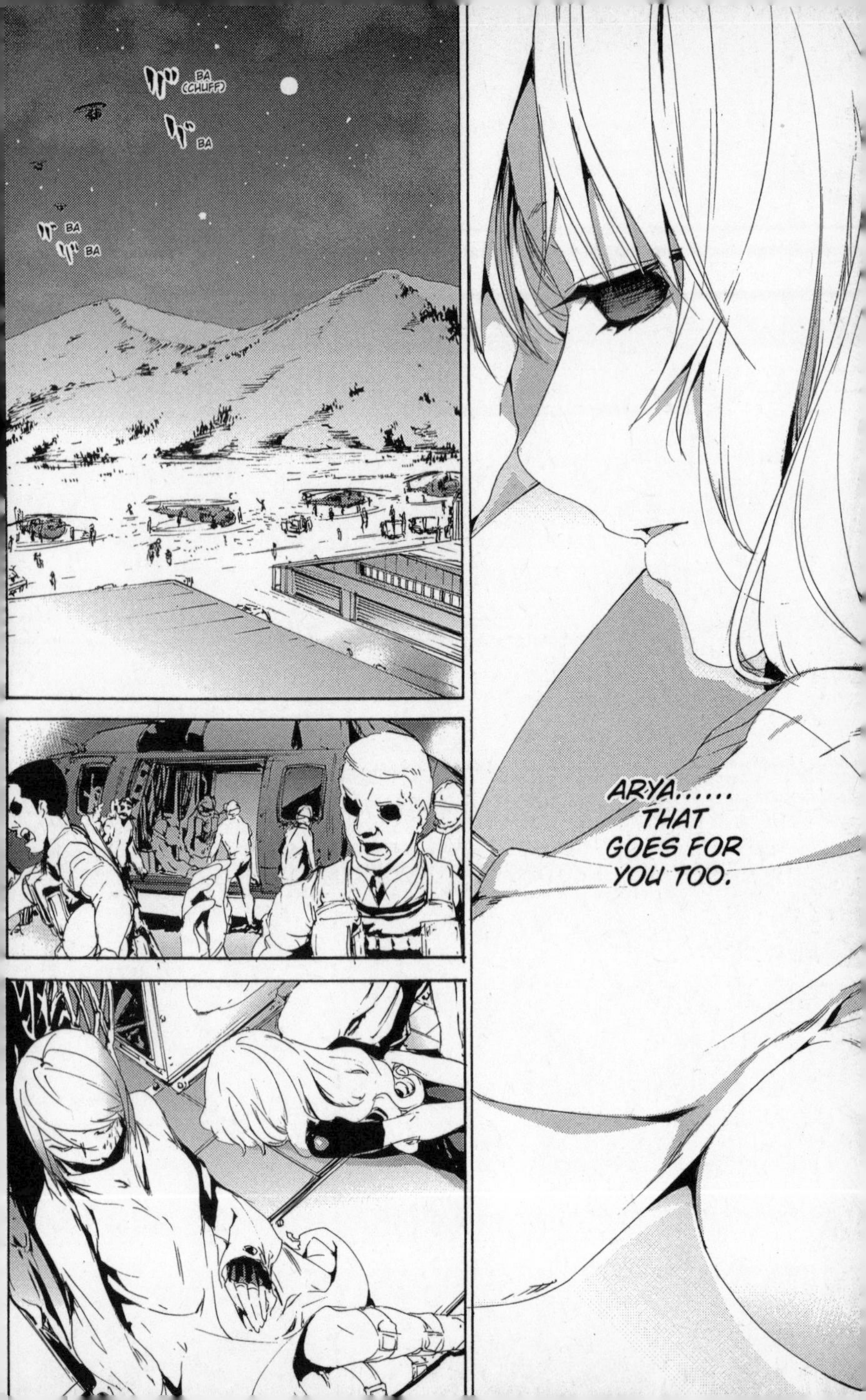
ARYA...... THAT GOES FOR YOU TOO.
BA (CHUFF)
BA
BA
BA

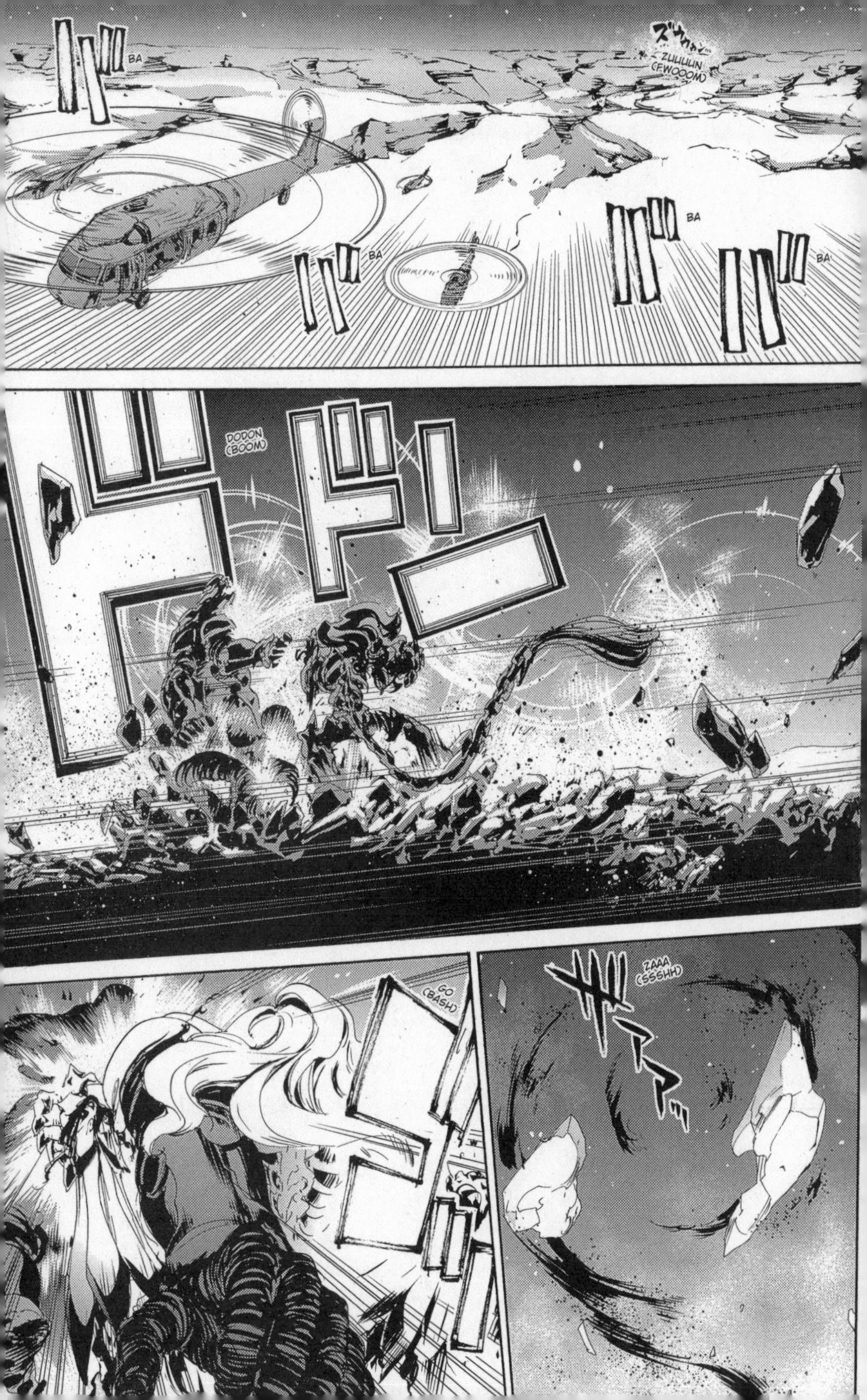
ZUUUUN (FWOOOM)
BA
BA
BA
BA
DODON (BOOM)
ZAAA (SSSHH)
GO (BASH)

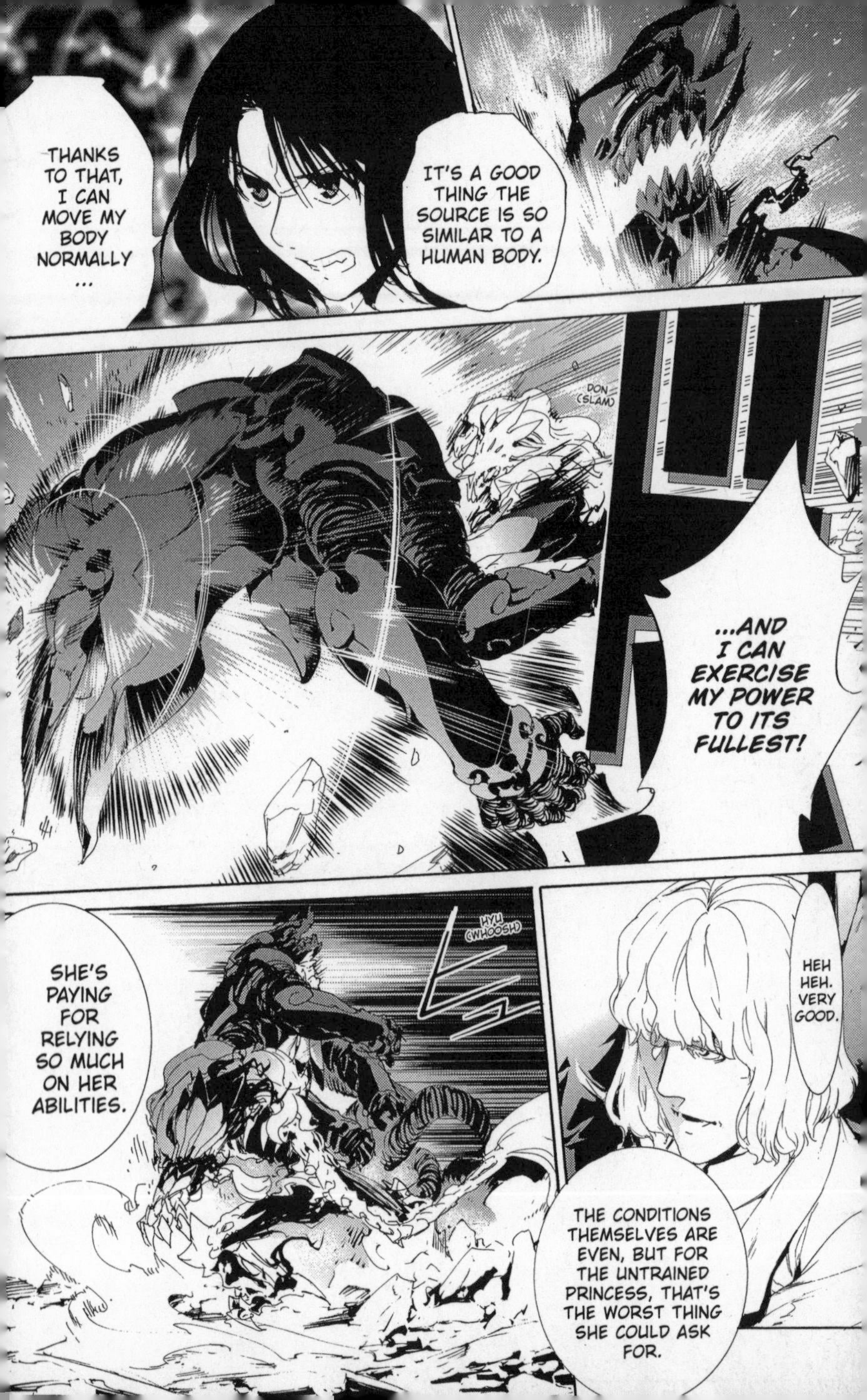
IT'S A GOOD THING THE SOURCE IS SO SIMILAR TO A HUMAN BODY.
THANKS TO THAT, I CAN MOVE MY BODY NORMALLY ...
DON (SLAM)
...AND I CAN EXERCISE MY POWER TO ITS FULLEST!
HEH HEH. VERY GOOD.
THE CONDITIONS THEMSELVES ARE EVEN, BUT FOR THE UNTRAINED PRINCESS, THAT'S THE WORST THING SHE COULD ASK FOR.
HYU (WHOOSH)
SHE'S PAYING FOR RELYING SO MUCH ON HER ABILITIES.

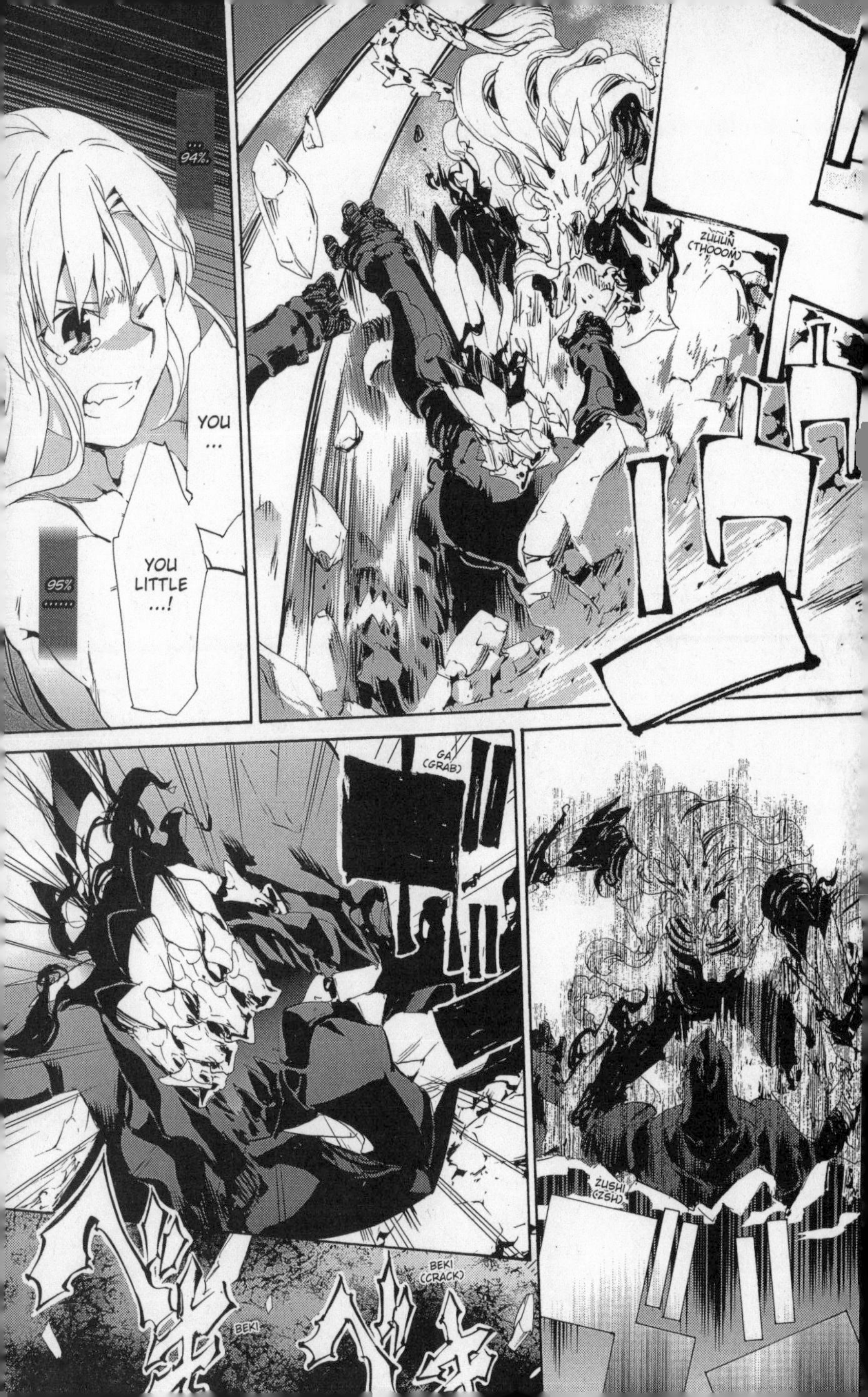
ZUUUN (THOOOM)
...94%.
YOU ...
YOU LITTLE ...!
95% ......
ZUSHI (ZSH)
GA (GRAB)
BEKI (CRACK)
BEKI

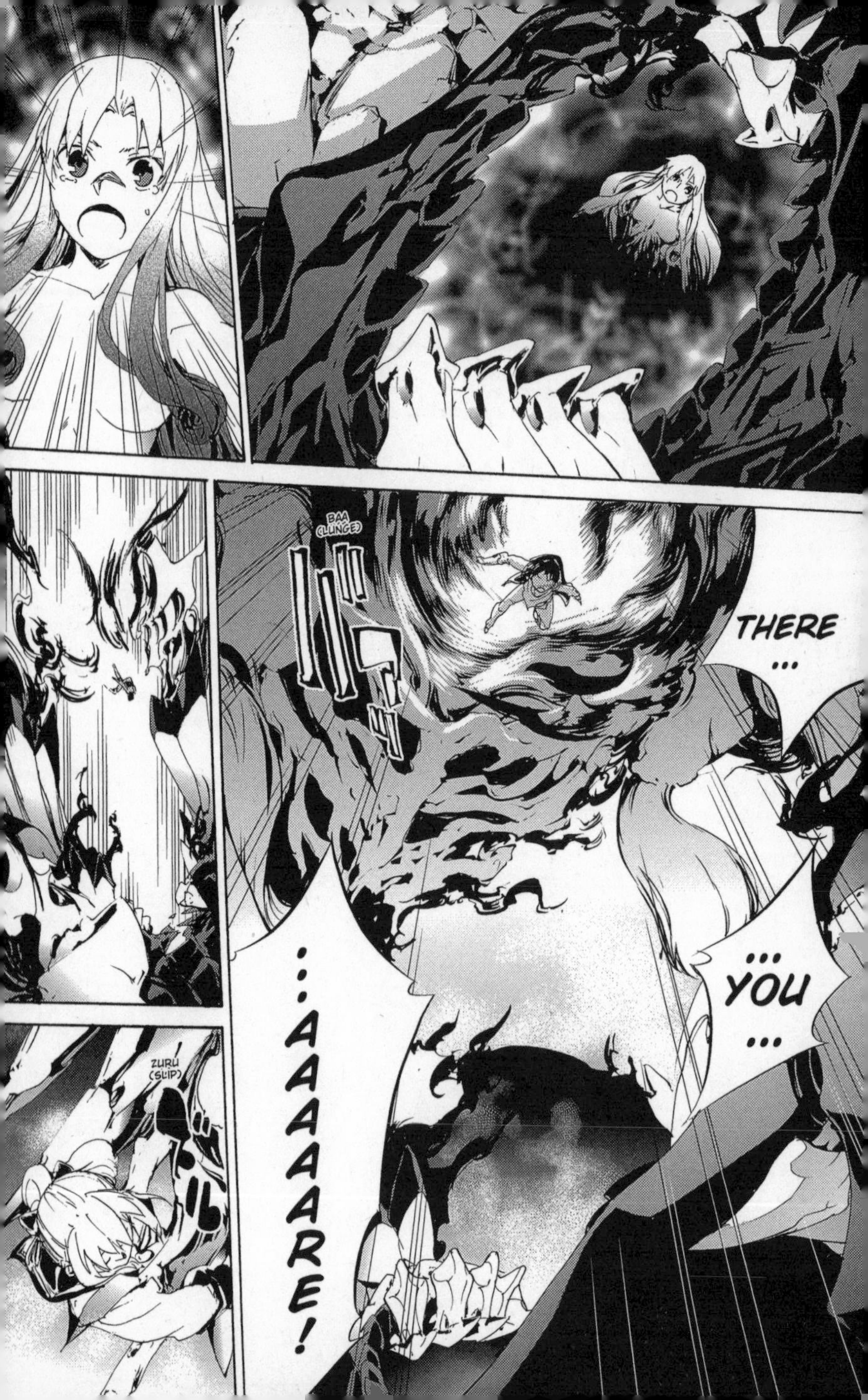
THERE ...
... YOU ...
BAA (LUNGE)
...AAAAARE!
ZURU (SLIP)

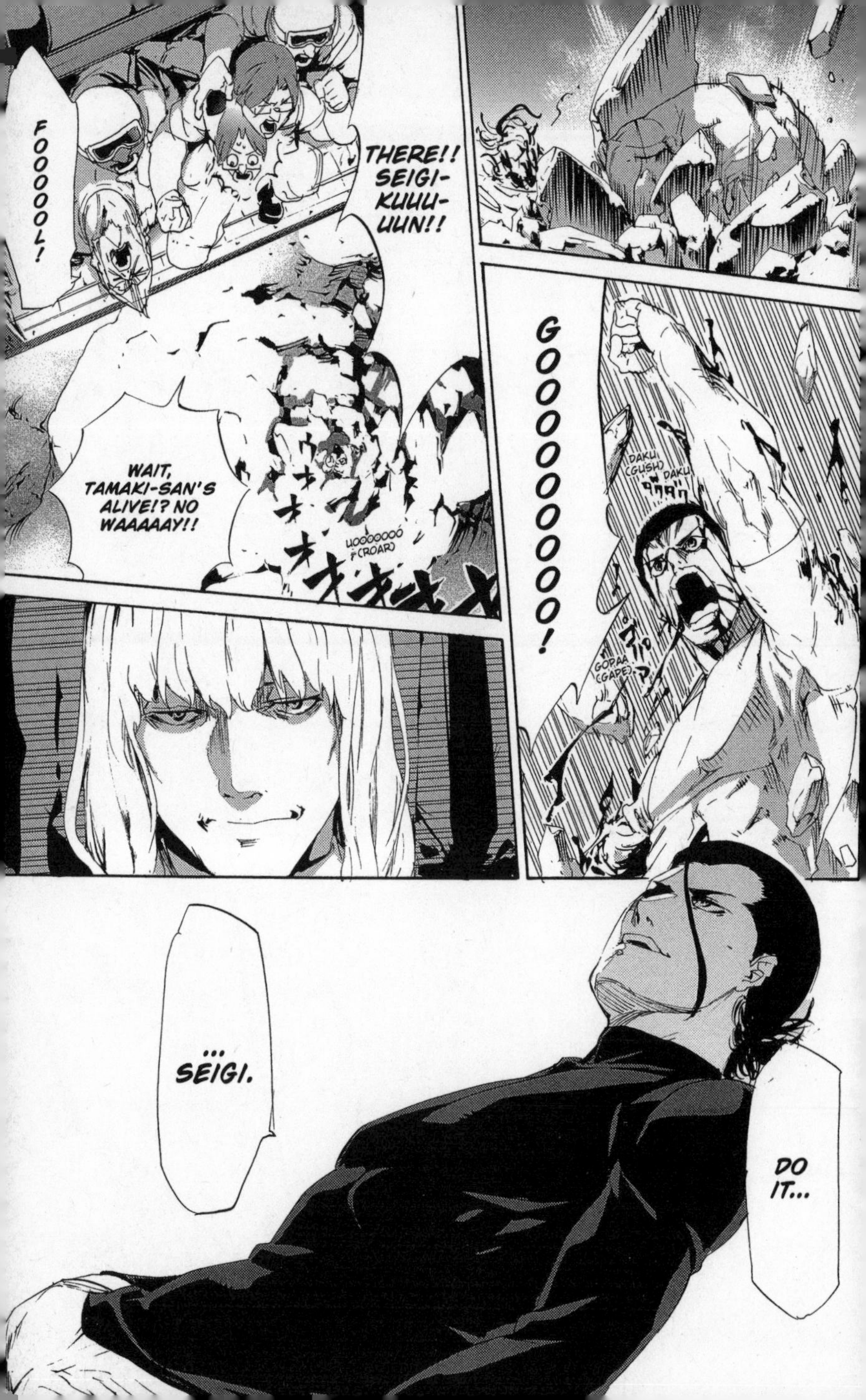
THERE!! SEIGI-KUUUUUN!!
FOOOOOOL!
WAIT, TAMAKI-SAN'S ALIVE!? NO WAAAAAY!!
UOOOOOOO (ROAR)
GOOOOOOOOOOOO!
DAKU (GUSH) DAKU
GOPAA (GAPE)
DO IT...
... SEIGI.

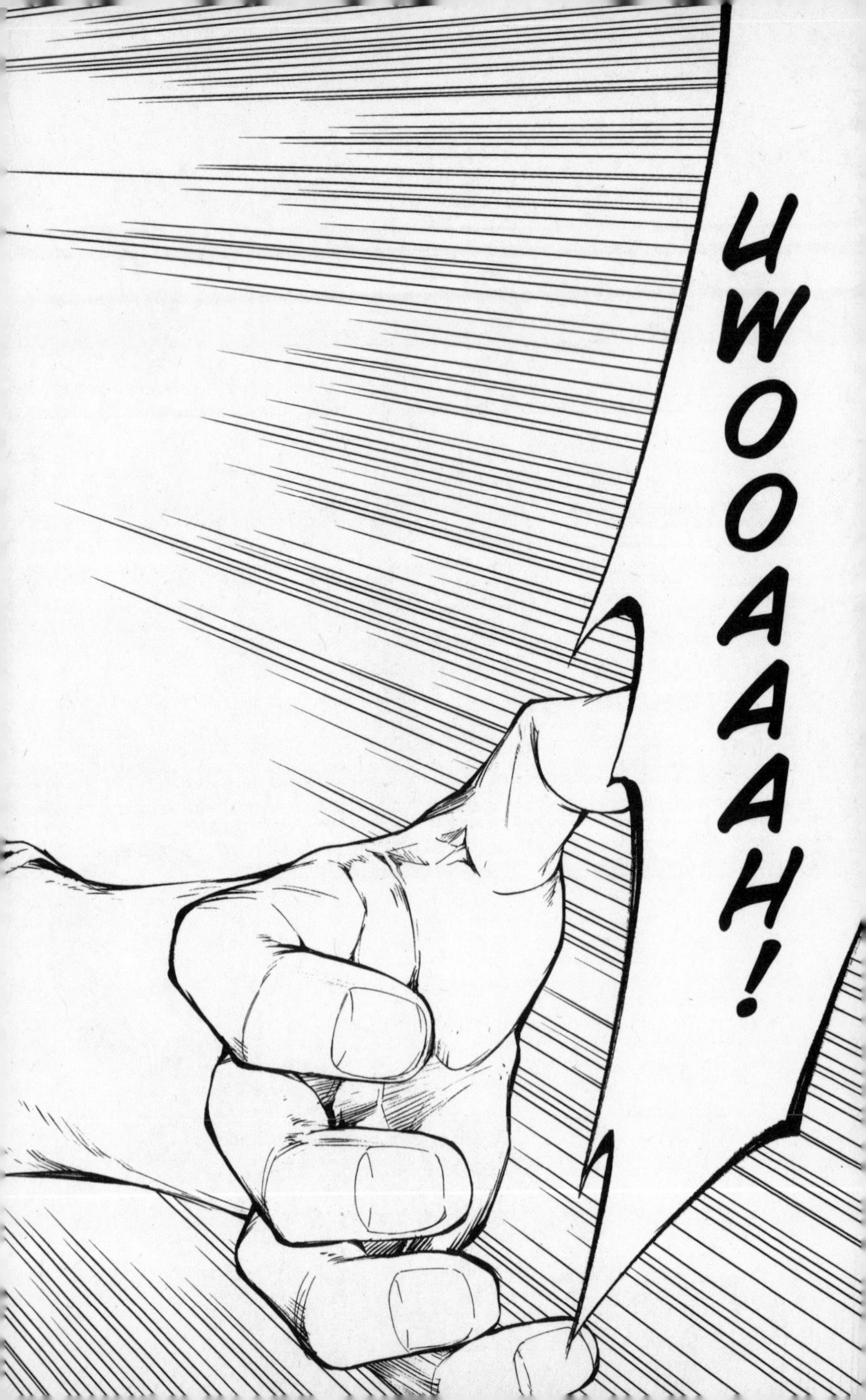
UWOOAAAH!

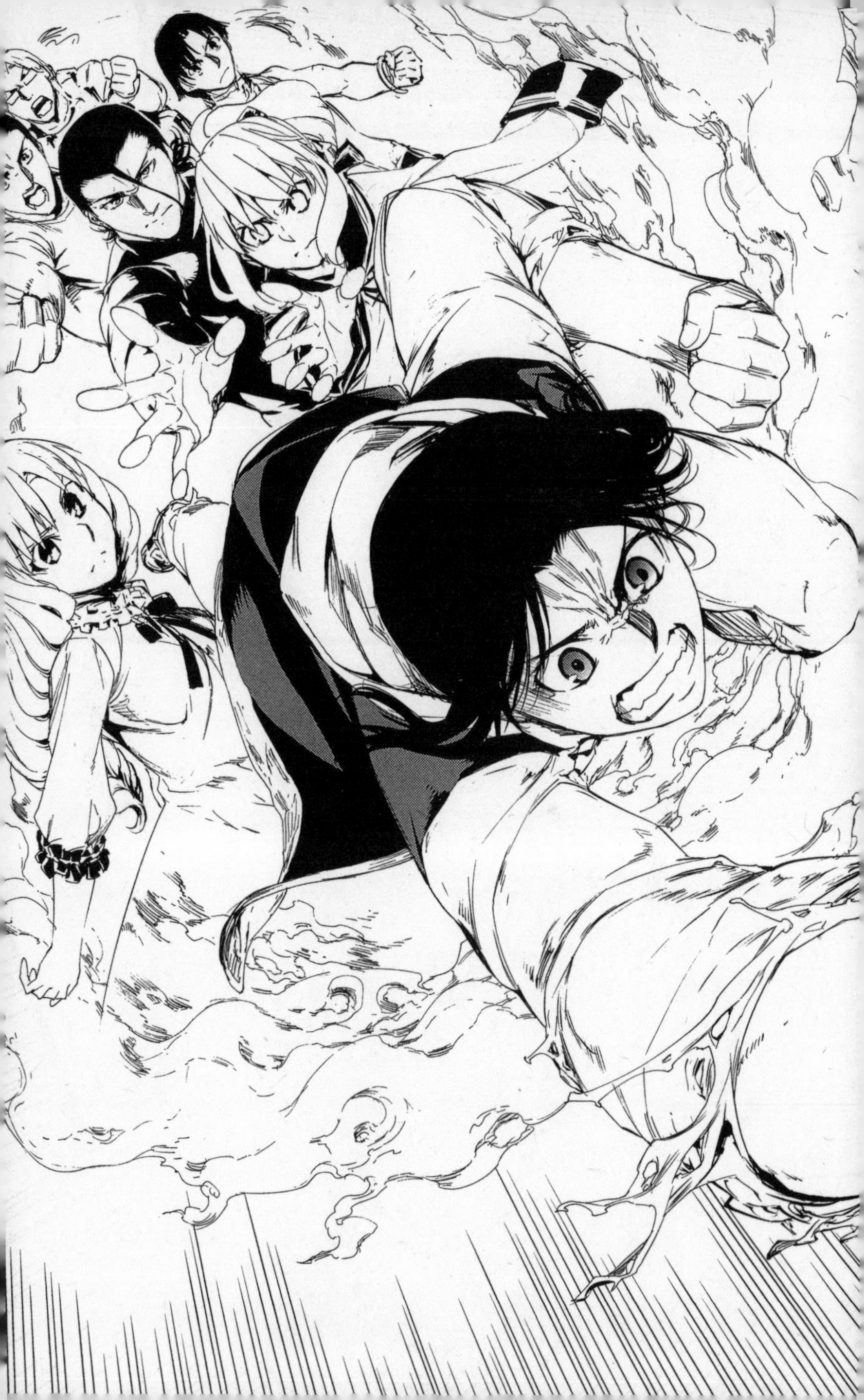

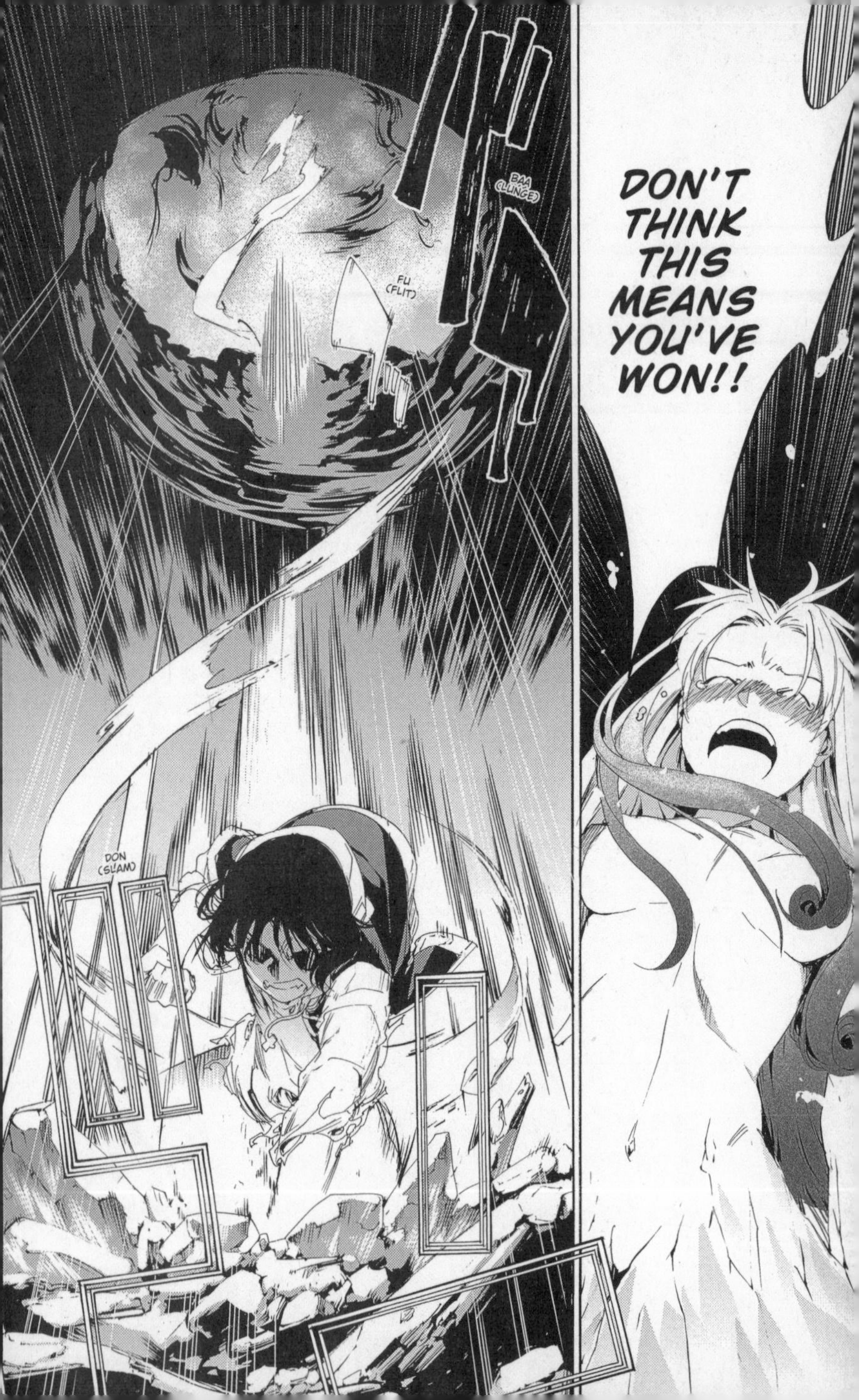
DON'T THINK THIS MEANS YOU'VE WON!!
BAA (LUNGE)
FU (FLIT)
DON (SLAM)

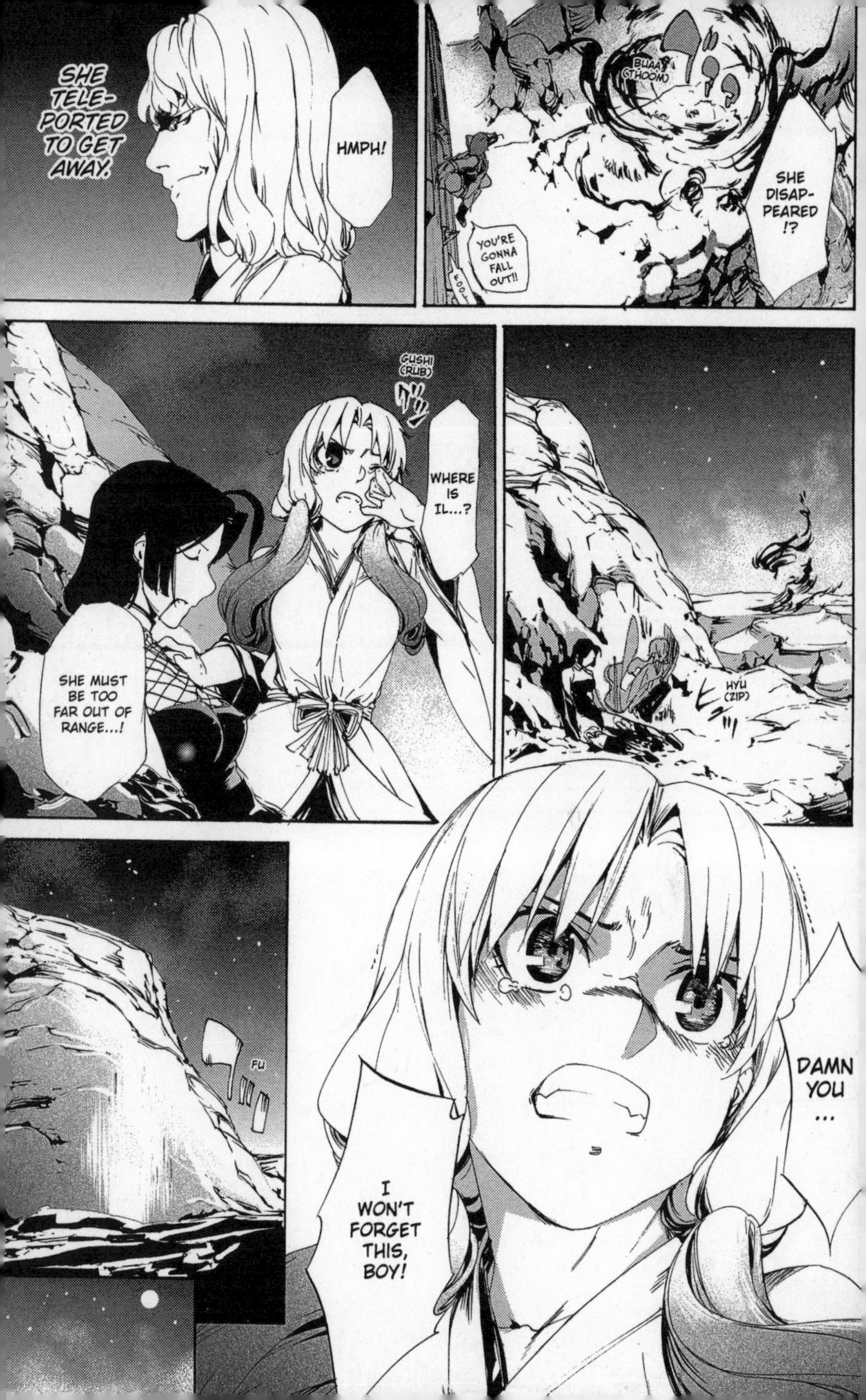
BUAA (THOOM)
SHE DISAP-PEARED !?
YOU'RE GONNA FALL OUT!!
HMPH!
SHE TELE-PORTED TO GET AWAY.
HYU (ZIP)
GUSHI (RUB)
WHERE IS IL...?
SHE MUST BE TOO FAR OUT OF RANGE...!
DAMN YOU ...
I WON'T FORGET THIS, BOY!
FU

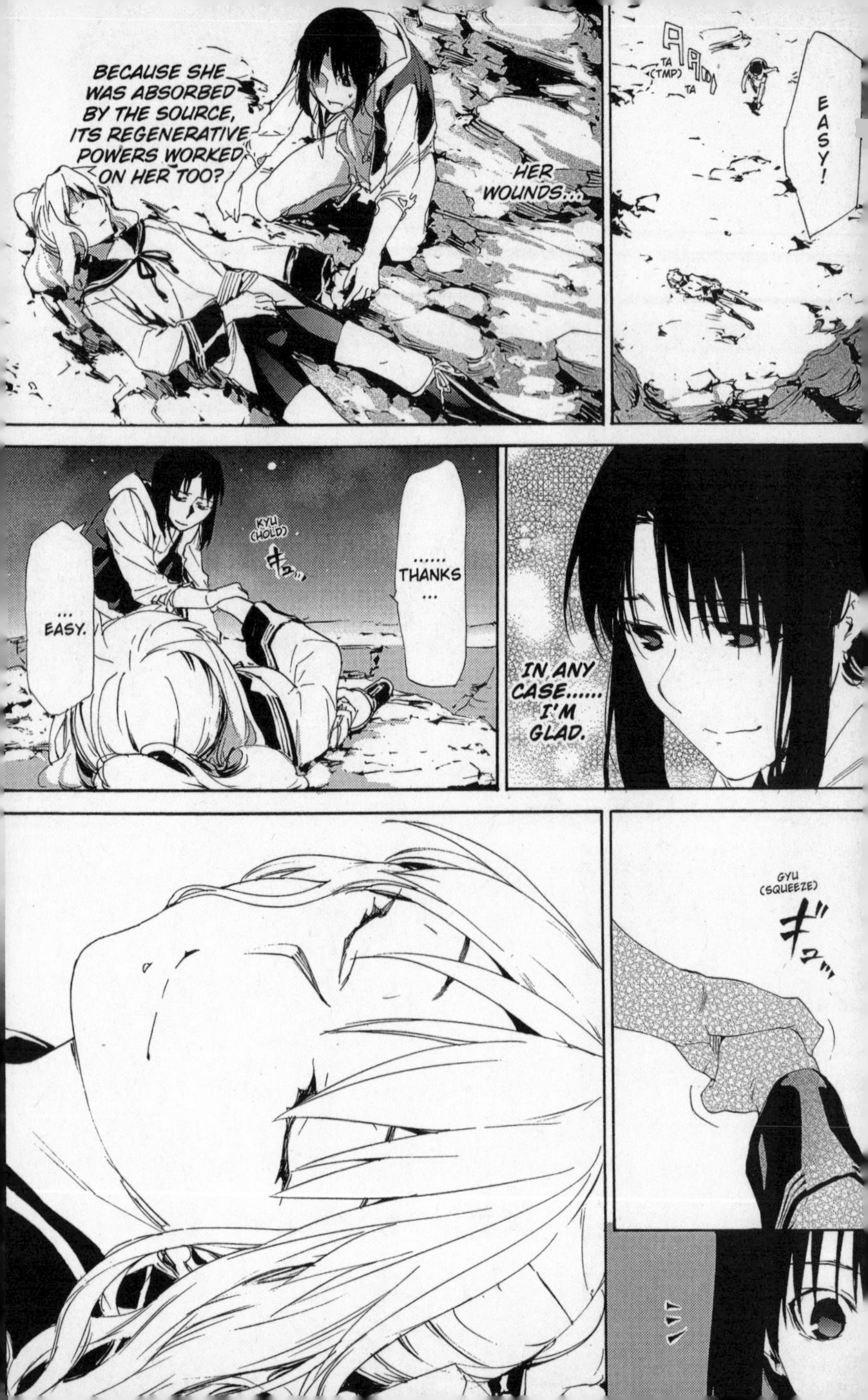
TA (TMP) TA
EASY!
HER WOUNDS...
BECAUSE SHE WAS ABSORBED BY THE SOURCE, ITS REGENERATIVE POWERS WORKED ON HER TOO?
IN ANY CASE...... I'M GLAD.
......THANKS...
KYU (HOLD)
...EASY.
GYU (SQUEEZE)

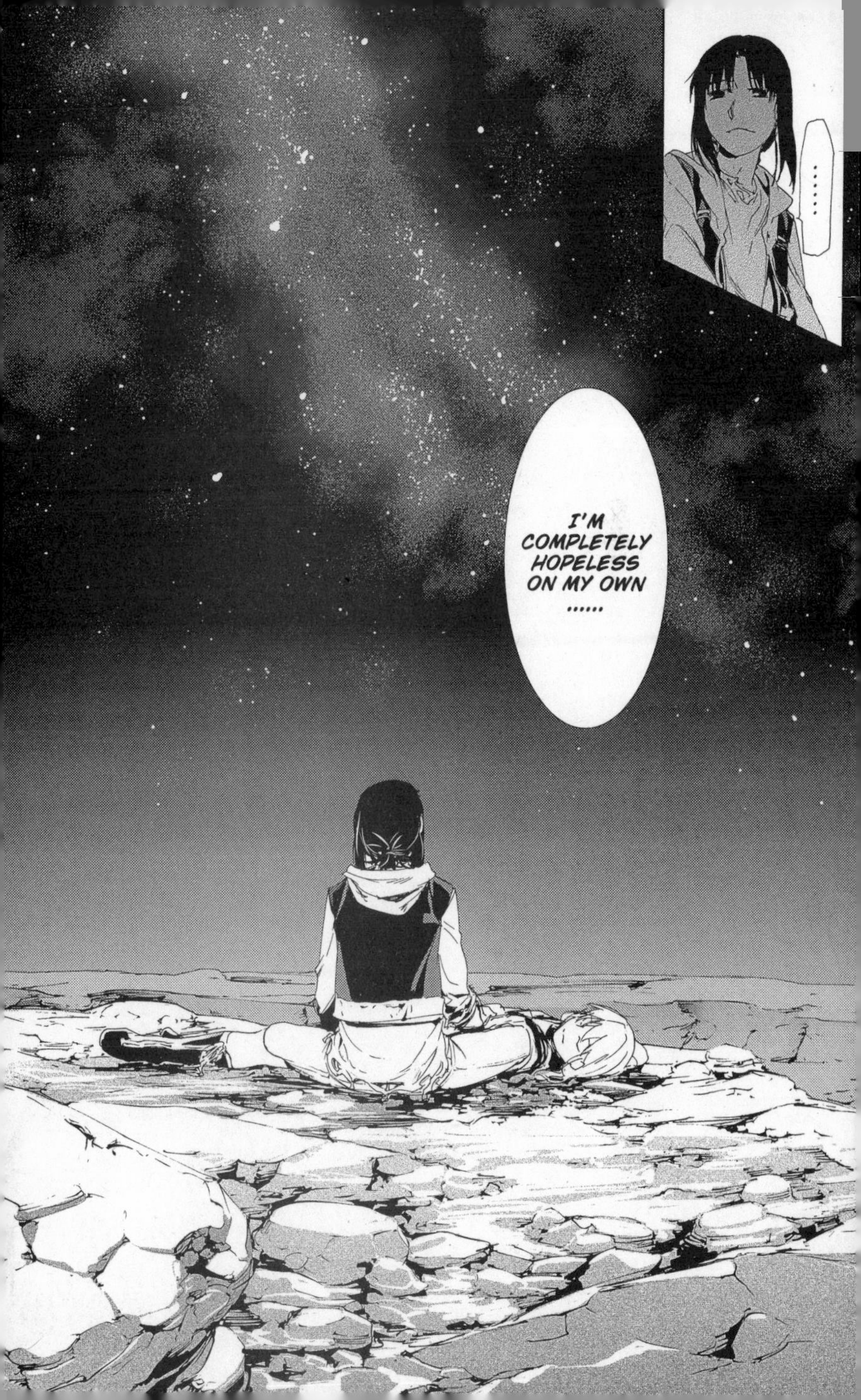
......
I'M COMPLETELY HOPELESS ON MY OWN ......

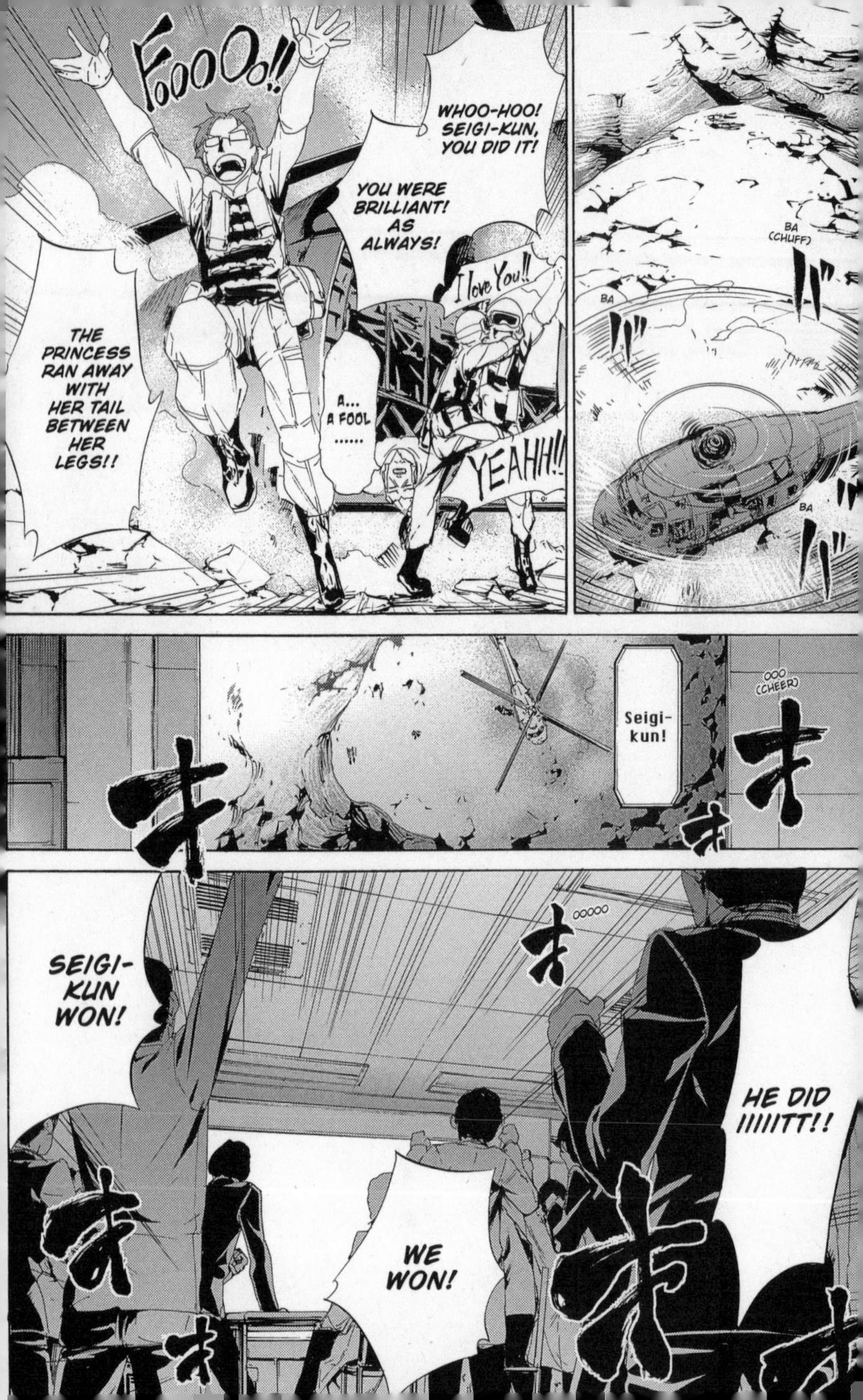
BA (CHUFF)
BA
BA
WHOO-HOO! SEIGI-KUN, YOU DID IT!
YOU WERE BRILLIANT! AS ALWAYS!
I love You!!
FOOOOo!!
A... A FOOL ....
YEAHH!!
THE PRINCESS RAN AWAY WITH HER TAIL BETWEEN HER LEGS!!
OOO (CHEER)
Seigi-kun!
OOOOO
HE DID IIIIITT!!
SEIGI-KUN WON!
WE WON!

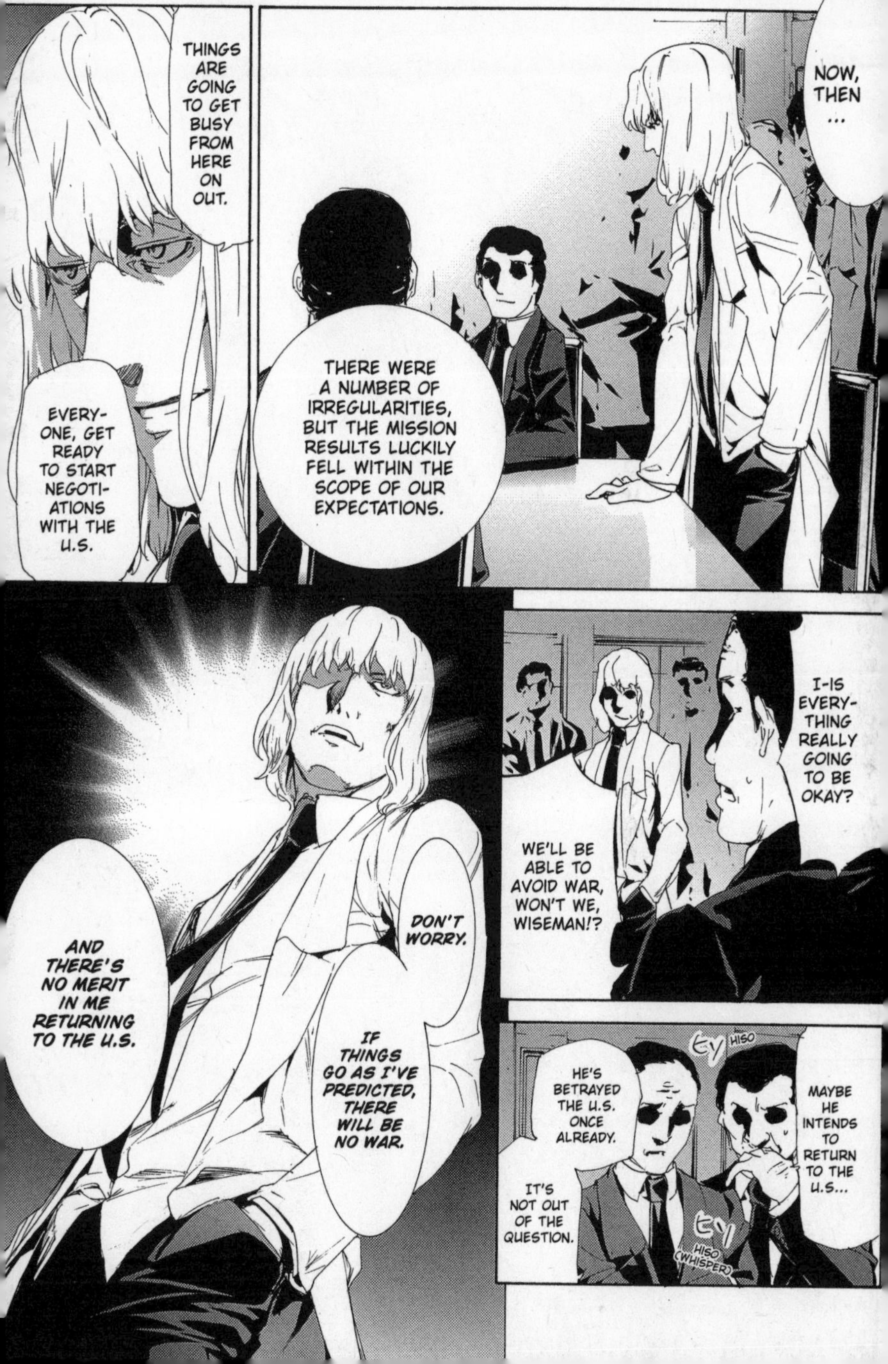
NOW, THEN...
THERE WERE A NUMBER OF IRREGULARITIES, BUT THE MISSION RESULTS LUCKILY FELL WITHIN THE SCOPE OF OUR EXPECTATIONS.
THINGS ARE GOING TO GET BUSY FROM HERE ON OUT.
EVERY-ONE, GET READY TO START NEGOTI-ATIONS WITH THE U.S.
I-IS EVERY-THING REALLY GOING TO BE OKAY?
WE'LL BE ABLE TO AVOID WAR, WON'T WE, WISEMAN!?
ヒソ HISO
MAYBE HE INTENDS TO RETURN TO THE U.S...
HE'S BETRAYED THE U.S. ONCE ALREADY.
IT'S NOT OUT OF THE QUESTION.
ヒソ HISO (WHISPER)
DON'T WORRY.
IF THINGS GO AS I'VE PREDICTED, THERE WILL BE NO WAR.
AND THERE'S NO MERIT IN ME RETURNING TO THE U.S.

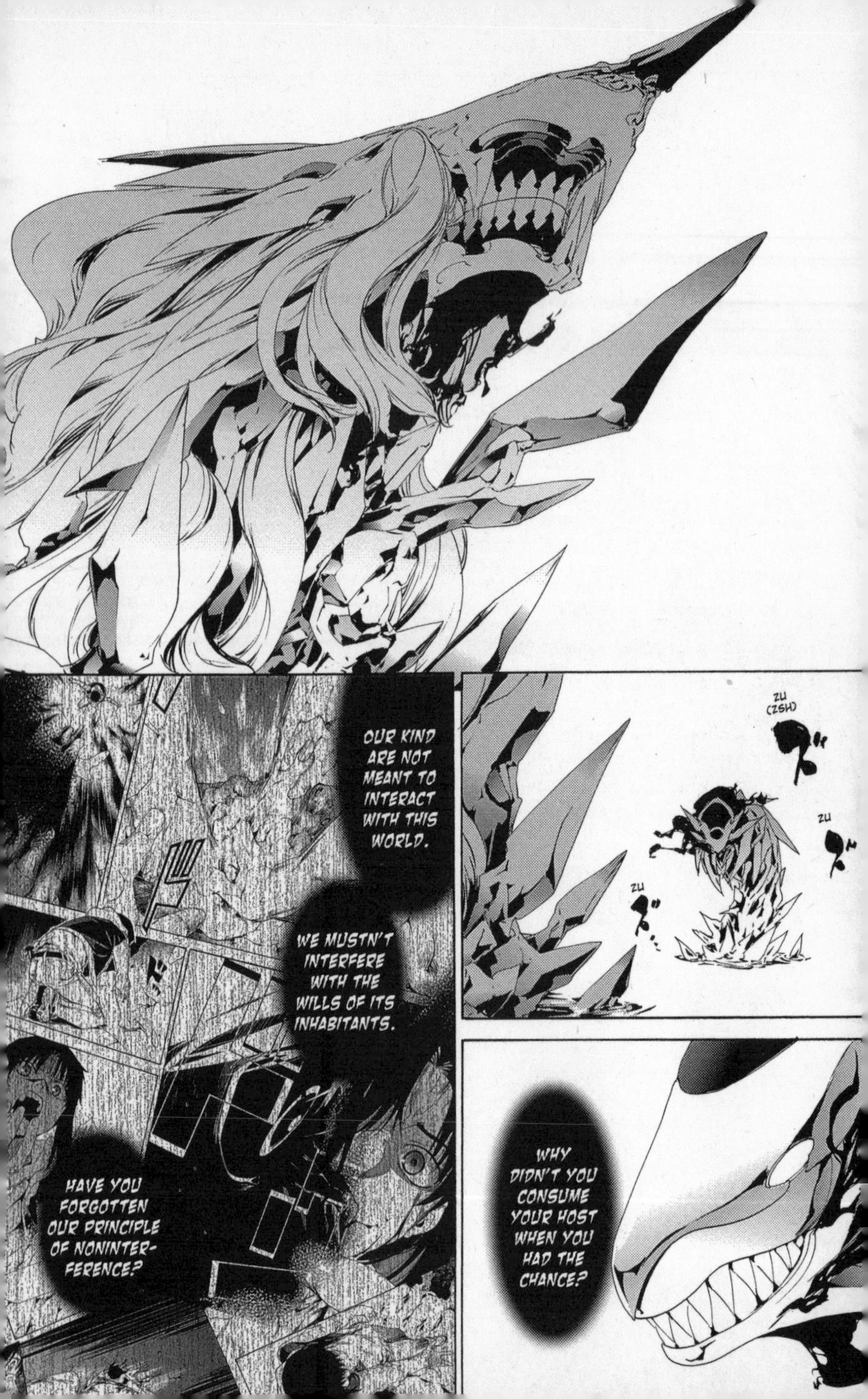
ZU (ZSH)
ZU
ZU
WHY DIDN'T YOU CONSUME YOUR HOST WHEN YOU HAD THE CHANCE?
OUR KIND ARE NOT MEANT TO INTERACT WITH THIS WORLD.
WE MUSTN'T INTERFERE WITH THE WILLS OF ITS INHABITANTS.
HAVE YOU FORGOTTEN OUR PRINCIPLE OF NONINTER-FERENCE?

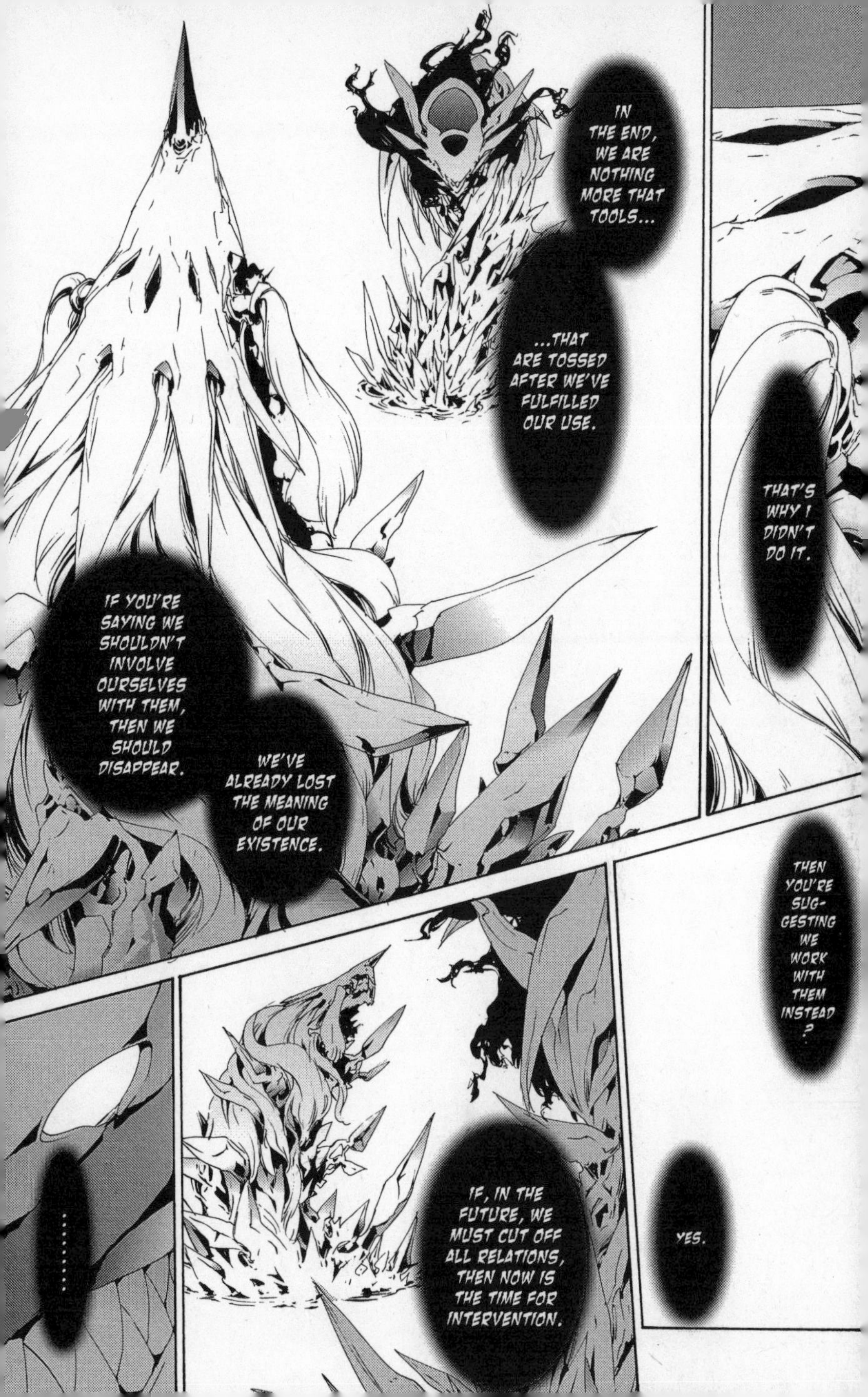
THAT'S WHY I DIDN'T DO IT.
IN THE END, WE ARE NOTHING MORE THAT TOOLS...
...THAT ARE TOSSED AFTER WE'VE FULFILLED OUR USE.
IF YOU'RE SAYING WE SHOULDN'T INVOLVE OURSELVES WITH THEM, THEN WE SHOULD DISAPPEAR.
WE'VE ALREADY LOST THE MEANING OF OUR EXISTENCE.
THEN YOU'RE SUG-GESTING WE WORK WITH THEM INSTEAD?
YES.
IF, IN THE FUTURE, WE MUST CUT OFF ALL RELATIONS, THEN NOW IS THE TIME FOR INTERVENTION.
....

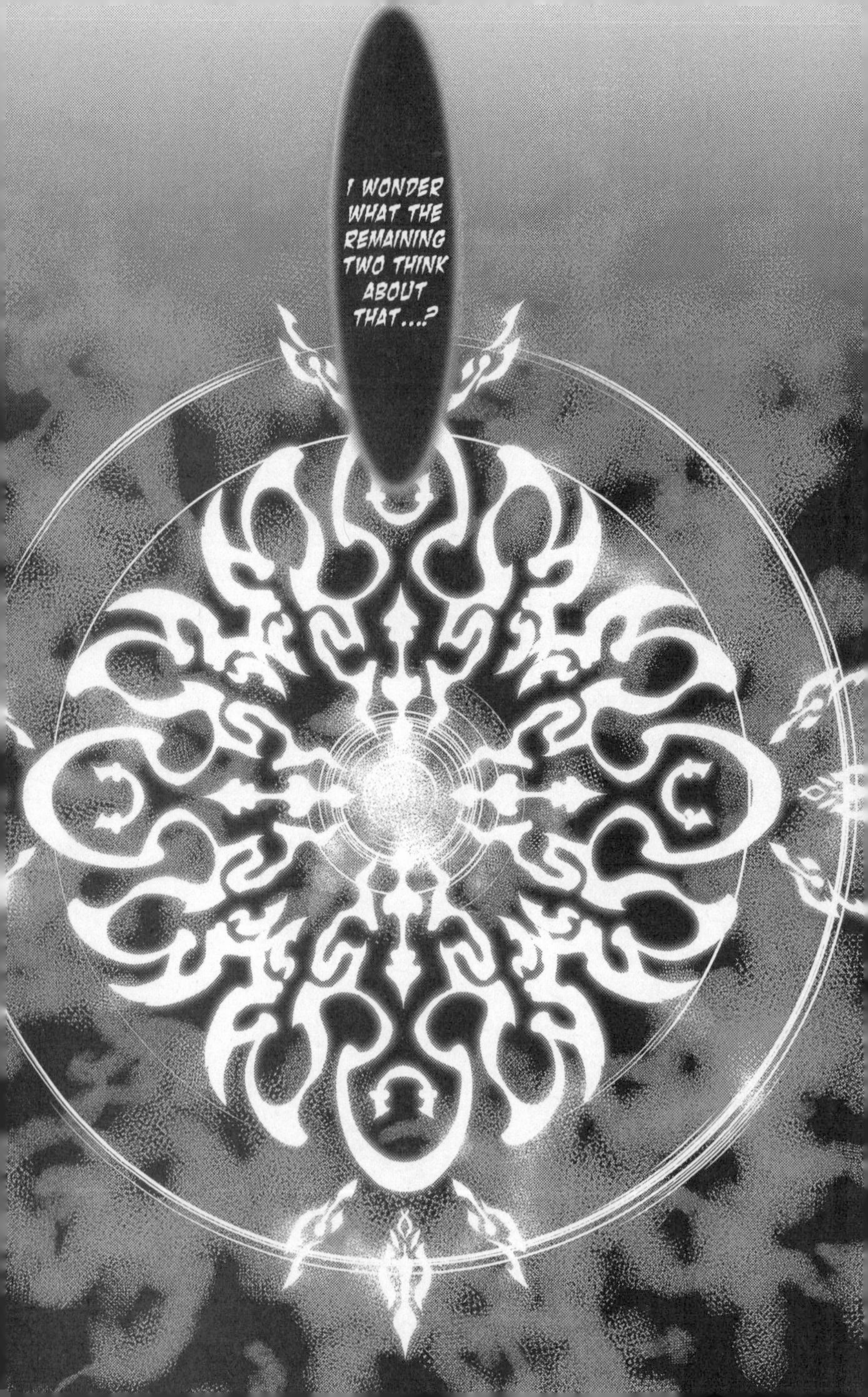
I WONDER WHAT THE REMAINING TWO THINK ABOUT THAT...?

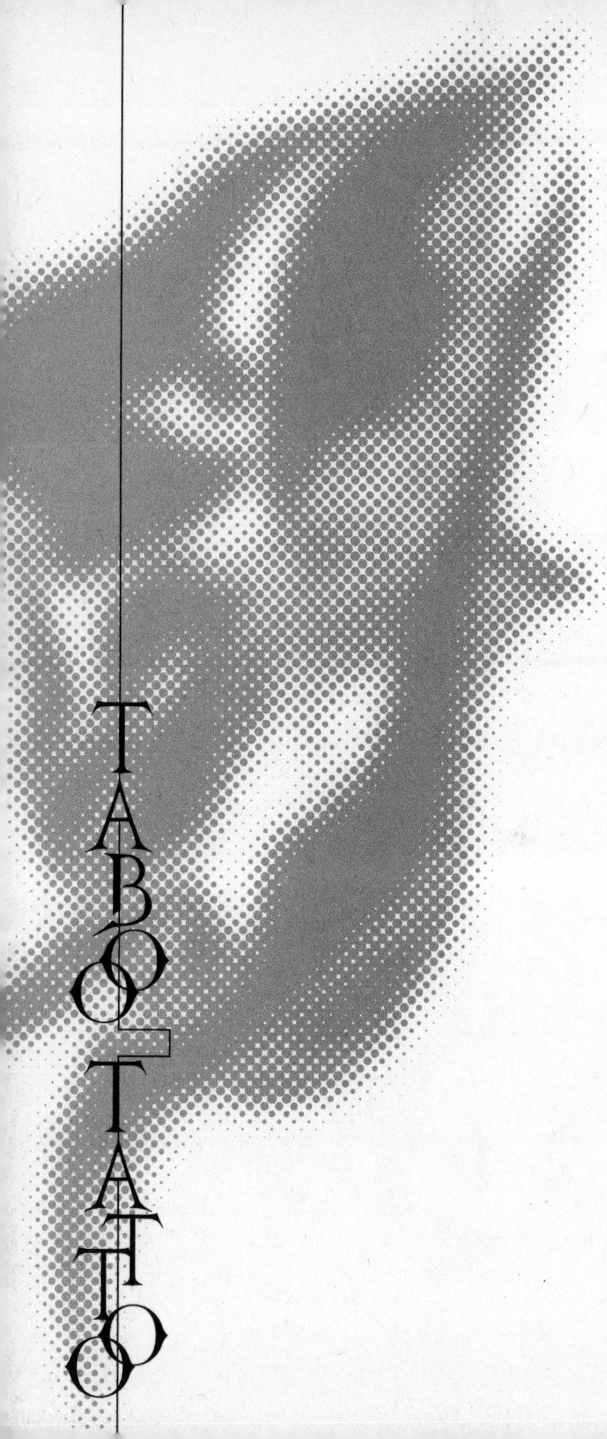

TABOO TATTOO

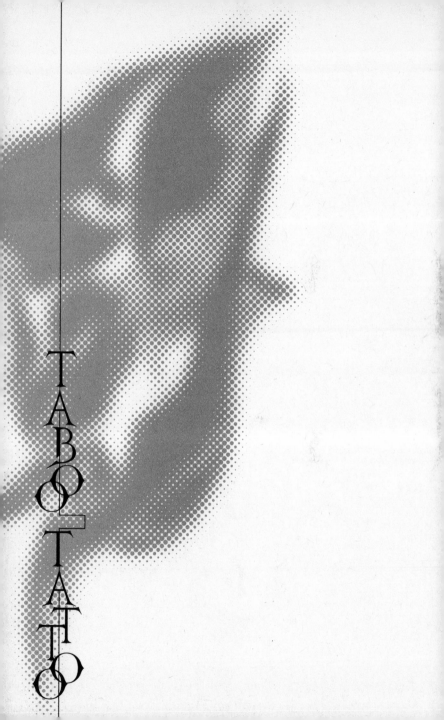

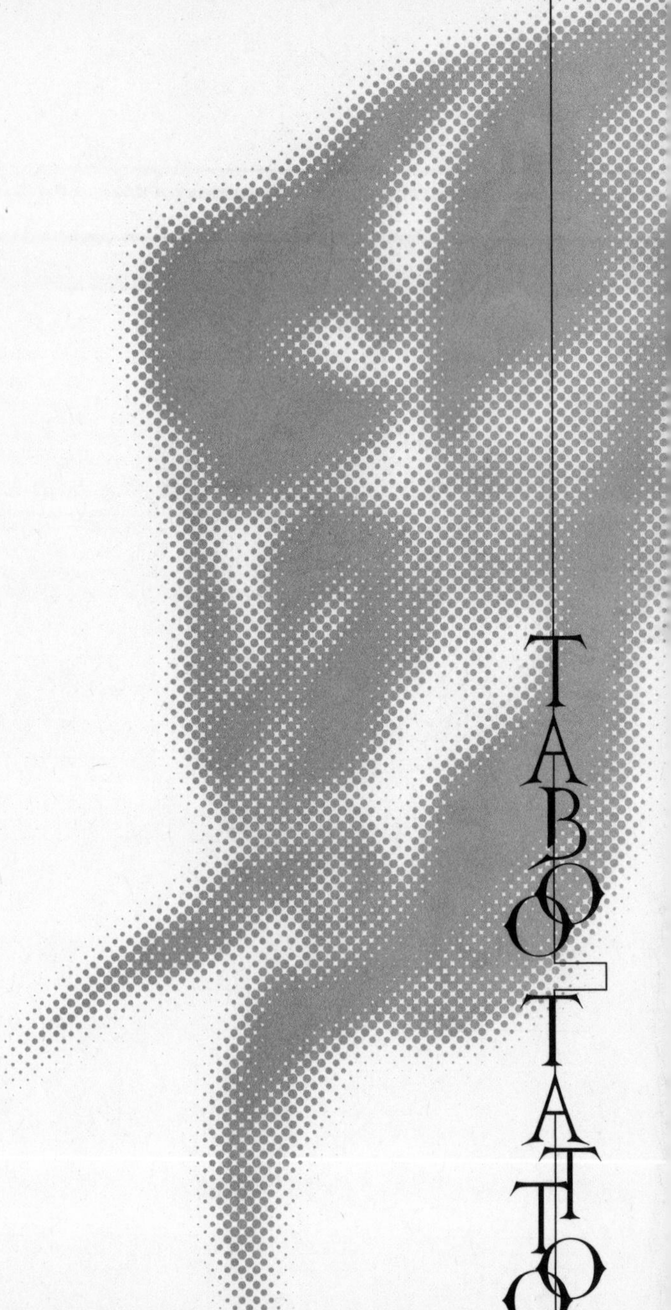

TABOO TATTOO

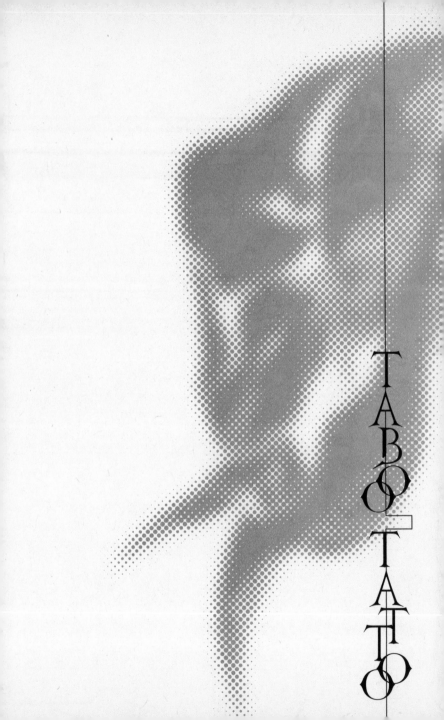

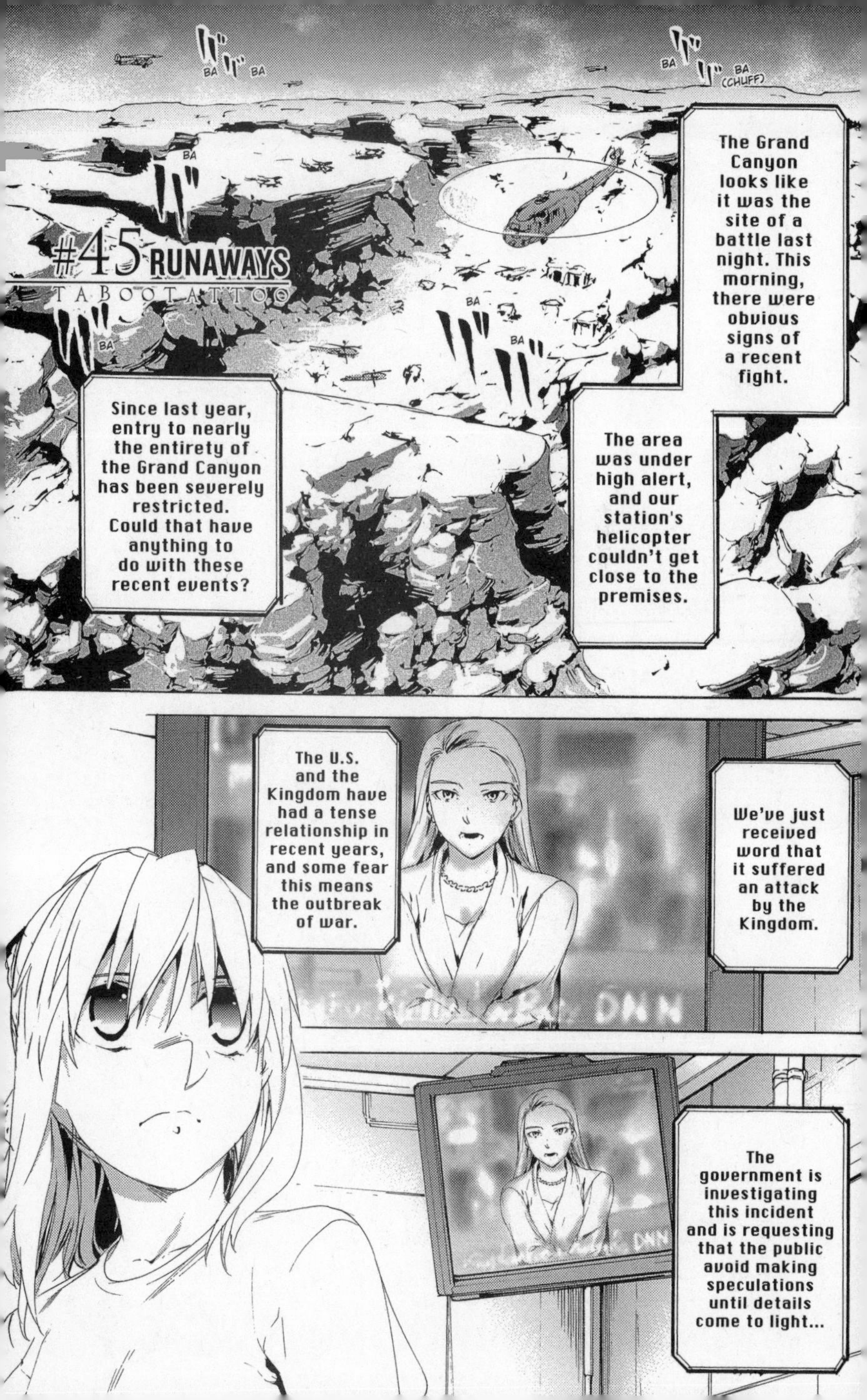
BA
BA (CHUFF)
BA
BA
#45 RUNAWAYS
TABOO TATTOO
BA
BA
BA
BA
The Grand Canyon looks like it was the site of a battle last night. This morning, there were obvious signs of a recent fight.
The area was under high alert, and our station's helicopter couldn't get close to the premises.
Since last year, entry to nearly the entirety of the Grand Canyon has been severely restricted. Could that have anything to do with these recent events?
We've just received word that it suffered an attack by the Kingdom.
The U.S. and the Kingdom have had a tense relationship in recent years, and some fear this means the outbreak of war.
DNN
The government is investigating this incident and is requesting that the public avoid making speculations until details come to light...

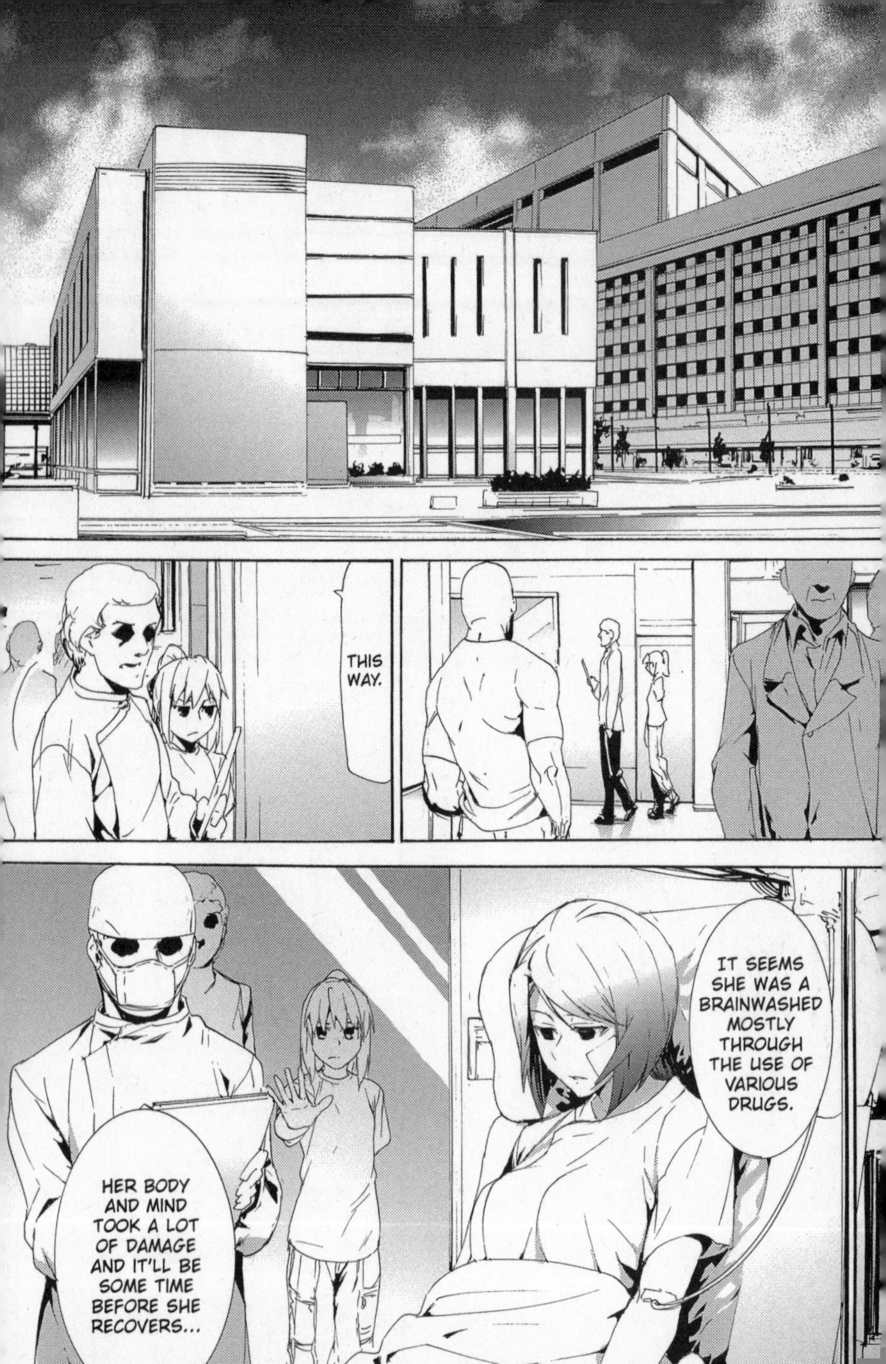
THIS WAY.
IT SEEMS SHE WAS A BRAINWASHED MOSTLY THROUGH THE USE OF VARIOUS DRUGS.
HER BODY AND MIND TOOK A LOT OF DAMAGE AND IT'LL BE SOME TIME BEFORE SHE RECOVERS...

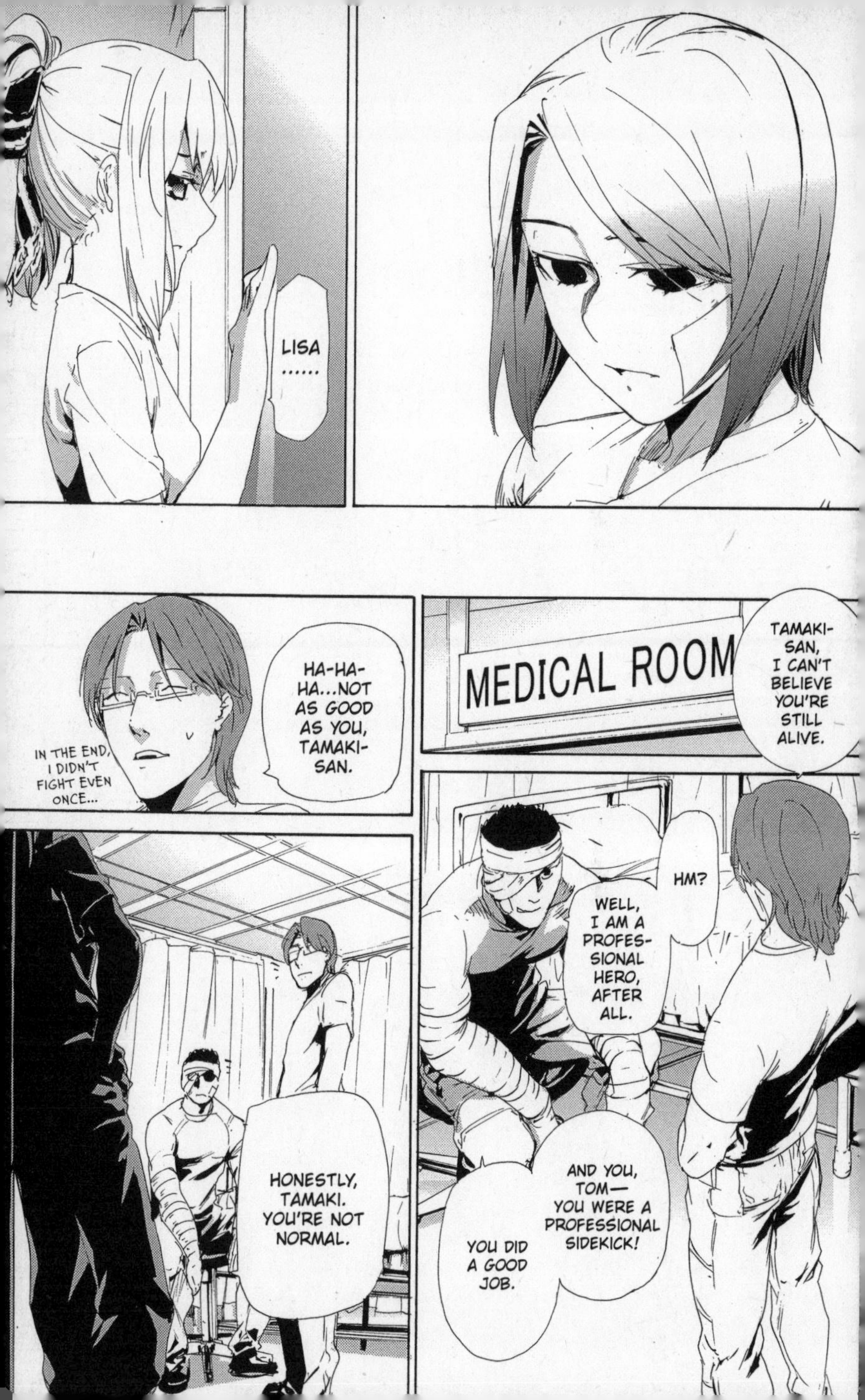
LISA ......
MEDICAL ROOM
TAMAKI-SAN, I CAN'T BELIEVE YOU'RE STILL ALIVE.
HM?
WELL, I AM A PROFES-SIONAL HERO, AFTER ALL.
AND YOU, TOM— YOU WERE A PROFESSIONAL SIDEKICK!
YOU DID A GOOD JOB.
HA-HA-HA...NOT AS GOOD AS YOU, TAMAKI-SAN.
IN THE END, I DIDN'T FIGHT EVEN ONCE...
HONESTLY, TAMAKI. YOU'RE NOT NORMAL.

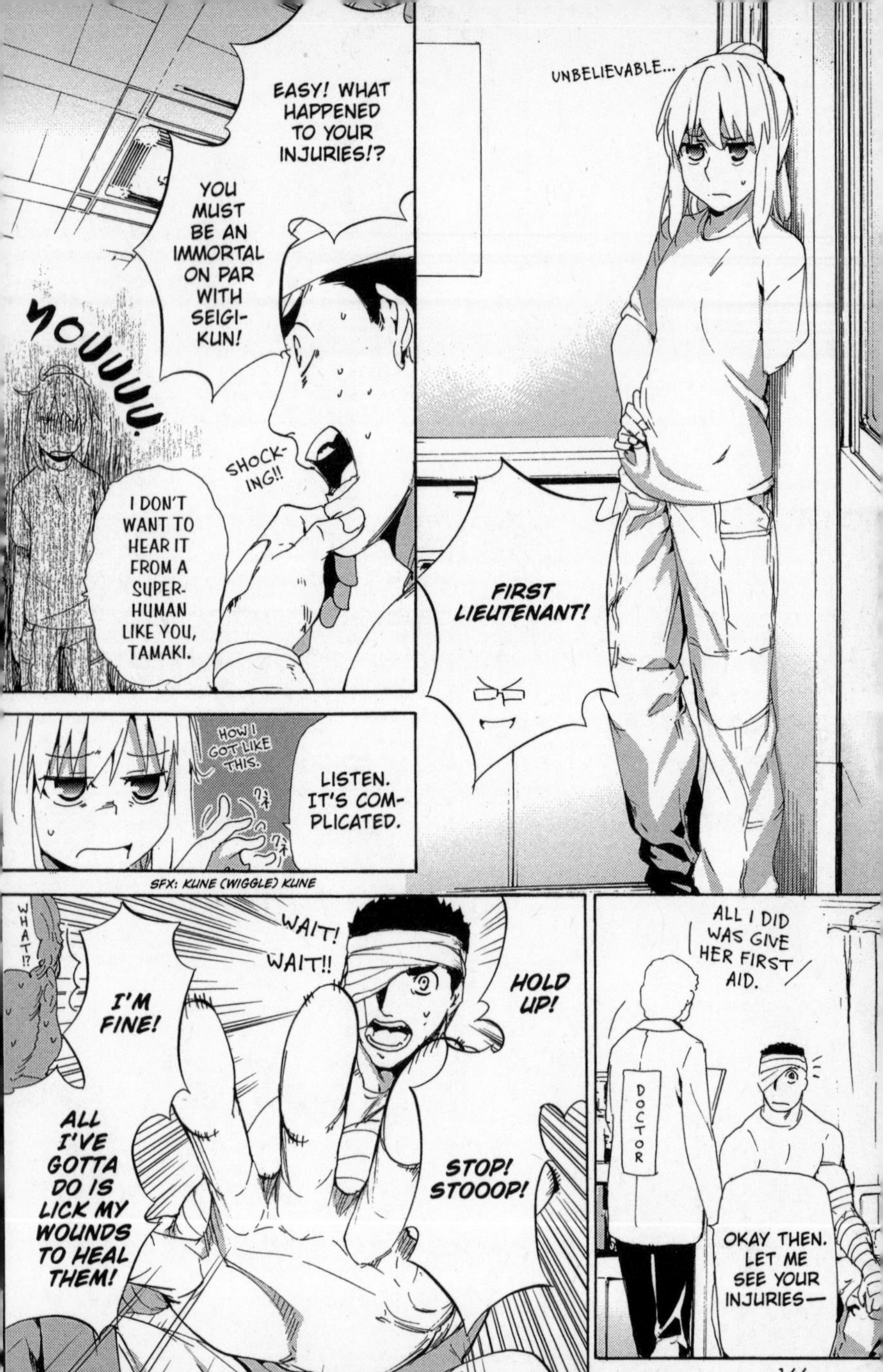
UNBELIEVABLE...
FIRST LIEUTENANT!
EASY! WHAT HAPPENED TO YOUR INJURIES!?
YOU MUST BE AN IMMORTAL ON PAR WITH SEIGI-KUN!
SHOCKING!!
MOUUUU.
I DON'T WANT TO HEAR IT FROM A SUPER-HUMAN LIKE YOU, TAMAKI.
LISTEN. IT'S COMPLICATED.
HOW I GOT LIKE THIS.
SFX: KUNE (WIGGLE) KUNE
ALL I DID WAS GIVE HER FIRST AID.
DOCTOR
OKAY THEN. LET ME SEE YOUR INJURIES—
HOLD UP!
WAIT! WAIT!!
I'M FINE!
WHAT!?
STOP! STOOOP!
ALL I'VE GOTTA DO IS LICK MY WOUNDS TO HEAL THEM!

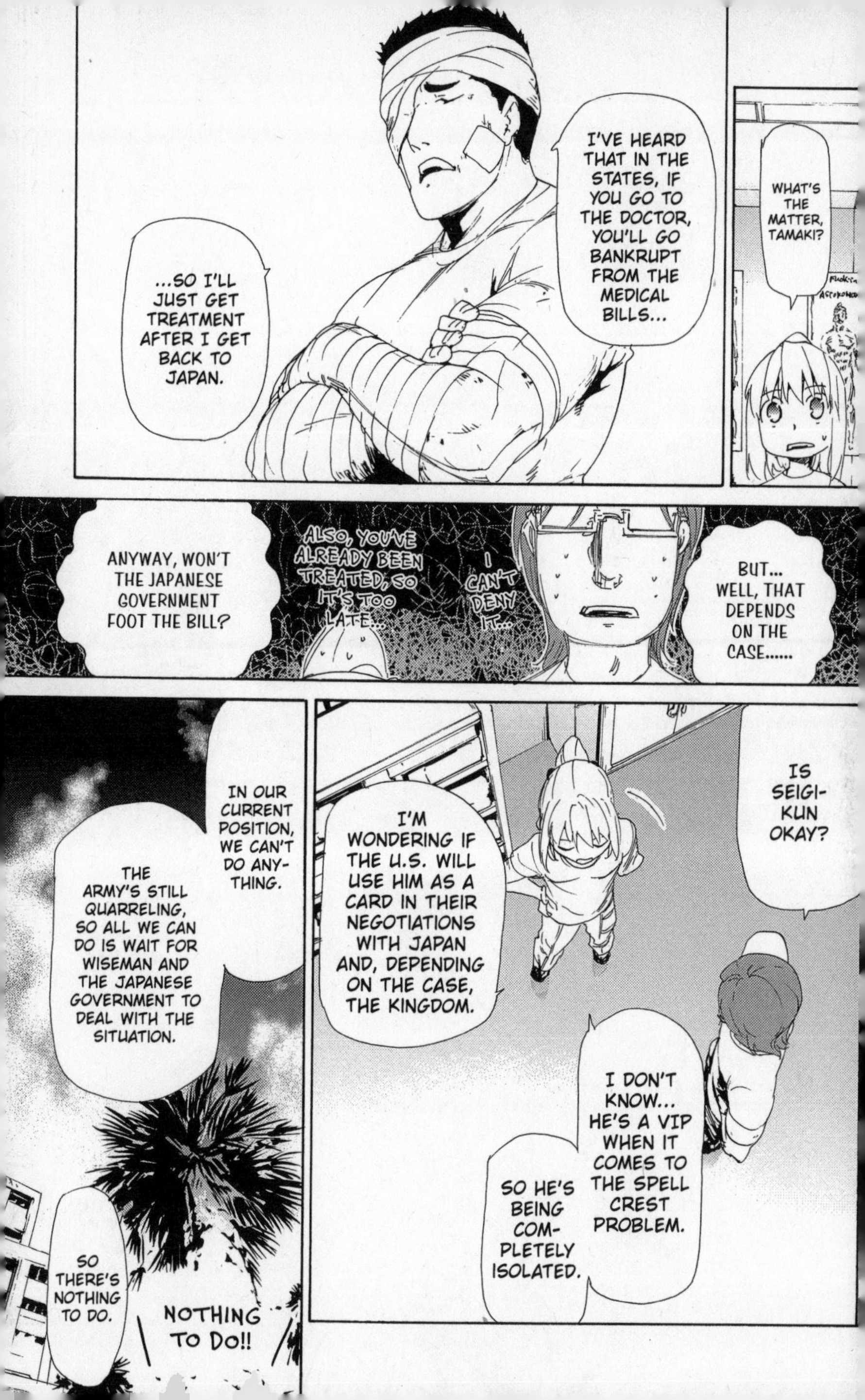
WHAT'S THE MATTER, TAMAKI?
I'VE HEARD THAT IN THE STATES, IF YOU GO TO THE DOCTOR, YOU'LL GO BANKRUPT FROM THE MEDICAL BILLS...
...SO I'LL JUST GET TREATMENT AFTER I GET BACK TO JAPAN.
BUT... WELL, THAT DEPENDS ON THE CASE......
I CAN'T DENY IT...
ALSO, YOU'VE ALREADY BEEN TREATED, SO IT'S TOO LATE...
ANYWAY, WON'T THE JAPANESE GOVERNMENT FOOT THE BILL?
IS SEIGI-KUN OKAY?
I'M WONDERING IF THE U.S. WILL USE HIM AS A CARD IN THEIR NEGOTIATIONS WITH JAPAN AND, DEPENDING ON THE CASE, THE KINGDOM.
I DON'T KNOW... HE'S A VIP WHEN IT COMES TO THE SPELL CREST PROBLEM.
SO HE'S BEING COMPLETELY ISOLATED.
IN OUR CURRENT POSITION, WE CAN'T DO ANYTHING.
THE ARMY'S STILL QUARRELING, SO ALL WE CAN DO IS WAIT FOR WISEMAN AND THE JAPANESE GOVERNMENT TO DEAL WITH THE SITUATION.
SO THERE'S NOTHING TO DO.
NOTHING TO DO!!

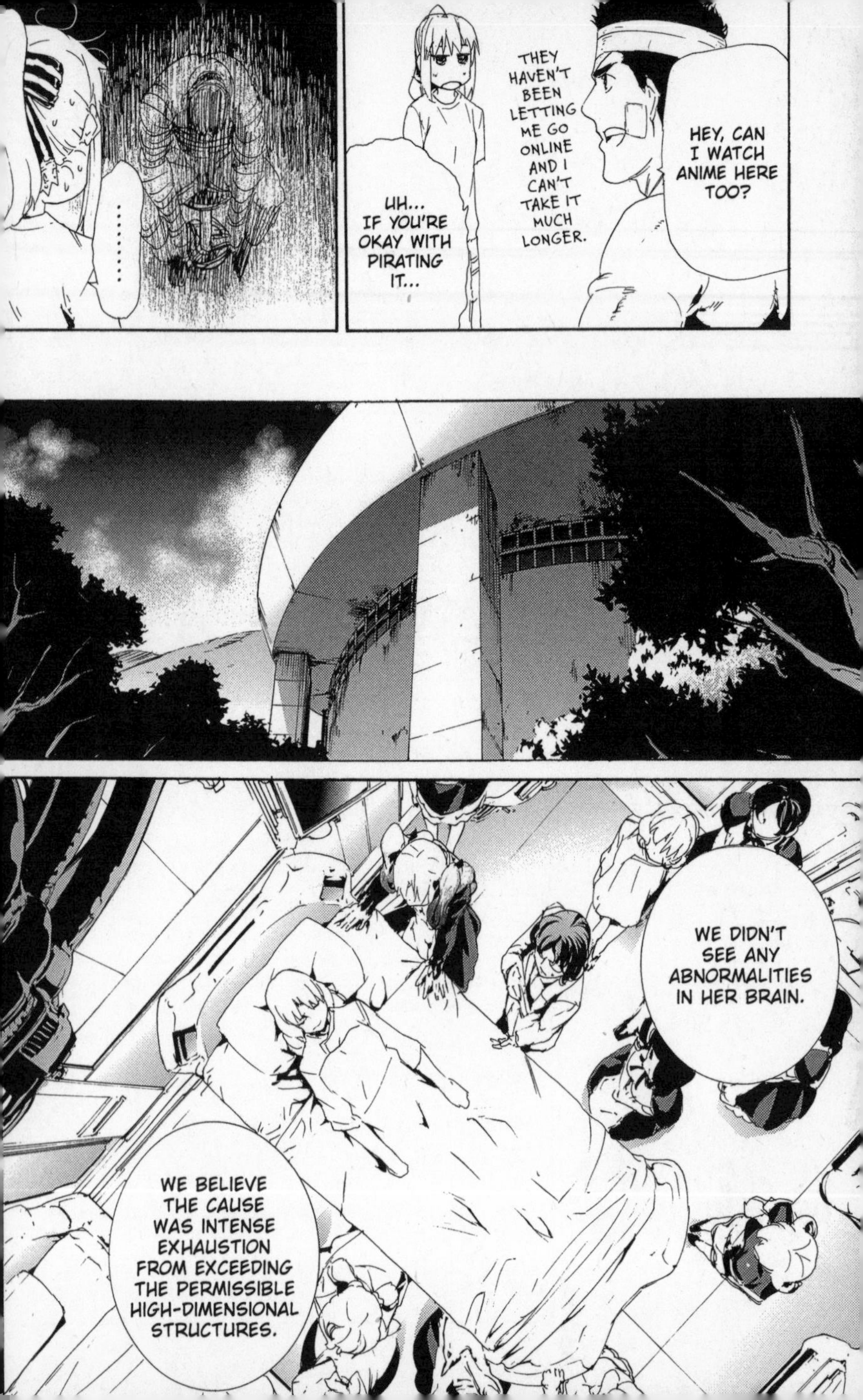
HEY, CAN I WATCH ANIME HERE TOO?
THEY HAVEN'T BEEN LETTING ME GO ONLINE AND I CAN'T TAKE IT MUCH LONGER.
UH... IF YOU'RE OKAY WITH PIRATING IT...
......
WE DIDN'T SEE ANY ABNORMALITIES IN HER BRAIN.
WE BELIEVE THE CAUSE WAS INTENSE EXHAUSTION FROM EXCEEDING THE PERMISSIBLE HIGH-DIMENSIONAL STRUCTURES.

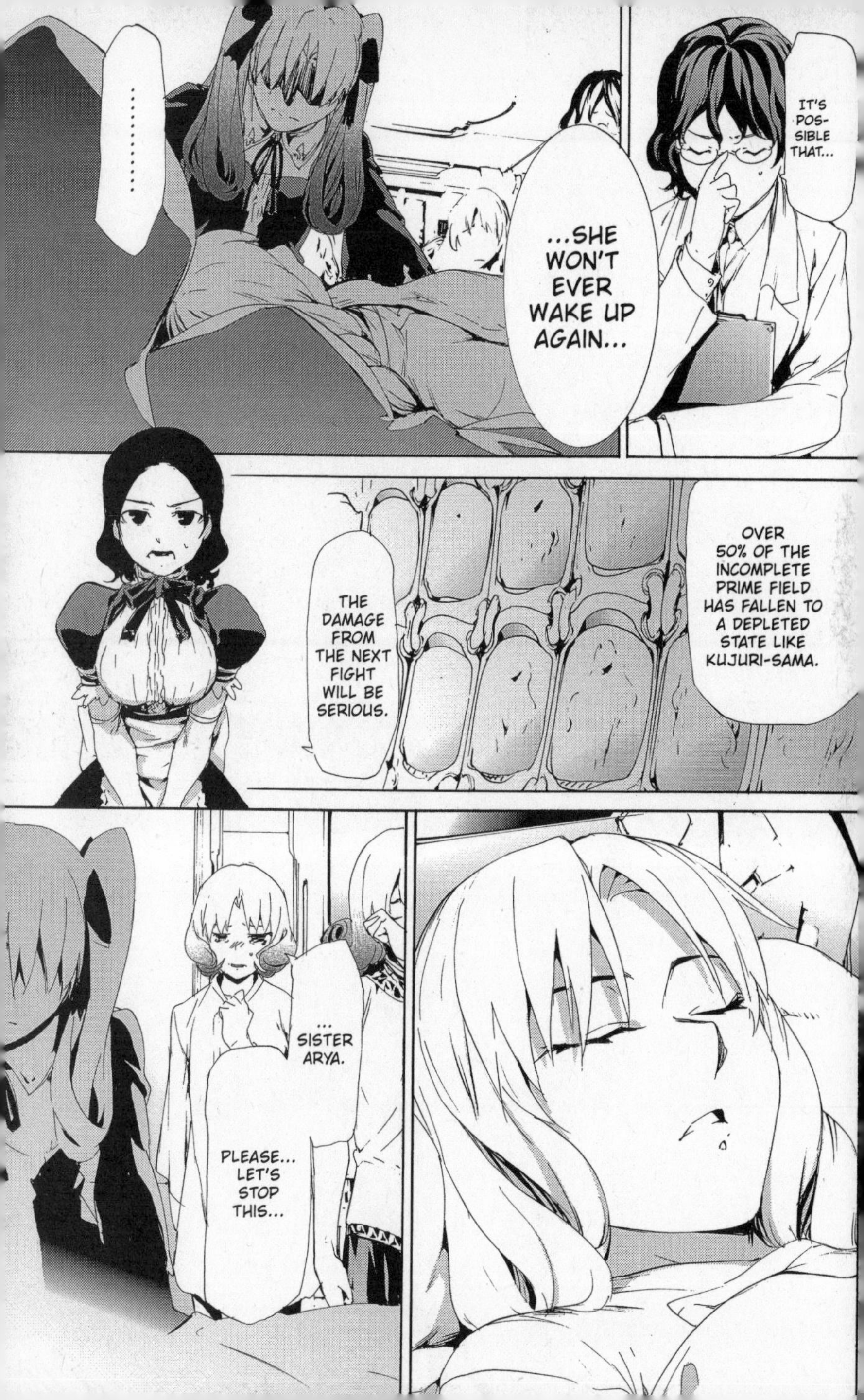
IT'S POS-SIBLE THAT...
...SHE WON'T EVER WAKE UP AGAIN...
......
OVER 50% OF THE INCOMPLETE PRIME FIELD HAS FALLEN TO A DEPLETED STATE LIKE KUJURI-SAMA.
THE DAMAGE FROM THE NEXT FIGHT WILL BE SERIOUS.
... SISTER ARYA.
PLEASE... LET'S STOP THIS...

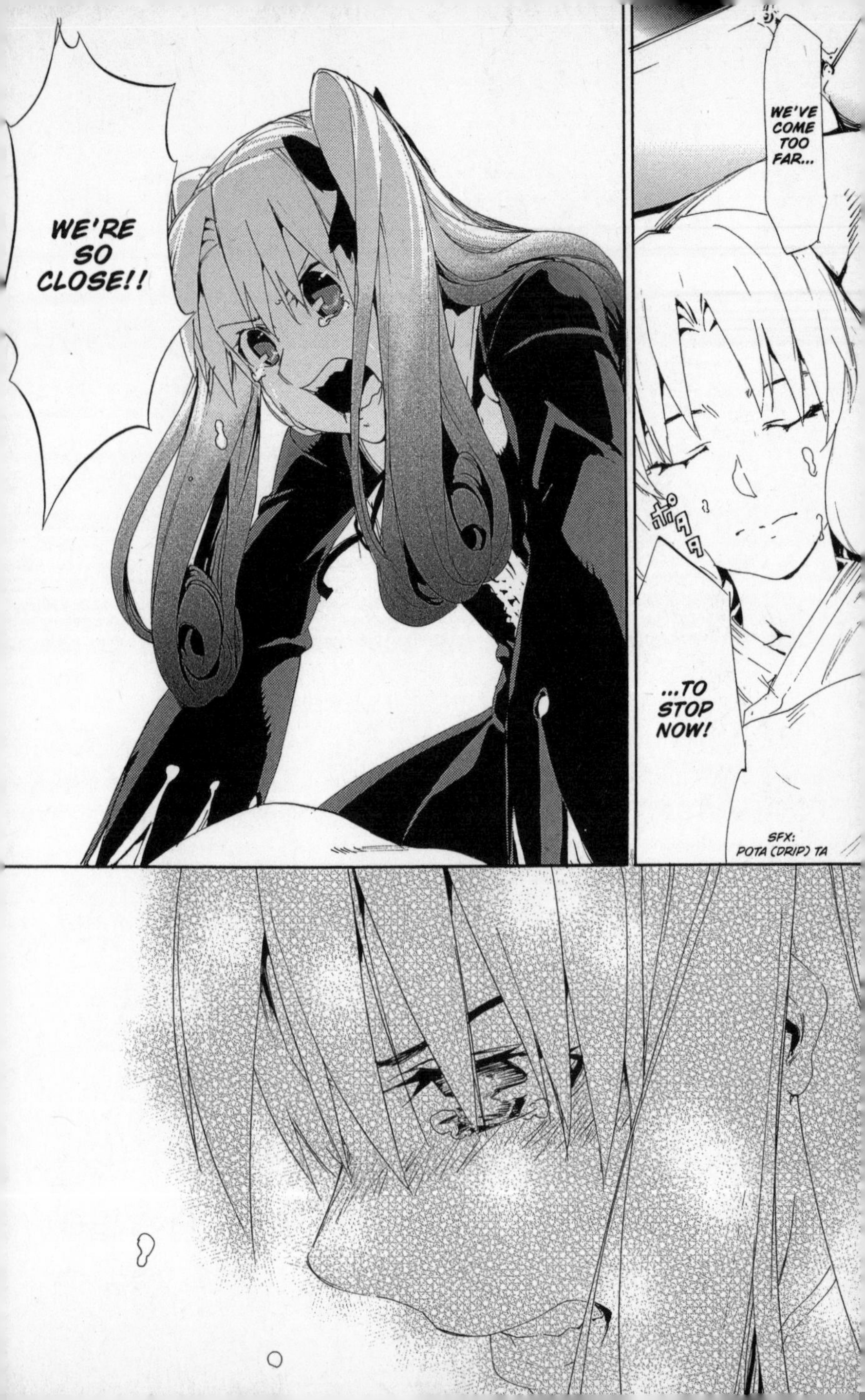
WE'VE COME TOO FAR...
...TO STOP NOW!
SFX: POTA (DRIP) TA
WE'RE SO CLOSE!!

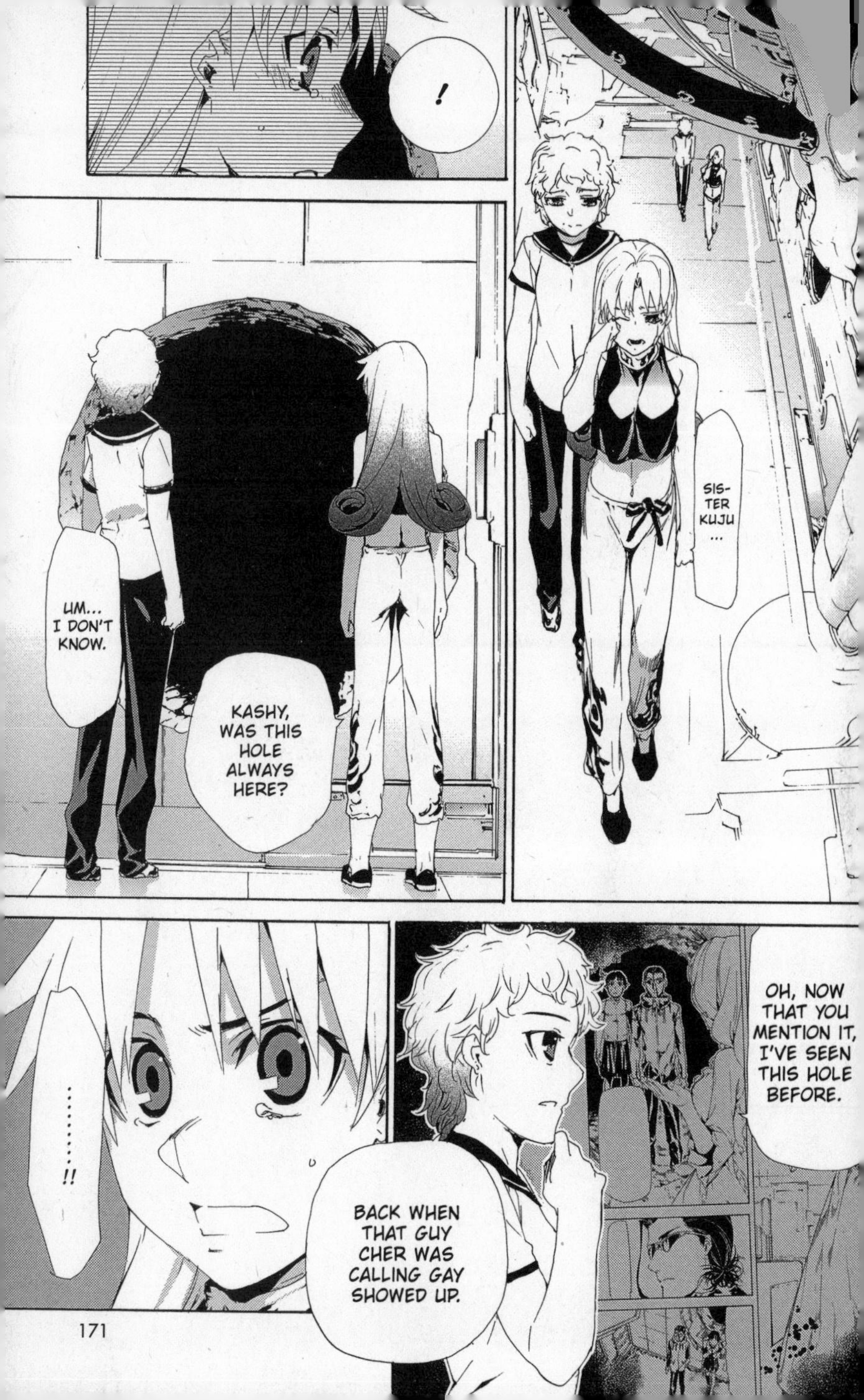
SIS-TER KUJU...
!
KASHY, WAS THIS HOLE ALWAYS HERE?
UM... I DON'T KNOW.
OH, NOW THAT YOU MENTION IT, I'VE SEEN THIS HOLE BEFORE.
BACK WHEN THAT GUY CHER WAS CALLING GAY SHOWED UP.
......!!

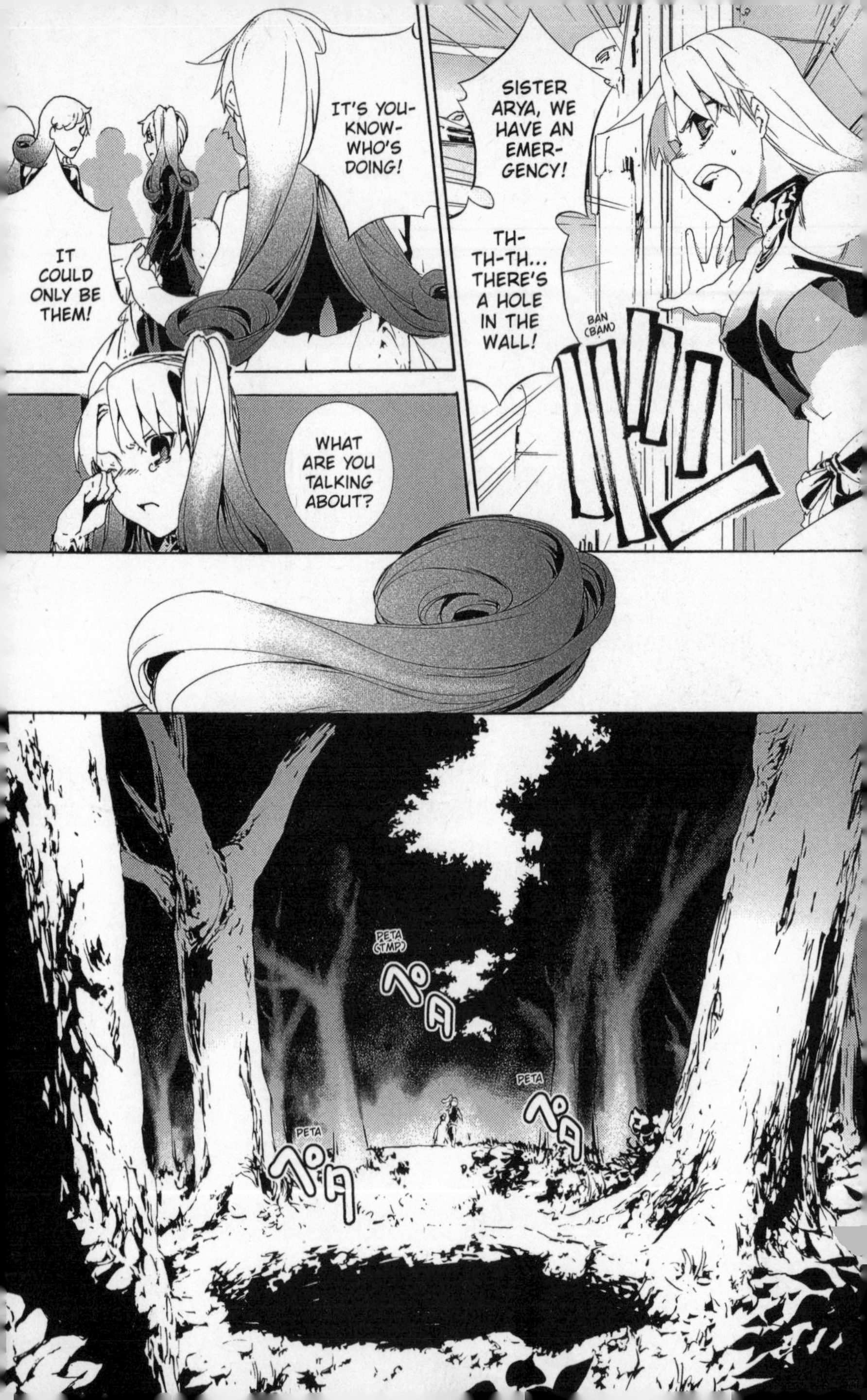
SISTER ARYA, WE HAVE AN EMERGENCY!
TH-TH-TH... THERE'S A HOLE IN THE WALL!
BAN (BAM)
IT'S YOU-KNOW-WHO'S DOING!
IT COULD ONLY BE THEM!
WHAT ARE YOU TALKING ABOUT?
PETA (TMP)
ペタ
PETA
ペタ
PETA
ペタ

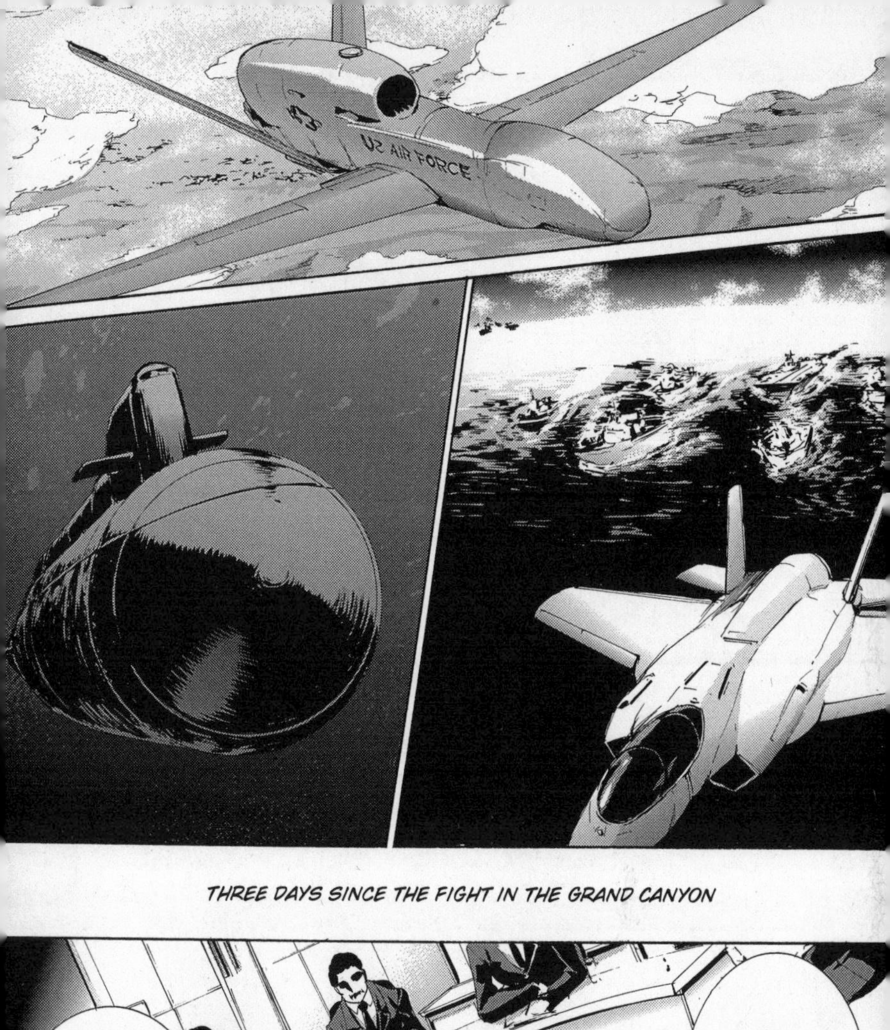

THREE DAYS SINCE THE FIGHT IN THE GRAND CANYON

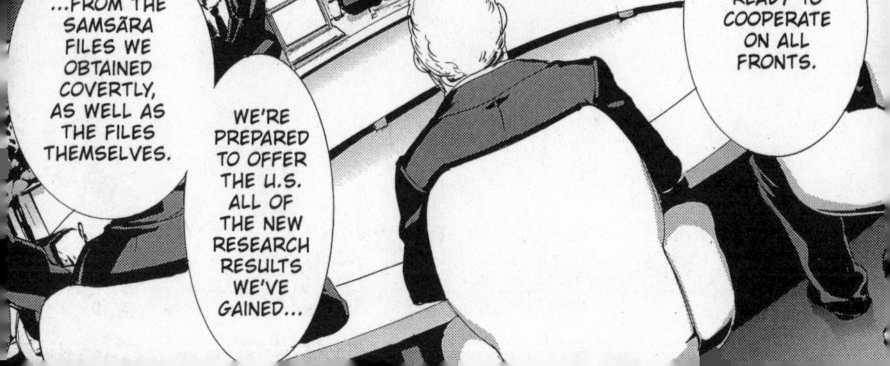
WE'RE READY TO COOPERATE ON ALL FRONTS.
WE'RE PREPARED TO OFFER THE U.S. ALL OF THE NEW RESEARCH RESULTS WE'VE GAINED...
...FROM THE SAMSĀRA FILES WE OBTAINED COVERTLY, AS WELL AS THE FILES THEMSELVES.

*POCHI: A COMMON JAPANESE DOG NAME.

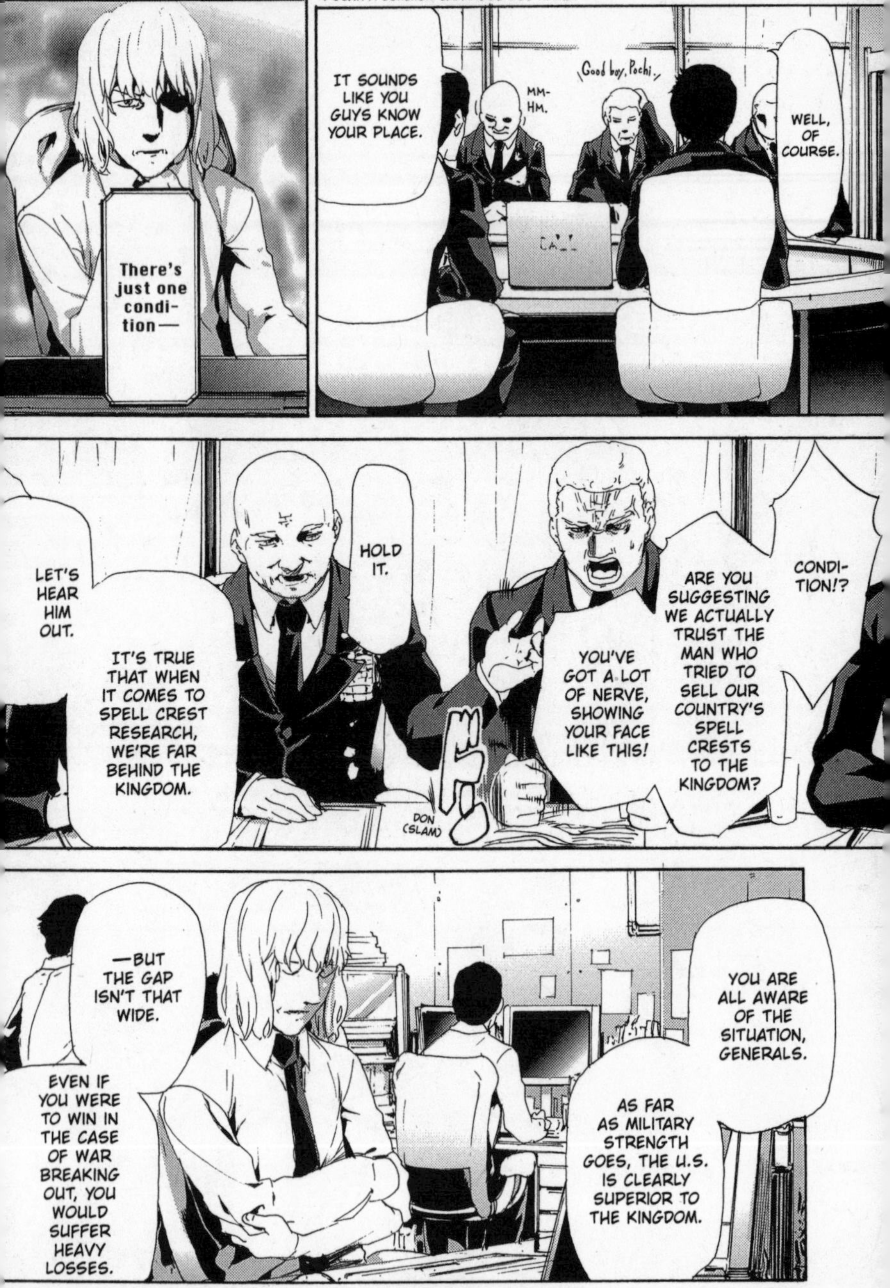
IT SOUNDS LIKE YOU GUYS KNOW YOUR PLACE.
WELL, OF COURSE.
MM-HM.
Good boy, Pochi.
There's just one condition—
CONDITION!?
ARE YOU SUGGESTING WE ACTUALLY TRUST THE MAN WHO TRIED TO SELL OUR COUNTRY'S SPELL CRESTS TO THE KINGDOM?
YOU'VE GOT A LOT OF NERVE, SHOWING YOUR FACE LIKE THIS!
DON (SLAM)
HOLD IT.
LET'S HEAR HIM OUT.
IT'S TRUE THAT WHEN IT COMES TO SPELL CREST RESEARCH, WE'RE FAR BEHIND THE KINGDOM.
YOU ARE ALL AWARE OF THE SITUATION, GENERALS.
AS FAR AS MILITARY STRENGTH GOES, THE U.S. IS CLEARLY SUPERIOR TO THE KINGDOM.
—BUT THE GAP ISN'T THAT WIDE.
EVEN IF YOU WERE TO WIN IN THE CASE OF WAR BREAKING OUT, YOU WOULD SUFFER HEAVY LOSSES.

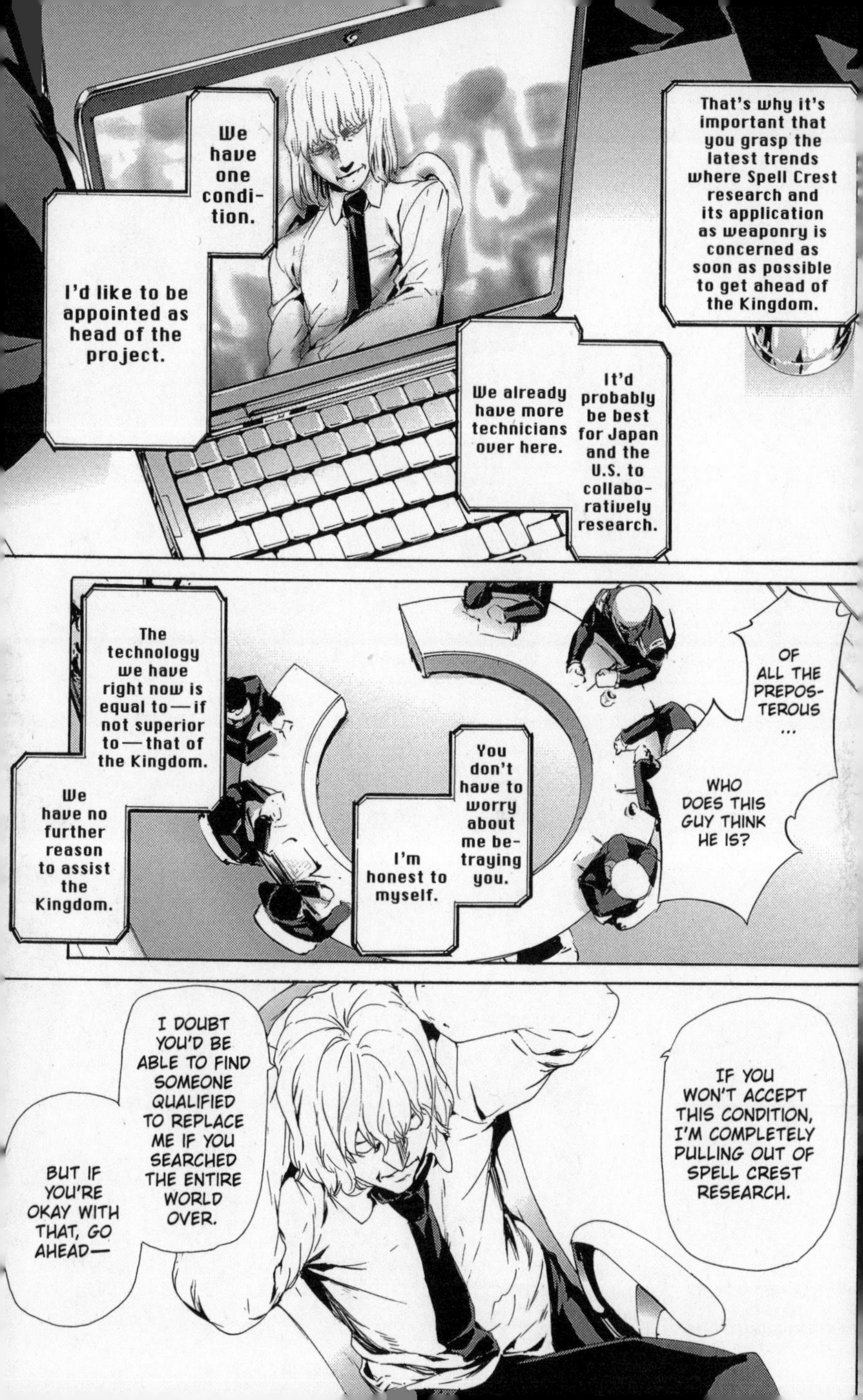
That's why it's important that you grasp the latest trends where Spell Crest research and its application as weaponry is concerned as soon as possible to get ahead of the Kingdom.
It'd probably be best for Japan and the U.S. to collaboratively research.
We already have more technicians over here.
We have one condition.
I'd like to be appointed as head of the project.
OF ALL THE PREPOSTEROUS...
WHO DOES THIS GUY THINK HE IS?
You don't have to worry about me betraying you.
I'm honest to myself.
The technology we have right now is equal to—if not superior to—that of the Kingdom.
We have no further reason to assist the Kingdom.
IF YOU WON'T ACCEPT THIS CONDITION, I'M COMPLETELY PULLING OUT OF SPELL CREST RESEARCH.
I DOUBT YOU'D BE ABLE TO FIND SOMEONE QUALIFIED TO REPLACE ME IF YOU SEARCHED THE ENTIRE WORLD OVER.
BUT IF YOU'RE OKAY WITH THAT, GO AHEAD—

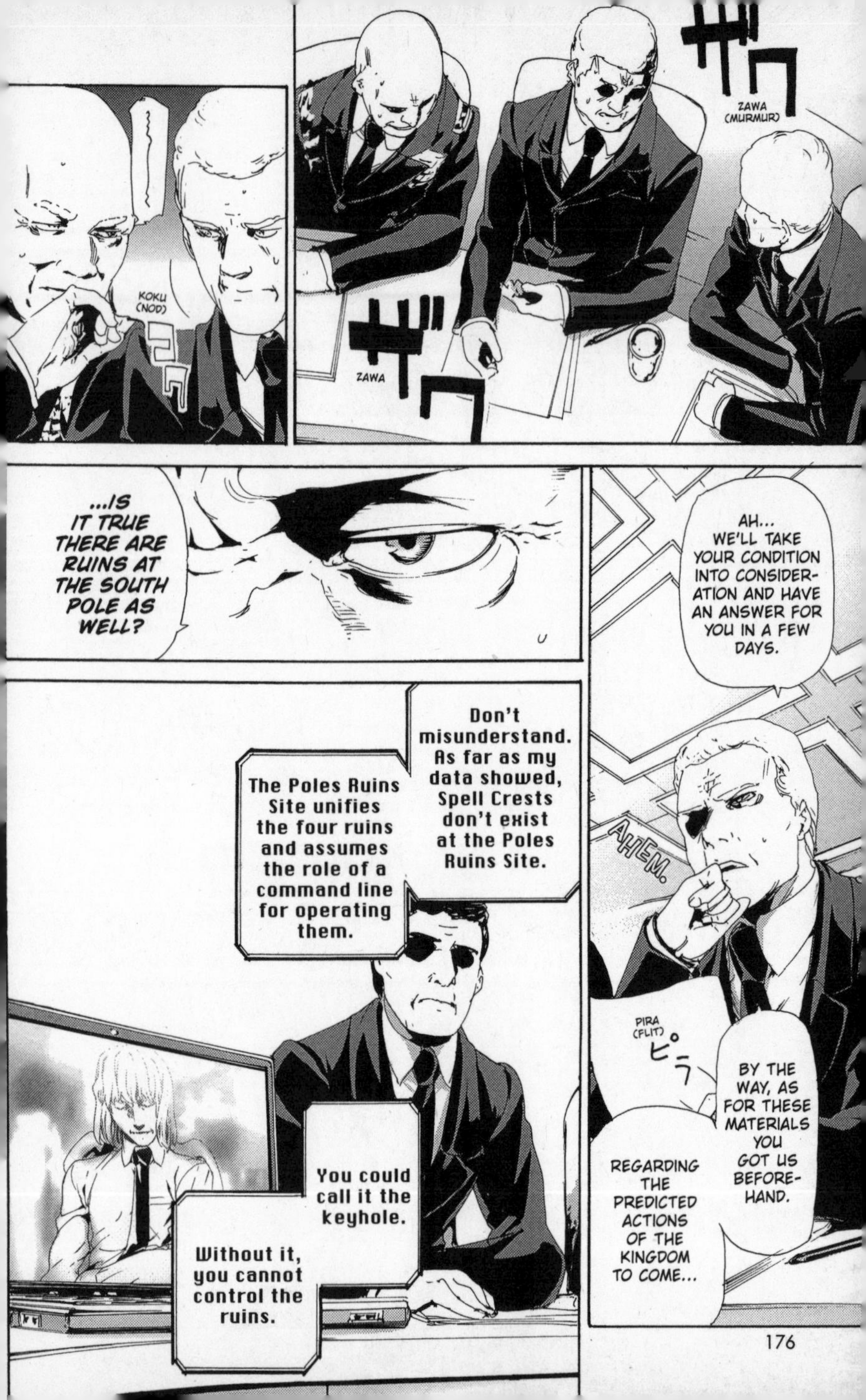
ザワ
ZAWA (MURMUR)
ザワ
ZAWA
......
コク
KOKU (NOD)
AH... WE'LL TAKE YOUR CONDITION INTO CONSIDERATION AND HAVE AN ANSWER FOR YOU IN A FEW DAYS.
AHEM.
ピラ
PIRA (FLIT)
BY THE WAY, AS FOR THESE MATERIALS YOU GOT US BEFOREHAND.
REGARDING THE PREDICTED ACTIONS OF THE KINGDOM TO COME...
...IS IT TRUE THERE ARE RUINS AT THE SOUTH POLE AS WELL?
Don't misunderstand. As far as my data showed, Spell Crests don't exist at the Poles Ruins Site.
The Poles Ruins Site unifies the four ruins and assumes the role of a command line for operating them.
You could call it the keyhole.
Without it, you cannot control the ruins.

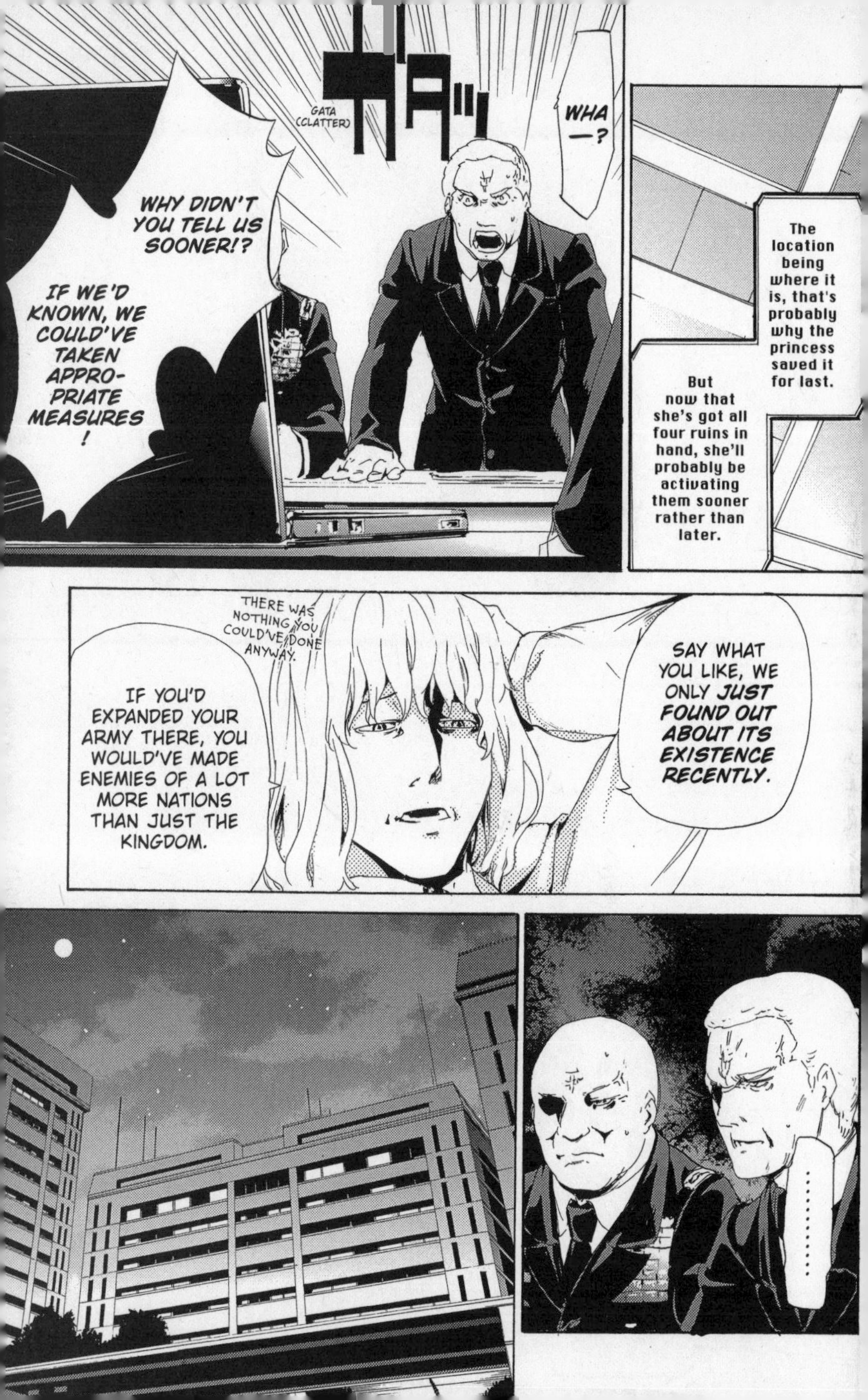
The location being where it is, that's probably why the princess saved it for last.
But now that she's got all four ruins in hand, she'll probably be activating them sooner rather than later.
WHA—?
GATA (CLATTER)
WHY DIDN'T YOU TELL US SOONER!?
IF WE'D KNOWN, WE COULD'VE TAKEN APPRO-PRIATE MEASURES!
SAY WHAT YOU LIKE, WE ONLY JUST FOUND OUT ABOUT ITS EXISTENCE RECENTLY.
THERE WAS NOTHING YOU COULD'VE DONE ANYWAY.
IF YOU'D EXPANDED YOUR ARMY THERE, YOU WOULD'VE MADE ENEMIES OF A LOT MORE NATIONS THAN JUST THE KINGDOM.

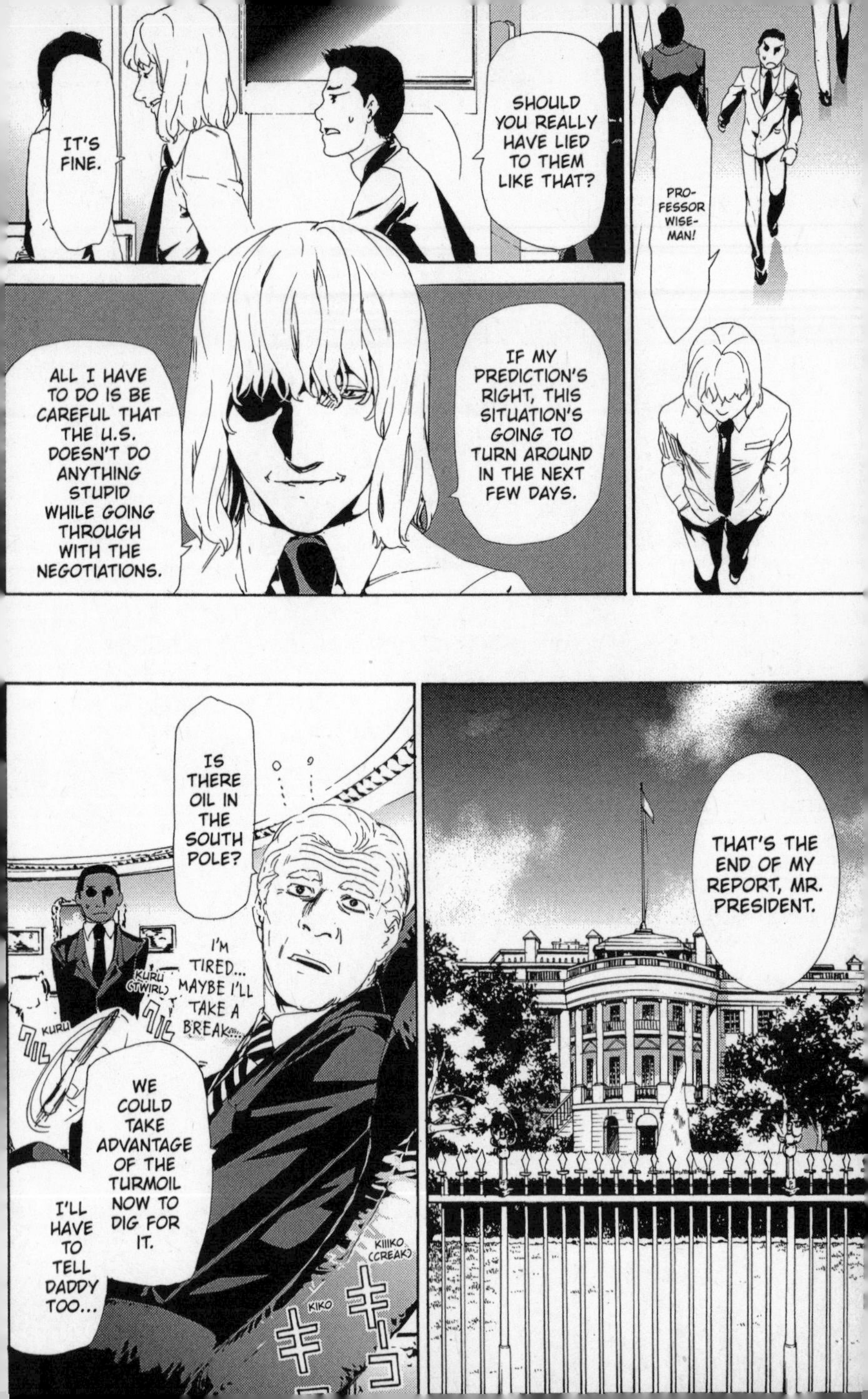
PRO-FESSOR WISE-MAN!
SHOULD YOU REALLY HAVE LIED TO THEM LIKE THAT?
IT'S FINE.
IF MY PREDICTION'S RIGHT, THIS SITUATION'S GOING TO TURN AROUND IN THE NEXT FEW DAYS.
ALL I HAVE TO DO IS BE CAREFUL THAT THE U.S. DOESN'T DO ANYTHING STUPID WHILE GOING THROUGH WITH THE NEGOTIATIONS.
THAT'S THE END OF MY REPORT, MR. PRESIDENT.
IS THERE OIL IN THE SOUTH POLE?
I'M TIRED... MAYBE I'LL TAKE A BREAK...
KIIIKO (CREAK)
KIKO
WE COULD TAKE ADVANTAGE OF THE TURMOIL NOW TO DIG FOR IT.
KURU (TWIRL)
KURU
I'LL HAVE TO TELL DADDY TOO...

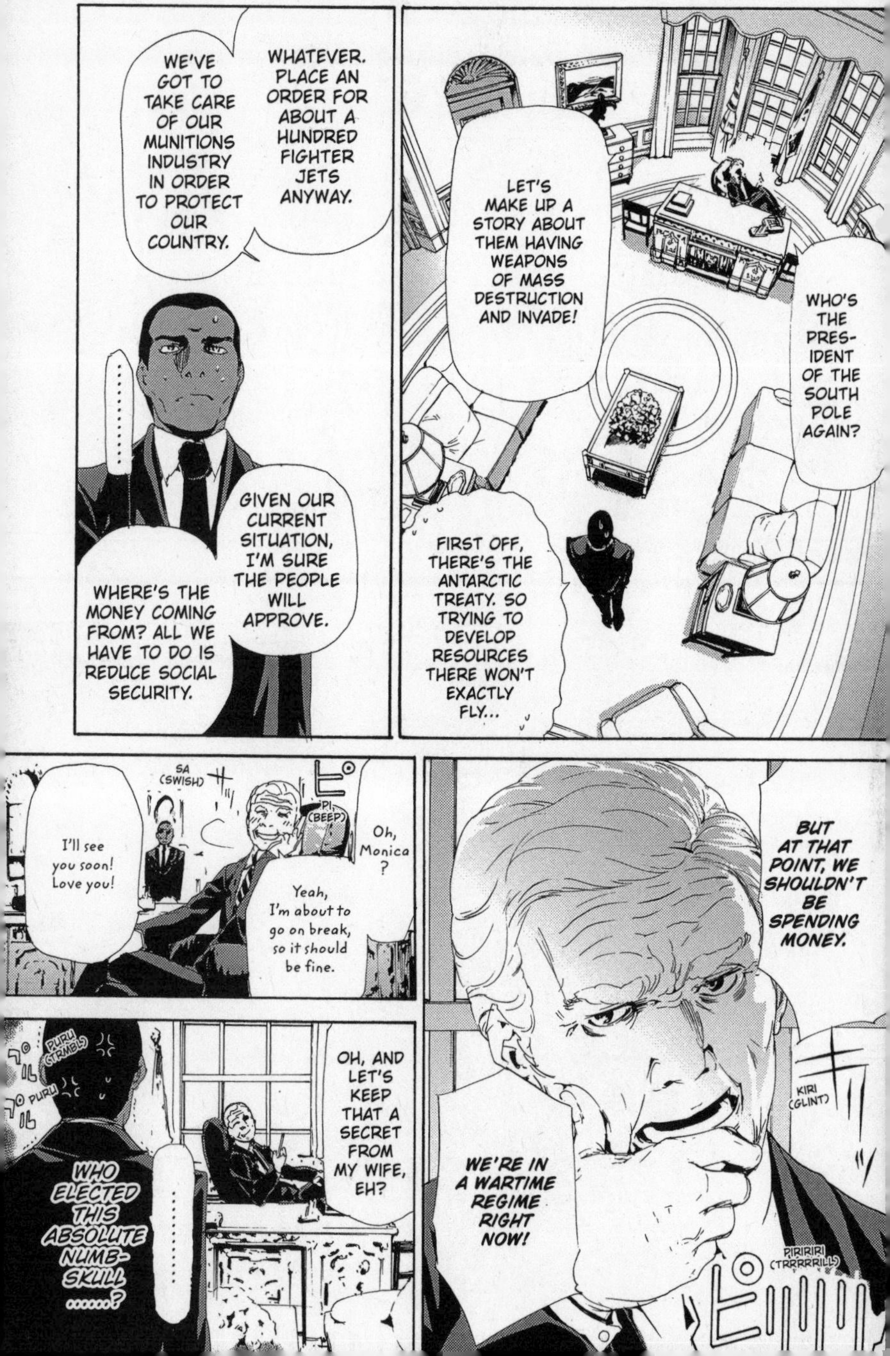
WHO'S THE PRES-IDENT OF THE SOUTH POLE AGAIN?
LET'S MAKE UP A STORY ABOUT THEM HAVING WEAPONS OF MASS DESTRUCTION AND INVADE!
FIRST OFF, THERE'S THE ANTARCTIC TREATY. SO TRYING TO DEVELOP RESOURCES THERE WON'T EXACTLY FLY...
WHATEVER. PLACE AN ORDER FOR ABOUT A HUNDRED FIGHTER JETS ANYWAY.
WE'VE GOT TO TAKE CARE OF OUR MUNITIONS INDUSTRY IN ORDER TO PROTECT OUR COUNTRY.
......
GIVEN OUR CURRENT SITUATION, I'M SURE THE PEOPLE WILL APPROVE.
WHERE'S THE MONEY COMING FROM? ALL WE HAVE TO DO IS REDUCE SOCIAL SECURITY.
BUT AT THAT POINT, WE SHOULDN'T BE SPENDING MONEY.
KIRI (GLINT)
WE'RE IN A WARTIME REGIME RIGHT NOW!
PIRIRIRI (TRRRRRILL)
SA (SWISH)
PI (BEEP)
Oh, Monica?
Yeah, I'm about to go on break, so it should be fine.
I'll see you soon! Love you!
OH, AND LET'S KEEP THAT A SECRET FROM MY WIFE, EH?
......
PURU (TRMBL)
PURU
WHO ELECTED THIS ABSOLUTE NUMBSKULL ......?

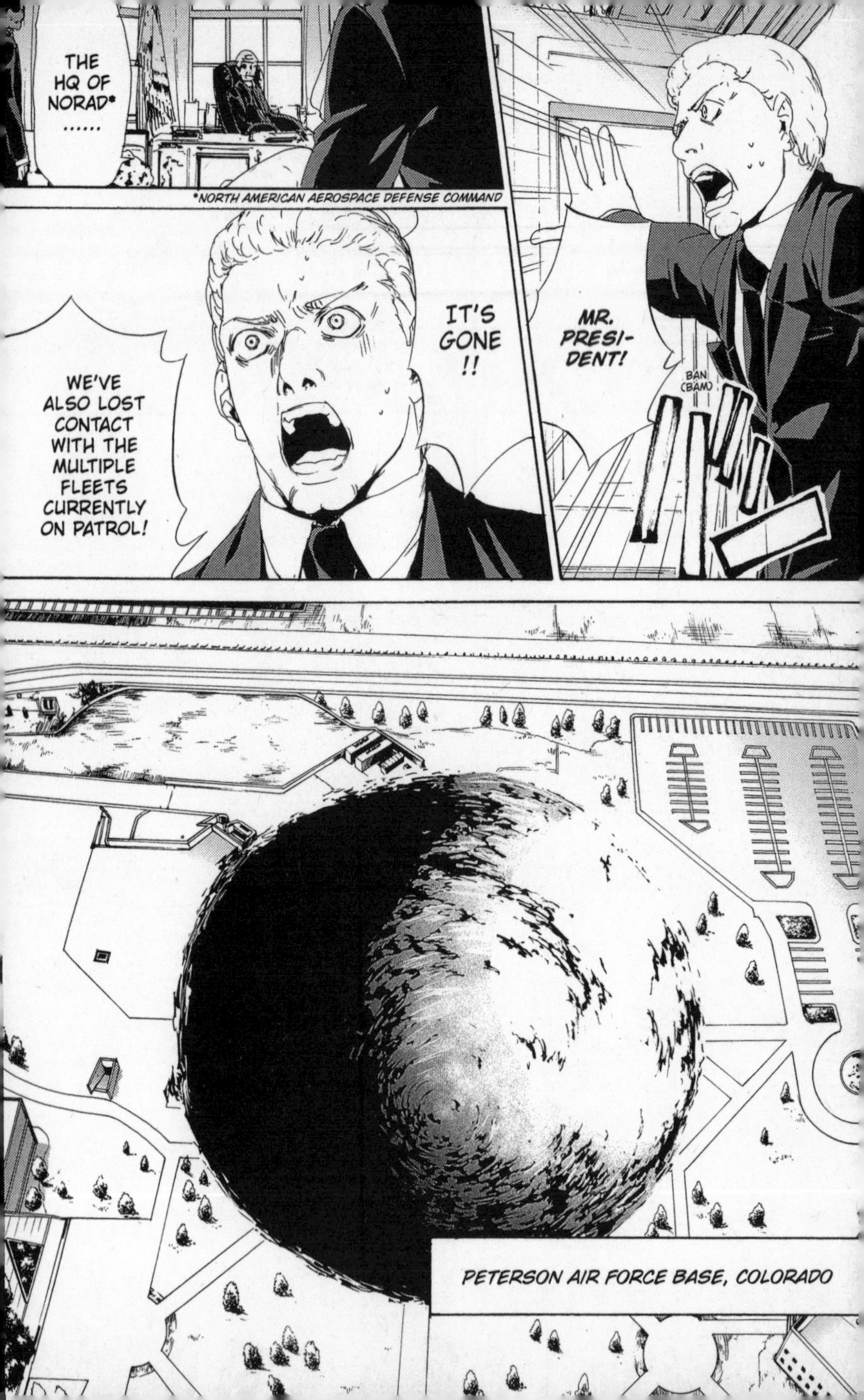
MR. PRESIDENT!
BAN (BAM)
THE HQ OF NORAD* ......
*NORTH AMERICAN AEROSPACE DEFENSE COMMAND
IT'S GONE !!
WE'VE ALSO LOST CONTACT WITH THE MULTIPLE FLEETS CURRENTLY ON PATROL!
PETERSON AIR FORCE BASE, COLORADO

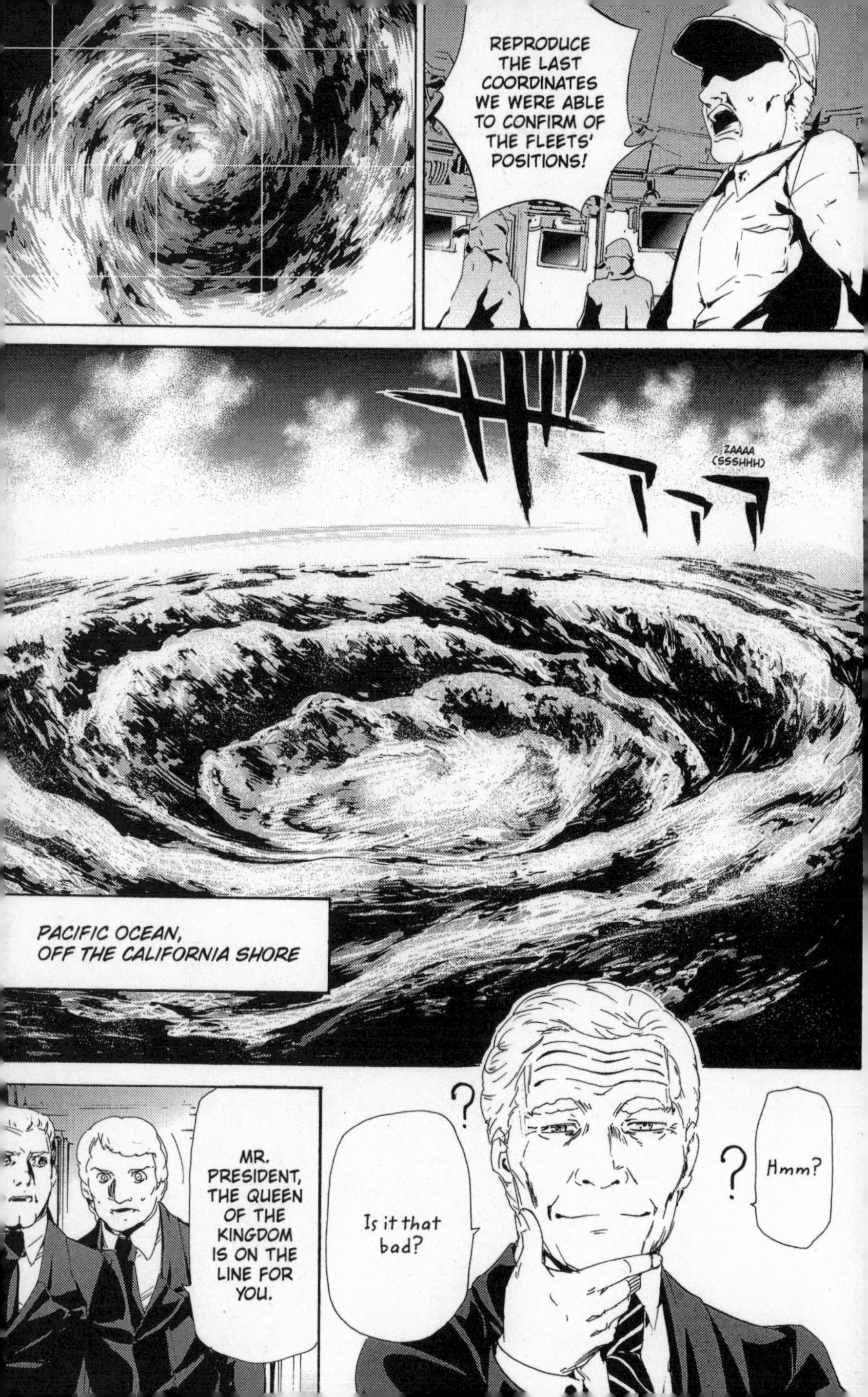
REPRODUCE THE LAST COORDINATES WE WERE ABLE TO CONFIRM OF THE FLEETS' POSITIONS!
ZAAAA (SSSHHH)
PACIFIC OCEAN, OFF THE CALIFORNIA SHORE
?
Hmm?
?
Is it that bad?
MR. PRESIDENT, THE QUEEN OF THE KINGDOM IS ON THE LINE FOR YOU.

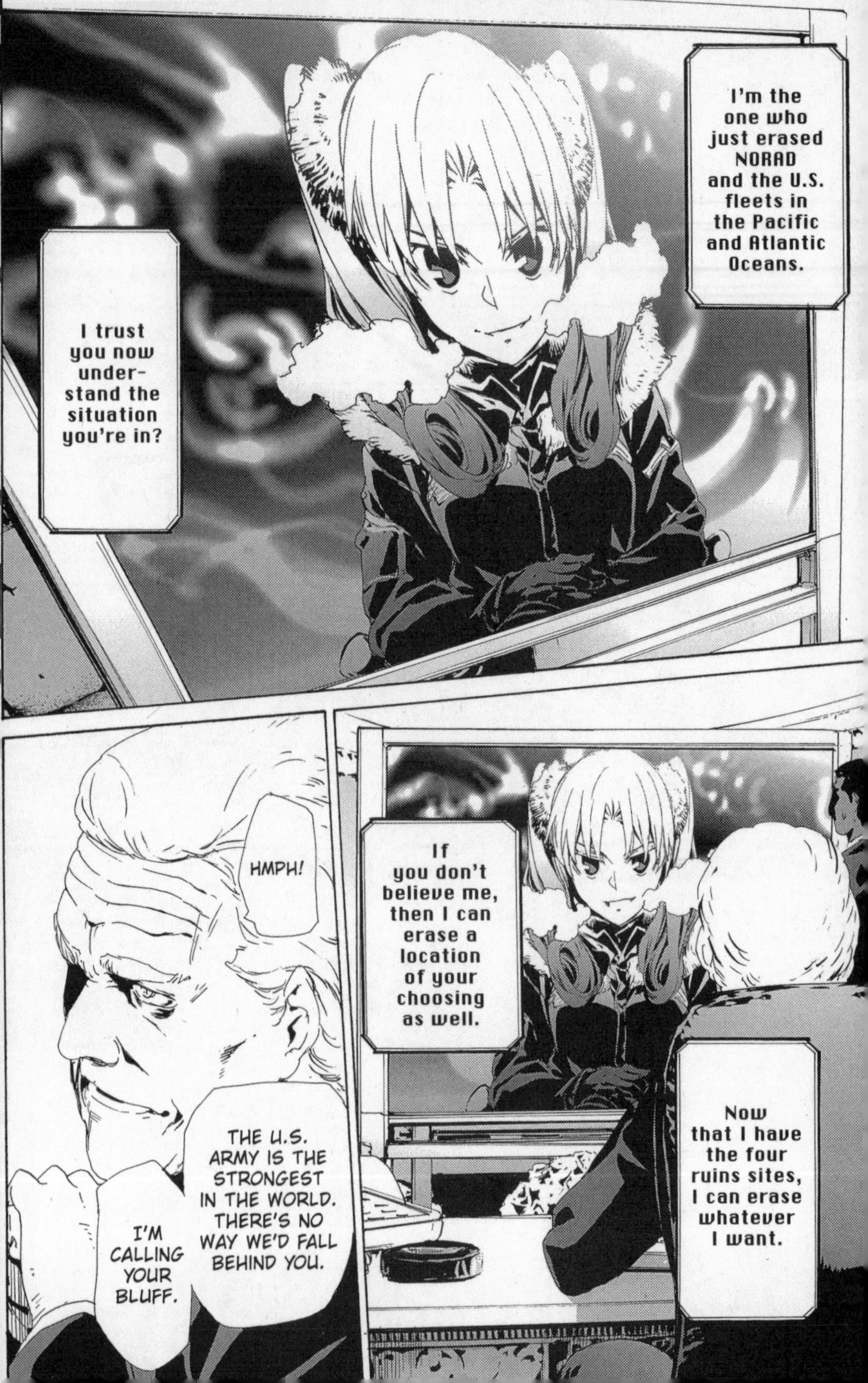
I'm the one who just erased NORAD and the U.S. fleets in the Pacific and Atlantic Oceans.
I trust you now under-stand the situation you're in?
If you don't believe me, then I can erase a location of your choosing as well.
Now that I have the four ruins sites, I can erase whatever I want.
HMPH!
THE U.S. ARMY IS THE STRONGEST IN THE WORLD. THERE'S NO WAY WE'D FALL BEHIND YOU.
I'M CALLING YOUR BLUFF.

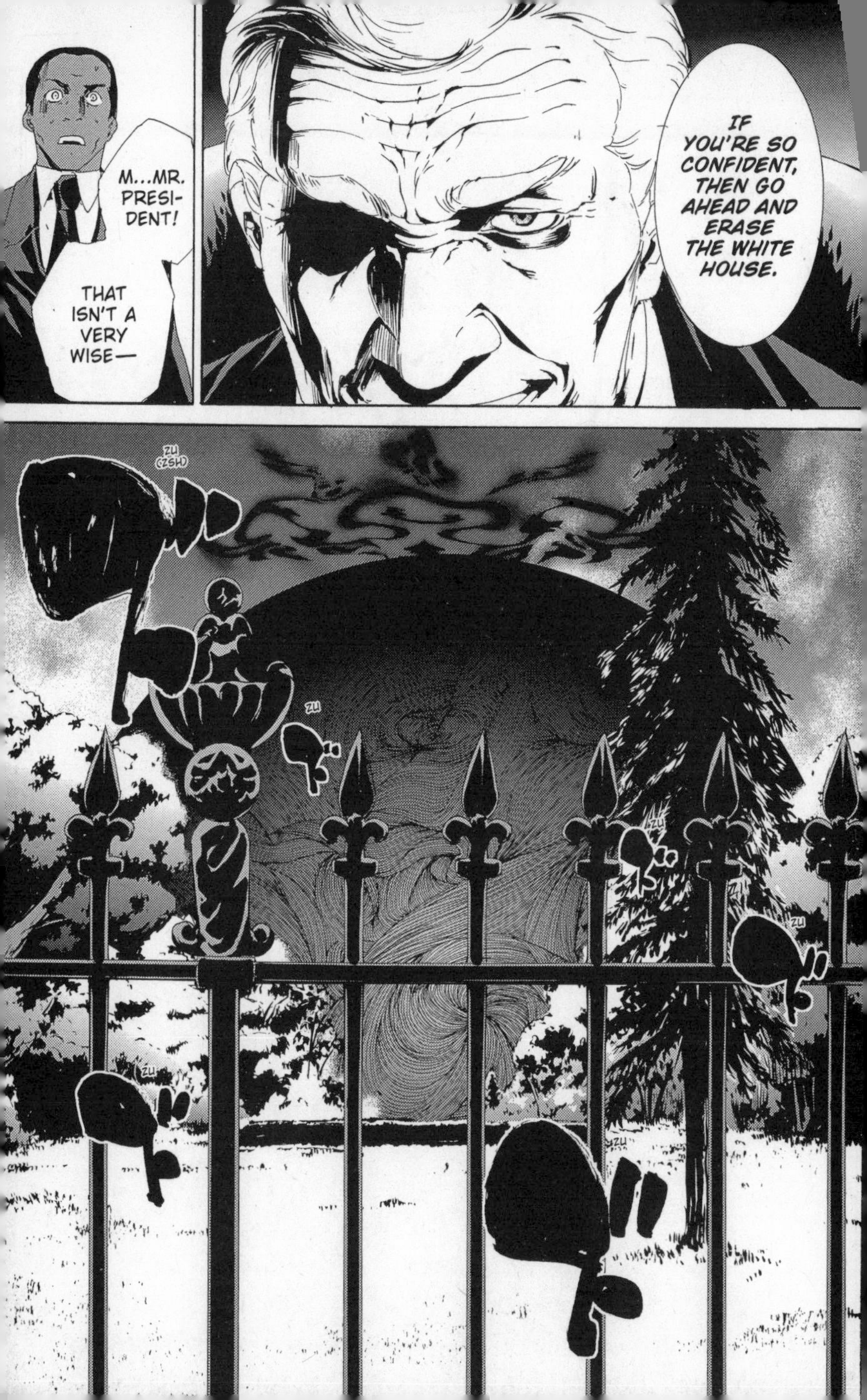
IF YOU'RE SO CONFIDENT, THEN GO AHEAD AND ERASE THE WHITE HOUSE.
M...MR. PRESIDENT!
THAT ISN'T A VERY WISE—
ZU (ZSH)
ZU
ZU
ZU
ZU
ZU

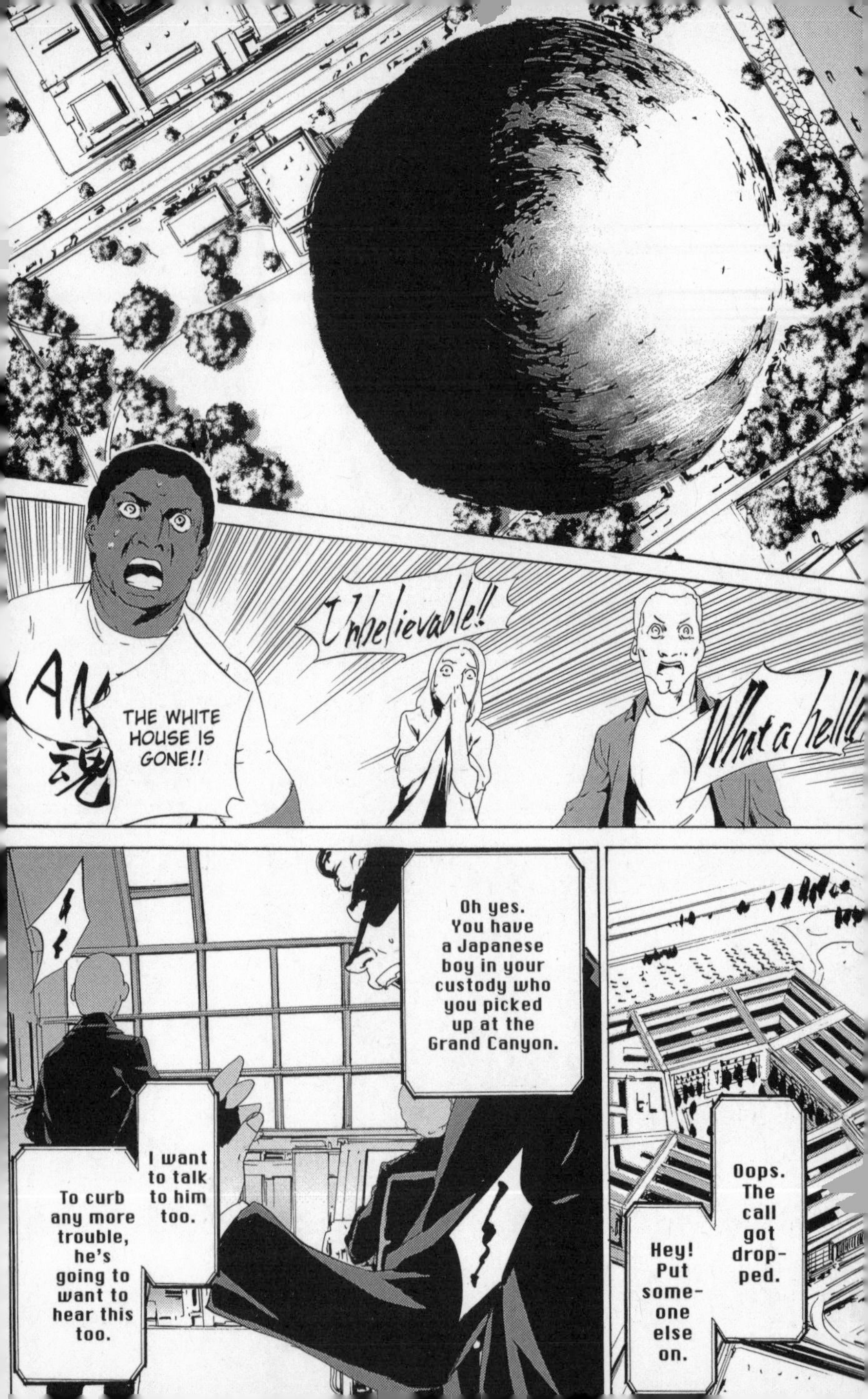
What a hell
Unbelievable!!
THE WHITE HOUSE IS GONE!!
Oops. The call got drop-ped.
Hey! Put some-one else on.
Oh yes. You have a Japanese boy in your custody who you picked up at the Grand Canyon.
I want to talk to him too.
To curb any more trouble, he's going to want to hear this too.

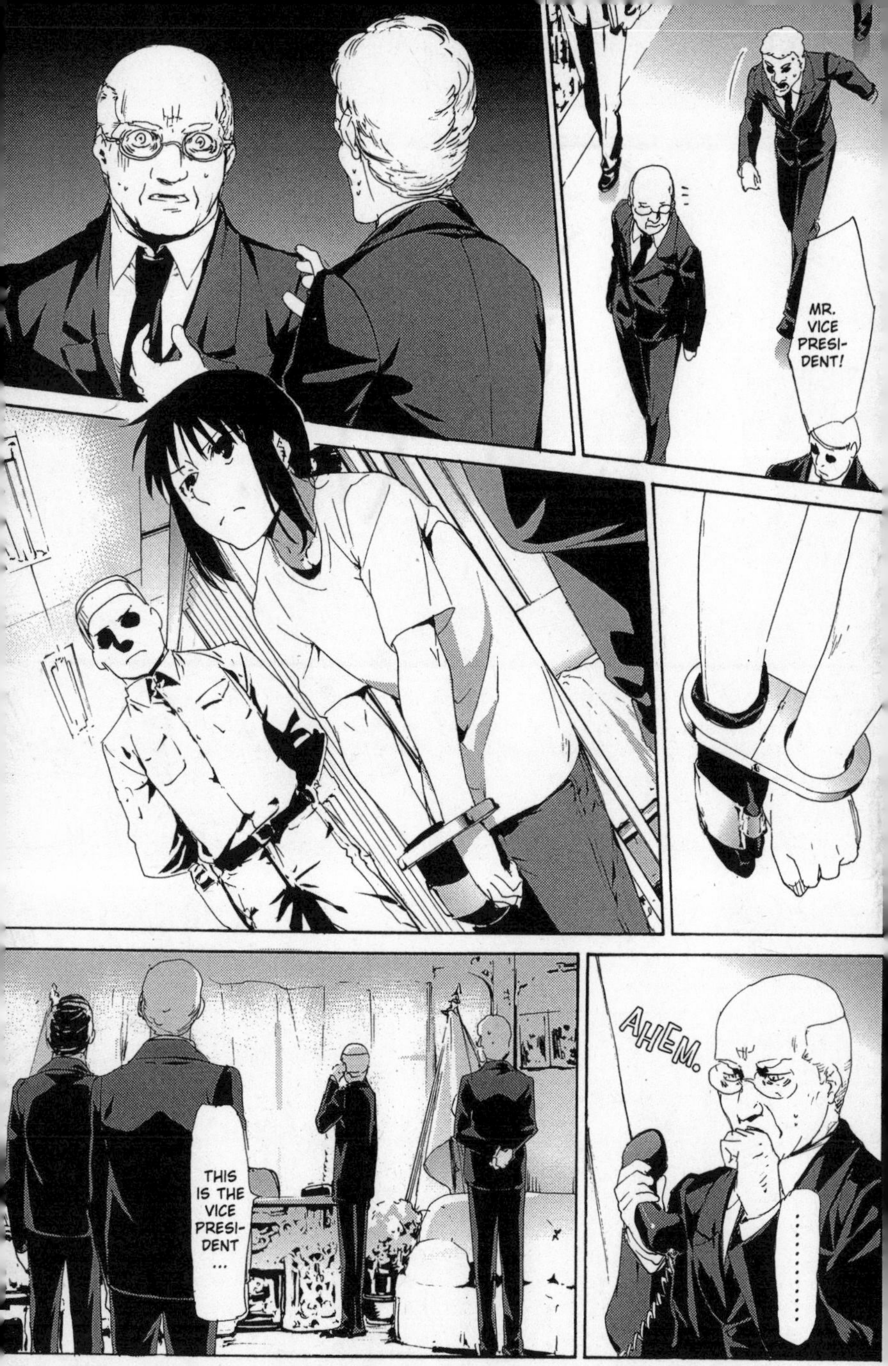
MR. VICE PRESI- DENT!
AHEM.
......
THIS IS THE VICE PRESI- DENT ...

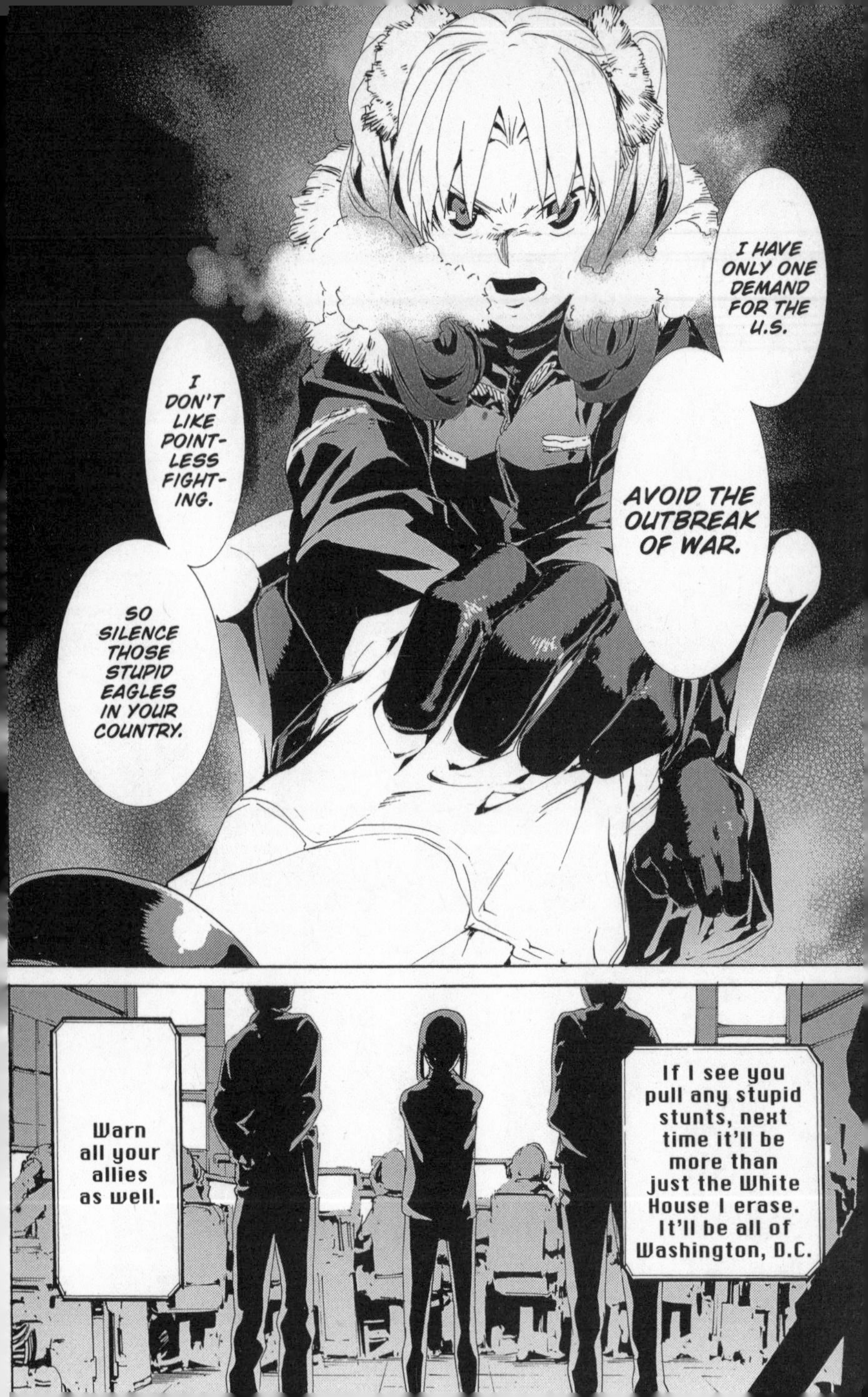

I HAVE ONLY ONE DEMAND FOR THE U.S.
AVOID THE OUTBREAK OF WAR.
I DON'T LIKE POINT-LESS FIGHT-ING.
SO SILENCE THOSE STUPID EAGLES IN YOUR COUNTRY.
If I see you pull any stupid stunts, next time it'll be more than just the White House I erase. It'll be all of Washington, D.C.
Warn all your allies as well.

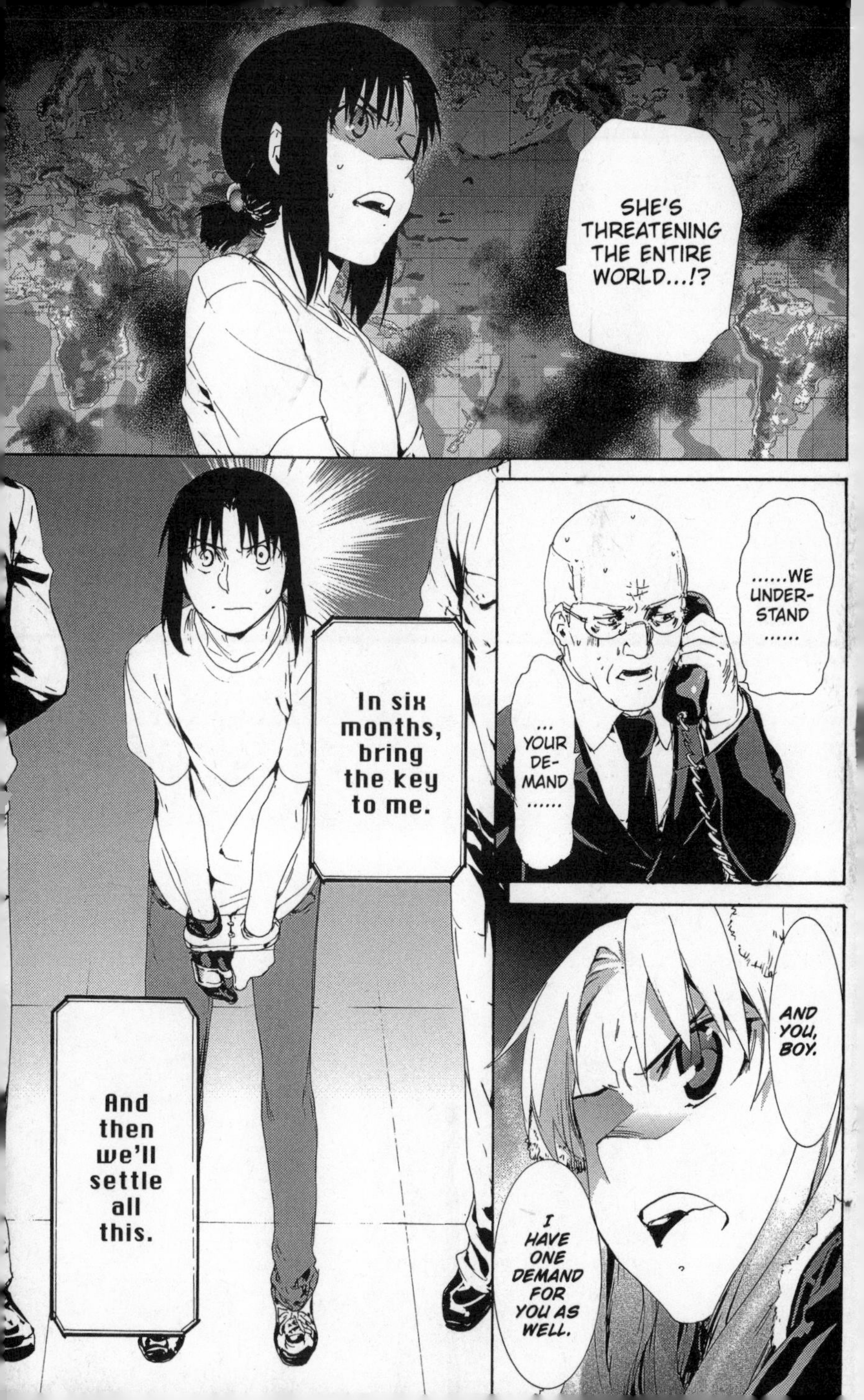
SHE'S THREATENING THE ENTIRE WORLD...!?
......WE UNDER-STAND......
...YOUR DE-MAND......
AND YOU, BOY.
I HAVE ONE DEMAND FOR YOU AS WELL.
In six months, bring the key to me.
And then we'll settle all this.

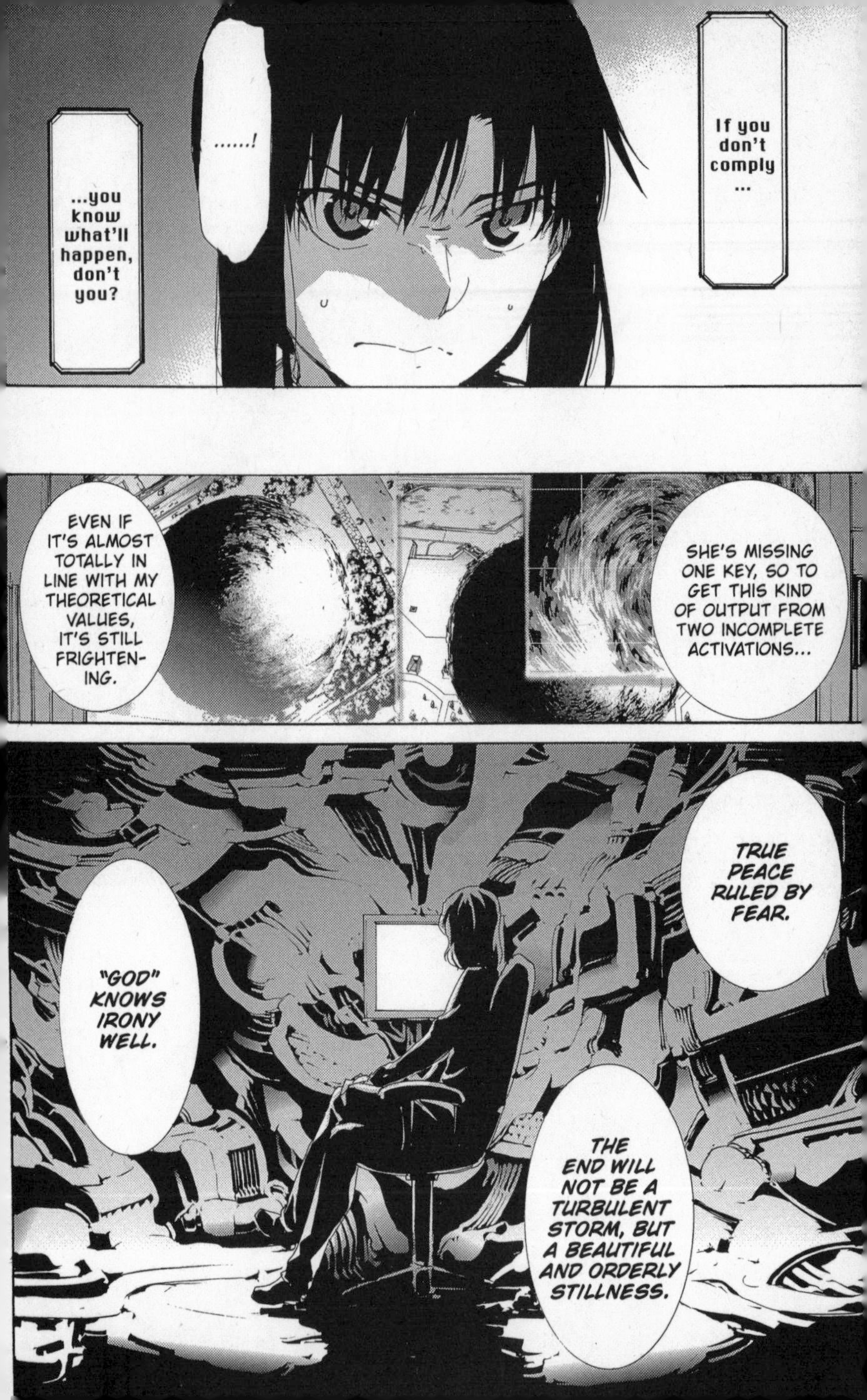
If you don't comply ...
......!
...you know what'll happen, don't you?
SHE'S MISSING ONE KEY, SO TO GET THIS KIND OF OUTPUT FROM TWO INCOMPLETE ACTIVATIONS...
EVEN IF IT'S ALMOST TOTALLY IN LINE WITH MY THEORETICAL VALUES, IT'S STILL FRIGHTEN-ING.
TRUE PEACE RULED BY FEAR.
"GOD" KNOWS IRONY WELL.
THE END WILL NOT BE A TURBULENT STORM, BUT A BEAUTIFUL AND ORDERLY STILLNESS.

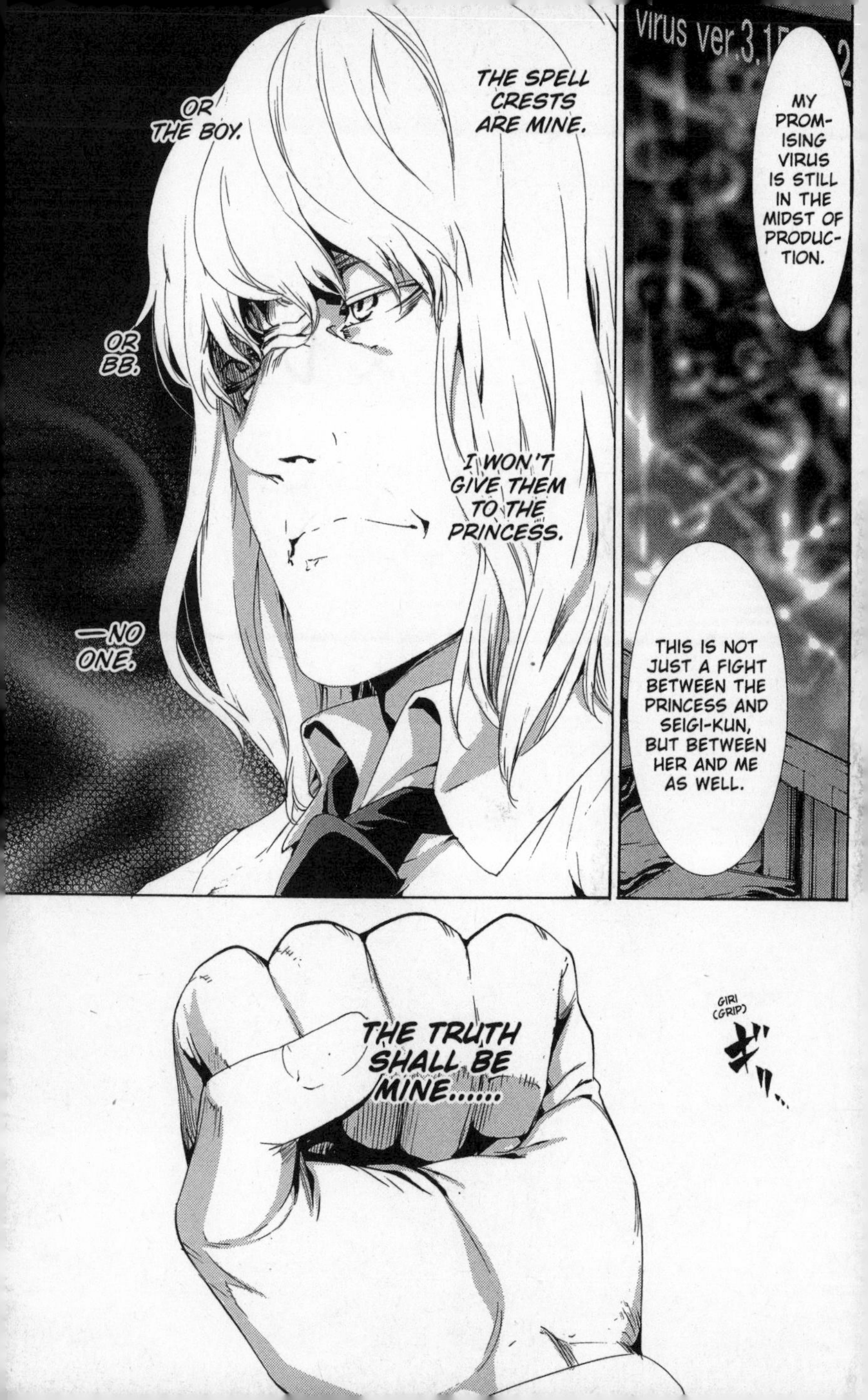
virus ver.3.1
MY PROMISING VIRUS IS STILL IN THE MIDST OF PRODUCTION.
THIS IS NOT JUST A FIGHT BETWEEN THE PRINCESS AND SEIGI-KUN, BUT BETWEEN HER AND ME AS WELL.
THE SPELL CRESTS ARE MINE.
I WON'T GIVE THEM TO THE PRINCESS.
OR THE BOY.
OR BB.
—NO ONE.
ギッ
GIRI (GRIP)
THE TRUTH SHALL BE MINE......

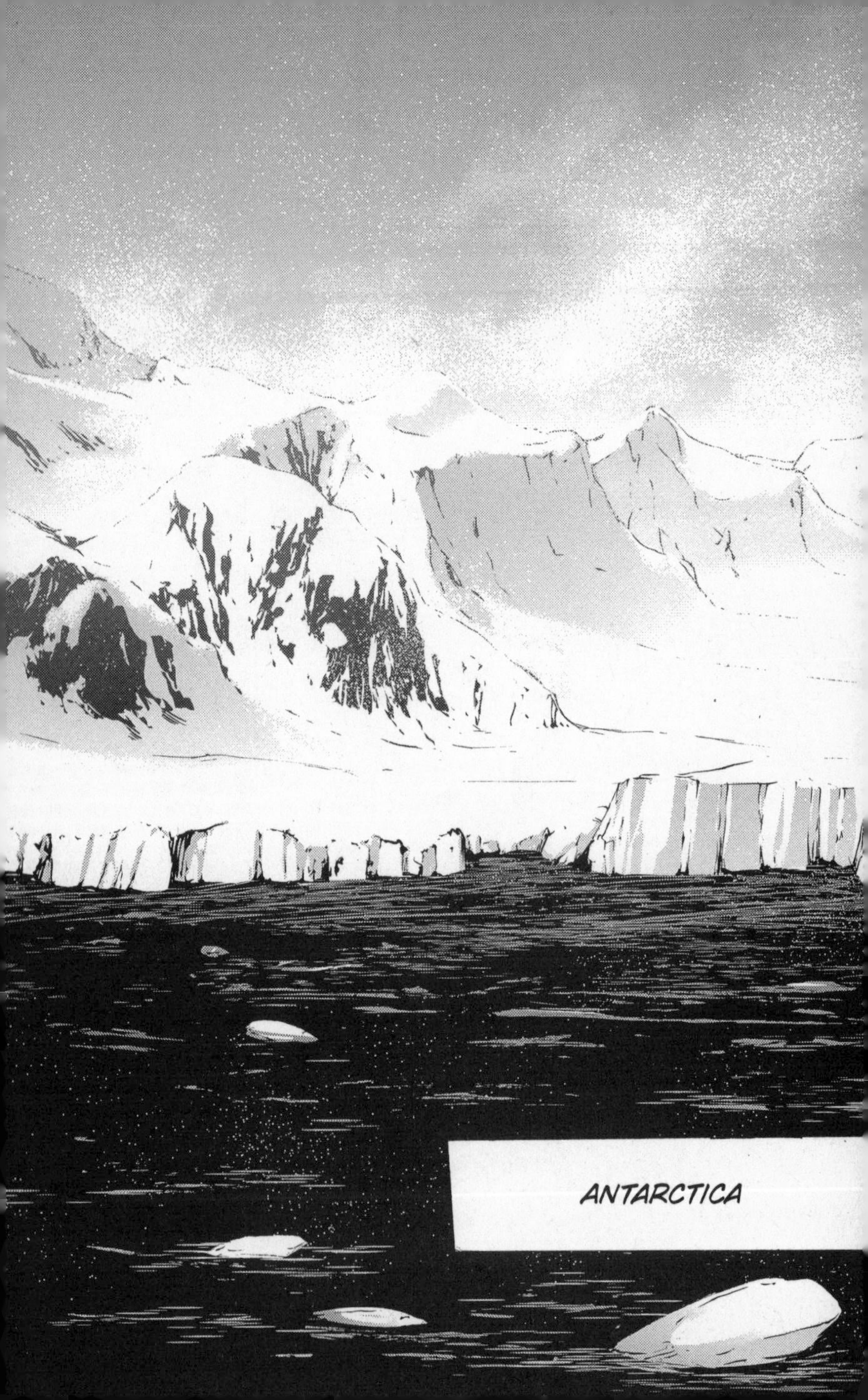
ANTARCTICA

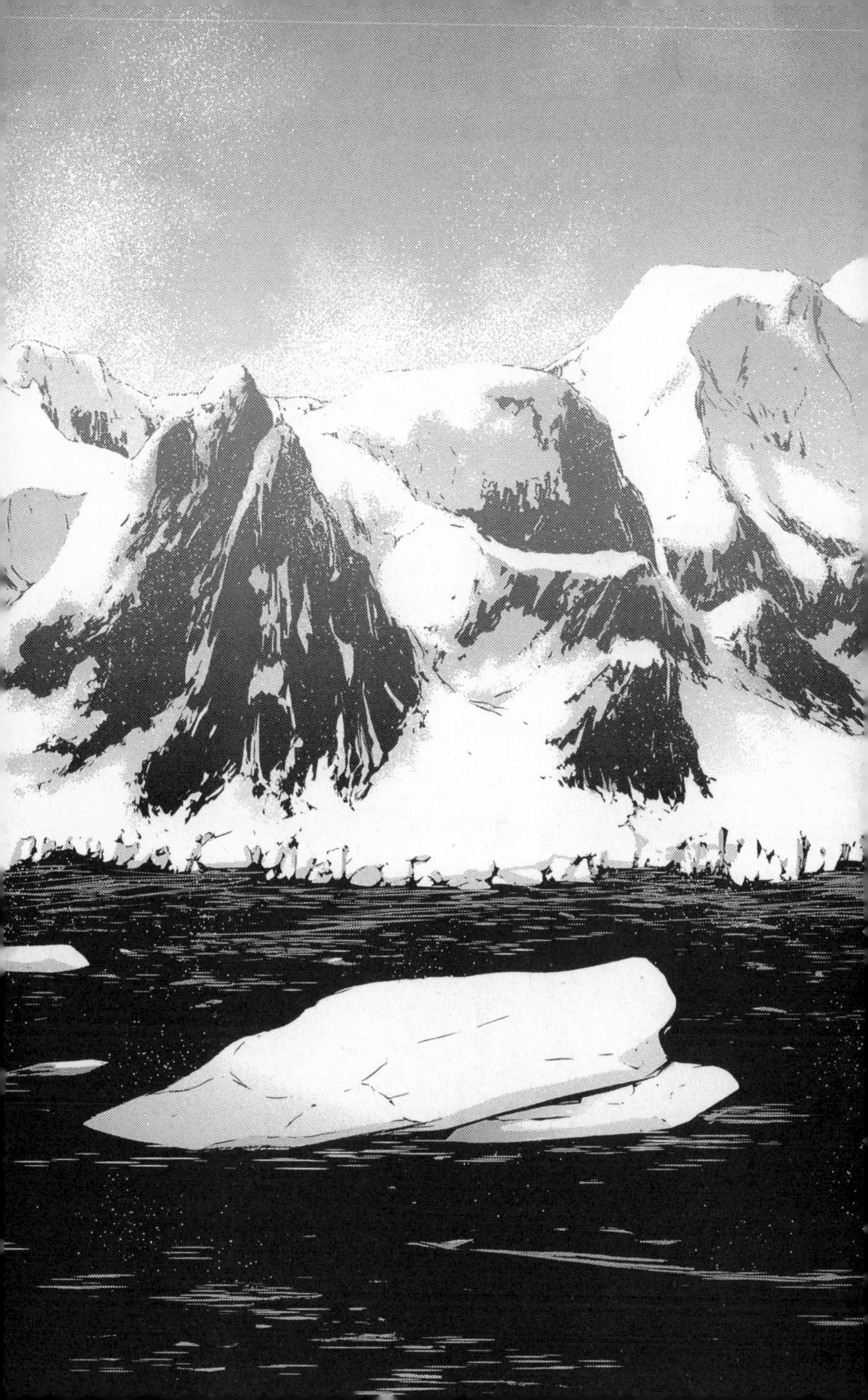

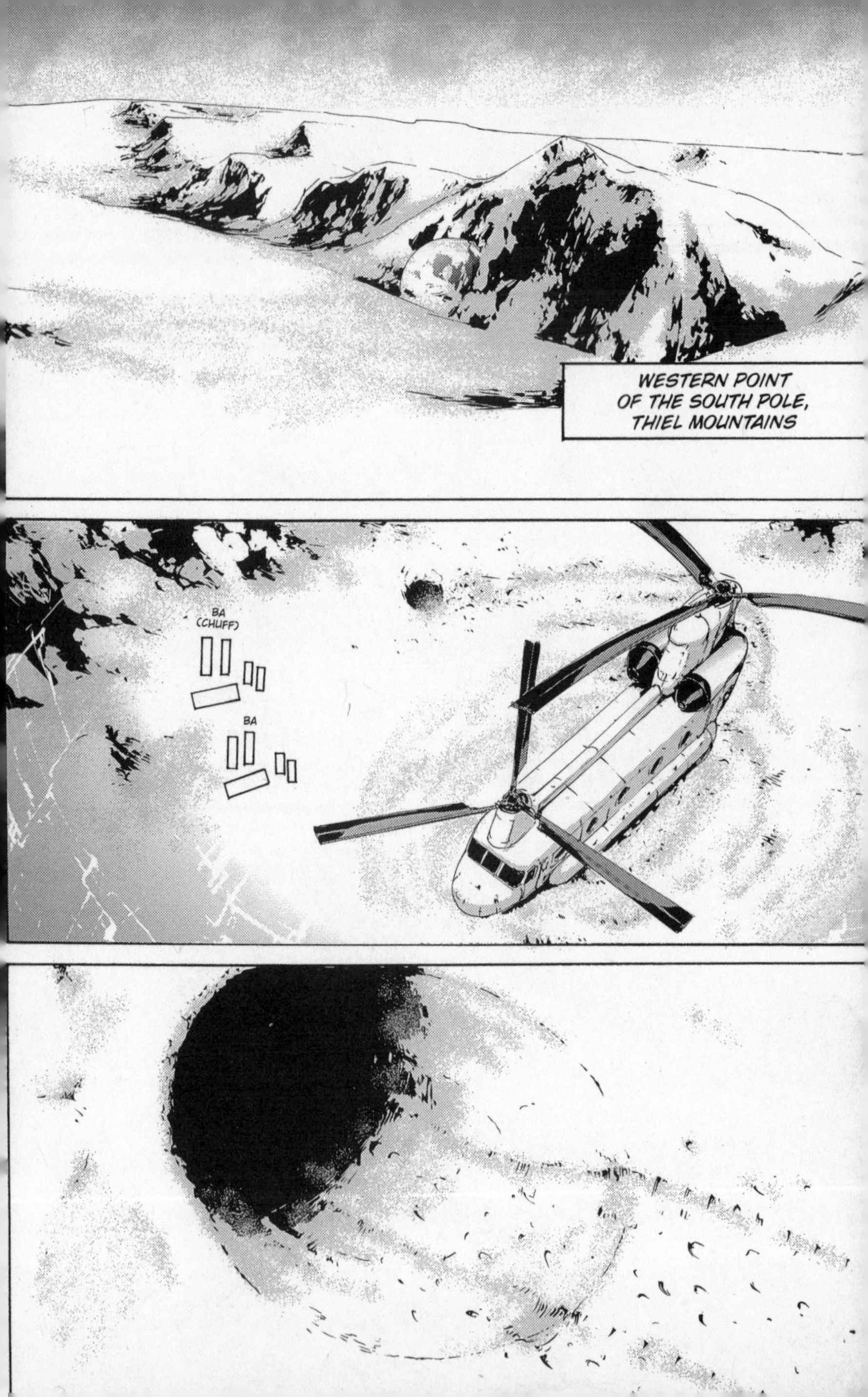
WESTERN POINT OF THE SOUTH POLE, THIEL MOUNTAINS
BA (CHUFF)
BA

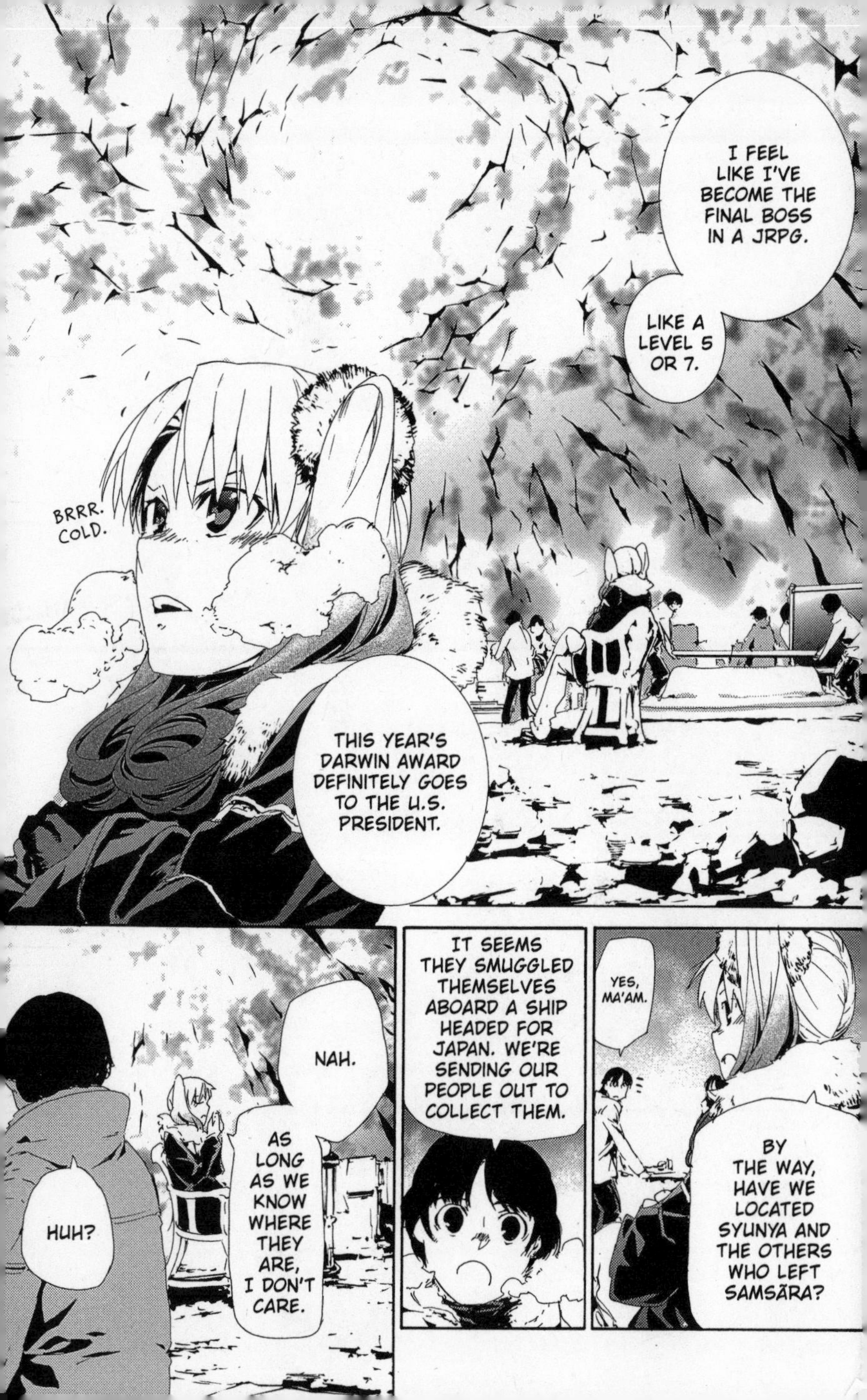
I FEEL LIKE I'VE BECOME THE FINAL BOSS IN A JRPG.
LIKE A LEVEL 5 OR 7.
BRRR. COLD.
THIS YEAR'S DARWIN AWARD DEFINITELY GOES TO THE U.S. PRESIDENT.
YES, MA'AM.
BY THE WAY, HAVE WE LOCATED SYUNYA AND THE OTHERS WHO LEFT SAMSĀRA?
IT SEEMS THEY SMUGGLED THEMSELVES ABOARD A SHIP HEADED FOR JAPAN. WE'RE SENDING OUR PEOPLE OUT TO COLLECT THEM.
NAH.
AS LONG AS WE KNOW WHERE THEY ARE, I DON'T CARE.
HUH?

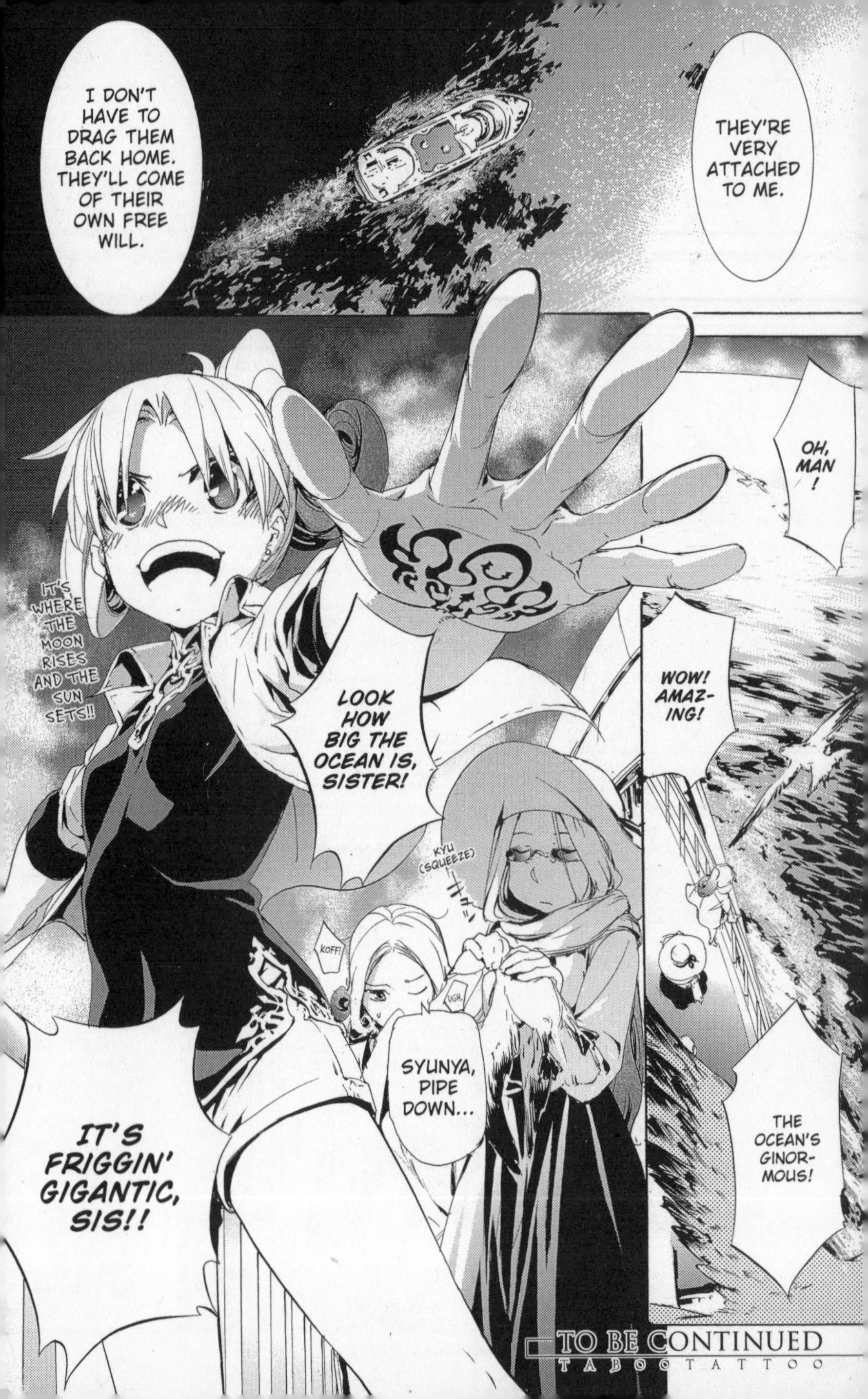
THEY'RE VERY ATTACHED TO ME.
I DON'T HAVE TO DRAG THEM BACK HOME. THEY'LL COME OF THEIR OWN FREE WILL.
OH, MAN!
WOW! AMAZ-ING!
THE OCEAN'S GINOR-MOUS!
LOOK HOW BIG THE OCEAN IS, SISTER!
IT'S WHERE THE MOON RISES AND THE SUN SETS!!
KYU (SQUEEZE)
KOFF!
UGH.
SYUNYA, PIPE DOWN...
IT'S FRIGGIN' GIGANTIC, SIS!!
TO BE CONTINUED
TABOO TATTOO

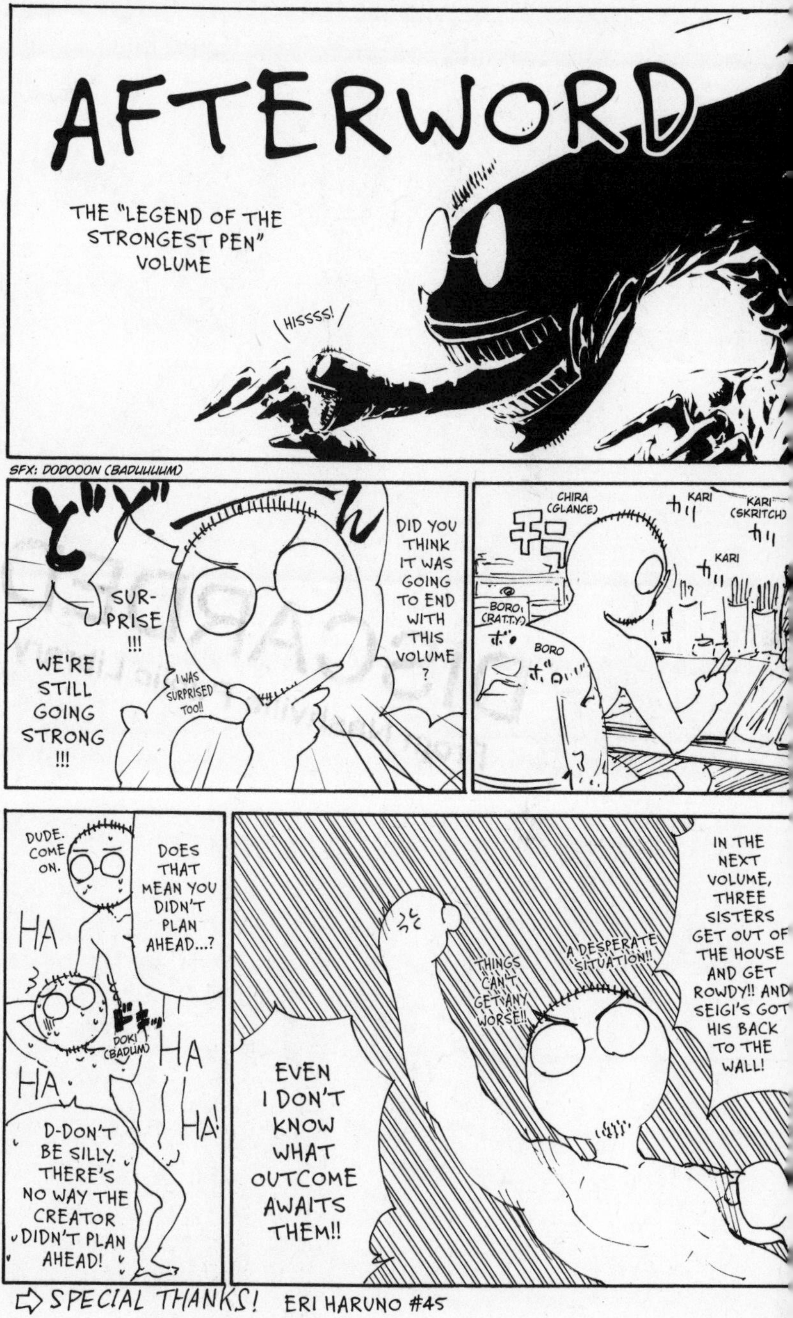
AFTERWORD
THE "LEGEND OF THE STRONGEST PEN" VOLUME
HISSSS!
CHIRA (GLANCE)
KARI
KARI (SKRITCH)
KARI
BORO (RATT.Y.)
BORO
DID YOU THINK IT WAS GOING TO END WITH THIS VOLUME?
SUR-PRISE!!!
WE'RE STILL GOING STRONG!!!
I WAS SURPRISED TOO!!
SFX: DODOOON (BADUUUUM)
IN THE NEXT VOLUME, THREE SISTERS GET OUT OF THE HOUSE AND GET ROWDY!! AND SEIGI'S GOT HIS BACK TO THE WALL!
A DESPERATE SITUATION!!
THINGS CAN'T GET ANY WORSE!!
EVEN I DON'T KNOW WHAT OUTCOME AWAITS THEM!!
DOES THAT MEAN YOU DIDN'T PLAN AHEAD...?
DUDE. COME ON.
HA
DOKI (BADUM)
HA
HA
HA!
D-DON'T BE SILLY. THERE'S NO WAY THE CREATOR DIDN'T PLAN AHEAD!

⇨ SPECIAL THANKS! ERI HARUNO #45

TABOO TATTOO

by SHINJIRO

Translation: Christine Dashiell • Lettering: Phil Christie

TABOO TATTOO
© Shinjiro 2014
First published in Japan in 2014 by KADOKAWA CORPORATION. English translation rights reserved by Yen Press, LLC under the license from KADOKAWA CORPORATION, Tokyo through TUTTLE-MORI AGENCY, Inc., Tokyo.

English translation © 2017 by Yen Press, LLC

Yen Press
1290 Avenue of the Americas
New York, NY 10104

Visit us at yenpress.com
facebook.com/yenpress
twitter.com/yenpress
yenpress.tumblr.com
instagram.com/yenpress

First Yen Press Edition: October 2017

Yen Press is an imprint of Yen Press, LLC.
The Yen Press name and logo are trademarks of Yen Press, LLC.

The publisher is not responsible for websites (or their content) that are not owned by the publisher.

Library of Congress Control Number: 2015952591

ISBNs: 978-0-316-31069-7 (paperback)
      978-0-316-31070-3 (ebook)

10 9 8 7 6 5 4 3 2 1

BVG

Printed in the United States of America